I0571687

MY BROTHER, MUHAMMAD ALI

MY BROTHER, MUHAMMAD ALI
THE DEFINITIVE BIOGRAPHY
RAHAMAN ALI

With FIAZ RAFIQ

JOHN BLAKE

Published by John Blake Publishing,
The Plaza,
535 Kings Road,
Chelsea Harbour,
London SW10 0SZ

www.facebook.com/johnblakebooks
twitter.com/jblakebooks

First published in hardback in 2019

Harback ISBN: 978 1 78946 171 8
Ebook ISBN: 978 1 78946 177 0

All rights reserved. No part of this publication may be reproduced, stored in a
retrieval system, or transmitted in any form or by any means, without the prior
permission in writing of the publisher, nor be otherwise circulated in any form
of binding or cover other than that in which it is published and without a similar
condition including this condition being imposed on the subsequent purchaser.

British Library Cataloguing-in-Publication Data:

A catalogue record for this book is available from the British Library.

Design by www.envydesign.co.uk

Printed and bound in Great Britain by Clays Ltd, Elcograf S.p.A.

1 3 5 7 9 10 8 6 4 2

© Text copyright Rahaman Ali with Fiaz Rafiq 2019

The right of Rahaman Ali and Fiaz Rafiq to be identified as the authors
of this work has been asserted by them in accordance with the Copyright,
Designs and Patents Act 1988.

Every reasonable effort has been made to trace copyright-holders of material
reproduced in this book, but if any have been inadvertently overlooked the
publishers would be glad to hear from them.

John Blake Publishing is an imprint of Bonnier Books UK
www.bonnierbooks.co.uk

I dedicate this book to my loving brother, Muhammad Ali.
He was my best friend and I'm proud of being his only sibling.
I was very fortunate to share his life.
I am forever grateful.

Contents

CONTENTS

FOREWORD

Muhammad Ali was bold, brash and courageous. He broke down so many barriers and created so many controversial situations. He was an international figure and a great fighter – a man who always fought against discrimination and always fought for equal rights. Muhammad and I could resonate with each other's attitudes, of being Americans, and of being outspoken about our equal rights.

Muhammad and I became very close friends. We had a lot of fun together and he was always joking around. I remember one day he said to me, 'Come on, let's take a walk in the community.' Somewhat bemused I asked, 'Take a walk in the community? Walk where? What are we going to do?' And Muhammad said, 'We're just going to walk in the community and talk to the people. And allow the people to talk to us.' So we would go on these walks on a regular basis. Muhammad would make people feel good about themselves. I thought to myself, 'How many celebrities of his stature would consider just walking among regular people, going around talking to them?' This, I felt, was very powerful.

One of the most important lessons we both mutually shared was that money is not God, and human dignity is very important. Your integrity is way up there. And as human beings, if you carry yourself in a certain way, you can defy all evil that comes at us. Muhammad was able to use the spotlight like nobody else in history.

I've known Rahaman personally for over five-and-half decades. I don't think there's anyone who was closer to Muhammad than his own brother. I am delighted that Rahaman has written the definitive biography on his brother Muhammad Ali, who was more than merely the most fascinating sporting figure of modern times. He was a lover of human beings, a warrior for the fight against discrimination, and not only did this great heavyweight champion transcend boxing, but he transcended all sports. He was bigger than sports. The Muhammad Ali story is an important part of history and I can say, with great conviction, that his legacy will live on for a very long time... hopefully forever.

Jim Brown
NFL Legend

PREFACE

To me, my brother was never just a boxer.

Muhammad Ali was, without doubt, the world's most loved sportsman, and perhaps one of its most adored humans. At the height of his celebrity my brother was the most famous person in the world, recognised on every continent. As an athlete, my brother transcended his sport, and as a man he seemed to embody some of our best instincts. When many people picture my brother, they visualise a lithe heavyweight slipping away from Sonny Liston's sledgehammers, or an older, wiser fighter letting George Foreman exhaust himself with body blows. But right from the start, I quickly came to realise that the sport of boxing was just a platform for Muhammad; he was the 'chosen one' to help unite people in the world through love, peace and respect.

No other human shared a closer bond with Muhammad than me – and our parents, of course. I was a near-constant fixture in my only sibling's company. I saw Muhammad at both his best and his worst: the relentless prankster and the jealous older brother, the outspoken advocate and the quiet family man behind closed doors. We grew up together, lived together, trained together, travelled together, socialised with celebrities, rubbed shoulders with presidents and even fought on the same fight cards.

But there's more to my brother's story than the sweet science and his days in the ring. Despite being diagnosed with Parkinson's, my brother never lost his zest for life in his later years. He continued to speak up and represent his religion and the human race as long as he was alive, dedicating his life to charity and helping others. His death in June 2016 caused an almost unprecedented outpouring of praise and emotion. More words have been written about Muhammad than about almost anyone else: most good, many controversial and some that seem intent on tarnishing his legacy. And yet, until now, the voice missing from the conversation has been the one belonging to the man who knew him best – me.

My brother's story has been told countless times via the medium of books, magazines and documentaries, but many accounts only consider the legend and not the man. I want to offer a fresh perspective and paint a portrait of not only the personality that most people already know, but of the human being that only I knew – a man who struggled with anger, fear and temptation like any other, but always did his best to make the world a little better every day. Like any other human being, Muhammad had his faults. He once said to me, 'If you ask any man when he's fifty years old if he would do things differently when he was twenty, of course he would. And if he doesn't then he's wasted thirty years of his life.' Muhammad, of course, didn't waste a minute of his own life – even those years that the government took away from his boxing career, he invested in becoming the magnetic speaker who would one day inspire a new generation.

As a young boy, my brother would say, 'I'm going to be the most famous man in the whole world.' We both always knew he'd be successful. I remember him once saying to me in his peak, 'Brother, isn't it wonderful how our dreams came true – how we accomplished all the goals we had as young children?' I have so much to tell the world about Muhammad Ali, and this book is my attempt to do it.

BROTHERHOOD

My brother almost killed our mom the day he was born.

His head was gigantic as a newborn, far too big to slip out naturally when Mom was giving birth to him. The doctors at the General Hospital in Louisville, Kentucky, tried every trick in the book to ensure they delivered my brother into this world without losing him, and it still almost didn't work. In the end, they resorted to using forceps, which caused Muhammad to be born with a lopsided head. Thankfully, our mom's own mother was there to console and help. Grandma reassured Mom that she would take care of her baby, and sat with my newborn brother, rubbing his head gently from side to side. Whether this played a role in the beautiful shape it eventually came to be I can't say, but those forceps left a mark on my brother's right cheek that would stay with him his whole life. Otherwise, as our mom always told us, you could see from the day he was born just how good-looking my brother would grow up to be – those fine features that punches seemed to slip off, and that face that launched a thousand newscasts – the one that almost everyone in the world would come to know. He was a beautiful boy from the first, and my mom loved him the instant she laid eyes on him.

Still, not everyone recognised my big brother so readily. Shortly after the birth, the nurses put the wrong baby in our mother's bed and Mom, still in a haze from the stress of the delivery, only realised that this wasn't her little baby boy after reading the name tag. Even though she must have been in a panic, our softly spoken mom would have barely raised her voice to say, 'Hey, this isn't my baby.' She had a way of taking such indignities quietly – one of many respects in which she was the opposite of our father. Finally, they brought my brother to her; she told us years later that all the babies in the ward were so quiet you'd have been hard-pressed to hear any of those little souls crying – except, of course, for my brother, who wouldn't stop. He went off like a rocket, already the loudest in the room after less than twenty-four hours in the world, and, of course, he eventually turned on the rest of the babies and soon they had started screaming too. Only my brother could set the whole ward off. Muhammad was loud, from the day he was born.

I've thought of my older brother as 'Muhammad' for the last five and a half decades, but when he came into the world, our parents named him after my father – Cassius Clay Marcellus Senior. He was born on 17 January 1942 and I was born eighteen months later. Our father was particularly fond of the Hollywood movie star Rudolph Valentino and decided to name me after him, Rudolph Arnett Clay. To my brother though, I was always Rudy, and to me and the rest of the family he was Gee, after his first words, 'Gee-gee', which he'd use when he needed food, his diaper changed or even just affection. In 1964, I would take the name Rahaman when he took the name Muhammad, but people in the family still called him Gee, and do even now. Our father was Cash, and Mom was Bird, inspired by the way she would burst into beautiful laughter when Dad sang for her or teased her or told her jokes.

Our mother was born Odessa Lee Grady on 12 February 1917. Her father, John Grady, was half-white with a black mother and a white Irish father. He had arrived in America in 1877 from a little town called Ennis in Ireland. After making the long and arduous journey across the pond, he met and married a freed slave woman. Blessed with beauty inside and out, our mom had a very soft and gentle demeanour. With a heavy framed body and very light skin, she was easily mistaken for a white woman, even in those days, when colour was so important to your opportunities in life.

Above everything else, you would be hard-pressed to see our mother angry or upset. Always cheerful, Mom had a kind of sparkle emanating from her that made her a very affable person. She constantly strove to treat others with dignity, and imparted those same values to Muhammad and me as soon as we could speak. We were taught to treat people with kindness, to embrace good manners and to respect our elders, regardless of their background. Without a shadow of doubt, my brother inherited his sweet and giving nature from our mother.

Mom was also a stickler when it came to neatness. She always kept us dressed sharp and smart, but her standards also extended to her surroundings. In our home, she made sure that we did our chores around the house – we had to make our beds every single day before we stepped out of the house, with the clothes that needed washing picked up from the floor and placed into the washing basket. General cleanliness was expected from every family member, young and old. Still, there was no favouritism. Although Muhammad was the first-born child, I can honestly say that Mom loved us the same and didn't favour one of us over the other.

Our father was, in many ways, the opposite of our mother. A talented artist who painted signs in and around the city of Louisville, he once told us that when he first began painting back in the early 1950s, there had been only one other black man painting oil signs in town. Initially, Dad started painting only in the black neighbourhoods, but as time went on, as a result of word of mouth, requests for his services from the white communities started to pour in despite the fact the town was segregated during that period. Even the pictures of Jesus Christ that hung in many of the churches in Louisville were painted by Dad. His name was stamped around the town.

Muhammad and I were his biggest fans, and were always absolutely amazed at his paintings. We would watch him work his magic and just be blown away by his artistic talent, so much so that I wanted to grow up to be able to paint like him. He would be the inspiration for me to take up the art of painting later in life, even if I don't think I ever quite reached his level.

He told my brother, 'You should become a lawyer or doctor,' but in the end, of course, it was Dad's other talents that Muhammad would end up emulating over the course of his career. Besides his artistic leanings, Dad was a natural actor and he loved to sing and dance. He had a showman's spark and would emulate the stars of the time, practising his vocals after work in the comfort of our home. Another thing he became known for was his flamboyant dress sense. This neat-looking, dark and handsome man would wear his freshly shone shoes, tight pants and crisp-laundered shirts and hit the jazz clubs where he would dance until the early hours of the morning. He had this way of speaking very fast, as if he was in a rush to get his words out. 'Cassius, slow your words down, because I hardly understand what you are saying,' Mom would say to him, perhaps not appreciating that hearing our father rattle off words at a hundred miles a minute would one day stand my brother's career in such good stead. Muhammad and I always thought that our father could have pursued a career in showbiz, but he told us that the racial barrier kept him from making a success because opportunities for blacks just didn't exist at that time.

Dad also, unfortunately, earned a reputation for drinking and being a ladies' man. He was a playboy, and Mom had to contend with his ways for much of her life. We would sometimes see our parents arguing and Muhammad hated it. He would hide under the bed or cover himself up with a blanket. He'd embrace me with an affectionate, protective hug with both arms wrapped around his little brother. Nonetheless, they still loved each other, even if they were polar opposites as far as their personalities went. Unlike our mother, our dad was very stern, not one of those fathers who emanated a lot of affection. Worst of all, when he was drunk he'd often get into arguments and even get physical with our mother. By and large he was a friendly man who endeavoured to treat people right, but those moments had a lasting effect on Muhammad and me, and I think we both attempted to treat the women in our lives better because of them.

One thing that both of our parents had in common was their faith. They were staunch Christians and followed the teachings of the Bible religiously. I remember how, without fail, Mom would dress me and Muhammad up on Sunday mornings to attend church to hear Reverend Wilson preach the gospel. Though she'd shower us with love and affection at home, our mother wasn't the type to express her feelings openly in the church by shouting and screaming like some of our fellow churchgoers. She was a quiet and peaceful lady in public, even if very little of that attitude rubbed off on her two boys.

★ ★ ★

When Muhammad was a small child he wouldn't sit still. He had what I guess you'd call 'an itch', an urge to always be active. He would try to talk at every opportunity he got, even opening his mouth when there was no reason to do it. He would be eating, stuffing his face with food and still saying to our mother, 'I want more.' At the age of five, he would be playing with the neighbourhood kids standing on a platform like a leader addressing a crowd – with me trailing after him, just as fast as my three-year-old body would allow. Our mom said she realised even then that my brother wasn't going to settle for being someone who'd be lingering at the back; he was just destined to be the centre of attention, always going to be heard. He was loud, proud and assertive. I came to think of him as a born leader, someone I'd follow into almost anything.

Mercifully for two boys so set on diversion, we didn't have too many opportunities to get into serious trouble when we were very young. We stayed in a rough part of town in South Louisville until a couple of years after I was born, but then moved to the West End of the city with our grandparents for a very short while, before moving again just four blocks away in 1947, to 3302 Grand Avenue. This is the house that is now famous for being Muhammad Ali's childhood home. In the beginning it was real rough where we were at, but there were worse places in the West End – Grand Avenue was, in some ways, considered upscale compared to most of the other areas close by. In the East End of the city, Smoke Town was really bad, but none of the black neighbourhoods in Louisville were as bad as the ghettos in the bigger major cities, where African-Americans were restricted to certain areas of the city, where the population density was often more than four times greater than white areas and where employment opportunities were often restrictive. The neighbourhood we grew up in was predominantly black, but there were some lawyers and doctors there, and we even had a few white families living alongside us.

Still, I'd like to debunk a myth that has somehow persisted for decades – that my brother and I had a middle-class upbringing. Although we weren't the poorest people in the neighbourhood – there were others worse off – most of our childhood in Louisville was spent in semi-poverty. That's the truth, and I know, because we lived it. Money was never easy to come by. There were plenty of times when we didn't even own a car, and when we finally did come by one, it was at least ten years old; when it was inevitably in need of some good tyres, Dad struggled to replace the old ones because of the cost. Our house, a bungalow, was a modest, two-bedroomed residence, with a living room and a small dining area with a kitchen and bathroom. We had a small front yard and a very long backyard that extended from the back porch to an alley behind the house. There were several tall trees in the backyard, with a pond that had goldfish swimming in it. It wasn't a bad place to live by any means, but there were still times when we couldn't afford to fix things in our home, and had to make do as a result. For several years, for example, our roof and walls were in such a bad state that rain was able to get through them. The front porch had been on the brink of falling apart almost since the day we moved in. Dad did try to get it fixed, but there were always more pressing financial concerns. Even most of the clothes that Muhammad and I wore when we were younger came from goodwill. We wore second-hand shirts and shoes that cost a dollar or less. So, no, I wouldn't classify Muhammad's upbringing as 'middle class' at all. Though our father was a painter of some renown and our mother had a job cleaning for some white families, in many ways we were always trying our best to make ends meet. But still, our parents would always put food on the table. And while my brother and I may not have had much money, have been showered with gifts, or got everything we wanted, the fact that we had each other was typically enough to make us happy.

Muhammad and I, for instance, shared a bedroom which was around twenty feet by sixteen feet – with his bed right next to mine. For some kids, that might have been a chore, but for us it just made us closer as brothers. He would have these late-night talks with me until we just fell asleep. He would tell me that he had dreams and he wanted to grow up and be something in life, and he would talk to me about one day becoming rich and famous. I remember he would tell me that he would buy our mother and father a big new house, a top-of-the-range Cadillac and have a quarter of a million dollars in his bank account. More specifically, he said that the quarter of a million dollars – always that number – would be saved so that if our family was in dire need, they didn't need to worry. Most people thought my brother's ambitions were far-fetched, but I had great conviction that Muhammad was the chosen one. I always knew he would make it big in the world.

While Muhammad was daydreaming about the fortune he would make one day, of course, he never lost his sense of fun, and the humour that he became known for in his adult life can be traced all the way back to when he was a young boy. More than anything, he got a thrill whenever he played a prank – endless variations on which he'd happily devise for anyone he thought might fall for it, but certainly for me in particular. One day he thought it would be a good idea to get me to squeal like a pig, through a grandiose plan in which he tied a long string around the curtains in our parents' bedroom. To get my attention he started pulling the string while he casually lay on his bed. 'Hey, Rudy,' he said, 'there's a ghost in our house!' The next thing our parents knew, I was yelling and screaming, trying to wake them up with the news that there was a ghost in the house. Dad rushed to our room to see what all the screaming and shouting was all about and, obviously, saw through the ruse straight away. 'Cassius Junior, will you stop playing tricks on your little brother Rudolph!' I remember him saying, still bleary-eyed for lack of sleep and using my brother's full name to show his displeasure – not that it would have ever discouraged Muhammad. 'I tricked you really good, Rudy,' he repeated, doubled over with laughter. It could have almost been his catchphrase.

★ ★ ★

Muhammad adored everything about our neighbourhood. The neighbours were nice enough and the general vibe was that of a close-knit community, but the best thing about it, for him, was that it afforded him endless opportunities for mischief and mayhem with a group of like-minded kids. My brother, as I've mentioned, was one of the leaders among the children, having risen to the top of that natural hierarchy that always occurs when enough kids get together. I was his constant companion, but I'd let him lead while I stayed in the background, hanging out at the front of our house, or by the little restaurant round the corner. There was another corner where we would play games and shoot dice, a little further from the watchful eyes of our parents.

Of course, we would play with whatever toys our parents could afford to buy for us but, like most kids, we also made our own. We would convert broomsticks into horses by tying a piece of string around the top and putting it in between our legs, and then hollering at the tops of our voices as we ran up and down the street with no care in the world. And, of course, like any growing boys at the time, our group of friends would all play cowboys and Indians. Muhammad, having typically taken charge, was always adamant on being the cowboy and would always say that I had to be the Indian. Back then, cowboys were portrayed as the good guys in the westerns and the Indians were the bad guys. My brother always wanted to be the good guy because the good guys always won.

That was fun and games, but even in the early days of our childhood my brother and I were very competitive. We were close in age, so we would challenge each other in almost anything we pursued. Muhammad, in particular, strove to triumph in whatever game or competition he took part in – it made no difference whether it was racing, trying to see who could run the fastest, who could jump the highest, playing marbles or jacks, or hide-and-seek. Losing was simply out of the question. Pro wrestling was popular in the 1950s, and our parents religiously watched it on TV, at least when the set in our house could be convinced to work. And so, of course, my brother would try to emulate the wrestlers on TV, usually at my expense. Sometimes the whole thing would get a bit boisterous as we grappled in the living room, but it wasn't always a one-sided affair. I always had a little more size on me when we were growing up, while he was a lot skinnier and quite lanky. My brother wasn't really that interested in athletic pursuits until after he took up boxing – there were other kids who were physically more imposing, even if he was quick and competitive.

And as far as sports were concerned, he never really enjoyed basketball or baseball, the games that almost every other boy of our age wanted to play as often as possible. Across the street from our friend Adrian's house there was a large plot of empty land which we'd congregate on, and although Muhammad didn't really care much for any organised sport, he would take part sometimes just for the fun of it. He didn't take a shine to tackle football because, ironically, he felt it was just too rough. He didn't mind playing touch football instead and he was very good at running and elusive with it, twisting away from our efforts to tackle him, the way he would one day dance away from the greatest fighters of his generation. And even back then, he was boasting – the thrill of a challenge just switched something on inside of him and he'd yell, 'I'm too fast for you!' even as he was sprinting away across the dirt. 'There's no way that you can catch me! Watch me score this touchdown!' And, thanks to his prodigious natural athletic talent more than any love of the game, he would back up this confidence – most of the time.

Luckily, more often than not Muhammad and I were on the same team, just as we would be through much of the rest of our lives, and those summer days growing up were very special and dear to our hearts. We were just innocent kids with boundless energy. Muhammad was always the life of the party and tried to inject a dose of enthusiasm into whatever he did. I, on the other hand, took things way too seriously – at least according to my brother. Though I was typically resigned to my role – I was eighteen months younger, after all – I sometimes let my frustration get the better of me. Even then, things would rarely get physical. Our mom's quiet disapproval and Dad's more hands-on discipline made sure of that. And, for the most part, sibling rivalry was nothing but good for me. Muhammad wanted to be liked and appreciated. He had that in him right from the word go. There was always an attempt to impress others and stand out from the group. There was, though, one area where I stood apart from my brother growing up, and as fate would have it that was the one that upset him the most.

To put it simply: I always found it easy to talk to girls. It often surprises people, but when we were young boys, I was more of a ladies' man than my brother. And I certainly started having girlfriends before he ever did. The girls in our neighbourhood and school knew us both, and Muhammad would always be making eyes in their direction, but he lacked confidence as far as approaching them went, and was absolutely petrified to ask them out. No matter how much he tried to conceal his bashfulness, it was always apparent. And as brash as he was, as radiant as his smile might have been, the occasional smile back was the closest he'd get to flirting, at least in those formative years. Almost unbelievably, some girls actually perceived my brother as what you might now call a 'nerd' – according to a few that I spoke with, it was because he didn't participate in football and basketball, the sports that were seen as being the preserve of the 'real' men. It certainly wasn't a lack of looks; it was more to do with his personality, which had its own stutters and starts, behind all that bravado. And if anything, Muhammad's attempts to rectify the situation made matters worse. He'd run alongside the school bus and call out the names of the girls and boys, and most of the girls would sink in their seats, embarrassed more for him than themselves.

Muhammad, of course, couldn't stand the fact that I was getting the attention from the girls, and back then it was maybe the only thing that had a chance of driving a wedge between us as brothers. On the way home from school, for instance, I would usually get off the bus early to walk my girlfriend home and hang out with her at her house. The same scene played out more than once: we'd be hanging out together, only to hear a knock on the door and answer it to find my brother there, his face a picture of innocence. 'Hey, Rudy, Mom wants you to come home now, you're in trouble,' would be the typical line. 'She told me to get you and said she wants you to come home right now!' I, fearing the worst, would apologise to my girlfriend and run back home, about four blocks in total, thoughts swirling in my head about what I could possibly be in trouble for. 'Mom, what's wrong?' I would ask as soon as we walked through the door, only to be met with a blank face, and the revelation that our mom, confused at my sudden appearance, didn't have the faintest idea what I was talking about.

I'd fall for this scheme of Muhammad's over and over again, with my brother repeating the charade whenever he got the itch. More than once I accused him of being jealous. On a couple of occasions, we exchanged a few words. And those days were really the only times in our childhood that I would really get mad at my brother. This wasn't a game he was going to beat me in, and it must have stung him to see his little brother outshining him in one of the few areas he still didn't quite understand. And yet, however heated our words became, there was never a time in our entire childhood when we came to blows. No girl was going to seriously ruin our relationship.

★ ★ ★

Whether we were chasing girls, playing touch football or coming up with games of our own devising, our parents had one golden rule that was strictly enforced, and that was to be back at home before it got dark. This was pretty common. Back in those days, it wasn't out of the ordinary for kids to leave the house in the early morning and roam the streets all day, not returning before dusk, getting up to whatever mischief they might throughout the day. Most people in our neighbourhood didn't have the luxury of wearing a watch, but Dad's solution was simple: 'Don't tell me you don't know what time it is. You'd better be home before the street lights turn on, otherwise you're in trouble.' And so every night a familiar scene would repeat itself. As soon as it started getting dark, street lights would start to come on and we would race them all the way home. We wouldn't always make it.

If we were late, we'd be treated to a good old-fashioned spanking. The bathroom was the typical punishment chamber. Muhammad would always go first, leaving me to wait outside for Dad to call me after he'd finished with my brother. Muhammad never really appreciated the harsh treatment Dad administered for lateness and other infractions, but our father had his own ideas of how things were supposed to be and he had what you might call a zealous attitude to keeping us in check, a way of raising his voice and a mean look that would etch itself across his face that confirmed what was coming. More often than not, seeing that would make us straighten up, but by then it would be too late. Rules were there to be obeyed and our dad was going to make sure we took heed. Perhaps because of this, and a few other things, Muhammad's relationship with our father became somewhat distant before he left his teens. When I say this, I don't mean they had a big falling-out, but that special bond that some fathers and sons are able to forge was lost before it could even begin.

Contrary to what some biographers have written, though, I'd never agree that our upbringing in Louisville had any element of what you'd call physical abuse. First of all, Dad never intentionally tried to inflict unnecessary pain. Most of the time, Muhammad and I didn't even take note of his discipline because we'd break the rules over and over again without giving much thought to the consequences. Of course Dad disciplined us physically now and again, but in the 1940s and 1950s the practice was deemed necessary. Giving kids a strapping was certainly nothing out of the ordinary in black communities, especially when the consequences of stepping out of line could be so grave. In hindsight, Muhammad realised that Dad had the right intentions all along, and he came to terms with the fact that it was for our own good. It *was* dangerous being out late, in our neighbourhood especially, and whatever else was on his mind, our father didn't want his kids to get caught up in the ugly scenarios that played themselves out on the streets nightly in our town. Even back then there were drugs to worry about, as well as robberies and fights and brutal stabbings, and as the father of two black boys, Dad had plenty of extra cause for concern.

Furthermore, in the 1950s, prejudice was spiralling out of control in parts of America. The violence instigated by the various racist groups that were creating trouble was particularly rife in the South, and in Louisville it never felt far away. As young boys growing up, it very quickly became apparent to Muhammad and I that being black made us different. In our town the blacks endeavoured to stay on their side of town in a sort of semi-isolation – we didn't encounter much trouble in our own neighbourhood, but elsewhere our race was shoved in our faces all the time. Tensions were high, and the potential for trouble was never far away.

One story in particular illustrates the kind of discrimination that was accepted as a fact of life during our formative years. When Muhammad was eight, Mom took him downtown, only to bring him home with tears running down his cheeks. It turned out that he had wanted a drink and stood outside a store crying for water – except that it was a store that didn't serve blacks. Mom took him in and asked the shop assistant for a drink of water regardless, but the woman, my mom told us later, was obviously afraid. She told Mom that she'd lose her job if she served 'Negroes'. Here was an upset kid, gulping back tears and only asking for something to quench his thirst, and his mother couldn't even buy water in a store in his own home town. In the end, the situation came to a head when the store's security personnel walked up to her and Muhammad and asked them to leave, in case the situation escalated. Mom was never a confrontational person so she didn't make a big fuss, but that incident and others constantly reminded my brother and me that we were effectively second-class citizens in our own town. Our race determined where we could eat, where our father could work, which parks we could play in and how we would be treated if we broke the law. That stuck with me and Muhammad for a long time. Even though our mother looked almost white to both of us, she was still treated as 'coloured' in everyday life, and even when we came to terms with it we would never be able to accept it. Muhammad in particular would often ask our parents why black people had to suffer so.

It was partly this climate that meant that, even when we were in our teens, it was rare that Muhammad and I would venture too far from the West End on our own. We had been warned – by our parents and by other members of the community – and knew what could potentially happen, even in a town as relatively 'enlightened' as Louisville. The only real trouble we encountered was outside the vicinity of the West End – if we were in the wrong part of town, the all-white part – but still, the fact that there was so little we could do never lost its sting. It wasn't uncommon for white boys in a car to pull up and hurl racial abuse. 'Hey, nigger, what are you doing here?' they would shout to us, trying to goad us into a situation that could easily turn ugly. It always hit home, but my brother and I did our best to stay out of trouble, only too aware of the beatings and lynchings that were still occurring in places like Mississippi. The Deep South was another world, but a world that our parents often brought to our attention, showing us pictures of Emmett Till's disfigured face when his killers were acquitted of murder, reminding us of what could happen if we dared to retaliate even in the face of hatred.

Despite those tensions, though, and even though he had his own frustrations to take out in life, Muhammad never bullied anyone. I can attest to that. Yes, he had a boastful side to him, and he certainly had the physical skills to back up his words, but to my knowledge no one ever said he bullied them or that he was a mean person in school or in our neighbourhood. Moreover, I never saw him do wrong by anyone who didn't bring it on themselves. He was extremely close to me, so anywhere he went, you could bet your last dollar that you'd see me with him. Our parents had made it clear to us at every step that we were to look out for each other whenever we were out of their sight, and Muhammad took pride in the fact that I was his little brother. He was very protective and every kid around us was aware of the closeness we shared. They knew that you couldn't mess with one brother; you had to mess with both of us. If somebody was going to bully Muhammad, or trying to instigate trouble with him, even if I was certain to lose, I would jump in there and fight wholeheartedly. There was no way you could've fought my big brother without me involved, and Muhammad would intervene if anyone tried hurting me. We got in our fair share of scraps that way, but it wasn't until Muhammad was twelve years old that we discovered we might both just have a talent for it.

THE DAWN OF
A DREAM

It was late October 1954 when my brother had his bike stolen. The bike, a white-and-red Schwinn, was a Christmas gift, and technically meant for both of us, though in practice my brother seemed to ride it more often than I did. Back in those days kids would ride their bikes everywhere – down to the grocery store, sure, but also with friends, around the town, searching for adventure in whatever form it might come. On this particular day, Muhammad and I, along with another friend, had heard about a Home Exhibition Show in downtown Louisville, taking place on Fourth Street, and we were eager to check it out. We left our bikes beside a rail next to the building assuming they would be safe, and then sauntered inside in anticipation of making the most out of our afternoon. And sure, it was a fine afternoon. There were stands with homeware and clothing, but also booths serving delicious foods and snacks, and fancy automobiles on display. Bands entertained the folk there having a day out with their families in a lively atmosphere.

After spending near enough three hours milling around we decided that it was time to head back home. Timekeeping, as I've mentioned, was a priority in our household. We walked back to get our bikes, but when we got there they had vanished, stolen. Shocked and extremely upset, my brother started to cry. This bike had been given to him by our parents as a Christmas present, but more than anything Muhammad was concerned we would be getting a good hiding from our dad when he learned of our negligence. Other people were coming out of the building, and so, both gulping tears back, we asked one guy where we could find a policeman. One man directed us to a building within the vicinity of the show, and so we made our way there to report our bikes stolen.

As we entered a large basement with tears still in our eyes, the first sounds we heard were thuds and groans, the thwap-thwap-thwap of skipping ropes hitting the floor and the sounds of gloved fists hitting heavy bags. There were about half a dozen men and older boys doing boxing drills in the basement, which clearly wasn't a police station but a gymnasium, though, sure enough, across the room we spotted a middle-aged man in a police uniform.

His name was Joe Martin. He was meticulously guiding some boys through the finer points of forming the correct boxing stance as we walked up to him. Muhammad, collecting himself, said, 'Mister, we were upstairs at the home show and when we went outside to ride our bikes home, someone had stolen them. Can you help us get our bikes back?'

Martin, who seemed like a gentleman, proceeded to take the description of the stolen bikes and told us he'd put in a report, but he wasn't going to let us go without making a sales pitch of his own. 'By the way,' he said, almost offhandedly after he was done with the official side of matters. 'Why don't you two little boys come back tomorrow, say around 6 o'clock in the evening, to this gym, so you can learn how to box?' Muhammad, who still had the traces of his tears on his cheeks, got that familiar challenging glint in his eyes, and told this big policeman that he was going to beat up the culprit as soon as he got a grip of him. Martin, who we'd grow to learn was a patient man, listened to a whole barrage of threats before suggesting to my brother that first he'd have to learn to fight, and in particular box, before he should even entertain this thought, let alone resort to these illegal tactics. We had limited knowledge of boxing and had never seriously contemplated taking up the sport in the past, but as it turned out Muhammad was so enraptured by the sights, the smell and the vibe in the gym that he almost forgot about his bike. Martin finished writing the report and reiterated the gym's opening hours, handing Muhammad an application to take home with him. Still worried about his bike but thrilled at the prospect of giving this new sport a shot, my brother happily took the piece of paper.

Muhammad never did get his bike back. Perhaps surprisingly, though, our parents were understanding when we revealed what had happened, with our father nonchalant in the face of our negligence. My brother, meanwhile, remained set on boxing for long enough to join Martin's gym, and I, of course, followed along with him.

Now, what most people are oblivious to is that one of our young cousins was a boxer. He was dabbling in boxing well before we entered a gym. Even before Martin's offer, he had enthusiastically offered to train Muhammad and teach him, knowing my brother's propensity for getting into scrapes and wanting him to be able to defend himself in case he ever got into an altercation with other kids. And it was our cousin who initially accompanied us to the gym and kept our interest when we otherwise might have been distracted by other childish things. As much as he was impelled to involve Muhammad in boxing, our cousin wasn't very successful and eventually quit. However, we brothers kept up our training.

I can recall Muhammad's first day at the gym with some clarity. He threw himself into the deep end almost immediately, getting into the ring with an older boy thinking he could hold his own without any real experience. It took no more than sixty seconds, though, for my brother to realise that throwing wild punches wasn't going to get him anywhere. Muhammad was trying ever so hard to knock the guy out. His training partner's superior experience and punching power left him dazed and bleeding from the nose. Martin, though, appreciated my brother's enthusiasm – this first, failed foray into the sweet science showed my brother's zeal and his heart.

Martin's gym, the Columbia Gym, was integrated, with black and white boxers training under the same roof. Despite the racial tensions in Louisville at the time, the sport brought both colours together in a way that not many other venues could. In the basement, every fighter was treated the same, and sparred together without prejudice. While training at Martin's gym, though, a black boxing coach by the name of Fred Stoner caught Muhammad's attention. Stoner had a gym on the other side of town, which pretty much catered for nothing but black boxers. Even though Muhammad's loyalty was to Martin, when Muhammad and I went to our first tournament we were very impressed by how Stoner's boxers dressed – their boots and shorts matched their robes, and they generally seemed well taken care of. Still, he didn't want to put a dent in his relationship with Martin, and so eventually, Muhammad found a way to work with both, while each remained oblivious to the other's influence. I, of course, followed my brother – something I was rather well practised at by that time. I let my brother lead and stuck to him like a magnet. We would train at Martin's gym in the early evening and then later we'd head to Stoner's dungeon for more physical and mental torture. It was worth the investment, though. Every trainer has their quirks, and being exposed to more styles and tricks certainly helped our growth in those early days.

The strength and size I had and Muhammad's fast-developing skills elevated us quickly in the ranks of both gyms. We both trained hard, but I have to admit that I was a little bit more lacklustre in regard to self-discipline compared with my brother. Boxing became Muhammad's life: he raced the bus to school and swore off soda pop in pursuit of greatness. I went along with it because he was my brother and I hung out with him, but his passion exceeded mine. He really wanted to reach the top and was willing to sacrifice to get there. He devoured boxing, falling in love with the sweet science and bragging to me about how he was going to be the greatest ever and in turn change our family status. It was there from the start; Muhammad, who was always aware of our family's struggles with money, had this ambition to become famous from the outset of his career. Later in his life, his early dreams about how much money he would accrue came to seem ironic – when he did get rich, after all, he didn't particularly care for his wealth, and gave it away as if he somehow found it distasteful. Still, at the time it was a big part of my brother's motivation. Then again, what teenager wouldn't be motivated to become a sports champion, famous and have all the money in the world? I was more motivated by money and fame than the pursuit of perfection for sure.

★ ★ ★

It didn't take long before we began to compete regularly. At school, kids knew we boxed because they saw us on the local TV show *Tomorrow's Champions*, which was broadcasting amateur bouts. We would earn $4 for each bout, most of them organised by Joe Martin. Apparently our amateur boxing careers were also being followed by the locals, and after just a few bouts we became minor celebrities in our little world – in the black community in particular. More surprisingly, the white kids that we had contact with also now had more of an amiable attitude towards Muhammad and I because they knew we were so popular. If you were white and prejudiced, and you were a kid, you were kind of still impressed when you heard or read about Muhammad or saw him fight. 'Hey, I saw your boxing match on TV last night,' kids would say to him in the street, the same kids who a year or two earlier wouldn't have even looked in our direction. It gave my brother a taste for fame early on before he was even considered for representing his country in the Olympics, which eventually would propel him to fame that went way beyond our local circle.

Schools were segregated in Louisville, like any other state in the south – grade school all the way up through high school. Muhammad and I graduated from an all-black school. Everyone was just about the same in that they came from humble beginnings. A lot of the young boys and girls that we grew up around had government support for their lunches at school, and no one had much in terms of material possessions. This segregation and poverty quickly taught us that being black meant you were different, but pretty early on in life my brother and I also came to the realisation that it was grossly unfair. We would switch on the TV and come across some horrific stories: dogs set on black people and lynching, accompanied by images that would stay embedded into our heads forever. As two young black men, Muhammad and I thought to ourselves, *Why are blacks treated differently here in America?* In our early lives, of course, we could do nothing about it, but I believe that, even back then, Muhammad was planning to help the world to change.

Schooling, on the other hand, wasn't something that Muhammad took seriously. He was the class clown. He was far from being the sharpest student in the first place and he didn't put much effort into his education even before boxing. Education wasn't something he consciously thought to be of great significance or value, and when he got introduced to boxing – when he was in middle school – he more or less gave boxing precedence over schooling. Muhammad had to stay somewhat motivated to make sure he didn't flunk, but since the chances of him becoming a success through schooling alone seemed slim, he dedicated his efforts elsewhere. He wasn't the only one.

If there was any one single person who was the driving force behind my brother, it was our father. Our mother was happy to go along with it, but Cash Clay had his foot on the gas. Neither of our parents had a really stable job, and when we both showed some promise in boxing our father saw it as the family's meal ticket; not just out of poverty, but to stardom and riches. Our father had the notion that both of his sons, no less, were going to be world champion fighters. He had great faith in us. Father took interest with intense earnestness and would be sitting ringside at all of our fights. He was a proud dad. Actually, he was one of our biggest fans. And it's worth repeating, Dad thought both of us were going to hit it big – not just Muhammad.

★ ★ ★

I don't think even my brother could tell you exactly how many bouts he notched up under Joe Martin's tutelage, from the ages of twelve to eighteen. I know he fought often – more than once a month, with me often alongside him – and barely took a break. Even in the early fights, you could see hints of the greatness he'd develop later, as he learned to circle and evade punches, pulling straight away from his opponent's swipes in a way that made some traditionalists wince. He notched up six Kentucky Golden Gloves titles and two national championships in what had to be over 100 amateur bouts, of which he only lost eight. In 1960, he entered the Golden Gloves as a light heavyweight to avoid the chance that we'd meet during the tournament, and won the tournament handily. Later that same year, he travelled to San Francisco to try out for a spot with the national team, and saw off a handful of outclassed opponents before winning a tough bout against Allen Hudson to secure a place on the team for the Olympics set to be held in Rome.

I didn't get to go to Rome, of course. My parents and I watched my brother battle on TV. In the early bouts, he looked like the world-beater we knew he was, easily outmatching opponents who seemed to have never seen a heavyweight so able to move, dodge and dance before. The finals, we knew, would be tougher, as he was facing an opponent of great pedigree. On 5 September, he stepped into the ring against Zigzy Pietrzykowski of Poland. Both fighters weighed in at 178 pounds. The Polish boxer was a tough southpaw fighter who was seven years older than my brother and had much more experience on his side. Nevertheless, Muhammad triumphed by beating him via a unanimous decision to clinch the gold medal in the light heavyweight division. This was a dream manifesting into reality, a day I'll never forget.

Upon his return to Louisville, a large home-town crowd eagerly awaited his arrival at the airport. My parents and I, the mayor of Louisville, the city aldermen, some local ministers and students from Central High School along with principals and the teachers had all made an effort to be at the airport to greet him. Numerous photographers from the local newspapers were waiting to snap pictures of the new champion. My brother, our parents and I were escorted from the airport by a motorcade through the streets of Louisville en route to Central High School. Students and members of the public were milling around outside the school holding the banners: *Welcome Home Cassius Marcellus Junior, Olympic Light Heavyweight Champion.* As our car approached the school, students and well-wishers rushed to see their own Louisville native, and Muhammad was happily taking it all in. We followed Muhammad to the school auditorium, where two seats onstage awaited my parents. My humble family knew that this would be a momentous moment, but it was even bigger than we could have imagined.

As everyone settled down, the Principal, Mr Alwood S. Wilson, was the first to speak. He shared with the audience how extremely proud he, the faculty and the students were of a former student bringing home the gold medal. After his heartfelt speech he beckoned Muhammad to come forward to speak and share his experiences at the Olympics. The audience stood up and gave him a standing ovation that went on for a few minutes. Muhammad rose from his seat and began speaking to the crowd. He spoke eloquently about his Polish opponent, a man who he admitted had given him a tough fight, pummelling him with heavy shots. My brother, though, was not too humble to note that he had been too quick and too clever for his adversary, and attributed his victory to the determination and boxing skills that he had spent years perfecting. He told us how proud he was to bring the medal back to America. He spoke of how he had dreamed that someday he would not only make it to the Olympics but triumph, and that, now that he had achieved his dream, he would use the Olympic podium as a platform to make his voice heard. The Olympics, he told the assembled crowd, would be the golden key to unlock many truths: a phrase that bemused many in the crowd at the time, who weren't aware of my brother's new-found interest in the politics of race in America. After Muhammad finished addressing the crowd, everyone in the audience, once again, stood up and gave him another standing ovation. Then exuberant students asked if they could see and touch the medal. Getting a glimpse of it was not enough; everyone wanted to get their hands on the gold. Muhammad graciously stepped down the stage, stood there with a smile all across his face as each student walked up to him and touched the fruits of his labour.

After an eventful time at the school, Muhammad was escorted out of the auditorium and we drove through downtown to our house. There were flashing lights and sirens as our motorcade passed through Louisville en route to our humble home. I was savouring the moment in the front passenger seat, while Muhammad sat and stood in the back waving with that signature smirk on his face at all the onlookers.

When we arrived outside our home on Grand Avenue, all our neighbours were milling around to give the new champ a hero's reception. The local newspaper was there to grab an interview and snap pictures. I remember gazing at the medal and how beautiful it looked hanging around his neck as he spoke to all those present. Eventually, the crowd dispersed, thrilled to have been in the presence of the Olympic hero. I began to reflect back on the years of us training together, running together in the early hours of the morning and discussing the best amateur boxers. Muhammad would always tell me with great conviction, 'Rudy, one day I'll win the Olympic light heavyweight gold medal.' I had faith in my brother's boxing ability so didn't for one moment let pessimistic sentiments overshadow the optimism. But still, there is no better feeling in this world than to witness the success of a family member. Our parents had always told us that we had to be dedicated to boxing in order to become successful. Our dad would explain that we would encounter obstacles along the way to success. Some parents aren't supportive of their kids, but ours encouraged us, and that's something I'll always remember.

Of course my brother's life changed from that moment, but mine changed too. I was sort of a celebrity in high school because of my brother's new-found status. The students would smile and wish me well as I passed by them in the hallways or sat with them in the classrooms. It was my senior year at Central High School, and I'll never forget it.

Now, for more than five decades everyone has known that Muhammad threw his gold medal away in the Ohio River because he wasn't allowed to eat in a restaurant in our home town after he won the Olympics. But I read somewhere that this is a false, fabricated story concocted by someone unknown to me and my brother and widely accepted. They said that my brother lost his medal and I did everything in my power to help to try and find it. They claimed that we looked everywhere in the house without any luck. As you can imagine, it was a symbol of prestige and something my brother was very proud of. Unfortunately, years later someone, for whatever reason, decided to spread that bullshit. I can put the record straight here: Muhammad and I went to the restaurant together when we were refused service. Muhammad said, 'I'd like a cheeseburger.' The lady replied, 'We don't serve Negroes.' My brother sarcastically said, 'I don't eat them, either. Just give me a cheeseburger.' Realising we weren't going to get served, we left disgusted and angry. And when we got to the Second Street Bridge, my brother tossed his beloved medal in the river. I tried stopping him, but my brother said, 'No, Rocky, I'm hurt. I've been so disrespected. It hurts me bad.' Next thing you know, I actually started to cry.

That was the last time we both laid our eyes on the Olympic medal. So, I witnessed it with my own eyes.

★ ★ ★

After the Olympics Muhammad turned professional and signed up with the Louisville Group – a group of ten millionaires – who became his management team. They had approached my brother after his victory in Rome, offering to cover his training expenses, travel, housing and food, as well as paying him a signing bonus and guaranteed income – in return for 50 per cent of the income from his fights and future activities.

It also meant saying goodbye to Joe Martin, who I'd like to say on the record, had guided Muhammad really well and had cultivated a great relationship with both of us during the course of their trainer-fighter relationship. Muhammad's professional debut was on 29 October 1960 against Tunney Hunsaker, a bout which took place in Louisville's Freedom Hall. After that fight – a six-round affair which my brother won on points – Muhammad's management team decided to employ the services of boxing's widely respected coach Angelo Dundee. This meant that Muhammad would have to relocate to Miami Beach, where Angelo ran the famous 5th Street Gym.

Interestingly, my brother's first ever encounter with Angelo, however, had come years before, in our home town. In 1958, Angelo was training light heavyweight champion Willie Pastrano, who was in town for a fight with George Holman. My brother followed the sport very closely, and would never pass up a chance to meet a fighter or trainer he respected, and so after the fight, which Pastrano lost, he called Angelo's room from the hotel lobby asking if he could see him and his fighter for five minutes. After a long pause, Angelo agreed and so Muhammad and I went to their room to meet him and his dejected fighter. Well, Muhammad more or less barged in there and barked at Angelo to take him on as a boxer. Dundee and his fighter were watching TV and drinking orange juice and eating potato chips when we interrupted. Pastrano, who was lying on the bed in his undervest indulging in a bowl of ice cream, initially dismissed my brother. He thought Muhammad was just this young enthusiastic teenager with a big mouth. And Muhammad, never reticent about getting his views across, immediately started bragging to Angelo that he was going to be the next heavyweight champion of the world. On one hand Angelo was taken aback by that kind of boastfulness because it was something no athlete resorted to back then. On the other hand, he was the kind of man who saw this sort of confidence as a positive in a fighter – a necessary quality for success in a tough sport. The five minutes turned into a three-and-a-half-hour conversation, consisting mostly of Muhammad peppering the coach and his fighter with questions. Muhammad was very inquisitive and his enthusiasm was evident to Angelo, and I think he was able to ascertain that this young man was something special.

Anyway, after my brother won the Olympic gold, Angelo happened to run into him in Louisville. Angelo was more receptive this time, telling him to join him in Miami to train with him. Much as it was a tempting offer at the time, Muhammad declined it – why, I don't know. When the Louisville Group hired the coach to train their new golden goose, it was an ideal move for Muhammad that would be the start of a new beginning. Before Muhammad made the transition, he had been training with Jersey Joe Walcott who had him mopping and sweeping the floor. Muhammad didn't like it there. In fact, he hated it. He had voiced his concerns to Jersey Joe to no avail, clearly stating that he wasn't there to wash dishes and do chores, but to train. This fell on deaf ears, so when my brother called Angelo, he wanted nothing more than to make a quick exit. Angelo was kind of expecting the call and all for it, and Muhammad, desperate, told him, 'I'd like to work out tomorrow.' 'Where are you?' asked Angelo. 'I'm in Louisville.' Angelo asked, 'Well, how are you going to get here?' Muhammad replied, 'I'm going to drive there.' So, he drove all the way to Miami, which was a fifteen-hour drive – long, exhausting but, in his eyes, well worth the trip.

The next day, Sunday morning, Muhammad made his way to the famed 5th Street Gym. Angelo's young son Jimmy would go to the gym with his father on Sundays. When the Dundees arrived at 10 o'clock in the morning they saw Muhammad patiently sitting on the stairs waiting for them. Muhammad swiftly made an impression on young Jimmy. They all walked up the stairs and into the gym so Angelo could show my brother the modest training facility. Muhammad caught Angelo off guard when he remarked that he wanted to have a sparring session and fight on Tuesday – two days after his marathon drive. Angelo's brother Chris, who was a promoter, would be in charge of setting up the fight.

Muhammad, of course, was keen to make up for lost time. Angelo paired him with Willie Pastrano and a handful of other heavyweights and they sparred – in a session that would go down in everyone's memory as another example of my brother's early brilliance. To be perfectly frank, my brother pretty much kicked the tar out of Willie and Angelo's other young heavyweights. He was nothing short of superb in the ring. Impressed with Muhammad's extraordinary performance, the coach turned to his star pupil Willie – who was the light heavyweight champion of the world mind you – and said, 'You had a bad day. You might as well go home. You're tired.' Muhammad was desperate to show his new coach his pedigree. He would normally take it easy on people he trained with, but he was all pumped up wanting to prove a point and didn't hold back on those guys at all. He gave them a very hard time. And his new coach, for his part, realised this was, as he would refer to my brother, 'the best kid'.

That wasn't the end of my brother's introduction to Miami, however. After that first workout Muhammad, along with Angelo and Jimmy, got together with some friends of Angelo's to have lunch at a place down the street. Angelo, of course, eagerly wanted to introduce his new Olympic champion to his friends. As the three entered an eatery near the gym, though, the man at the counter met Muhammad's smile with a glare and said, 'We don't serve Negroes here.' Well, he followed up with something worse than that, derogatory remarks that didn't go down well with my brother. It was as if an alien had walked in. Muhammad would've been within his rights to want to teach this man some manners, but at this moment Angelo entered.

'We're not having any of those,' he said, looking the man right in the eyes. 'We're having hamburgers. We're sitting here and we're having lunch.' At this point, there was nothing the guy could do. It was in his best interest to break the rules and keep his mouth shut. Anyway, after this little mishap they all sat down and had lunch and Muhammad's trainer introduced him to several of his friends.

Due to the segregation laws, finding a place for Muhammad to stay in became problematic. Muhammad initially stayed at the Mary Elizabeth and Sir John hotels in Overtown, a whites-only zone, before his coach found him a place. Angelo was concerned about his well-being, and he had every reason to be. Just being in those areas was enough to attract unwelcome attention, and my brother wasn't one to keep a low profile. Eventually, Angelo locked down a place for him on 7th Avenue and 118th Street, which was right down from the street where Angelo lived, a grey one-floor home with a front and backyard. Not exactly an Olympic champion's quarters – and even then, his troubles with race didn't end.

Muhammad, when he ran to the gym as part of his daily exercise, would periodically get stopped by the police. Angelo would get phone calls from the police almost daily, always variations on a theme: they didn't believe my brother was training at the fabled 5th Street Gym and were adamant on checking out his story. 'Angelo, is this young man your fighter?' the policeman would ask. 'Yes, he's my fighter,' Angelo would tell the officer, often irritated. 'Please let him go and train.' Miami wasn't necessarily better than any other place in the United States surrounding prejudice, but thank goodness my brother was at least staying within the vicinity of Angelo's home. As the fighter-trainer relationship started to gel, Muhammad would spend every holiday together with the Dundee family.

I was a senior in high school when my brother signed his contract with the Louisville Group and left for Miami Beach. After turning professional he spent a large amount of the money he received from his sponsoring group to purchase our parents a new home. Mom had often spoken about some of the things she desired to have – a new home being one. I can vividly recall how happy our mother was. Now our family could afford some luxuries as my brother's future looked bright.

It wasn't long before I got the call to follow Muhammad. Despite his close bond with the Dundee family, my brother didn't trust a lot of folks at the time, and, consequently, in 1962 he sent for me because he wanted a close family member with him. For my part, I never really had a regular job, so I jumped at the chance. My first job was to be a member of Muhammad's entourage and training camp. Needless to say, I wasted no time packing my bags and moved out there to be with him. I quickly settled in with my brother. Muhammad and I would often spend time watching movies in our front room and just relaxing. We both would usually go to bed at 11 p.m. because we had to wake up early in the morning to do our roadwork.

Quite apart from his patience in dealing with police officers, Angelo was just what my brother needed. He was a wonderful character, combining the warmth you'd associate with a favourite uncle and a mastery of fighters' psychology that bordered on the supernatural. He could get into his fighters' heads and urge them to accomplish things without them even knowing he tried, which, at that point in my brother's career, was exactly what he needed. Early on Muhammad was very stubborn about his own ideas, and so the game became for Angelo to find some way to convince his fighter that whatever he wanted to do was his own idea. He spent a lot of time kind of manipulating Muhammad, getting him to think that he was the one deciding to train more, train less, work a specific punch or whatever. If he wanted my brother to throw an uppercut more, he'd heap praise on him for the one time in a round he threw it, and the next round Muhammad might throw it half a dozen times.

One of my favourite anecdotes concerning Angelo, though, comes from a different fighter that he was training at the same time as my brother. The guy's confidence in his punching was ebbing, specifically his confidence about hitting with power. That kind of worry, as any fighter knows, can be death – if you aren't convinced you can hit, you'll be afraid to trade, and you'll only get hurt. So one day, before a training session, Angelo unscrewed the top of the peanut bag, and the first time this boxer hit the bag it came right off its moorings and flew across the gym and it was knocked off. The stunned fighter suddenly thought he had this explosive punching power, and started hitting with confidence again. Imagine having a guy like that on your side, helping you out behind the scenes. And I knew the difference it made – we'd occasionally fight between ourselves. Sometimes he'd whup me, and other times I'd whup him. But I could feel him becoming better, faster, stronger.

It was two-way traffic, of course. Every boxer works hard, but Angelo had said over the years that he never had a boxer who worked that hard in the gym as Muhammad did. This was a man, mind you, who in his career coached more than fifteen world champions. In fact, Angelo felt

Muhammad worked too hard sometimes. It was very clear, even early in his career, that Muhammad took too many punches in training. Angelo knew, as did I, that he allowed his sparring partners to hit him in the head. Even after donning a head guard, he would welcome the sort of severe punishment that most boxers would do everything in their power to evade. He was convinced that being pummelled would toughen him up for real fights, which, in those days, didn't sound as crazy as it does today. Any way you look at it, my brother was a consummate professional, who worked hard and did everything he could to prepare for each one of his fights. And, of course, his toughest fights were yet to come.

A BROTHER ON
A MISSION

In the 1960s, prejudice and segregation was a fact of life for every black man in America, but some places it was more prevalent than others. And while you would certainly feel racism's insidious effects in Louisville, in Miami it was inescapable. Segregation, for instance, extended not just to nightclubs and cafes but to beaches. Miami's white residents kept its most pristine stretches of sand for themselves, while leaving black people to swim near sewage outlets or excluding them entirely. Restaurants stayed segregated well into the decade, and even when schools were officially declared desegregated, many residents pushed back.

This was the mood in Miami when my brother relocated to the city in 1960. If you were a person of colour, these rules were part and parcel of your existence in what was supposed to be a free country – even if you were an Olympic athlete. While Muhammad would never allow another man's prejudice to impede his progress in training – he was too thick-skinned for that – there were certainly occasions when Muhammad and I would have a run-in with the uglier side of the country while we socialised in Miami. Any time that you stepped out of your lane, someone would be there to tell you, openly or behind your back, that you forgot your place. It wasn't limited to the general populace, either; you drew attention from the established institutions and authorities in mainstream America too. Muhammad said to me, 'As long as our people stay in their place, they're

OK. But as soon as they get out of their lane, then they might get killed.'

Muhammad, with his trademark confidence, was ready to meet this kind of treatment with open disdain. As a knowledgeable student of boxing history, he traced this contemptuous attitude towards black athletes in particular back to Jack Johnson, who was hounded and put in jail on trumped-up charges of taking a white woman across state lines for illicit purposes. He was also aware of the tribulations of Joe Louis and Jesse Owens, both of whom were hounded by the Internal Revenue Service for most of their lives over tax issues. He was also only too aware of the perils that had faced Jackie Robinson, who received death threats when he became the first black player to compete in Major League Baseball in the modern era.

Jim Brown, who forged an enduring friendship with Muhammad, was seen as the angriest, meanest black man in America and was served with all kinds of trumped-up charges in terms of claims from women in particular. The message was clear: any time you got out of your lane in American society, if you were black you were going to be attacked and pilloried. That most certainly was the case with Muhammad, who had garnered no end of media attention in the wake of his Olympic victory. But at the same time as my brother was being told to know his place, it was seen to be critically important that the heavyweight champion of the world be a tool for white political, economic and other interests. When Muhammad decided to fight against that system, he knew he would become a target. But, just as every other black American athlete found themselves, in some way or another, under attack by the white American mainstream, he also knew that it was likely to happen whatever he did.

With all of this in mind, it might be easier to understand what piqued my brother's interest in the Black Power movement, and specifically the Nation of Islam. There's a misconception that Malcolm X introduced my brother to the Nation of Islam and was responsible for converting Muhammad, but that's not entirely true. Malcolm was influential, no doubt about it, but he wasn't the one who invoked Muhammad's interest initially. It was an assistant minister named Captain Samuel X Saxon who first introduced my brother to the Nation's teachings, after a chance meeting on Second Avenue just before he left for the Rome Olympics.

Captain Samuel was the captain of a mosque in Miami, and this was where my brother went frequently when he first moved there. This was the first time he had listened carefully to what the Nation were teaching, and Miami was the place where he slowly realised that this was what he had been searching for all his life. In the early days, it was definitely more politically related than religious, even if that feeling shifted over time. My brother and I decided to join this controversial group because Muhammad wanted to feel a part of something, a cause, not because of any underlying spiritual quest.

Whatever our reasons, though, alarm bells started ringing out back at our parents' residence once Muhammad and I embraced the teachings of the Nation of Islam. Dad and Mom were gravely perturbed, to say the least. They felt their children should be good Christians, and this new religion was well beyond the scope of their experience, so they were, understandably, very upset. Growing up, Muhammad had a burning itch which told him there had to be something better than the racism he experienced as a young boxer – a light at the end of the tunnel. And while my parents had taught us that the Lord would provide, the religious beliefs we were both brought up with didn't seem, at least to my brother and I at the time, to be the solution. My brother, who possessed an inquisitive mind, had spent half his life questioning why black people should suffer the conditions that they were in, why anything black was associated with negativity. This even seemed to be the case in Christianity: anything good in the Bible was made white, with Jesus and the Lord himself portrayed that way, whatever country they had first been born in. We were shown images of the saviour of mankind as a benevolent white man, with seemingly no place for other skin colours in the hierarchy of heaven. Well, that wasn't enough for us. My brother didn't want to be a run-of-the-mill Negro, throwing himself at the mercy of Christians who'd often already shown they thought of black people as second-class citizens. He refused to accept that.

★ ★ ★

Our parents, of course, weren't the only people to worry about our new affiliations. Most people in the United States abhorred the Nation of Islam, and anyone associating themselves with the organisation was regarded with suspicion. Even among the black community, a lot of people maintained their distance from the movement. In the beginning, no one really knew we were gravitating towards becoming Muslims, because Muhammad and I had resolved to keep our intentions quiet until the right time – it was our dark secret. We both agreed that we would proclaim ourselves Muslims when the time was right, but publicly we were forced to be careful by the prying eyes of the press, which was predominantly white, and even a few individuals around us who might have given away our secret. If we exposed ourselves, we knew that boxing's governing bodies, public opinion and even the United States Government might become obstacles in Muhammad's quest to become a world boxing champion. Muhammad, it was decided, had to keep his loyalties secret until the night he got his hands on the coveted heavyweight title. He had to be, in his own words, 'Wise as a serpent but harmless as a dove.'

As the game of hide-and-seek continued, though, certain individuals close to my brother became more and more aware of his links to the Black Muslims. After amassing a 19–0 professional record with fifteen knockouts, Muhammad had been given the opportunity to challenge the heavyweight champion Sonny Liston, a fight he knew he would have to take more seriously than any of his bouts to that date. Three months before the Liston fight, Muhammad and I were at Angelo's house for Christmas, and the family was out in the backyard. Back in those days there wasn't much integration, and my brother wasn't yet a famous face, so every time Muhammad visited the Dundee family they'd open the door and laugh about it with the neighbours, who found it rather strange that a young black guy was visiting next door. As time went on and Muhammad was thrust into the media spotlight and he would show up at Dundee's home, the neighbours would willingly come over to see him, but at this stage they would almost reel in disbelief when they saw two young black men knock on the door in an all-white area.

Anyway, on this particular occasion, Muhammad and I joined in as the Dundee family unwrapped their gifts. Since Muhammad was missing our family back in Louisville, he saw Angelo's family as kind of his surrogate family, and he enjoyed playing with Angelo's young son

Jimmy, whom he'd spent some time with over the years, in particular. Muhammad was quiet as we tucked into the meal and lounged around enjoying the family atmosphere, but when Jimmy started playing with a pair of walkie-talkies he'd been given as a present, his more playful, energetic self emerged. Little Jimmy was running around screaming on his walkie-talkie, 'Cassius! Cassius! Where are you?' Muhammad replied, 'There's no Cassius here, it's Muhammad Ali.' The bemused young kid kept on shouting, 'I don't know Muhammad Ali!' The point is, Angelo knew what was going on with my brother and his involvement with the Nation of Islam, even though he rarely delved into what Muhammad was up to as far as his political tendencies were concerned. But Angelo, one of the few people Muhammad could trust, endeavoured to keep it all hushed up because he had a growing fear that the boxing commission would pull the fight if it got a sniff that his fighter had joined a widely reviled religious group. The dream of becoming the heavyweight champion would be put in jeopardy, and Angelo, more than anything, wanted him to be crowned heavyweight champion of the world – this was the ultimate goal.

Not many people are aware, but initially my brother became Cassius X – this was the name he was given by Elijah Muhammad. Then he gave him his name Muhammad Ali in time for my brother to announce it immediately after his victory over Liston. Muhammad, we were told, means being the one worthy of praise, and Ali means the most high. Although Muhammad had initially been given his name over the phone, when he came to Elijah Muhammad's house he went upstairs. The great spiritual leader said to Muhammad, 'I have the meaning for it' and he came down and he revealed what it meant. I was given mine, Rahaman Ali – meaning 'Merciful' – at the same time.

When we submitted to the Nation of Islam we were also submitting to the teachings of the leader, honourable Elijah Muhammad, who went on to have a profound influence over my brother. And, almost from the beginning, the teachings that Muhammad was exposed to seem to fit him in a way that little of his education had until then. Muhammad resolved to channel his emotions into something much deeper, something that he felt would be a potent force in his life, since by this point he had gone beyond seeing the Nation as a religious group and begun to embrace its deeper teachings.

Membership of the Nation had other profound effects on my brother's life too, of course. When Muhammad became part of the Nation, he spent time with Elijah Muhammad, but also came under the thrall of one of the leader's nine children. Jabir Herbert Muhammad was a devout Muslim but also a businessman, who ran a photography studio on Chicago's 79th Street as well as the Nation's official newspaper *Muhammad Speaks*. It wasn't until later that my brother actually met and befriended Herbert soon after the Liston fight, and Muhammad asked his spiritual leader if his son could collaborate with him and assist him in managing his boxing career. Herbert's father gave his permission readily, signalling the start of a long-lasting relationship which would benefit Herbert personally as much as it would the Nation. At the time Muhammad was being managed by the Louisville Group, under a ten-year contract, so Herbert would have to wait until 1966 before he could fully get his claws into my brother, but he still took every opportunity to increase his control. However, Muhammad and I didn't see it that way at the time; as we saw the relationship, we operated on the basis of mutual respect and had his utmost trust.

Elijah Muhammad, meanwhile, was not interested in sport and play at all – his interest and single greatest objective lay in reaching the black men living in a white man's White America. He was happy to use any vehicle he could, and, as an outspoken, charismatic celebrity, my brother certainly fit the bill. So yes, in a sense he certainly exploited Muhammad, but the relationship to some extent went both ways. As Muhammad primarily forged both a personal and working relationship with Herbert, my brother had access to the leader of the Nation of Islam through his son.

* * *

While side distractions involving religion were playing a pivotal role in Muhammad's life, in his quest to conquer the heavyweight division he tirelessly continued to work towards a better future. He also continued to make time for friends. A day before the Liston bout, which was scheduled for 25 February 1964, Muhammad and I went into the hospital to visit Jimmy, who was only ten at the time, because he had had a hernia operation which was going to prevent the young boy from attending the fight. By that point, Jimmy had been to every one of Muhammad's fights from the age of five onwards, so the young man was understandably upset. What was interesting, though, was that the hospital ward for white children was full so the staff had asked Jimmy if he would mind being housed in the Negro ward. 'Why?' the young bemused boy asked. 'Well, because it's the Negro ward,' the doctor replied. Jimmy, of course, said that this was OK with him, and so he was the only white patient in the black ward, right next to another kid who was the same age. And so one day he was talking to this other kid about how upset he was about not being able to go to see Muhammad fight for the belt when he heard someone shouting out aloud in the hallway, 'Young Chief, where are you!?' Muhammad used to call Angelo 'Chief' and so Jimmy would sometimes be referred to as Young Chief. 'Little Dundee, where are you!?' came the shouts. The next thing anyone knew, my brother and I, along with a couple of Muhammad's camp members – Bundini, Howard Bingham and Patterson the bodyguard, in denim jackets with our bear-hunting gear on – barged in. Can you imagine the look on the nurses' faces? We gave them a big scare.

Anyhow, we walked into the room and there lay Jimmy. Muhammad kissed Jimmy on the head. And as his eyes met the black kid's, who was lying down next to Jimmy, Muhammad said to him, 'What are you doing here? You're lying around doing nothing!' Next, Muhammad put Jimmy in a wheelchair. Then we took the other kid and put him in a separate wheelchair, and then we wheeled them both down the hallway making a chaotic scene as the other patients looked on. We spent plenty of time with Jimmy, but everyone in that children's ward got an autograph from Muhammad. My brother did the Ali shuffle, did magic tricks and impressions, and put a smile on those kids' faces for the whole afternoon.

Despite my brother's whimsical sense of humour, he had more serious issues to contend with if he was to get his hands on the title. At that time in particular, the Mafia definitely had an influence on boxing. There were certain boxers that they had a firm grip on, and the heavyweight title, being the most valuable in the sport, was never far from their concerns. There were those who preferred it that way, though. Certain people have always liked the concept of the criminal fraternity running boxing. I think certain business people and gamblers were comfortable with them though, since in their eyes they knew where they stood. However, by the 1960s the Mafia had a problem: they faced considerable opposition from the Black Muslims. From early in his career, even before Herbert could wrest full control away from the Louisville Group, Muhammad had the protection of the Nation of Islam. The Mafia, even if they were vying for control, could not infiltrate his camp as easily as they normally could with other prize fighters thanks to the Nation's presence, and so, compared with other champions of the era, my brother was a free man who could do whatever he wanted and go wherever he pleased. Without being under the Nation's umbrella, who knows what fate would have had in store for my brother?

As for Angelo, he preferred to keep things legit. The nature of heavyweight boxing at the time always meant that some degree of interaction with the criminal fraternity would be necessary, but in the case of the Dundees, rumours persisted that it was Angelo's brother Chris who dealt with organised crime and not necessarily Angelo. Why would Angelo? After all he could acquire what he wanted through his brother. So the connection with the Mafia was stronger with Chris, but they didn't really control either brother. Around the time of the Liston fight, Angelo was negotiating with the notorious mobsters the Nilon brothers (Jack and Bob) and endeavoured to keep them from controlling the judges and the referees. Angelo was astute. He would not let it be known until about twenty minutes before the fight who the judges were. And there was a big argument about that. The Nilon brothers and organised crime figures Frankie Carbo and his partner Blinky were determined to get their claws in the fight. These were dangerous men. Apparently Angelo didn't have anything to do with them or his brother Chris as far as aiding them. Muhammad's coach and his brother stood up for boxing and did their best to make it a clean sport.

Obviously, the Mafia had their hooks in Liston. From the start of his pro career in 1953, Liston had been 'owned' by St Louis mobster John Vitale.

By 1959, Frankie, who'd once operated as a hitman for the Mafia group Murder, Inc., owned a majority interest in Liston's contract alongside his partner Palermo. They, alongside a group of other promoters known as the 'Combination', had complete control over him, and were well known for fixing high-profile boxing matches. Mercifully, Muhammad was in the safe hands of the Dundee brothers. They kept Muhammad free of talk of the Mob so his mind was focused on the job at hand with as little distraction as possible. Not only was I helping my brother train, but I was a moral support system. Maintaining some distance, my brother basically left the Mob situation to the Dundee brothers. We received anonymous threatening phone calls a week before the first Liston fight and even on the morning of the fight at our house, but we paid them little heed. In our way of thinking, God would protect us – and if he didn't, the Nation was there to help.

My brother finally fought Liston in Miami, but before he entered the ring he had one final tribulation to contend with. I made my professional debut with a hard-hitting fight against Chip Johnson. My opponent was a more experienced pugilist with six pro fights to his tally – even in the amateurs he had fought far more times than I had. It was a tough fight, and I took some heavy shots. When I was fighting in the ring, I later found out, Muhammad sneaked out of the dressing room and stood in the hallway and watched me fight. The forever concerned older brother, he wanted me to prevail with as little damage as possible. That meant a lot to me when I found out about it, a lot more than the fight. The feeling I had, knowing that my brother was more concerned for my well-being than his own on the most important night of his career, has stayed with me since that day.

In any case, I got beaten up really badly, but nevertheless I fought my way to the end of four rounds and was awarded the decision. Winning my first pro fight made me ecstatic, but the feeling wouldn't last. The ring announcer announced me as Muhammad's brother and the crowd started booing me. They still weren't enamoured with Muhammad, and were happy to make their feelings known to anyone sharing his name. As the boos continued, my brother was shouting for me to exit the ring and telling me that he'd do my fighting for me.

After the fight I went back to the dressing room, and he put his arm around me and explicitly told me that I didn't need to fight any more, and that he was going to be crowned the champ tonight. 'Rudy, that was your last fight,' he empathetically said to me. 'I'm going to take care of you for the rest of your life, don't worry about it.' I had a quick shower and got changed. I rushed back to the arena to watch my brother in action, in the ringside seat I'd been assigned. As my brother made his way to the ring the tension and excitement in the air was reaching its climax – there's always a hum, a buzz, a way the air changes at any fight, but this feeling was something else. However much he clowned and joked, we both knew that this was a very dangerous fight for my brother and it was scary, to be honest. I had butterflies in my stomach, a sense of nerves that never quite left me in any fight he had, but threatened to unseat me that night.

Maybe I didn't need to worry so much. From the opening bell, my brother showed that he could back up every word he'd said in the press, in his confrontations with Liston, to supporters and detractors alike. He danced away from Liston's punches, swayed out of range with the leans and slips that most commentators had said would get him killed, and peppered Liston from a distance from bell to bell. Round after round, Liston was barely able to stand and land against my brother, let alone hit him with the kind of shots he was famous for.

The only rough moment in the fight, famously, came when Liston's camp resorted to dirty tricks, smearing something on their man's gloves that affected my brother's vision, almost costing him the fight. I realised that something was wrong almost immediately, and the situation sent all sorts of thoughts spiralling through my head. My first concern, of course, was for my brother's safety, and I'd have pulled him out of the ring in a second if I thought his well-being was at stake. At the same time, I knew that this might be the only chance he ever got at the world championship, that the humiliated Liston would never give him another shot if he lost now. Confusion at what exactly happened, the roar of competing emotions, the swell in the crowd as they saw Liston making what many perceived as a comeback – my adrenaline was out of control.

This moment was almost as dangerous for Angelo as it was for

Muhammad. The Black Muslims in my brother's corner instantly got their hackles up, assuming he had something to do with it and casting doubt on his loyalty. While Angelo was reassuring them, he was also taking action – he knew from past experience the kind of tricks Liston's team were prepared to pull, and calmly washed out my brother's eyes in between rounds.

'You're not quitting!' I remember him barking, as he sent my brother out for what would turn out to be the final round. Angelo wasn't like some coaches who would shout and instruct their fighters to throw certain punches, expecting them to follow their advice to a tee – Muhammad had licence to conduct the fight himself, using the initiative he'd shaped over years of training. Where Angelo shone, however, was in this sort of crisis – he stayed cool and collected, and probably kept my brother from losing his only shot at the title. Muhammad was Angelo's golden boy and he knew his fighter had a chance to be the heavyweight champion of the world. By then, Muhammad's relationship with his coach was almost like that of a father and son connection. There was no way, I knew, he would have double-crossed his golden boy. Not a chance.

After the incident with Muhammad's eyes, the Black Muslims and I redoubled our efforts in the corner, looking out for any further interference of an illegal nature. And I, of course, was Muhammad's personal bodyguard, always up close to Muhammad. Before the fight in the dressing rooms I had been under strict instructions to keep my eyes on the water bottles in case anyone walked into the room and put something in them. If I took my eyes off the bottles for even a few minutes I had to empty Muhammad's water bottle and fill it up with fresh water in case it had been tampered with. I wasn't taking any chances. If the fight went to a decision, I was certain then the judges would have been influenced by the Mob. That was the way boxing was at the time.

In the event, Muhammad cleared his eyes and Liston quit in the sixth round, just as things were heating up outside the ring. After that fight, I later found out, members of the Mafia went up to Herbert after the fight and told him, 'We're going to come after you with twenty men if you don't come and work for us.' Herbert straight-up ignored them at the time, but by my brother's next fight, I heard, there were 2,000 members of the Nation in attendance. Both parties threatened each other but nothing ever materialised.

Meanwhile, I learned that my brother didn't even trust Angelo as far as I thought. Sometime after the first Liston fight, while we were lounging around at Dr Ferdie Pacheco's home, Muhammad stunned his camp members. He divulged that he didn't trust anyone – Angelo, Ferdie or anyone else for that matter – at the fight. This may have stunned some of these men who thought Muhammad trusted them 100 per cent, while others understood the dilemma. However, Muhammad had doubts about all his cornermen. 'I only trusted my brother and Captain Sam,' he told the assembled crowd. Although my brother and I had forged a strong relationship with Angelo by then, there was still something of a shred of doubt in his mind. I mean, at the time no matter how friendly or close any white guy was to my brother, there was always that chance of being double-crossed.

The fight had brought the sport into widespread public disrepute. In a way, Muhammad winning that first fight against Liston helped to push the Mob out of boxing. Liston, even if he didn't want any part of them, had been the biggest money-maker for the Mafia, holding the most valued prize in the sport and its biggest earning potential. When his star faded, they lost their hold on things. The rematch on 25 May 1965 only cemented things and, to me, the suggestion that Liston took a dive in the second fight against Muhammad is ridiculous. The Mob was counting on him to win the title back. They were in the game to control boxing and rake in money using boxers. Liston's life and livelihood were on the line – the Mob only had one use for him and that was to fight. I think after Muhammad regained the title it kind of got the Mob to back off a little bit more because they said they wanted Angelo and Chris to come on board, and the Dundee brothers said, 'No way!' But before anyone could breathe a sigh of relief, there was something else to trouble mainstream America.

* * *

It was just on 6 March, less than two weeks after my brother claimed the heavyweight crown that Elijah Muhammad officially announced to the world that he would be honoured with a new name. My brother had been answering questions about his relationship with the Nation since before the fight, and now they were reaching a crescendo, with endless reporters calling him a 'card-carrying' Muslim and calling the organisation's credentials into question. We were all expecting the backlash, of course, but it exceeded even our worst expectations. Some of the black population were of the opinion that Muhammad had made a grave mistake in joining the Nation of Islam, a grievous error both in terms of his career and his role as a representation of and the image of black society. Meanwhile, the death threats began immediately – it seemed like anyone who could get hold of a crayon and a piece of paper was lining up to promise my brother that they were coming for him. He was getting threats from people promising to petrol-bomb his house, shoot at his car or murder him. More hatred was directed towards Angelo and his family because of their association with my brother. Everyone around Muhammad, we knew, was a target for the worst elements in America.

Being Muhammad's brother, it wasn't nice at all to see him in such a vulnerable, threatened position. My primary job at the time was to keep my eyes on my brother, and I did everything from literally watching his back to making sure no one tried to poison Muhammad. Did it make me a little paranoid? Absolutely. Did it enrage me? Certainly.

Let me be clear: death threats, whether they're frequent or rare, are a fact of life for anyone who is moving up in black American society. I don't care whether you're a boxer or an outspoken TV commentator or President of the United States. If you're black you're going to get a certain amount of attention from politically malignant degenerates. Between 1967 when activist Dr Harry Edwards first proposed the Olympic project for Human Rights and 1972, he received a staggering 300 death threats. This was just part of life back then for those of us who spoke up. So when Muhammad announced his allegiance to the Nation, and later when he refused to go into the military, there was no shortage of cowards sitting on their couches ready to write something negative to a black man who was standing on his constitutional rights and principles in society. You got used to it. After a while it even got more tiresome than frightening. But it never stopped making me angry.

Another thing – this one more a nuisance than a source of fear – was that, as a member of the Nation, the FBI was going to be tapping your phone, opening up your mail and following you around everywhere you went. If you look at the FBI counter-intelligence programme and freedom of information requests from the time, they had files on the Nation of Islam which consisted of hundreds of thousands of pages. The FBI monitored mosques and wire-tapped everyone from Malcolm X to local ministers, officials and lieutenants of the Nation of Islam in various cities. They accumulated information on parents of members, vehicle licence plates, meetings. They really saw the Nation of Islam, for some reason, as a threat to America. This federal law and enforcement agency spent an inordinate amount of money to watch the Nation of Islam – and, mostly, it was in vain. The Nation of Islam was so careful of their reputation that they warned us repeatedly not to carry a weapon, and instructed us carefully on how to conduct ourselves around officers of the law. Elijah Muhammad, I remember, told us not to carry even a penknife. Muhammad was happy to comply, saying, 'I don't believe in violence… unless you're jumped.'

Still, the FBI endeavoured to keep track of what we were doing and saying, apparently expecting to uncover some grandiose plot against America. We were always aware that spies were there; our privacy was invaded in a way you'd scarcely believe. I remember Muhammad was told by his advisors and people around him, 'Always be careful what you say on the phone. If you want to discuss anything have a meeting.' There were certain things, certain information, that we were forbidden from discussing on the phone to minimise potential interuptions by the authorities.

During his later trial for refusing the draft, it even emerged that my brother had been recorded during conversations with Dr Martin Luther King, whom he'd been in touch with since Dr King wished him the best before the Liston fight. FBI notes released later showed my brother telling King that he was keeping up with his work and that he regarded him as a brother. Later, the law enforcement agencies put out misinformation about my brother, fake letters that quickly became tabloid fodder, anything to undermine this young black man who was causing waves. I don't believe for a second that FBI director J Edgar Hoover seriously thought of Muhammad as a threat to America. And yet, still, FBI agents, it emerged, went through my brother's school records. FBI agents were visible virtually everywhere Muhammad went. Maybe they were satisfying their own curiosity? Not much about the whole thing makes sense.

More recently, it's been claimed that Angelo was an informant for the FBI. This is just absurd. True, the FBI pulled Angelo in before the first Liston fight, but that only showed how loyal to Muhammad and his friends the man was. They showed him pictures of the Nation of Islam, men whom Angelo would easily have recognised, asking, 'Angelo, who's this guy? Who's this guy?' and every time Angelo responded with, 'All these Muslim guys look the same to me.' Angelo wasn't going to give up anything – not on a man who wasn't just a fighter, but a part of his family.

MUHAMMAD & MALCOLM

Long after Malcolm X left this earth, Muhammad was giving a speech at a gathering in Los Angeles when a black man, who looked somewhat older than the typical crowd there, barked from the back, 'If you don't believe and preach what Elijah says, you are going to die.' This individual was referring to Malcolm's murder. Muhammad, who had become outwardly disenchanted with his late friend, responded, 'No. You ain't going to die if you don't believe what Elijah says. But I know some people who'd kill you if you talk bad about me! And I don't have to tell them to kill you.' There was a loud burst of laughter at that, but my brother wasn't laughing – far from it. 'I know some people who'd kill you!' Muhammad continued. 'Listen, listen. Let me tell you. Any man who is powerful, who's loved by hundreds of thousands, he doesn't have to say, "Get him." You're not safe talking about him. I know some brothers who'd kill you if you talk about their mama. They'd kill you! You call his mama a no-good whoring bitch and see if you don't die. I know some people who'd kill you for their mama! A brother would bump you off so fast Muhammad doesn't have to be around.'

The guy in the audience wouldn't leave it as he persistently tried to needle Muhammad to justify Malcolm's death. Muhammad finally got so tired of him he said, 'I ain't bumped off nobody, why you asking me?' But whether he was aggressive or defensive, the questions about

Malcolm's death continued to dog him for some time. It was partly his own fault. Around eight months after Malcolm was assassinated, Muhammad went on a Chicago radio station, WVON, appearing on a show called Hotline hosted by Wesley South. Muhammad, not holding back, declared publicly that Malcolm was going to be 'taken care of' by the Nation. Later, some believed that my brother should be arrested on suspicion of complicity in the killing of the former member of the Nation of Islam. But my brother said a lot of things publicly. He was like that. What he said may have been misinterpreted.

Muhammad gravitated towards Elijah Muhammad when Malcolm had parted ways with the leader – the latter two being embroiled in a bitter feud. The Nation, of course, had advantages – Malcolm was an individual, whereas the Nation of Islam had evolved into an institutional cult that had structural as well as spiritual influence over my brother. Muhammad, at this stage, was firmly in the camp of Elijah Muhammad against his former friend Malcolm. Malcolm, my brother said, had claimed Elijah Muhammad had got twelve women pregnant, that he had discovered that the esteemed spiritual leader wasn't holy and he was having a dozen babies. According to some prominent followers, Malcolm was trying to steal followers and overthrow Elijah Muhammad – hence his tirades against the Nation's leader. But there were more practical reasons for the side my brother chose, too. You're talking about choosing between an individual who had left the Nation of Islam hoping to start a new organisation for Afro-American unity, as opposed to the Nation of Islam where the sons of Elijah Muhammad were my brother's business managers, boxing managers, public relations managers, handlers and so forth, along with spiritual and financial commitments that it was very difficult to walk away from. Had Muhammad decided to stick with Malcolm, he would have left his religious institution behind, alongside hundreds of thousands of dollars if not millions. That would have been a very difficult break to make for any man. This was a sentiment some shared. But I personally felt Muhammad, at the end of the day, would never turn his back on the Nation no matter what.

Of course, at one point, Muhammad still held Elijah Muhammad in the highest regard and clung on to his every word like it was the gospel truth. But once Malcolm broke with the Nation, Muhammad *was*, at least briefly, confused about where his allegiance should lie, even if he didn't show it publicly. Malcolm had been a tremendous force for Elijah Muhammad. He did great work, and perhaps should have been better rewarded for it. But some people felt that he also turned on his benefactor, especially those who were part of the Nation. He went around the world trying to undo some of the things he did, and it was seen as a grave threat. In the eyes of some, Malcolm may not have been a threat to the Nation of Islam, but the point is: he was.

Malcolm, for his part, maintained that he had been exposed to the true religion of Islam when he made a pilgrimage to the holy city of Mecca a couple of months after my brother won the title. What he learned there, he said, conflicted with the teachings of Elijah Muhammad. As a consequence he started to speak up, and that was the root of the problem. The Nation has a general rule, rule number nine, which is to allow no one to make a nuisance. Malcolm, essentially, became a nuisance. He said that if the Muslims would have left him alone then he would've left them alone, but, according to some prominent members, that's not true. He was constantly calling Muslims, constantly asking people to come to his side. He became an interference, and, in the eyes of many, a threat. And Muhammad was aware of the fact. Eventually, Malcolm believed that he had reached a dead end. He even said he was surrounded by these comedians, these actors and he wanted to come back to the Nation. And he was bitter and angry, just as you would be if you were fired from your job. And sometimes you may cuss your boss. Maybe he wanted to come back but his pride wouldn't let him.

Perhaps Malcolm felt he had made the wrong decision by turning his back on Elijah Muhammad. My brother and others in the circle certainly thought so. You have to remember that the Nation had been going twenty years before Malcolm ever came on board and well before my brother and I became members. Malcolm was a helper, not a leader. Elijah Muhammad used him just like he used my brother to get the message out to the people. Malcolm was from the streets and he was good at his job. Elijah Muhammad promoted him, brought him to the biggest stage and he went to work and did what he was supposed to do.

Malcolm, evidently, is a hero to many people. He did some good things and this will never be taken away from him, but some felt he made a foolish decision by his benefactor, who gave him his home. Malcolm was the only man given the honour of using Elijah Muhammad's car – no other minister had that privilege. He was given a salary. He was given $1,000 a month. No other minister was given money like that. He was given special privileges.

Whatever enmity existed between them, though, Muhammad was crushed when Malcolm passed away. Muhammad never, I think, turned his back on his friend completely. Deep down he cared, and his tone started to reflect that, later, in 1975 after the death of Elijah Muhammad. When Malcolm was thrown out of the Nation, Muhammad and the rest of us weren't allowed to speak to him. And when he used to call it was hard for Muhammad not to talk to him because they both had forged a long friendship based on trust. We used to visit Malcolm at his house and spent a lot of time with him. But during his time in the wilderness, Muhammad said to Malcolm, 'You know we can't talk to you right now. We have to wait till this is over. Just hang in there and keep up the faith.' This was his initial attitude. Now, I know that in the movie *Ali* they made it look like that my brother hated Malcolm after they parted ways, but deep down there was always some ambiguity there, the same as you'd have for any good friend who'd gone astray. There was an element of ambiguity attached to their relationship at that point, and I think that the movie got that wrong because Muhammad didn't really hate him. We simply had to respect the wishes of Elijah Muhammad. Muhammad had nothing bad to say to Malcolm. I think that, deep down, he hoped that one day they could be friends again.

At the same time, we kind of knew that something bad was likely to happen to Malcolm sooner or later, based on how many enemies he made. When he was shot, we were surprised, don't get me wrong, it felt extreme, but it also made a kind of sense that it was coming. I don't believe it was the Nation of Islam members who were responsible: Malcolm had a lot of enemies, both among the mainstream authorities and elsewhere. Muhammad and some of us agreed, for instance, that Malcolm praising Kennedy's death wasn't a good idea. It's something

Muslims don't do – pray for somebody to die – especially somebody who cared about black people.

There's a belief in some circles that Malcolm staged his own death. He knew something was going to happen and he always kept a photographer who captured everything. It is the viewpoint of some that he wanted to go out the way he did. How true that is, I couldn't say. Malcolm was told to leave the country, let things cool down, give calmer heads a chance to prevail but he wouldn't leave. At the other end of the spectrum, he had also received warnings not to go. Seven days prior to his death his house was firebombed. The next day Malcolm is on a plane and he's in Michigan. The day after, he's speaking somewhere else. Then he's speaking on a radio station in New York. He was constantly working, even after his house was firebombed, and he said, 'I'm going to name who the people are this Sunday.' To some, he was making it dramatic. And his wife at the time said they were getting seven, eight threatening phone calls a day. But apparently when the FBI came to his house they couldn't find one recording in his house of somebody's voice to analyse who was calling.

As time went by – after the death of Elijah Muhammad – Muhammad would move away from the version of Islamic philosophy that he had first been introduced to, Elijah Muhammad's version, to the more orthodox version that Malcolm had been exposed to before his death. At that point, I think, he began to sort out a lot of the contradictions and conflicts that he was wrestling with. Fast forward to Muhammad's memorial service, and Malcolm's daughter spoke about the fact that my brother had come to a better understanding of what Malcolm had gone through in terms of his transformation from the Nation of Islam to a more Orthodox Islamic commitment. By that point, Muhammad had actually made up with Malcolm's family with regard to some of the earlier conflicts he had been wrestling with in terms of his relationship with Malcolm and Elijah Muhammad. In hindsight, at least, my brother realised that he had made a mistake by turning his back on his friend.

Why didn't my brother leave the Nation earlier? Supposedly Muhammad once told sportswriter Dave Kindred that had he left the Nation of Islam they would have killed him. He would often say, in relation to the Nation, 'A fool can act a wise man but a wise man can't act a fool.' It was a habit of his – to throw things out there without spelling out his feelings, and let you ruminate on them. According to the Muslims from the Nation, they would not have touched Muhammad had he left the organisation. If he left, according to them, there would be no repercussions. If Muhammad had gravitated towards bad-mouthing them like Malcolm did then perhaps things would have been different, but it's true that some Muslims came and went from the Nation with no ill feeling attached, even if they weren't as high profile as my brother. I personally feel that the Nation of Islam wouldn't have touched a hair on my brother's head, let alone attempted to take his life. And I'm sure our family share the same sentiment as me. Besides, Muhammad and Herbert, despite the latter's financial interests in my brother, were like brothers and truly cared for each other.

WAR & CONDEMNATION

At the outset of the Vietnam War, my brother wasn't especially for or against it. In that, at least, he reflected the outlook of the rest of the United States. Plenty of people had a vague idea that communism needed to be stopped before it could take root in this small South East Asian nation, but plenty more argued that America didn't need to interfere. Then again, there was patriotism to consider – like most other children, Muhammad and I were taught in school that any war America fought was to preserve peace making the world a better place for democracy, or for freedom. My brother would have had no problem joining the armed forces had he been drafted back when he was a teenager – he said so himself. But his thought process completely changed when he became a man and able to think for himself.

Muhammad first refused to be inducted into the United States armed forces in March 1966. Not long after that we went to Canada where he fought George Chuvalo. Chuvalo was a tough, come-forward fighter, a guy who didn't mind taking a punch to land one, and more than a few fans were hoping to see him put my brother on the canvas. Chuvalo talked about how he wouldn't fold under the same kind of pressure Liston had, boasting a forty-seven fights record in which he'd never been knocked out. The fight had to be held in Canada after several American venues refused to host us, prompting my brother to tell the world that he was being punished in the pursuit of his cause. In addition to our usual camp members, Jim Brown, Howard Cosell and Bob Arum tagged along. A couple of months earlier, Muhammad, along with Jim, Bob, Herbert and John Ali, formed a boxing promotion company Main Bout Inc. to promote Muhammad's fights. So Jim had come on board. Bob Arum, a lawyer of Jewish descent, really had no clue about the sport of boxing, but had represented my brother in legal matters.

Even if not many commentators gave Chuvalo a chance, it was a great opportunity for Canada to get a glimpse of the champ. Fans and media packed in Sully's Gym in Toronto to get a glimpse of the brash boxing champion who had come to wipe out their national boxing treasure. The gym, which was on the first floor, was a very large training facility. I remember it had one ring, six heavy bags, a couple of speed balls, and the walls were plastered with posters and pictures of the greats like Sugar Ray Robinson, Rocky Marciano and champions of yesteryear. Downstairs was a parts collision business where they fixed cars. Boxing promoter Earl 'Sully' Sullivan ran the training facility, and had arranged for Muhammad to come and fight in Toronto because he was having a problem fighting elsewhere, even in Canada. Initially, he was supposed to fight in Montreal, but they turned him down. Eventually, with a little help from Sully, the guys who owned Maple Leaf Gardens in Toronto conceded, and at last he got his licence to fight in Ontario.

The atmosphere on a typical day was euphoric as Muhammad dazzled the audience during his daily sparring sessions in the ring. Fans paid from $1 to $5 to watch the heavyweight champion spar, and all proceeds would go to support neighbourhood children. Muhammad was working with several of his own sparring partners including myself. He'd just finished working with Jimmy Ellis when Angelo Dundee asked a young local boxer named Spider Jones if he wanted to move around and do a couple of rounds with Muhammad. The young man couldn't miss an opportunity such as this. Jones was nervous at first because the gym was jammed with spectators and media alike from all over the world. So, it was quite an experience for this then 22-year-old boxer to be thrown in at the deep end and be given attention. Muhammad, meanwhile, was ready to go some hard rounds, after starting his fight camp in less than prime physical condition. As they proceeded to spar, Muhammad started pushing his sparring partner towards the ropes, urging him to pound on him. Jones, somewhat astonished, welcomed the invitation. Muhammad would be blocking and slipping the onslaught, and then he'd flick out a couple of jabs and lightning fast punches. However, he didn't try to pummel his partner, or in any way push hard.

One thing about Muhammad was that he typically didn't go hard in sparring. Unlike George Chuvalo, Joe Frazier and Sonny Liston, who went very hard in sparring, as if it was a real fight, my brother was typically very relaxed, experimenting, trying out new things, giving his partners a chance. Angelo used to say that he didn't think Muhammad ever won a sparring session because he was the sort of guy who didn't take it seriously, but he worked hard. Then again, the Muhammad Ali I saw spar in the gym wasn't the same Ali fighting in the ring in front of thousands. When I say this, I mean observing him in sparring you'd think he was 'losing'. But when he fought for real, he was serious in performing. Boxing was a passion for him, but I can tell you that he didn't have the propensity for hurting people. He was somewhat strange in that despite being a fighter in a brutal sport, who faced some of the roughest and toughest fighters in its history, he didn't enjoy wilfully inflicting pain. Muhammad wasn't a finisher like Sugar Ray Robinson or Sonny Liston, or like Mike Tyson later became. He was just a straight-up guy who outboxed you and got into your head. When he got in your head, he'd use that to defeat you as you made mistakes and felt the overwhelming pressure.

There was more to it, too. Muhammad was more than just a smart fighter; he had heart. He was a warrior. And no true warrior is in the game to hurt their sparring partner, the man who's supposed to help him train for his real fights. I'm sure that when Jones first got in the ring he expected to be humiliated in front of the close to 700 people in attendance. I mean, my brother was big news in Toronto. He had come to fight their champion. In spite of the fact he was the outsider, he was embraced by the Canadians like their own. That gym was jammed up with people, so you'd think Muhammad would be inclined to show off in there, try to hurt this boxer who was doing his best to pummel him into oblivion. Of course, Jones had accepted his challenge by climbing in the ring, and he admitted later that he really expected to be humiliated and beaten up by Muhammad – but no such thing happened. They went a gruelling three rounds, in which Jones tired himself out as much by trying to land a clean shot as by taking shots of his own, and afterwards my brother still had waves for the crowds.

After the workout, there was another surprise. Muhammad sat with Jones in the dressing room, which all the fighters shared. Jones, a keen singer, started a rendition of 'Stand by Me', which invoked Muhammad's interest. 'It's a great song,' Muhammad said to him. 'Who is that by?' Jones replied, 'Ben E King!' Jones proceeded to shed light on King – how he began his career and how he'd become the lead singer in a group called the Drifters. My brother seemed intrigued, as he rarely missed a chance to expand his knowledge in an area he found interesting. Both men ended up spending an inordinate amount of time discussing music as they sat there drained from exchanging blows earlier. One of the most prominent singers who was a good friend of Muhammad was Sam Cooke – Sam was also his favourite singer, he told Jones. As it happens Jones knew much about Cooke too and shed light on the elements of his history that my brother wasn't well acquainted with. I had met Sam too: he had been in attendance at the victory party following my brother's victory over Liston, and though he wasn't an active member of the Nation of Islam, he was certainly aware of their teachings. But Spider offered up more background knowledge on Sam: on his musical career, and his time with the group the Soul Stirrers. Sadly, Sam had been killed in 1964, shot in what the police called a justifiable homicide but his friends contended was anything but. Muhammad had his own doubts about the verdict, and discussed them with Jones.

Amazed at this young man's impressive knowledge about music, my brother said, 'Man, you should be in radio.' Coincidentally this had been Jones's intention all along and he eagerly told my brother as much. Muhammad said, 'I was born to be heavyweight champion of the world; you are born to be the radio champion of the world! You need to get in radio, that's where you belong!' Jones said, 'I know.' This sort of stuck with Jones and my brother remembered the day he left – it was just before he went to the airport after the fifteen-round brawl against Chuvalo, which

Muhammad won via a decision – and he gave him a big hug. 'Next time I come here I want to be on your radio show,' said Muhammad. 'If you don't have a radio show then I'm going to whup you!'

So, Muhammad shared a mutual passion with his new Canadian friend. From then on he would always converse about music every time he crossed paths with Jones, He would say, 'Sing "Stand by Me"! Look, Spider Jones, man, you know all about music, man!'

Jones would go on to interview Muhammad twenty years later. My brother, as most people know, was great to interview and anyone who spoke to him quickly realised that behind his physical prowess lay an amazing intellect. He had a tendency to cut interviewers off in the middle of their questions. He'd get up in the middle of the interview and start sparring with them, it was insane. Muhammad always came across as very intelligent, and always talked about his religion and social issues when he was given the media platform. He moved towards what he considered very important subjects, but he'd always find time to joke around. A thing he never resorted to was bad-mouthing his opponents unless he was promoting a fight. Before a fight he would just tear into them. When the fight was over, he treated his opponents like friends.

One time, during a conversation about the music fraternity, I heard Muhammad say that he believed his friend Sam Cooke was murdered. After Cooke's death, a conspiracy theory had formed around the shooting, and it seemed fairly plausible. Back then, certain powerful people didn't want black folks to own their own record labels. However, Sam had started his own record label and was producing most of his own songs, as well as keeping the publishing rights to his songs. Well, this state of affairs didn't go on for long before he was shot under circumstances that were odd to say the least. Bertha Franklin, the manager of the seedy Hacienda Motel in Los Angeles, had shot him, claiming he had tried to rape her, but most people claimed it was a conspiracy. Sam could've had any woman he wanted. He was a good-looking guy. He was only thirty-three years old and he was at the top of his game as a musician. He was one of the greatest singers around.

My brother took his death very badly. He loved Sam. They had become really good friends. Sam would often visit us in Miami in the early days and we would all lounge around and have a great time. Back in those days a lot of the record companies were owned by the Mob, especially in the big cities such as New York and Chicago. Otis Redding started his own record label and a few months later, in 1967, his plane crashed in mysterious circumstances, killing him, the pilot and four of his band members. That could have been a coincidence, who knows, but Muhammad talked about Sam several times and about his death. My brother eventually recorded his own version of Ben E King's 'Stand by Me', which went on the market to moderate acclaim. Could Muhammad have been a decent singer if he had pursued this path? I think with practice he had some potential to succeed. He generally had an aptitude for anything he might put his mind to.

★ ★ ★

Muhammad was scheduled to appear at the Houston Induction Board on 28 April 1967. He phoned Herbert that morning. He would always ask his manager for advice. Most mornings or nights I would find my brother on the phone to Herbert. Somewhat unsure of what lay in his fate, Muhammad asked, 'What's going to happen?' He didn't ask what Herbert expected him to proclaim at the hearing – there was no doubt in his own mind, I sensed, that he was going to spell out his principles. He wasn't ready to surrender to the government. I knew that, too. Muhammad had a tendency to confer with Herbert to get his input. To be honest, he barely questioned his manager, even if others around my brother felt Herbert had control over most issues if not all – he played a pivotal role throughout his career in dictating what Muhammad should do. Anyway, we weren't oblivious to the consequences that the refusal could have on Muhammad's career moving forward.

Meanwhile, Arum was trying his utmost to steer my brother away as he tried to convince him to take a deal he had presented the government with – if Muhammad enlisted, he would take part in exhibition fights entertaining the troops. Furthermore, it wouldn't have a detrimental effect on his boxing career; Muhammad would continue to box professionally. Behind closed doors Arum warned my brother that he was walking right into a suicide if he refused what was supposed to be a lucrative deal. With the exception of me almost everyone else around Muhammad felt the probability of my brother stepping into a boxing ring again was literally zero. And Arum – who knew my brother's career would be over if he didn't embrace the deal – didn't hold back telling him bluntly that he was being foolish. Everyone around my brother – including our father and even Herbert, even though he was following his own father's instructions – wanted my brother to actually submit to this deal. Muhammad, of course, was lining the pockets of all those around him. Not surprisingly, it was in their best interest. Arum, in later years, has gone on record saying that the reason he pressured Muhammad to submit to the offer was because he didn't want my brother to go to jail, that he cared for him. Of course, the promoter was really concerned about losing his cash cow.

Early in the war, then, Muhammad's response to the draft was largely dictated by that of the Nation of Islam – many black Muslims refused to serve, and my brother was simply following their lead. He was acting on his religious beliefs, sure, but he didn't particularly think of it as an unjust war. This somewhat changed, however, when Muhammad was reclassified in the middle of the conflict. Muhammad wasn't much of a reader – his level of literacy was never more than adequate in those days, and it was very difficult for him to take the tests that the draft board had set as part of their criteria for enlistment. It wasn't until the army required more soldiers, after several years of tough, bloody jungle warfare, that the qualifications for being drafted were lowered. But at that point, they never gave him another test, just reclassified him with lower scores. You can imagine how this sat with my brother. He had been made out to be stupid, but then suddenly he was smart enough because they needed more bodies to send to Vietnam.

When he found out that he'd been classified so he was liable to serve – we were at his Miami concrete rented bungalow when he received a phone call – I think my brother's initial reaction was, *Why me? I'm heavyweight champion of the world. My taxes pay for so many guns, tanks and soldiers' salaries. Why don't they draft other boys who don't pay tax?* So his first response wasn't in principle – but there was more to it, too. From what I saw, Muhammad didn't initially understand that he would not be sent to the front lines to kill anybody. Sports celebrities who went into the army before him were given easy jobs, giving exhibitions to entertain the troops, and I think the widespread assumption was that if he enlisted, he would not be sent to the front lines, either. At first he apparently didn't realise this, and that honed his anger to a point, prompting the public objections to the war that made him a pariah to much of America. By the time he became aware he was in no personal danger, he wasn't willing to surrender his principles. 'Why should a black man be sent by white men to go and kill brown men?' he said. 'I am a member of the Muslims and we don't go to wars unless they are declared by Allah Himself. I don't have no personal quarrel with those Viet Congs.'

Our parents were concerned. I remember my brother saying to them, 'I follow the Honourable Elijah Muhammad. I'm a Muslim. Elijah Muhammad says I cannot fight for this country. I cannot go kill innocent people who don't kill me. They don't call me nigger. I cannot go there and fight. I will not do it.' Mom and Dad said, 'If that's the way you feel, go ahead and do what you think is right. Go ahead, stand your ground. We are with you one hundred per cent.'

Even now, many people overlook the fact that blacks were disproportionately drafted into the military to fight in Vietnam. This caused a conflict in its own right: you had people who were confused, conflicted and unsure about America's purpose in the Vietnam War, but many of them had sons, uncles, brothers and fathers who were in the military fighting against communism. So some supported my brother's decision while still wondering why their relatives should have to serve, but others wondered why Muhammad thought he should be above the law.

White mainstream America, in particular, saw Muhammad as an oaf, but also as an uppity black man who didn't know his place. He had occasionally been called 'The Kentucky Clown' and 'The Louisville Lip' since early in his career, but after joining the Nation and changing his name to Muhammad Ali, the criticism of him took on a new, more aggressive tone. Now that he refused to step forward and be inducted into the military he became an athlete who was openly detested, with commentators and newspapermen lining up to spit their bile at him.

HARD TIMES

Meanwhile, Muhammad continued to protest in public after the American Government revoked his licence to box two months after he refused to be drafted for Vietnam. As a consequence, his financial situation quickly became bad as he was plunged into dire financial straits. Nobody would license him to fight domestically. Although the Nation of Islam lent something of a hand in so far as supporting him financially at this time of hardship, my brother was compelled to do something himself to get back on his feet. And because they also confiscated his passport, needless to say, he could not fight overseas either.

One reason that this was a problem was that Muhammad had just married for the second time. In 1964, he had married Sonji Roi, a cocktail waitress introduced to him by Herbert Muhammad after our trip to Africa. We toured Egypt and Ghana and in Egypt we met President Nasser. In Ghana hundreds of frantic fans ran towards us just to get close to Muhammad, and Herbert actually ran away fearing for his life. Initially, Sonji felt she wouldn't like my brother because she didn't like the way he bragged, it turned her off – but Muhammad, persistent in this instance, zeroed in on this beautiful young girl. After a whirlwind five-week romance they tied the knot on 14 August 1964, and a couple of days later she visited us in Louisville to meet our parents.

However, trouble reared its head almost immediately. One of

the biggest problems Muhammad had with his first wife was that she completely refused to adhere to the teachings of Islam in terms of embracing modesty. I recall my brother countless times shouting at her telling her to wear modest clothing. He would say, 'You can't be walking around in short dresses.' My brother had a huge problem with his wife wearing miniskirts and showing flesh – it was against our religion. He believed he had to set an example, and if his wife wasn't setting an example then what message would this be sending to others? Muhammad and Sonji clashed and she said to him she wasn't ready to submit to his rules. She said to my brother he thought the male was the 'superior' one in a home who really knew what he was talking about, and it was difficult for him to disagree. Roi constantly quarrelled with my brother over her actions and dress, but also because of her constant questioning of Elijah Muhammad's teachings. They divorced in 1966, and my brother was determined that his next wife would be a more positive influence on his life.

Eventually, he married Belinda Boyd in August of 1967, when she was seventeen. It was more or less an arranged marriage. Muhammad had to get permission from her parents and they played an important role. My brother was living in the South Side of Chicago in a modest two-bedroomed house, which Herbert had given to him and his new wife, while I had my own place that I was renting several blocks from my brother. But they had first met when he was eighteen years old and she was only ten. He was visiting Muhammad University of Islam Number Two, which was a Muslim school in Chicago she would eventually go on to graduate from, during his tour after winning the Olympic gold medal. 'I'm going to be the heavyweight champion of the world before I'm twenty-one,' he told the group she was part of. 'So get your autographs now! I'm going to be famous.' Muhammad walked up to Belinda and said, 'Here, little girl, this is my autograph. I'm going to be famous one day. My name is going to be worth something.'

'How do you know you're going to do it before you're twenty-one?' a bemused Belinda asked, looking over the piece of paper. 'Wait, your name is Cassius Marcellus Clay? Do you know what the Romans did to people? You've got the word Clay, which means dirt you mould, and you're proud of this?'

This, I guess, was all a little much for my brother. In so far as Belinda was still a little girl, she already exuded confidence and maturity, and he was still scrambling for an answer when she followed up.

'Brother, I'm going to tell you something.' She proceeded, tearing the paper into pieces as she edified my brother with her quick wit and words. 'If you want to talk to me you need a name of respect, a name of honour. As a matter of fact, you need a Muslim name. Then we can talk.' She returned the autograph in pieces. 'You can take that back with you.' At the Muslim school she was attending, she explained, students would read the stories of the Caliphs – Abu-Bakar, Usman, Umar and Ali – who were seen as champions, great men who fought for their religion.

'You're one of the Caliphs,' she told my brother. 'You need to fight for Islam.'

Then she was gone. Muhammad, who had never experienced anyone talking to him like this before, let alone a ten-year-old girl, was left in complete shock. 'She tore my name. She tore my autograph.' He murmured. 'Who is she?'

The response from those in attendance was immediate, and discouraging. 'You can't mess with her,' my brother was told. 'She's the Princess of Islam. That's what Elijah Muhammad calls her. And her father – you do not want to go there.'

Belinda's father, to be sure, was a man of few words, but when he gave you that stern look you knew he meant business. Despite that, though, this young girl left a lasting impression on my brother. At some point, someone told him her age, which of course stunned him. 'She's only ten?!' 'Yes,' came the reply. 'But Muslims are very advanced, very educated.'

Just before Muhammad fought for the title, when Belinda became a teenager, she decided to do her own research on my brother. She started to learn more about his boxing career, reading up on his past fights and his Olympic performances. At the time he was preparing for his first fight against Sonny Liston and his face was plastered all over the TV. She saw what Liston was saying about Black Muslims and heard my brother say, 'I'm going to whup that guy,' and I guess it left an impression on her. At some point, she sat down to write a poem that she would eventually hand to my brother. It read:

This is the legend of Cassius Clay.
The most beautiful fighter today.
His fist fights are great he's got speed and endurance.
But if you try to fight him it'll increase your insurance.
This kid's got a left, this kid's got a right.
Look at him carry the fight.
All the crowd is getting frantic, there's not enough room,
Cassius' law of boom.
Who would have felt when they came to the fight
They'd see spooks set alight.
No one would have dreamed when they put down their money
They'd see a total eclipse of Sonny.

When Belinda got the opportunity to give her poem to Muhammad, he was overwhelmed. 'You wrote this for me?' he asked her. 'I love it. You're smart.' He'd go on to use it in interviews, giving rise to some of his most famous quotes, but very few people would have guessed that those lines were penned by a thirteen-year-old.

Anyway, my brother kept an eye on Belinda, and would try to see her whenever he was in Chicago. Eventually, she wound up working in the bakery, where he would drop in to flirt and talk, with Belinda always holding her own in the conversation.

Belinda would quickly become the backbone of their relationship. She quickly realised that behind closed doors Muhammad wasn't an extrovert; he was a quiet individual. Belinda brought a lot out of him and, to an extent, increased his confidence. This made him open up. She played her role well and showed him new parts of life and told him that, when it mattered, he was invincible. She was full of all this insight telling him, 'You can beat this, you're going to be great one day,' when the magnitude of everyday life got on top of him. All these things kept his self-esteem up when exterior forces were bringing him down. You have to understand that Belinda keeping his spirit up was a large part of why my brother was able to pass the test set him by those years in the wilderness. As the saying goes, behind every great man there's a great woman, and my brother was lucky to have met her – even if she was a girl at the time.

Belinda, sadly, never really benefited from Muhammad being the heavyweight champion because when they tied the knot he had already been stripped of his title, and when he recaptured it, of course, their relationship was falling apart.

Still, for the time being, Muhammad had a wife to support, and he had to get himself out of the financial hole he was sinking ever-deeper into. Louis Farrakhan – high-ranking member of the Nation – let my brother stay in his home for a while and took care of his first wife Sonji when he was training for Sonny Liston. Now, Farrakhan sponsored Muhammad's and Belinda's honeymoon, which was generous but did nothing to solve my brother's long-term financial problems.

By this time he had fought twenty-nine times professionally, including nine title fights. Out of those nine fights his cut was $2 million after everybody got paid – from the manager to the janitor – before taxes. And after the $2 million the ten white men in Louisville who backed him made a deal, oblivious to Muhammad, with the government where they would give the government 90 per cent of all his earnings before Muhammad received any money – under an arrangement known as the Joe Louis Law – to keep him from being broke. That only left my brother with a meagre 10 per cent of his $2 million to live on. Out of that he had to pay between $150,000 and $200,000 to Sonji when they divorced – and in addition he was paying $1,200 a month in alimony. Then there were legal costs that had mounted up requiring attention. Muhammad paid a staggering (for the day) $96,000 in fees for the lawyers representing him against his fiercest of foes – the United States Government. And after that, of course, he had to live and pay bills. Small wonder that there wasn't much left in the bank to do it with.

Not that my brother took this too seriously. 'I don't know why people are so confused over one Negro boxer getting low in funds,' he'd say, laughing. 'Even America's broke. America is cancelling trips abroad to save money. So, you know, if big powerful America can be broke, well, it's no surprise that a little Negro boxer can go broke.' It takes a special kind of man to laugh at the situation my brother found himself in – stopped in his prime when he was ready to make big money in a sport he had immersed himself in since he was twelve.

Whatever the state of my brother's finances, it certainly didn't seem like it deterred him from spending. In one interview, he told Bud Collins – host of a public affairs TV programme – that he was planning on purchasing an aeroplane of all things. The sole reason for this mammoth purchase was that he travelled all around the country, always moving and on the road. Muhammad always received requests to make appearances ever since he dethroned Liston, and driving was literally killing him. Now, the man who had famously almost missed the Olympic trials because of his fear of planes was considering investing in his own wings. The interviewer, who seemed stunned, followed up, 'I don't mean to pry in your personal affairs, but there's been so many stories that you've been like Joe Louis, that you're broke. You owe $280,000 on one hand and on the other hand you're talking about buying a jet.' Muhammad always had an answer for you. You could never derail him whether you were engaged in a deep philosophical conversation or a member of the media was grilling him. He replied, 'I say lease. I'm just about broke. I'm not allowed to work here in America and I'm not allowed to leave. I'm not like Joe Louis. I didn't fight for thirteen years.'

On top of all this Muhammad had to contend with the people closest to him, who weren't above taking advantage of him financially. Herbert was getting one third of Muhammad's total earnings and the Nation was getting one third. That left my brother with a meagre one third. And, almost astonishingly, all expenses came out of Muhammad's share. And there were a lot of expenses, believe me. I can't remember what the expenses budget was back then, but later, in the 1970s, a training camp budget of $100,000 was the norm, and often it would go over budget. The management cut was just plain ridiculous and inequitable, yet Muhammad had readily agreed to what any right-minded individual would have seen straight away as an abysmal business decision. The problem was, when it came to business, literally anything Herbert wanted Muhammad to do my brother would agree to. Herbert had a firm grip on Muhammad from day one and saw him as a commodity as much as a friend. It was worse than unacceptable in the eyes of those who deeply cared for Muhammad – it was crazy. When certain individuals questioned Herbert about the fact that out of a $6 million purse Muhammad would make $4 million and he had to fight, while the manager got $2 million in one night and never fought, Herbert would respond with, 'I said it was part of the contract and we agreed on it. People might say, "Yeah, but that was too much money for you." All the people around him would say it, but that was our agreement.' Our family would often complain, however, that Herbert made no effort to re-evaluate the situation so that the financial side was fair.

To put it frankly, I think my brother's own management could be said to have taken advantage of him and the situation would repeat itself right throughout his career. Muhammad was the most famous athlete around, but most of his earnings would benefit others around him. He was fighting to make others rich. My brother didn't really understand money in those days. I remember at times he didn't put it in a bank because he feared if the banks got robbed or went broke his money would go down the pan. Instead, he took the cash and hid it here and there, feeling that it was much safer out of the bank than it was tucked securely in it. He thought a briefcase full of cash, let's say $50,000, had greater value than a cheque worth $100,000. To him, the latter was a piece of paper. That was his mindset back then.

★ ★ ★

As my brother's financial situation spiralled out of control, his associates finally came up with the idea of booking him on the American college circuit. This would entail him going around from college to college giving speeches, which he would get paid for. These days, the after-dinner circuit can be a lucrative avenue for retired athletes, but for my brother, who should have been in the prime of his career, it was a necessity in the face of financial disaster, and a way to feed his family.

In the beginning, Muhammad was terrible at speaking engagements. By this stage, he had come out against the war in Vietnam, which of course was a huge issue on college campuses at that time, so he was very well received at first as most students shared his sentiments concerning what was increasingly perceived as an unjust war. But he also repeated the Muslim dogma that very few people in the audience would connect with, even in liberal-leaning colleges. For starters, he would make disparaging remarks about marijuana, and it's easy enough to imagine how that went down in the early sixties. He would talk about religion, which further alienated audiences who were more likely to be atheists than the rest of America. More than anything, though, he alienated audiences by attacking interracial couples. Despite the prejudices that existed in those days, there were still plenty such couples around, and frequently the kinds of places Muhammad chose to lecture would be more tolerant than the general populace towards them, only to be confronted with the heavyweight champion telling them that they were against his religion.

The single speaking engagement that stands out most in my mind came very early on at Berkeley. Muhammad gave an outdoor speech at a large plaza. There were thousands of people there. He stunned the audience from the word go, launching straight into a series of moral platitudes: he prided himself on being black and beautiful, he said, and he was shocked by the amount of interracial couples in the crowd. At this point, a large part of the audience stood up and sauntered off. A somewhat rattled Muhammad made a show of sipping from a bottle of water to take a mental breather, and more people got up and walked away. As he resumed his speech, Muhammad shifted into a long tirade about the Koran, talking about the necessity of keeping 'red birds with red birds' and 'blue birds with blue birds', only to see more of his audience slip into the ether.

I think my brother fast realised that it wasn't working. You can't overestimate how excited these students had been to see their hero in person, but by attacking them so openly he immediately turned off a huge chunk of the crowd. I'm not saying everybody walked out on him – or even most people – but the effect was enough to be notable, and embarrassing for my brother, even though he continued to address those who remained. After the speech, the sportswriter Robert Lipsyte talked to Muhammad about his disparaging remarks, but my brother denied that the audience had reservations about him. He was just too strong, he told Lipsyte, his message was just too potent – it was beyond the capacity of the audience to absorb it. Lipsyte disagreed straight to my brother's face – it was quite obvious, he said, that nobody was really interested in what Muhammad had to say about segregation, or about not smoking grass. You have to remember this was in the middle of the civil rights campaigns, and a lot of these kids were very much involved in integration. To them, Muhammad seemed to be on the wrong side of the fence. He wasn't endearing himself to the public there.

With the benefit of hindsight, Muhammad grew to understand that his early speaking style was more or less a disaster, even if he wasn't prepared to personally take the blame. His excuse persisted – those present weren't able to handle it. He would never admit that he was lousy, but rather the strength of the speech was something the audience could not deal with. You couldn't beat my brother verbally – he was resolute in his fight to uphold his principles and what he believed in – but he began to accept, after a few more engagements, that he should at least be prepared to listen to other points of view. He took to including a question-and-answer period after his speeches where the students were given ample opportunity to confront his views head-on. Often, yes, this would lead to a certain level of conflict, but that only mirrored what was happening in the world, and in the end it exposed my brother to a number of viewpoints he might otherwise never have considered. He also practised hard for his speeches. At first, Belinda would write many of them out for him using white cards, printing everything out on them so that he could read from them until he was confident enough to deliver his message unaided.

In the beginning it was a slow and painful process, but as time went on, and he became more self-assured, he stopped reading from the cards and started just talking, which was much easier and more natural for him. As he got more comfortable in his role, he would inject a dose of humour. He'd talk about how black is beautiful, ask why angels are always portrayed as white while devils are black – still making his points about racial discrimination, but in a way that his audiences could respond to. By the end of those three years in the wilderness, he became a compelling campus speaker, doing the Ali shuffle and telling some jokes while toning down – if not excluding entirely – his more extreme viewpoints. He was always an entertainer, but I feel like his college speaking gave him an edge in public speaking that would help in press conferences and publicity tours for years to come.

★ ★ ★

Another aspect of my brother's university speaking career that soon paid off was that it gave him a chance to perfect his poetry. He would often spout his poetry as he addressed students, penning a lot of it as he went from college to college. At one stage in his career, he was actually invited to teach poetry at Oxford University – though that plan never quite came to fruition. He did, however, go on to give a speech at Harvard University where he received a tumultuous standing ovation. And although Belinda had helped him with his verse earlier in his career, he came to know another poet well over the years – the television personality and activist Nikki Giovanni.

When my brother first met Giovanni, her career was just beginning to take off and she was travelling extensively. She used to fly every place she went, which was the most practical for long distances. Belinda, who was aware of Muhammad's inclination towards extracurricular activities, knew she could trust this particular female friend of his, and was thankful for it. It was somewhat funny because Belinda would question Giovanni, 'How was the trip?' And Giovanni would say, 'It was wonderful.'

Not that the two friends had too much temptation to get close, in any case, since they both chose different modes of travel. Muhammad would be travelling on his own on his bus, which he owned and he had his driver, while his friend would take the plane. Muhammad absolutely hated flying, even by then. It's a well-known fact that my brother purchased a parachute from an army surplus store and wore it on the plane when he first flew across the pond to Rome for the Olympics. In fact after the Olympic trials my brother was supposed to fly back to Louisville from San Francisco, but refused to get on the plane. Instead, he asked his coach Joe Martin to lend him some money so he could take a train back home. The plane flew back leaving my brother behind. Muhammad was told to fly or walk back. Stubborn, Muhammad happened to have a watch which he had no choice but to pawn in order to get the money for the train ticket. I'm glad he eventually made it back.

Giovanni, for her part, wasn't going to get in the middle of Muhammad's marriage – even when things started to sour between my brother and Belinda; she thought it wasn't any of her business. Muhammad might have started to deviate somewhat when it came to being faithful, but whenever my brother saw the poet he always endeavoured to be very kind to her, nothing more than that. And she was good for him, too – my brother being a Muslim and Giovanni a Christian, women's issues were something Muhammad often broached. Muhammad held the view that women should follow certain principles and guidelines, but Giovanni ardently believed that women should be independent. It was no point having a deep discussion with my brother about this, and so she often claimed not to have an opinion. She believed that everybody does what's comfortable for them.

'I don't think it's my business to have any opinion on anybody's religion,' she would tell my brother. 'I think your religion comforts you and I'm glad my religion comforts me. So I don't have an opinion.' Muhammad obviously had his own somewhat polarising attitude and would always challenge people, but, at least with Nikki, things never got too heated.

★ ★ ★

During the period Muhammad was battling the United States Government, specifically in 1968, *Esquire* magazine planned an audacious stunt for a cover story about him. The publication wanted to produce a symbolic cover, and so they invited him to their studio to take part in a special photo shoot. Muhammad agreed to do the shoot and dropped by the studio in New York by himself. I usually accompanied him literally everywhere, but there were times when I wasn't by his side. He really did think that it was merely going to be another of the type of photo shoot he had sat through countless times before. He was relaxed when he got to the office, right up until the photographer, a man named Carl Fischer, briefed him as to what was going on – the idea behind what they were trying to achieve. Apparently they had conceived an idea that they would portray my brother as a martyr – a man who was being crucified by the Establishment. The photographer told Muhammad that they wanted to put him on the cover being crucified like St Sebastian – the Christian saint and martyr who had died in AD 288 at the height of the Roman Empire.

It was a controversial idea, to say the least, and the first opposition to it was my brother's spiritual leader. Before they could pursue the idea any further, Muhammad felt it was imperative to get the OK from Elijah Muhammad because of what St Sebastian represented – specifically, Christianity. My brother rang Elijah Muhammad and put him on the phone to the photographer, in a call that eventually included art director George Lewis. They explained what they aimed to achieve and why it would be in Muhammad's best interest to do this, as a way of drawing attention to Muhammad's cause and the way he was being treated. Elijah Muhammad initially had some reservations as he deeply cared for Muhammad's image. It was vitally important, of course, for him not to get entangled in something that would be degrading to the Muslims. However, when he understood that this was going to be for a mainstream magazine cover, which would result in good publicity not only for Muhammad but what he represented, he didn't waste much time in doing a U-turn. Suddenly, the religious element took a back seat. It really was no longer indispensable to him. The Nation of Islam craved publicity and used my brother, who was their biggest connection to the masses, to propagate their ideology.

The magazine intended to put Muhammad on a cross and use arrows to signify the way he was being crucified for his refusal to fight for the US Government in a war which he ardently believed was unjust. The biggest hurdle, as far as the shoot goes, was in relation to these arrows. Fischer, apparently, had practised using them before Muhammad's arrival, but when he pasted them on to Muhammad's body, they would fall off because they were too heavy to stay stuck on. As my brother lounged around the photographer came up with an idea wherein he set up a bar across the studio and hung clear fishing line across it to hold up the arrows. The shoot was very slow, mundane and tedious and Muhammad was required to stand there for a prolonged period. My brother showed signs that gave the impression it was very uncomfortable for him. Being a consummate professional eventually they got it done. Nowadays they wouldn't have that problem; they would simply do it on the computer.

During the course of the shoot, Muhammad was his usual jovial self, kidding around with Fischer. He was always in a buoyant mood every time he was in the presence of people who he felt would be receptive to his ideas and conversation. He understood the complications they had in shooting the pictures, and so he was very much patient in dealing with them. Besides, my brother enjoyed being famous and he rarely shied away from working with members of the press. I would always relegate myself to the background. He'd be soaking in the attention and I'd be standing quietly by his side.

In general, photographers enjoyed photographing my brother, and this time was no exception. Muhammad was very helpful and very nice to the staff, and it was appreciated. Fischer, we came to learn, had photographed a lot of famous people over the decades and from his experience he found some of them to be very cranky and extremely demanding if they were put under pressure. It wasn't often, Fischer told us, that people who were very famous were not merely very receptive, but willing to mingle and chat with the staff. My brother in no way showed any diva behaviour, even when technical difficulties arose. The whole shoot took almost two hours, after which Muhammad took a shower and got dressed, still chatting with the team.

The cover, which was a very simple one, had no advertising lines on it, a far cry from today's news-stands that are jammed with words. What was great in those days was the cover could be very simple, just the photograph. This meant that the message being conveyed became very powerful. My brother would always stand up against the slings and arrows of fortune, America was to learn – whatever the cost.

THE GREAT COMEBACK

By the time my brother's licence to box was revoked, a lot of Muhammad's money was being sucked in by the Nation of Islam. This was an especially troubling development for our mom and dad – both of them had always had their doubts about the organisation because they thought it was taking advantage of Muhammad, and my dad in particular could never reconcile himself to the Nation's way of thinking. I would hear Dad scream and shout, 'Damn, those Muslims are stealing my son's money!' He absolutely despised the organisation at the time. As much as my brother loved our dad, though, he felt he had a loyalty to the organisation that had changed his life. And I, naturally, followed.

The Nation, for their part, had their own reasons for laying claim to my brother's earnings. When Muhammad was stripped of his title and plunged into financial difficulties, the Nation of Islam, acting under the orders of the honourable Elijah Muhammad, gave my brother a high salary and a loan of $100,000. Belinda's parents had saved up enough money for her to go to college, but were gracious enough to hand over their savings when their daughter and her husband found themselves in dire financial straits. Elijah Muhammad certainly took care of my brother for a while, but it was Belinda's parents that made a difference.

Muhammad, then, freely admitted that he owed the Nation money, but what he never took into account is that he had lined the pockets of the Nation in the past – especially when they came looking for their money back. The Nation expected my brother to repay the loan as soon as he was in a better position financially, which was at least one reason why, after over two years of inactivity, Muhammad was eager to get back in the ring.

Here, though, my brother incurred the wrath of the Nation's leader. On hearing that his most famous disciple was going to re-emerge in the boxing ring because he needed money, Elijah Muhammad was aggrieved. He rebuked my brother – saying, in effect, 'God was able to provide for you while you were outside the ring and now you're crawling back to do that. You're going to be carried out of the ring eventually.' The prize ring, he felt, glorified violence and distracted men from religious service, at the risk of corrupting their souls. My brother, he felt, was a minister in the Nation first and foremost, and should be working for its advancement. After meeting with my brother to explain his grievances, Elijah Muhammad put out a statement in the newsletter *Muhammad Speaks* announcing that he was suspending Muhammad for one year. Further, he was taking back his name. My brother had legally changed his name, of course, but this was standard for the Nation – to them at least, my brother would be Cassius Clay for the duration of his suspension.

Herbert Muhammad, meanwhile, had ambivalent feelings about this process. On the one hand he certainly respected his father and tried to follow his decrees, but on the side he was trying to get fights for Muhammad almost constantly. He had even suggested to my brother that he could do exhibition fights if he consented to the draft, as a way to keep active during service, but Muhammad had always stood firm in his refusal to enlist.

In any case, Muhammad accepted the suspension, going so far as to publicly admit that he was wrong and privately say to me, 'When I think about it, he was right to suspend me.' Whether he truly meant it or not, I can't say. But he certainly tried to work his way back into the graces of the Nation of Islam, and was finally welcomed back by Elijah Muhammad. He would bring busloads of people to Elijah Muhammad's home in Chicago, and the leader of the Nation would greet them – one of the few ways for him to meet his followers, since he so seldom ventured outside his home.

Muhammad, at this point in his career, never shied away from giving credit to Elijah Muhammad for his own success. He would, on occasion, make him out to be some kind of an angel, proclaiming in both public and private that he would have been nothing had it not been for this man. He was an average boxer, my brother explained, who had barely got out of school, and been very lucky in his Olympic victory. 'Elijah Muhammad was the man who gave me courage, the man who gave me strength, the man who made me stand up and be proud,' he told others. For his part, Elijah Muhammad would call Muhammad up before every fight and say, 'Brother, you cannot lose because Allah's on your side. The other guy doesn't have Allah on his side.' That was Muhammad's booster rocket. Had it not been for Elijah Muhammad, he wouldn't have been what he became, Muhammad believed – a notion which is arguable. And so, their dispute over Muhammad pursuing the prize ring again was one of the only times he went against Elijah Muhammad, which to an extent for a while put a dent in what had been an extremely solid relationship. The fallout was short-lived, however, and both men reconciled their differences.

★ ★ ★

By mid-1970 Muhammad had been inactive for more than three years in the ring and was itching to get back. Herbert, his lawyer Chauncey Eskridge and I were all collaborating with him to get him back into the ring as soon as possible, but Muhammad wasn't prepared to relinquish his principles to do it. It was at this point, though, that we made another useful contact: a lawyer named Jonathan Shapiro, who was working as a civil rights lawyer with the NAACP Legal Defence Fund. This organisation was, of course, interested in dealing with racial discrimination from the government – the problems that black people were facing in dealing with all kinds of government activity, but also the discrimination that black Muslims specifically were being subjected to. Shapiro was working in Mississippi, but he knew Chauncey from working on similar cases, and was also involved with the Southern Christian Leadership Council, which was Martin Luther King's organisation. In 1970, when Muhammad's case was in the courts, Eskridge made contact with Shapiro because he wanted the Legal Defence Fund to get involved, which would bolster my brother's chances of prevailing in court. After conferring with the other lawyers in the organisation, Shapiro obliged.

At that point, Muhammad's case had recently been lost at the court of appeal. To take it further, Shapiro had to apply for what was called a 'petition of statuary' to the United States Supreme Court.

When Muhammad refused induction into the armed services, virtually every state revoked his licence. However, now Muhammad's team found a loophole. In light of new evidence, the Legal Defence Fund decided to sue the New York Boxing Commission to require them to give Muhammad his licence back. The logic was simple: the commission had first denied the licence on the basis that he was a convicted felon, but my brother's legal team discovered, in the course of the work that they did, that the New York Boxing Commission had licensed convicted felons who had been convicted of all kinds of heinous crimes to box in the state. In the view of the legal team, this made the suspension utterly bogus and undeniably discriminatory, and the boxing commission were told by my brother's legal representatives, in no uncertain terms, that he should get his licence back.

Another issue that had been raised in Muhammad's case was that he was being drafted into the army, and here, again, the spectre of discrimination was never far away. The draft boards in each community, which decided who should be drafted, were almost exclusively white: blacks had been systematically excluded from the boards. Muhammad's lawyers asserted that this was a violation of his rights – that people of colour should serve on draft boards, just as they were legally expected to serve on juries. The team lost on that issue, unfortunately.

A plethora of issues were united in the case against my brother. Not only was he a lightning rod for racial and religious discrimination, but as a supporter of the anti-war movement, all of the pro-war elements of the population were against him. The country was fighting a war on the back of black people and the court was concerned that if they allowed one member of the Nation of Islam to avoid the draft then it would set a precedent allowing every member – maybe even all black Muslims – to do the same, undermining the law, the draft and the war. Hence they didn't want to make a decision that was going to have such an impact on the country. At the same time, it was difficult to deny that in denying him an exemption as a conscientious objector the Department of Justice and the draft boards had acted illegally, since they had acted on political and not religious grounds.

There was abundant evidence to support Muhammad. The court was in a dilemma, and they eventually resolved it by deciding in his favour by overturning the conviction, but doing so on very narrow grounds that didn't have any precedential value. It didn't create a precedent that would allow black Muslims across the nation to get an exemption from being drafted. The court case certainly played a part in raising all these issues, but achieved little legally that would affect black men across America.

When my brother refused the draft, literally everybody thought his boxing career was over and were convinced he would end up in prison. However, I had a totally polar opposite view. I personally believed that this was the start of another level in terms of Muhammad's career and that it would skyrocket, that he would soon be a bigger name than before and make even more money. Muhammad and I put trust in Elijah Muhammad and God and we had no doubts clouding our minds.

In June 1971, the court overturned his conviction unanimously. In the meantime, Muhammad prepared for his first comeback fight, which would take place in the state of Georgia. This might have seemed unusual: that the state of Georgia, a Deep South state where there was so much racism and opposition to the stance my brother was taking, would allow him to fight. The thing was: Georgia didn't have a boxing commission. From that point of view, it was an easy fix. But at the same time, unbeknown to anyone, making the fight happen was going to be a battle in itself. A variety of obstacles lay ahead.

★ ★ ★

I'd spent an inordinate amount of time with Muhammad for virtually every bout he prepared for before his suspension, and I can say with great conviction that he was typically upbeat and exuded confidence before his fights. The first time he fought Jerry Quarry, though, in the first fight after his suspension was lifted, he was nervous. There was work to be done in the gym to eradicate his ring rust, he knew, and a slip-up in the ring would give his detractors the excuse they needed to write him off as a has-been.

In training, he was certainly sharp enough. I worked hard with him, sparred with him regularly, stepping up the pace in the final weeks before the fight. He felt as tough as ever to me, but doubts still clouded his mind; his nerves were getting the better of him because there was so much at stake. If Muhammad was defeated, he knew it could be all but done. He had lost millions of dollars and a huge amount of prestige while out of the game, and now there was both an opportunity to rise again and a chance to be humiliated by an opponent who, he knew, was both fast and very tricky. Muhammad never cared about anyone's reputation as a fighter as long as his performance and condition were up to scratch, but with so much at stake, he still worried – and the circumstances around his comeback fight didn't make things any easier.

Wherever I accompanied my brother in the world we attracted attention, and the social mores of the time virtually guaranteed that some of it would be bad. When he was training for the Jerry Quarry bout, which was scheduled to take place in Atlanta, he faced considerable opposition – the Ku Klux Klan started showing up, fully prepared to cause pandemonium. Then still allowed by many police departments to operate with impunity, the race-hate group proclaimed to all who would listen that this fight wasn't going to happen on their patch, sending everything from admonitions to all-out threats. They conducted marches and rallies up on Stone Mountain, the vast monolith that the town near Atlanta was named after, and threatened enough people that we genuinely struggled to find a venue for the fight. At one point, things got so bad that people around Muhammad were telling him he should wear a bulletproof vest for his own safety. But my brother said his faith would keep him safe. 'I'm never going to stop fighting for what I believe in,' he told me. 'Allah will protect me.'

Aside from the threats and intimidation, there could barely have been a better venue for my brother's comeback fight. In Atlanta, which was predominantly a black city, the general feeling was that even King Kong couldn't beat my brother. We felt the love on every side as the city rallied around the fact that Muhammad was back and outsiders flocked to what was considered the Mecca of the United States. The issues surrounding the Ku Klux Klan might still have had some effect on my brother's mindset, but amidst all of the furore Muhammad's entourage all did their utmost to keep him apart from the negativity and hate being pushed by the white supremacists. We were as revitalised as my brother by his upcoming fight. We formed a wall keeping him from distractions as much as possible, and after a few weeks in our care I couldn't wait to get in there and kick butt. For my part, I had as much reason to be excited as my brother. I was going to be fighting on the undercard.

One memory from those days stands out in my mind as a testament to the kind of man my brother was. A couple of days before the fight we were having a weigh-in session in front of a packed auditorium, and it turned out that our former next-door neighbour from Louisville Larry Montgomery had made an effort to come down and offer support, bringing his own brother along. Muhammad, as usual, was being loud and boisterous, and Larry was trying hard but couldn't get Muhammad's attention. Eventually, to get his attention he hollered out, 'Gee-gee!', my brother's childhood nickname – and, well, the reaction was instantaneous.

'Everybody quiet, somebody knows me!' called my brother, turning around and immediately recognising our neighbour standing among the crowd. 'I want everybody to know this is my next-door neighbour, Lawrence Montgomery, from Louisville, Kentucky,' Muhammad shouted. 'He lives on 3300 Grande Avenue and I lived at 3302 Grande. I want everybody to know he's one of our best friends. I used to take care of his children when they were small.' This was true, Muhammad and I would often babysit our neighbour's kids – and my brother was like that, he would give people attention. He never forgot those he left behind when he moved out of Louisville.

Still, he had more important issues which required his attention. At that point, my brother and I were very spiritual and we believed that the Nation of Islam and Allah was going to bless Muhammad and reinstate his title, despite the intense pressure Muhammad was under. We both believed that there was no way one of us brothers was going to lose – this was the affirmation we practised.

As I mentioned earlier, I turned pro when my brother fought Liston the first time in 1964. I fought only twice after that, and then Muhammad was exiled. At that point, I started to lose interest in boxing. I had developed kind of a disdain for the sport because of the government's actions, and I lost some of the fire for competition that lived in me when I could compete alongside my brother. Then along came my brother's reinstatement, by which time it had been five years since I had had a professional fight, and suddenly I was back in the ring like nothing had happened. I started to get that old feeling again; I was just revved up. We were at the training camp and we were working together leading up to the fight, and the whole place was just humming with built-up energy. Quite honestly, we could not wait for the bell to ring, so we could take out our frustrations on our respective opponents. I went out and won my fight. I was all excited and couldn't wait to see my brother back in the ring and cheer him.

I wasn't the only one. A who's who of black celebrities turned out to watch his comeback fight, from Sidney Poitier and Diana Ross to the Reverend Jesse Jackson. People were calling and sending letters to him, rooting for him and telling him to be careful, or to show the government that they hadn't beaten him. As the fight approached, we slowly became aware that even a sizeable chunk of the white population was rooting for my brother, many of them for the first time. This was new: my brother was used to playing the loudmouth, the braggart, the guy that everyone wanted to see beaten, and now he was being cheered. It was quite something. And all he had to sacrifice was millions of dollars and three prime years of his career.

On the night of the fight, my original opponent, Tom Cohen, was abruptly replaced by a boxer billed as coming from the Bahamas, 'Hurricane' Grant. He might have been nicknamed the Hurricane, but I brought the thunder that night, putting him on the defensive almost immediately as I came out strong. He survived the first round and attacked a little in the second, and after six minutes of action we touched gloves in mutual respect. But almost at the start of the third, I caught him with a combination that dropped him, then followed up to finish him when he got back to his feet. I wouldn't lose on my brother's comeback night.

Quarry, meanwhile, hit hard, looked mean and could take a punch, but had very little for my brother. Muhammad came out fast, firing out hard rights behind his signature jabs, evading Quarry's attempts at counter-punching almost as if they weren't there. He was heavier now, and tired a little faster, but he threw dozens of punches and Quarry found them difficult to answer. In the end, a cut stopped the fight in the third round, probably not soon enough for Quarry.

That wasn't the end of the evening's drama, however. Directly after the fight, Belinda received an anonymous phone call. 'Now that Muhammad Ali has won, you lose,' said the gruff voice at the other end of the line. 'The bomb goes off at 12 o'clock.' Ultimately, nothing happened and the call was declared a hoax, but given the circumstances of the bout, it was something we could have all done without.

I'm glad there were no kidnapping attempts on Muhammad's family. You would certainly think maybe somebody would be crazy enough. A little-known fact was that my brother prepared for such eventualities: for instance, with a safe room under the kitchen at the Deer Lake camp, a trapdoor under the big table. By this stage, Belinda and Muhammad had three children – Maryum aka 'May May' born in 1968, and twin daughters Jamillah and Rasheda, less than a year old. Unknown to most, Muhammad and his wife also previously had a premature baby, a son, who lived a mere three hours. So when the twins were born the parents had meticulously followed the doctor's orders. Losing a son, understandably, put a strain on Muhammad and Belinda. Now with a threat directed at my brother's family, he had to take it seriously even if it turned out to be a hoax. Nonetheless, nothing materialised.

★ ★ ★

Forty days later on 7 December 1970, Muhammad despatched Oscar Bonavena via a technical knockout in the final round in Madison Square Garden – I improved my own record to 7–0 on the same night. In January Muhammad moved his family to Cherry Hill in New Jersey.

Suddenly, my brother was eyeing up Joe Frazier, who was holding the title at the time. It was the fight everyone wanted to see, and there was a tremendous amount of cash on the table: both fighters were guaranteed $2.5 million each, an unheard of amount back then. Herbert had been flooded with offers from around the globe, from Europe, Japan, to Texas and the Big Apple. Even a major TV network was keen to get on board and made an offer of a couple of million dollars. Muhammad, who was content, talked over the offers with his manager who argued that they could do a lot better. After further discussions Herbert 'went to work'. Not long after the phone rang, with Herbert bringing the news that there was a staggering $5 million offer on the table and it would be split between Muhammad and Frazier so both fighters receive the same amount. Without any hesitation Muhammad said to Herbert, 'Take the $2.5 million.' What he was oblivious to was he'd end up pocketing a meagre 16 per cent ($400,000) as his share. Herbert felt it was the ideal time to explain to my brother how the finances would be broken down. So he proceeded to carefully explain to Muhammad that a large chunk of it would line the pockets of Federal Government and the state of New York. Of course, then with Herbert's cut – something that could never escape Herbert's mind – and training expenses, the mega purse would be shrunk dramatically. I mean, you could equate that to daylight robbery. Nevertheless, as usual, Muhammad didn't make a big deal of it. I must add, several years earlier Muhammad had enlisted the services of a white man by the name of Gene Kilroy to act as his business manager. But all fight negotiations and contracts were handled by Herbert who had the final say in virtually everything.

Angelo, meanwhile, was reluctant to take the fight at all, showing his ring savvy. He felt that my brother still hadn't recovered from the ring rust after his layoff, and that Quarry and Bonavena weren't exactly a test of his skills. Despite him looking dazzling in the gym, Angelo tried to insist that Muhammad have a couple more fights to ensure he was ready, both physically and mentally.

This was a tough argument for Angelo to make. In spite of the layoff Muhammad was still a freak of nature. He was so good at what he did that it was difficult to deny him the shot he so desperately wanted. The training regime he put himself through to get back to peak physical condition was unbelievable, and I say that as a man who worked with him almost every day. Nevertheless, Angelo felt he just didn't have that extra element required to prevail. Muhammad had fought twice already – the short fight with Quarry and a tough fight with Bonavena – but it was the latter bout that fuelled Angelo's concern. Sure, Angelo said, my brother scored a TKO, but Bonavena took him to the fifteenth round, and Bonavena wasn't half the fighter Frazier was.

Sharing Angelo's sentiment, Belinda predicted a defeat for her husband if he went ahead with the fight. As concerns mounted, Belinda realised her husband was believing all the hype to the extent that he was taking training less seriously. 'Look, you're not training,' she said to him. 'You're not running. Don't be trying to convince yourself you're going to win.' Belinda continued, 'This man wants it more than you do. And if you don't stay focused you know what, you're going to lose this one. It might even be good for you to lose this because it's going to teach you to stay on track instead of taking things lightly.' At this point, Muhammad did something that was, in my eyes, completely out of character for him, and went after Belinda. He came at her, not seriously but just to show her he was in great shape and that he didn't appreciate her sentiments.

As her instincts kicked in and she ducked, she shouted, 'Are you kidding me?' Realising the chances of reasoning with her husband were slim, she turned her back on him as far as the Frazier fight was concerned, and refrained from offering her support from that day forward. Although it was a very upsetting time for her, that moment when she completely backed off and let Muhammad run loose to do what he wanted marked a significant moment in their relationship. After that, there was no going back.

Despite their well-publicised rivalry pre-fight, believe it or not, Muhammad actually liked Joe. He thought Joe was a great fighter, a very tough warrior. Joe had great movement and he was like an animal on the loose, always pressing forward. My brother knew his adversary's calibre. He saw it when Joe smoked Jimmy Ellis, who was Angelo's heavyweight champion while my brother was out of the ring. Jimmy had some big right hands, but he didn't budge Joe. And in retrospect Muhammad would,

I think, look back and admit that he did have ring rust even after two comeback fights. It's a difficult balance for any fighter, for any athlete: we live with our egos and use them as a driving force. Muhammad certainly had an inflated opinion of himself, but at the same time he was the Olympic and returning heavyweight champion, and without thinking he was the best he might never have stepped in the ring with Frazier at all.

In the event, the Fight of the Century was set for 8 March 1971. The announcement sparked unprecedented attention globally, a storm of the biggest hype in sporting history up to that point. Reportedly, $25 million revenue was generated and $1,352,851 gate revenue, which was a record-breaker for an indoor event at the Garden Arena. I heard some ringside seats were going for $150, which in today's currency inflation rate is equivalent to just under $1,000. The event began to live up to its hype before either of the fighters even stepped into the ring. *The Wall Street Journal* predicted a $40 million box office when all the figures were finally in.

Despite the hype, Muhammad prepared for the fight as much as he would any other. It was not out of the ordinary for people to converge into Muhammad's hotel room up until a few hours before a fight, and on this occasion I was there with a larger entourage than usual. Three hours before the fight, I remember, Angelo's son Jimmy, daughter Terri and about half a dozen other kids from the camp were being treated to a magic show by Muhammad 'The Magician' while the rest of us waited with what felt like much more anxiety than my brother was showing. He spent a whole hour with those kids. This is what he did before every fight; nothing changed. It just calmed him down and forced him to control his nerves. He had one favourite trick where he would face the corner and stand on one leg to make it appear that he was levitating. That was his favourite thing to demonstrate, and that day the kids went as crazy for it as ever.

Beneath that confidence, though, I knew that he was certainly battling nerves. His stomach would get so nervous he'd throw up before every big fight. He'd run into the bathroom and do dry heaves from nervous anticipation, as many boxers do. Other than that, there were no visible nerves before he fought Frazier. If he had them, which I'm sure he did, he did a damn good job of concealing them. Often, he'd devour sweets before a fight, which he knew would upset his stomach; he'd be so worked up and ready to go.

Finally, all the integral members of Muhammad's camp congregated into the dressing room. Muhammad preferred to have some of the closest members of his team around him before the fight – typically Angelo, Gene Kilroy, Howard Bingham, Herbert Muhammad, Youngblood, Bundini, Pat Patterson the bodyguard and, of course, me. It wasn't unusual to see celebrities, who were eager to meet him before the fight while others waited until the fight was over, then pop into the dressing room.

The rest of the pre-fight ritual was always the same. Bundini would wrap Muhammad's hands and help him put on his gloves. Muhammad would give Angelo a hug, and there would be quiet for the last moments in the dressing room. At these moments, Muhammad was very introspective. He would sit there on his own for a while, in his own zone mentally. In those moments, no one could watch him, let alone talk to him.

Muhammad always felt that being in the dressing room getting ready was the scariest moment of fight night. All your thoughts, all the advice you've been given, they're going to be left behind when you enter the ring. Neither your coach, nor anyone else for that matter, is going to be holding your hand when your adversary comes in like a steam train trying to knock your head off your body. That's when you react and do what you've trained to do. But those moments before the fight? Those are the times when fear can get you, if you let it. Muhammad knew that and he was a consummate professional and the fear, the adrenaline rush, was something he understood well and knew how to control. All the brash talk and act was left behind in those moments before the fight. As it was time to make his way into the arena, just before the fight, he'd have his team members make a little bit of noise, but that was about it.

I was fighting on the undercard, which marked my fifth and final undercard fight under my brother. Danny McAlinden, with a record of 14–1–2, won via a unanimous decision. The defeat was a setback as far as my boxing career went, but I was more upset than anything because of the tone it set – I knew it would give my brother something else to worry about, a little mental trouble he didn't need to be dealing with.

Finally, Muhammad made his way to the ring with me close by his side. Madison Square Garden arena was packed with 20,455 screaming fans, but that was nothing to the amount of people watching around the world. My brother guessed that 10 million people might watch the fight, but I've heard more recent commentators put the final figure closer to 300 million, more than the population of the United States. As the atmosphere reached fever pitch one fan died of a heart attack. It was just unbelievable.

From the opening bell, my brother fought like he had something to prove. Maybe that was the problem – instead of dancing and floating as he had against Liston, he planted himself on flat feet to fire power punches at Frazier, who came in low, bobbing and weaving, always looking to land his power left hook. In the opening rounds, my brother took first blood, but every so often Frazier would slip through, and by the sixth he was still coming strong. The ninth was maybe the most violent round of the fight, both men landing big punches. And if my brother could have kept up the pace he set in the ninth and tenth rounds, he might have finished Frazier. But he was tired, the kind of tired you can only know if you've ever stepped in the prize ring yourself, and by the eleventh, he had to back off. By now my brother was dancing again, but Frazier was planting himself to punch, throwing shots to the body and head from close inside that I could feel even from my spot at ringside. Shots to the head hurt, sure, but you can fight through them. It's the ones that land low that sap your will, and stay with you all night.

By the fourteenth round, you could tell that both men were exhausted. I was thinking to myself that perhaps Joe was going to run out of gas because he had been throwing that left hook of his repeatedly with a lot of force, and it was just a matter of time before Muhammad was going to catch him with a great punch and knock him down. Instead, much to my surprise, the opposite happened.

In the fifteenth, my brother was knocked down. It was a perfect punch, a hook that Frazier lined up as my brother threw an uppercut, and it snapped Muhammad's head to one side with shocking force, sending him to the canvas. Unbelievably, he bounced up almost as soon as he went down, back on his feet before the referee could count to four. But it was enough. When the bell rang after a gruelling fifteen-round battle, Muhammad's nemesis was given the decision, leaving him retaining his coveted title. Frazier ended Muhammad's undefeated winning streak, which at the time was thirty-one wins with twenty-five knockouts.

After the verdict, Muhammad was hurried back to the dressing room, eluding any quick attempts to secure a post-fight interview. He took it all in good spirits. He was, without a shadow of doubt, upset, as it was his first ever loss as a professional, but he didn't seem shocked, or even surprised. In terms of injuries, the worst was a swelling on his right cheek, which looked horrible but soon disappeared. After spending half an hour in the dressing room, he emerged for an interview.

'I didn't want to lose,' he told the press, 'But since I have lost I just have to make the best of it, just like a man who's been sent to prison for ninety-nine years has to make his world in prison.' He believed that he won on points and urged everyone to examine his and Frazier's face to ascertain who had taken the worst beatings, but he was ultimately graceful in defeat. 'You know, I've always been handing out defeats, now I'm defeated,' he said. 'Now I can see how other people felt. Sometimes you are lost in the intoxication of greatness and the feeling of being always victorious. There comes a point you let your guard down.'

He could talk all he wanted, but after the fight Muhammad only grew more upset when he realised he'd been the architect of his own downfall. 'I was wrong,' he told his family. 'I was lazy. That's not going to happen again.' The defeat left such an indelible mark on him – he was so mad at Joe Frazier – that at one point, Belinda had to leave the family bed because he was pummelling his pillow in his sleep, just hitting it with one-twos like it was a real opponent. The loss haunted him, playing on his mind constantly. He kept talking about the defeat, expressing his dismay and his disdain for his foe.

It was a bad time. But sometimes, great things come from bad times, and I can confidently say that Muhammad wouldn't have become the man he went on to mould himself into, as far as the boxing ring is concerned, had he not lost the Frazier fight. You can disagree, but many of us in his camp felt it was a prelude to kind of putting everything else into place. You can't put it any better than Angelo did immediately after the fight. 'I can tell you one thing,' he told the reporters, as my brother left the room. 'Muhammad will be heavyweight champion of the world again.'

CHALLENGING ALI

As my brother was settling in his Tuscan-style villa in the upcoming and exclusive suburb of Cherry Hill, I'd visit him whenever I could. Prior to this he had a brief stay, about six months, in Philadelphia. Muhammad's commitments on the East Coast, which included two weekly trips to New York, drove him to move from the windy city of Chicago. And back then he was still absolutely terrified of flying. College campus commitments weren't the only reason for his hectic travel itinerary. Although Muhammad had been out of the ring for several years, he had been eking out a living on the speakers' circuit, giving lectures in educational institutions and making seemingly endless TV appearances. It might not have been as lucrative as the prize ring, but he still had the means to buy a home that seemed like the height of luxury compared with the one we grew up in. Besides, my brother had fought twice by the time he bought the Cherry Hill residence. Set on a secluded one-and-a-half-acre plot located on 1121 Winding Drive, the one-floor house was built in 1965. Ten years earlier, the leafy suburb it was situated in didn't even exist; now, by the time Muhammad moved in it was one of the more prosperous neighbourhoods in the area. For Muhammad, of course, relocating brought him into contact with old and new acquaintances alike. Some had his best interests at heart. Others' motives were more suspect.

It wasn't hard for anyone, whatever their motives, to meet my brother. After he moved to Cherry Hill, it was only a matter of days before it became common knowledge that the great Muhammad Ali had moved into the neighbourhood: word spread rapidly, and my brother helped things along by welcoming guests with open arms. Even though he eventually hired a butler, his hands-on approach meant that more often than not he would attend to the doorbell himself, and so it wasn't uncommon for random strangers to knock on the door and be greeted by the man himself. And, of course, he was always obliging: whether the person at the door was a young fan requesting an autograph or a well-wisher asking him to pose for a picture, I never saw him turn anyone down. Often, before anyone else in the house knew it, Muhammad would be standing on his own doorstep engaged in conversation for a prolonged period with a group of total strangers. Moreover, if you were lucky enough and he wasn't busy, he'd beckon you to step inside and make yourself at home. The next thing you'd know, you'd be lounging in the former world heavyweight champion's living room, with the champ himself treating you so cordially that any observer would think he'd known you all his life.

It wasn't just tourists and well-wishers who dropped by to chat, of course. When brothers Bernard and Howard Pollack, a pair of mink furriers who dabbled in boxing management, invited Muhammad to visit their area, he had jumped at the chance. The brothers were from Reading – a modest town in Pennsylvania – and Bernie religiously sat on the front row at every fight Muhammad fought, cheering as loud as anyone for the champ. He also managed several lesser-known fighters, several of whom would come down to train at his newly installed training facility on a nearby farm, where he had built an outdoor ring. One of Pollack's fighters, Ernie Terrell, boxed my brother for the heavyweight championship in 1967 — and lost a lopsided fifteen-round decision. Pollack used the occasion for an introduction, and Muhammad quickly came to prefer his spacious, open-air gym to the premises where most of his fight prep took place.

Back in the early 1970s, it was accepted practice in the pugilistic world for boxers to retreat to sequestered mountain camps as they prepared for their bouts. The mountain air, it was thought, was conducive to a relaxed atmosphere, the clean water and fresh food would be nourishing for the fighter, and the seclusion allowed for an environment free of distractions away from the crowd. Muhammad himself felt there was something more to the mountains. He was of the belief that they were mystical and magical. After he first moved to Cherry Hill, he trained at Bernie's outdoor training facility for his first fight against Frazier. But more importantly, even in those days, he was working on a contingency plan – his own training camp up in the hills, which would become a hotspot for visiting fighters for years to come. It would also be the location for some of the oddest encounters of his life.

★ ★ ★

On 28 March 1967, six days after despatching Zora Folley, my brother had an interesting, if not bizarre, encounter in New York City with a somewhat supercilious man by the name of George Dillman. And I was there to witness it for myself. Coming from an impoverished background, this short, stocky extrovert had dabbled in the sweet science of boxing, but devoted the bulk of his training time to studying the then-mysterious martial arts of the Orient.

Muhammad's first meeting was accidental. My brother had received an invitation to a sports banquet taking place in the Hotel New Yorker, near Madison Square Garden. The charity bash, which attracted numerous sports celebrities of the era, was jammed with high rollers. Several prominent names from tennis, golf and baseball were in attendance, alongside celebrities from other spheres. Muhammad was there representing the boxing world; Dillman was representing the martial arts fraternity. As it happened, Muhammad would end up sitting next to this bespectacled, physically non-imposing man. Dillman may not have been the most intimidating person you'd set your eyes on, but when he opened his mouth, he more than made up for it. He was far from bashful, even if he lacked my brother's flair for the dramatic. And when they struck up a conversation, it was clear he wasn't lacking in confidence.

'You know,' he said turning to Muhammad, 'I think we should start training together.' This wasn't an uncommon offer for my brother –

dozens of people wanted to train with him, as well as pursuing him in a business context or trying to attach their name to The Greatest in some other way. But Dillman persisted, suggesting that the two of them could hit bags, do roadwork together or whatever else my brother wanted. Muhammad was the most famous sportsman in the hall, and asked why he should entertain the thought of enlisting this little man. He, after all, was the heavyweight champion of the world. Naturally, he wondered what this man's motives were and was less than enthusiastic about the prospect of collecting another trainer in a camp that was already full of opinions.

Martial arts at the time were far from thriving in the West. It wasn't until six years later that the kung fu boom kicked in when the then-late Bruce Lee exploded on to the big screen in his smash hit Hollywood epic *Enter the Dragon*, and the masses flocked to learn the secrets of the arts of the Far East. By then, arts such as karate and kung fu were starting to receive more mainstream exposure, but boxing was normally viewed as the most brutal of the fighting systems, and pugilists were still seen as the most feared of all fighters. In 1967, you'd have been hard pressed to find any prominent fighter of repute from the Oriental arts who was even recognised by an average American, let alone revered like my brother.

To Muhammad then, Dillman was an unknown. The organisers had invited him to participate at the charity event because of his martial arts credentials, but in those days there were no mixed martial arts events where he could exhibit them. Still, Dillman persisted: he claimed that he had some new concepts to offer Muhammad, which the boxer could integrate into his repertoire to make him a leaner, meaner, even more lethal fighting machine in the ring. Dillman, apparently, earnestly believed he could bring something to the table, if only the Ali camp was willing to give him a chance. What mystical magic this master claimed to possess, my brother had no idea and, as a matter of fact, wasn't remotely interested.

Dillman, at least, was humble enough to commend Muhammad's boxing prowess. He admitted that Muhammad would prevail if they both shared the ring together. 'You'd beat me and there's no doubt about that,' he conceded over dinner. 'But I think I'd give you a good run for your money.' Less modestly, however, he claimed that my brother had no chance outside the sports arena. 'If we go out here in the alley,' he boasted, 'I'm going to be able to use my hands and feet and I won't have gloves on. I will kick the living daylights out of you. I don't care what you know. I will beat you so badly that you won't know who you are.' Muhammad was stunned, naturally. 'You think so?' he asked, still treating the matter as a joke.

'I know so!' Dillman replied, grinning. 'Should we go in the alley?'

Normally, my brother would have welcomed a challenge, which would've resulted in a playful spar, but here my brother demurred. 'No, let me think about that,' Muhammad said. He was, at the very least, curious as to whether this big-mouthed little man could back up his words, even if he didn't entirely believe him.

Dillman, who was now coming across as a confounded nuisance, went straight on to claim that he could improve the heavyweight champion's hand speed. He would teach Muhammad what he referred to as a 'back-fist', which he explained was a quicker move than the standard boxer's jab. Now, boxers have the fastest hands in the business – even in those days, disciples from other combat sports would seek out boxing gyms to work with professional coaches, aiming to improve their own hand speed. Muhammad himself had some of the fastest fists the heavyweight division had ever seen, and here was this man promising he could do better. He was either crazy, I decided, or cocky…or just plain confident.

Muhammad, meanwhile, couldn't get his head around this one. In the end, he took a business card from Dillman, and as soon as the event came to an end, we all sauntered outside. My brother's presence, not surprisingly, drew plenty of attention from members of the media who were milling around and snapping pictures, and Dillman left.

At the time, my brother still had his apartment in Miami, Florida, and was thoroughly caught up in the Vietnam War controversy. Two weeks after this event, he was arrested for avoiding the draft, his face plastered all over the TV screens across the globe. At the time, Dillman resided in Washington DC, where he was a serving officer with the United States Military Police. Due to these circumstances as much as he was tempted to get in touch with Muhammad, he refrained from contacting him. Dillman could no longer be associated with Muhammad. Being an officer in the Military, he had top secret clearance status. If his phone call ever got traced and intercepted, it could potentially result in dire consequences leading to his dismissal. A year later, Dillman was transferred to Bernie Pollack's town of Reading where he would cross paths with my brother again.

★ ★ ★

By the early 1970s Dillman had opened up his own martial arts training facility downtown on Jersey's 5th Street. I later found out that he was boasting to everyone who would listen about challenging the great Muhammad Ali – his now ex-wife Kim, his students, anyone who was around him when a TV was on. 'You're not going to believe this,' he would brag, 'but I told him I could kick his ass.' Everyone's entitled to their opinion, I guess.

The next meeting between my brother and this braggart, though, was a pure coincidence. Across the street from his school was a nice little restaurant, which is no longer in business, which he frequented two or three times a year. Since Muhammad was in town, he and Bernie decided to grab something to eat before delving into business discussions. They walked into the eatery, and there was Dillman, sitting with his back to the door.

'Don't turn around now,' whispered his wife, 'but Muhammad Ali is behind you.' 'Yeah, right!' said Dillman, spinning around to see my brother and his partners standing right behind him, as if they'd heard all his big talk and come to make him back it up.

To his credit, Dillman didn't flinch. He stood up, greeted my brother and shook his hand. 'Champ, do you remember me?' he asked. 'I don't remember your name,' said Muhammad. 'But you're that karate guy who said he could whup me!'

'That's it! George Dillman.'

'That's it. You said you could whup me. You still think you could whup me?' Dillman replied that he could – he hadn't changed one bit. Amused, my brother told him that he was going to be training in the locality. Dillman revealed that his own training school was just across the street, right up this street from the restaurant, not even half a block.

'Look, we have to eat,' Muhammad said. 'But I don't want you to get away from me this time.' He asked Dillman if he could wait around until they ate because he wanted to converse with him. They got their food and then they all walked out together and made their way to the karate school. Dillman wanted to show Muhammad his own, rather modest-looking, facility.

For Dillman, it was time for round two. Muhammad was still rather dubious about the whole thing as his thoughts shifted to Dillman's attitude towards fighting. Although Dillman seemingly could talk the talk, Muhammad hadn't quite been swayed by this man who had had the audacity to challenge him. This guy hadn't just thrown down the gauntlet challenging the greatest boxer of all time, but was willing to have a punch-up in the street.

After pondering the situation, my brother decided to further probe Dillman to test the waters. 'What about if I shot a left jab at you?' he asked as Bernie and Dillman's wife stood there, not quite sure whether to be nervous or not.

'Well, you can go ahead if you want,' said Dillman, without any sign of apprehension.

Now, my brother was used to playing around at sparring with strangers. Exchanging blows with fans, fighters and everyone in between was well within his comfort zone, and the fear of looking bad never really crossed his mind. So, they squared off and Muhammad fired a left jab at his face, only for it to be met by Dillman's right-hand parry. At the same time Dillman countered, following up with what is referred to as a left roundhouse kick – aiming low at groin level, he didn't quite kick my brother in the groin, but tapped his pants just enough that he doubled the bigger man over. As soon as Muhammad bent double, Dillman stepped in with a right hand. 'Now do you want me to finish the job?' he quipped, somewhat sensing Muhammad's reluctance to continue as the situation was on the verge of intensifying. 'No,' Muhammad conceded, 'we're going to start training.'

As the adrenaline ebbed, Muhammad told Dillman that he was getting ready for a fight and asked if he wanted to join him while he prepared.

This, needless to say, was something Dillman had longed for ever since both men's initial introduction. Needless to say, he was on board. Muhammad, meanwhile, didn't have access to any sparring partners at this stage, and no real equipment had been installed at Bernie's place. He was doing roadwork and working the bag, but I guess he thought it would be fine to have some extra company with a mind for fighting.

'Get Bernie Pollack's phone number,' Muhammad said to Dillman. 'I'm staying at his house. You've got to call Bernie on Thursday night to find out where we are. What do you want to train me in?'

Dillman chuckled. His plan, as he relayed it to my brother, was to improve his hands – the way he hit. Apparently, he had some unique ideas in his bag of tricks, including an array of unique breathing exercises that he claimed would allow my brother to absorb heavy punishment for twelve to fifteen rounds and, in the process, not gas out. But Dillman's interest also lay in introducing the prize fighter to a whole new world of combat. 'I would like to teach you how to block kicks,' said Dillman. At this, my brother stopped him in his tracks before he could utter another word. 'I don't want to learn how to kick!' he exclaimed. 'If I kick somebody in the ring, I'm disqualified!' Dillman explained that he wasn't particularly interested in converting Muhammad to his own sport; he wanted to show him additional defensive manoeuvres purely for self-defence purposes. You have to remember that at the time, the terms 'kick-boxing' and 'mixed martial arts' were not coined, and mixing combat styles wasn't prevalent. Thinking outside the box was not encouraged. 'Well, I'd like to teach you how to block kicks when they're coming at you,' said Dillman, 'in case anybody ever tries to sucker punch you or kick you in the street. You're the world heavyweight champion, so you ought to know how to fight anyone.'

This, at least, tickled my brother.

'That's great.' he said. 'You're on.'

To be honest, Muhammad had a habit of befriending anyone and everyone, and it wasn't unusual for strangers to tag along when he was doing his roadwork, or interact with him while training. It wasn't unusual for me to see a total stranger bump into my brother in, let's say, a restaurant and the next thing you know he'd be best buddies with the man. Gene Kilroy, who was stern and, equally, blunt like me, had a hard time trying to keep strangers and so-called 'friends' away from my brother who he felt were invading his space. And Gene, later, would fume when he heard Dillman boasted about how he 'taught' Muhammad. In fact, the mere mention of Dillman's name would light a fuse. I don't think my brother really felt that this man was going to in some way really accelerate his skills drastically. Angelo Dundee, when we weren't in full fight camp mode, stayed in the background and let Muhammad do his own thing. For my part, I was happy to indulge him, as long as these tricks didn't interfere with our regular training.

★ ★ ★

And so, that Friday morning at 6 a.m. sharp, Dillman promptly reported to the gym accompanied by his wife. It was a pretty basic set-up back then – Bernie had put up an outdoor boxing ring with a tent over it, a far cry from the state-of-the-art gyms that we have access to nowadays. But it served its purpose. It was good enough to get a gruelling workout done.

Training kicked off with a three-mile run, Dillman's wife driving the car behind the fighters. When they returned to the tent gym to continue their workout, my brother didn't put on gloves to spar because, as I said, he had no equipment yet because it was being shipped in. Muhammad worked with Dillman on the action of a back-fist, the move Dillman had been referring to all those years previously. Muhammad's new 'training partner' held the view that a boxer and a karate exponent can throw the same move, but the latter can get the move out a little quicker by the way he positions the elbow. But boxers don't do that. Muhammad had strong reservations initially. 'I can't hit with the back of the fist!' he protested. A back-fist, you see, is an illegal blow in the sport of boxing and he wasn't going to risk being penalised. Dillman, reassuring him, said, 'I know, we're going to change it and you're going to do the same motion.'

Embracing the idea, Muhammad started working on that move. You look at Muhammad in action in any of his fight footage in the 1970s, and you'll see the martial arts back-fist in action. More precisely, if you look at any Ali fight before 1972, and you look at any fight after 1972, you will perceive, without a doubt, the transformation. Especially if you're a martial artist, you'll be able to figure it out. You'll see Muhammad is moving somewhat differently. In fact, in one of the fights – the second George Chuvalo fight – if you watch carefully, you'll more clearly see a back-fist in action. You'll notice the arm extended. And you'll see the elbow action of this blow as opposed to a round punch favoured by the boxers. Now Muhammad started hitting using a more direct route. He was firing his jab straight out like a battering ram.

He's also breathing differently. Muhammad went over to his own corner and performed a breathing exercise when he fought Chuvalo. Then he proceeded to do a stare down. He didn't even take a rest for the full two minutes in his corner. He went over and stared his adversary down, waiting for him to get up to psych him up.

Consequently, Muhammad did some serious training for George Chuvalo, Jerry Quarry and Floyd Patterson. And he won all of those big bouts. When he beat Floyd Patterson, he publicly gave Dillman credit for being the man that taught him the move that closed Floyd Patterson's eye. However, he refrained from referring to the technique as a 'back-fist'. Instead, he said it was a move he utilised to constantly batter the same spot of the eye so badly that it almost popped out. Patterson couldn't see; he was blinded. Muhammad pulverised him and it led to the fight being stopped and he triumphed.

So, Muhammad had started working with Dillman whilst Deer Lake camp was being set up. At the time, neither man realised that a tender new friendship would ensue – one that would forever transform and benefit the cocky martial arts exponent's life. Soon, a storm interrupted his training, which got Muhammad contemplating. He now felt a permanent training complex was required.

Finding the countryside to his liking, my brother eventually decided to purchase the land on Schuylkill Hill Mountain in Deer Lake, Pennsylvania, from Bernie's brother. He liked the proximity to the major cities – most notably New York, Philadelphia and Jersey City. This, as I mentioned earlier, had influenced his decision to move to Cherry Hill in the first place. It wasn't long before the rest of the entourage joined Muhammad. When he bought the land it was just a wood-covered hill. Now he could begin to build a training complex instead of training out of

Bernie's outdoor gym. The team – Dillman, his wife, Larry Holmes, Gene Kilroy and several others went up the hill in Wrangler jeeps for a final assessment of the land. It was a hell of a hill. Muhammad walked back down where the work started. 'I think we can build a gym right here,' he said. Once the camp was completed, Muhammad's training there began to take on a more settled pace and feel. Deer Lake would serve as the training oasis for some of his most memorable bouts.

THE OUTDOOR
ADVENTURES

When the idea first came up, my brother said he'd rather go to jail than move into the hills. He was certain that he wouldn't last a week. You have to understand that Muhammad was born and raised a city boy. He genuinely enjoyed being in the cities surrounded by the masses. Looking out at the endless, quiet woods, sitting around waiting for workout time and being away from his fans and well-wishers, the people who'd motivated him through every fight in his career up to that point... that, he thought, would drive him insane. Being around people injected him with the enthusiasm he needed, my brother thought, and he'd never be able to get that in the mountains. Little did we all know that this thought process would soon change.

From the first day of construction at Deer Lake, it was clear that my brother knew exactly what he wanted. In that era, western movies had made log cabins a cultural icon, and my brother, being a great fan of the genre, loved the look of the old West. He favoured the rustic setting and the solitude: it was exactly the image he wanted to give his camp.

Then there were the materials themselves. Nowadays, cabin builders have a tendency to use pinewood, which doesn't last long because it's too susceptible to moisture and rot. At Deer Lake, eighteen predominantly wooden buildings were erected to my brother's specifications, and every one of them was made with hardwood that had the durability to last over a hundred years. When the camp was complete in its entirety, it included a fully equipped gym, spacious kitchen, mosque, cabins that housed sparring partners and visitors, a bunkhouse and a horse barn. It wasn't just a place to train: it was a place for people to congregate, and it was built to last.

Still, there were teething problems. When the camp was first built, some of the cabins had been put up on the hill, while Muhammad occupied a cabin below. But, eventually, this came with the inevitable result that everyone would congregate into Muhammad's cabin, spending more time there than in their own quarters. 'I can't have that,' my brother finally said, thinking of his training. 'If I have to take a nap I can't have people keeping me up.' And so, he ordered a bunkhouse be built for the rest of the team, up on the hill. This housed eighty people, but soon even more cabins would need to be built.

Among the additional cabins, at Muhammad's request, a two-bedroomed log house was built for Bundini Brown and Angelo Dundee. Soon enough other members of Muhammad's entourage spoke up, asking for separate quarters to accommodate their own families when they visited. This resulted in more cabins being put up to keep everyone happy.

Muhammad was going to have his own family members join him from time to time, so a chalet was built on the other side of the gym. Our parents would stay there whenever they visited. By then, our father had cancer so my brother wanted him close. Eventually, a bigger three-bedroomed ranch house on top of the hill overlooking the chalet was constructed, and that was where my brother would reside in the months before his bouts. As fight date neared and my brother's mind went into fight mode, however, he would move out of the comfort of the ranch house and back into a rustic cabin. The only real luxury this provided was heating.

My brother's wife Belinda and the kids often visited the camp, even though they spent less time staying there than our parents. This wasn't due to a lack of amenities: outside the house Muhammad had a playground built for his kids, and in the summertime he would have a blow-up swimming pool put up for them. Deer Lake was no California, but it would get really humid, especially in the gymnasium. Still, my brother always strove to not only take care of his immediate family, but everyone else there. It was just another example of his constant efforts to make the people around him happy.

Anyway, the family soon settled in and Belinda acclimatised herself to the rural area and took the kids to every amusement park in the vicinity. She embraced the loving mother role while her husband immersed himself in his boxing. When Muhammad and Belinda went shopping or out, a friend would babysit the kids: up at the camp, there was never any shortage of volunteers. Deer Lake became their second home, thus it was imperative to be organised and have access to virtually everything, as they would at their main home in New Jersey.

Wherever I happened to be – whether I was staying with my brother on the East Coast or in Chicago or Louisville – I would always make time to spend at the camp. Once I was driving my brother's limousine from Louisville to Deer Lake camp. It's an eleven-hour drive. I was very tired as I had been driving for hours and I should have pulled over, but I didn't. I kept driving to make it to the training camp in time, and I fell asleep at the wheel. The next thing I knew, my car had run up on the guard rail. My eyelids opened and I yelled, 'Oh my God!' Instead of my car completely going over the guard rail and over the cliff on the other side, it literally straddled the rail and was just stuck on top of it, rocking back and forth, inches from falling over the cliff. My heart was beating faster as I tried to hang on for dear life. However, I was able to open the door and crawl out. I just began thanking God for saving me. If the car had gone down that cliff I wouldn't be here today. From that day, I took time to rest a little more on my trips to the camp.

Although the principal purpose of Muhammad moving to Deer Lake was to prepare for fights, he also took time out to relax. There was no other option: back in those days, fighters fought much more often in a year than they do now. Muhammad fought a staggering six times in 1972 alone – the first year the camp was open – compared with the two or three that most of today's top pros average. To descend into a monastic state for every week of every fight camp would have been unthinkable.

Before long, my brother came to love Deer Lake. He even admitted that he enjoyed staying at the camp more than his home in New Jersey. Spending time at the retreat gave him an opportunity to appreciate the outdoors more. Besides, he could escape the bustling city life for the tranquillity of the rural countryside. I sensed that he seemed to enjoy nature and the serene landscape. I've since learned that being in the great outdoors has been scientifically proven to reduce stress levels, help to find clarity and rejuvenate your mind and body. I can attest to that personally. The feeling of bliss that washes over you when you're outside the city, in the relative quiet of the countryside, is second to none. Deer Lake did Muhammad a world of good. It recharged his batteries and reinvigorated him.

Sitting outside on his deck, the two of us might watch a deer run by or watch wild turkeys trot through the camp. It was like a mini safari park. There were big black bears up in the mountains, and every now and again a bear would run through the camp. At least one was still living there after my brother sold the camp. And from what I hear, a mother with two cubs lived there for years in a little cave. All the neighbours fed her, developed an affinity with her and tried to keep her a secret. Despite their efforts, the authorities somehow found out, and came and whisked her away. She was far from a threat to anybody. But the authorities had a rather different perception. They always have to know better, I guess.

There was also a lake that my brother and I would frequent, sitting on the bench and just watching the local fishermen. Muhammad didn't fish, but he would watch them and take pleasure in watching the ducks float by. He would gaze off into the distance and just enjoy the view. After devouring a little snack there, we would come back to the camp feeling relaxed. At the time, although Muhammad had all these fancy cars – a total of six, which included three Rolls-Royces – something he had a penchant for, he profoundly enjoyed riding horses up and down the hill with his kids. He immersed himself in outdoor activities, which stood as a stark contrast to the lively, unpredictable social life he'd been famous for.

When Muhammad wasn't savouring the outdoor experience, he would shut himself in his ranch house and watch TV movies, which became one of his favourite pastimes. Back then there wasn't the array of TV shows and movies that we have access to today: there were only three TV stations. But my brother really liked to watch films, watching them for hours alone or with others. He declared Saturday nights a movie night: we would set up a big screen which hung on the wall in the gym, the entourage would congregate and we'd all have a great time. It wasn't out of the ordinary to have visitors over, and they were never turned back, whether local or someone who had travelled hundreds, if not several thousands of miles from out of town. Often, total strangers, who were in no way, shape or form associated with our camp, would be rubbing shoulders with the heavyweight champion, watching *Shane* on the big screen and munching popcorn. His absolute favourite movies were scary movies like the classic Hammer Horrors, but he also loved westerns. Later in his life, a friend asked him, 'Who's the actor you admire the most?' 'Clint Eastwood,' he replied. 'He can act, he can direct, he can produce, he can compose music, he can fly a helicopter, he can sing, and he's seventy-five years old and he's still going strong!' And he said, 'The most important thing, he's humble, just like me!'

The cinema screen wasn't all for fun, however. My brother had also accumulated fight films of some of boxing's greatest champions, acquired so that he could study the fights and prize fighters of the past. His favourite pugilist of all time was Jack Johnson, the first black heavyweight champion of the world, who fought in an era when racism was even more prevalent in the prize ring than it was in the 1970s. Our father had told us stories about this fine specimen of a man when we were both growing up, keeping us enthralled with tales of an era where fights might be scheduled for forty-something rounds, and we both thought Johnson was the greatest thing in the world. Muhammad had been enthralled by the heavyweight champion ever since he was a kid, and studied his fights whenever he got the chance – more than once, he attributed the 'anchor punch' that knocked out Liston in their second bout to Johnson – but it was in these Deer Lake sessions, when he spent an inordinate amount of time analysing his movements, that he really found an appreciation for Johnson's physical prowess.

★ ★ ★

For my brother, the best part of Deer Lake was the mindset it allowed him to get into as he approached a dangerous bout: relaxed, but focused.

'I've got everything I need here,' he told one visiting reporter. 'I don't have those hotels where in the lobby people can bother me. I'm eating good country-cooked food, breathing good air, drinking clean spring water.' There were distractions, sure, but none of them endangered his discipline as he put himself through the same arduous regime to peak for each fight. My brother worked hard. He never complained.

Even at the dinner table everyone was welcomed. The kitchen was big enough to accommodate the entourage and a lot more. Again, total strangers would be walking in and out of the camp kitchen. A large custom-made table, twenty feet long and five feet wide, was set up to accommodate everyone. Two chairs were always reserved for Muhammad and a companion, whether it was Belinda joining us for a meal or any other prominent visitor.

My brother was ahead of his time, always following a healthy diet. Our Aunt Coretta used to cook breakfast and lunch. She was a superb chef, and she did a commendable job, even catering to the amount of people who would show up to camp. The food that she made was wholesome and healthy, with fruits and vegetables, a good balance of carbohydrates and protein to give Muhammad and the boxers the right amount of required nutrients. I remember one of her specialities was what we called Coretta's stew, made up of big chunks of meat, celery, potatoes and carrots. She'd just get it going and leave a big pot of stew on a board out there, and you'd see her making home-made rolls coming out of the oven. If any visitors came up and we were eating, Muhammad would say to them, 'Come on and eat with us!' He didn't care who it was. 'Go on, grab a bowl of stew,' he would say to them. There was no special treatment for camp members; everyone was on the same vibe and treated with the same dignity.

You didn't want to get on the wrong side of Aunt Coretta, however. She didn't take any shit from anyone – camp members or otherwise. A special sign hung in the kitchen that read, 'This is my kitchen. If you want a bowl of soup, you don't complain about what's in it. You eat it the way it is or you get out.' Often frustrated, she would complain, 'A lot of kids come in from the poor neighbourhoods and they stand there and tell me, "Oh, I don't like carrots in my soup." "I don't like celery," or "I don't like onions." Well, leave! There's no way that I can take out the carrots just for you.' She was dismissive of those who complained. Needless to say, they would end up eating it and savouring it. Now, Muhammad didn't complain because he loved her cooking. His weakness, which wasn't a weakness to him, was ice cream. He could sit down and eat half a gallon of ice cream in one sitting. He kept a freezer full of half gallons of vanilla ice cream.

Aunt Coretta wasn't the only chef there. We had a whole host of culinary experts feeding us. There was a chef named Lana Shabazz and another, brother Abu-Bakkar. They were the ones who often handled the meals too.

One day in the kitchen, Muhammad was sitting there and a few more people, including Lana, were around. My brother used to devour melons. He absolutely loved them. Lana was slicing the melons up, as she always did, and he was sitting there eating them. He would take a couple of bites and swallow. Lana would always tell him to chew his food correctly so that it would digest better. Anyway, he was sitting there enjoying his melon, like he always did, and suddenly it got caught in his throat.

Next thing you know, he was choking to death. Those around him weren't sure if he was really choking or joking around. Eventually he managed to cough it out, and instantly remarked, 'Wouldn't it be something if the heavyweight champion of the world died from eating a melon?' Despite nearly being choked, he saw the funny side to it all, which wasn't surprising since he had a penchant for injecting a dose of humour into everyday life. If you knew Muhammad, you knew that he was endowed with a strong sense of humour; whether you were a young kid, someone his own age or an old person, you found my brother affable and you could resonate with him. If you were around him, the atmosphere was never mundane. You could hobnob all day with him and you'd still want to do it again the next day. His company was contagious.

Deer Lake, and especially the kitchen, was also another place for my brother to perfect the magic tricks that he already loved. Every so often, a visitor at the camp would teach him a new trick – how to make a coin or a card disappear, or how to pick your chosen card out of a deck. The next thing you'd know, we'd all be eating and he would stand up to mesmerise those who were present with his latest bit of trickery. He'd shrink a piece of rope, appear to cut it in half and then present it whole, or tie it in knots and have it magically unravel. He wasn't a professional magician, but he had a flair for showmanship that added to everything he did, and an obvious joy in performing that just made the fun infectious.

★ ★ ★

Basing himself in a rural setting was more about getting away from the hustle and bustle of the city than avoiding his well-wishers: the fans were always welcome. Notwithstanding his fame, Muhammad's workout sessions were open to the public at the camp. There were no rules to conform to, in contrast to the stringent protocol that modern fighters – and celebrities – are inclined to have in place. The fear of being harassed and having their privacy invaded is something many of those in the fame game can't get over. And others, who are more amenable to meeting fans, might set up black-tie events where a quick picture and a hello might set you back up to $3,000. If luck's on your side, then you might get to ask a question or two before the management move you on as they shield their commodity. But my brother was giving himself away for free. No other star, even in those days, would have countenanced the idea, let alone give personal access to fans in the way he willingly did. There would sometimes be fifty or sixty fans at the gym – sometimes just a handful. The numbers fluctuated, bearing in mind the place was out in the middle of nowhere. Had the camp been in a major city, the place would've been swamped. A prominent city such as Philadelphia, which is just over eighty miles away from Deer Lake – one can only imagine how much attention Muhammad would've received if he had based himself there. I'm sure the sheer number of visitors would have posed a problem in controlling the situation.

Still, people would often drop in to watch Muhammad from far beyond the boundaries of the local towns. If there was a fair amount of them milling around during a sparring session, it wasn't an unusual sight to find Muhammad walk over to the ropes and initiate a conversation in between rounds. He'd be peppered with questions as the curious youngsters and older men and women alike stood in awe of him. He would answer as many as he could and then take a sip of water and go back to the business of sticking and moving with his sparring partner for the day. Afterwards, if he was in the mood, he might regale the audience with his magic tricks and stories. Ali the flamboyant entertainer and larger-than-life character would kick in, and the atmosphere was euphoric. Even the coaches and I, there for the serious business of boxing, would sometimes come up behind the fans and make funny sounds behind their ears, goofing around, as they stood there watching Muhammad pound his partners in the ring. But we all knew that it was my brother they were there to see. He endeared himself to everyone, but it came naturally to him. To my brother, everyone was to be treated with the same dignity, whether they were a fan or a fighter.

Mindful of all this extra attention, I and the few genuine friends and long-time associates of Muhammad at the camp had a tendency to be somewhat protective. Although he was always approachable, a core group of people who really cared for him surrounded him, five or six guys, and would act as intermediaries – directing the people to come in when the champ was ready to spar, and asking them to disperse when he finished his workout. You'd hear, 'That's it! Ali's done for the day! Thanks very much!' and that would be it. We had to stay disciplined, because my brother would have stuck around all day mingling with the crowd, without a thought to his own rest and recovery.

I, of course, was the biggest gatekeeper of all. I was pretty quiet, but I was also a little bit bigger than my brother, and with me being a former pro boxer and a Golden Gloves champion out of Kentucky, I guess you could say I had a reputation for being somewhat mean. But that's what Muhammad needed because back in those times, especially in the 1960s, there was a certain level of paranoia. How could we know that all these people flocking around Muhammad were going to be nice? How could I know someone wasn't going to try to sneak up on my brother and hurt him? That's why every time you saw me I was right by his shoulder. That was my job: to protect him far beyond the point he could trust anybody else to. I'm in almost every photo of my brother from those days, like his shadow. I had to be like the secret service, but unarmed – all I had was my persona, size and meanness. In the end, Muhammad felt comfortable at fight camp because he knew his brother was right behind him, and you were not going to mess with me.

This wasn't just paranoia, either. Sure, there were adoring fans who just wanted to touch the champ, but also I had to keep the crazy fans off, and a lot of them really were crazy. Sometimes you'd get someone who'd taken issue with his religion or his attitude to the draft... or someone even crazier who just thought they might be able to get a clean shot at the champ. Sometimes, you'd get a sense of someone just from the way they acted, twitchy or a little off, even if they weren't cussing or yelling. Not everyone loved my brother, but all those years I was at my brother's side you couldn't get past me to get at him. Even journalists who came to camp in search of an impromptu interview and tried to get close to Muhammad would have trouble getting past me, and more often than not be saved by my brother. 'Rahaman, let it go,' Muhammad would say to me. 'He's OK. We'll do the interview.'

★ ★ ★

Although he'd do his best to find time for interviews, one group that my brother *always* made time for was young people, and that led to one of the most memorable incidents up at Deer Lake. The Snowell kids were a group of eight siblings – mostly teenagers, some younger, and a couple of them in their early twenties – from a black family residing in a nearby town called Pottsville, which is about six miles from Deer Lake. They always caused havoc when they came to the camp, but my brother was rarely too busy to take time out to converse with these kids, and often got into the ring with one or more of them, to give them a few pointers on the sweet science of boxing. I know from experience that spending time with a well-known personality allows you to see them as they actually are, as opposed to the idealistic or notional idea of them. Muhammad, though, looked as impressive in actuality as he did on TV, and these youngsters held him in great esteem. They were aware that they were in the company of a man who was adulated, but they realised this man treated them – and everyone else at the camp, for that matter – like he'd known them for a million years. For somebody of that stature to treat a group of kids from the projects like that, it was special. It really meant everything to them.

Anyway, on one particular day, he was in the gym working out and giving the Snowell kids boxing tips, talking about the sport and life, and even bringing in a little of his preaching. Often, visitors were given further access to Muhammad after he'd finished his workouts as his handlers rubbed him down. Members of the entourage would let two or three people at a time into the back room, where they could spend five minutes or so in his company. So on this day, after my brother finished mingling with these kids in the gym, he invited them into a room and sat them down. He told them to wait in there as he stepped out for a minute. He returned with a big black briefcase. Placing the briefcase on the table, he flicked it open so that they could clearly see bundles of money stacked inside. And then, he left the room for ten whole minutes.

I can only imagine the scene inside. In the case would have been more money than they'd ever seen in their lives, sitting there unguarded as all the brothers and sisters silently stared at the neatly bound stacks of bills. It wasn't out of the ordinary for Muhammad to play around, but I guess he was testing these kids to see what they would do – how they would react. He was probably waiting outside looking through the window or keyhole or something. After ten minutes ticked by he reappeared in the room, sat down on the bed, counted all his money…and then, he was all smiles. 'You mean to tell me you're all from the projects and you don't steal? Take me to your mother!'

Though the Snowells' mother was warned in advance that Muhammad would be driving down to the projects to pay her a visit, the family still got a surprise when he turned up. Whether they thought my brother's promise seemed far-fetched or not is anyone's guess, but anyone Muhammad spent time with knew that he was a man of his word and a man who loved surprises. He had a tendency to randomly call strangers up at Christmas time wishing them all the best, scrolling through the phonebook to pick out random numbers, and more often than not being hung up on by someone who assumed it was a prank call. One time, two teenagers from Pottsville bumped into him in a deli while he was eating with Angelo Dundee. After signing autographs for them, Muhammad asked what their plans were for the evening. They told him that they were going to the cinema across the street to watch a movie. The next thing those young men knew, Muhammad and Dundee were watching a film in the cinema with them, munching on popcorn, like they'd known each other for years. My brother could shock you, and shock you big time.

Still, although the kids had already related the story of the briefcase to anyone in the neighbourhood who would listen, their tale was mostly met with disbelief. So, when Muhammad arrived in his fancy car, parked up outside this family's modest house and made his way inside, he gave the whole neighbourhood a big shock. It didn't take long for the naysayers to come out and flock to the Snowells' household, but little did they know that the champ had come calling with an even grander scheme in mind.

Moved by the actions of her kids, he told Mrs Snowell to choose any house, the biggest house in the area, and explained that he would purchase it for her, a reward for a good mother from a man who was all too aware of the grim reality of life in the projects. But there were even more surprises in store: much as Mrs Snowell was taken aback by this once-in-a-lifetime offer, she declined. She said that her children didn't do anything beyond what they were supposed to do. 'Find a house and I want to buy it for you,' Muhammad insisted. 'No,' Mrs Snowell repeated. 'The good Lord has taken care of us to date and he will continue to do that.'

My brother was further touched by this woman's humble attitude. Not only had her kids demonstrated a trustworthy attitude that not many would, but their mother refused to accept a handout. 'This is beautiful,' he remarked. Muhammad had, throughout his life, crossed paths with all sorts of people. Most took advantage. Others who didn't would never say no if he offered them financial help. Mrs Snowell actually advised him to save his money because one day he might need it.

Since Muhammad wasn't in a great deal of a hurry, he decided to spend several hours at the house mingling with the family. He was enthusiastically welcomed, of course. By this point, several neighbours had invited themselves in to get a peek at a famous face, but Muhammad, for his part, just wound down like he was in his own home. As the evening wore on, he spent the time joking around and had a meal with the family. In the kitchen, he even had a playful sparring match with some of the kids.

'Who you looking at?' he'd yell to one of them. 'I'll beat you up!' he would shout in jest. The kids, of course, were ecstatic. Having Muhammad Ali at your house was a dream you would think would never expect to come true, and yet my brother made that dream a reality for more people than I can remember.

★ ★ ★

As much as Muhammad was inclined to fool around, he was very serious when it came to religion. Islam was the topic of much discussion between Muhammad and his closest family members, and he could easily transition into a more serious frame of mind whenever the subject arose. Straight after beating Sonny Liston to capture the heavyweight title, he had delved deeply into the teachings of the religion he had embraced, and by the time of the move to Deer Lake he had a burning desire to preach at every possible opportunity. The decision to convert to Islam signified a fundamental change in his priorities, and was a life-changing experience that brought him much fulfilment as it did problems.

Despite the fact he wasn't a highly educated individual, my brother was a man of great wisdom. His knowledge of Islam's teaching was all the more remarkable when taking into account his circumstances, and he used it frequently to educate others and invoke the interest of people who might otherwise have kept their minds firmly closed. 'Islam means peace,' he told the family as we listened to him during these moments, showing a man of great learning and experience beneath the fighter and practical joker. One day, he might talk about the Five Pillars of Islam: the profession of faith, the ritual prayers, showing charity to the poor and the needy, fasting during Ramadan and the pilgrimage to Mecca – Muhammad had performed the pilgrimage in January 1972, just before moving into Deer Lake camp. Another, he would hold forth on the Holy Koran. 'Once you've read it,' he would tell us, 'you should go out and teach it to people.' This is what the Koran emphasises, and it was also what my brother believed. Everything he talked about in these more serious moments was, in one way or another, designed to improve you, whether morally, spiritually or educationally.

Zakat, or charity, was one of the central tenets of Islam that was always in my brother's thoughts. Everyone who knew him on a personal level, or met him, would attest to his giving nature – it was a deeply ingrained tendency throughout his fighting career and long after he retired. He gave millions away to charity, and even more to people that he saw in need. To some, this probably seemed like he was throwing his money away, but my brother had a rather different notion. What compelled him to have such a giving heart? How many other celebrities would exert themselves to that level, make money the least of their worries and instead pour millions of their own hard-earned cash into charitable causes or give it away to random strangers?

Certainly, Islam had played a major role. Part of the reason why Muhammad was so inclined to help people was down to the fact that he believed with all his heart that God had blessed him. God had spread his name all over the world, given him fame and money, and in the eyes of Muhammad, if God had put you in a fortunate position, you had a responsibility towards those who were less fortunate. My brother and I regularly came into contact with people trying their best to make their way through life with no visible means of support. Directing his efforts towards relieving the plight of our brothers living in poverty would become a lifelong mission for my brother.

I must add that the goodness in him, inevitably, attracted the attention of devious people. Random strangers trying their luck at Deer Lake were, sadly, a common sight, and, without doubt, he was easily swayed by people. Even so, he never changed. He couldn't change, he didn't know how. Muhammad would sometimes sit down in the gym after a workout and people from all over the country would approach him with all kinds of fabricated stories, needs and wants. And, as much as it may sound unbelievable, he used to sit there with his chequebook in his hand. And he'd write them cheques for thousands of dollars, like a benevolent king. Often he'd take out a whole wad of notes and hand it over to total strangers. I mean, among these leeches were people whom Muhammad didn't know personally, or had just met for the first time. My brother, in all honesty, would never question the motives of these individuals, whatever the people who cared for him told him. Muhammad didn't care about the money. It was frustrating for me, because I was always so wary

Above left: Muhammad at age four, and me at age two.

Above right: My brother at twelve years old, remembering to keep his fists up.

© *Bettmann / Getty*

Below: In his first fight at Madison Square Garden, at eighteen years old, my brother put down Gary Jawish in the third round at the Intercity Golden Gloves. Veteran Jawish outweighed him by 50lbs.

© *New York Daily News Archive / Getty*

Left: A first taste of glory on the podium at the Rome Olympics, in 1960. That famous gold medal made history in more ways than one.

© Bob Thomas / Gett

Right: My brother and our parents being driven through the streets of Louisville after he returned from the 1960 Olympics. He just soaked up all the attention he received.

Left: We are flocked by students in our hometown after his historic gold medal win.

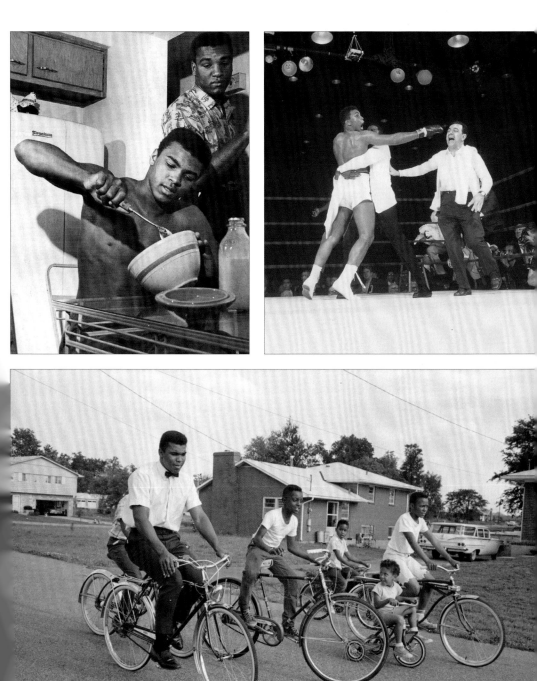

Above left: My brother makes a breakfast mix as I look on in our Miami apartment, in the early 1960s.

Above right: Cassius Clay, as he still was then, celebrates with Bundini Brown and his legendary trainer Angelo Dundee after defying the odds and beating the intimidating Sonny Liston.

© *Herb Scharfman / Getty*

Below: Cycling with neighbourhood kids near our parents' home in Louisville. Taken not long before he took the name Muhammad Ali.

© *Steve Schapiro / Getty*

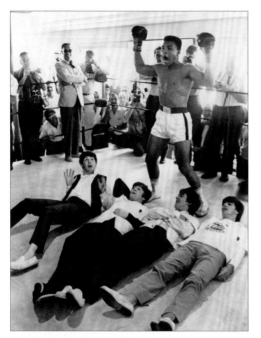

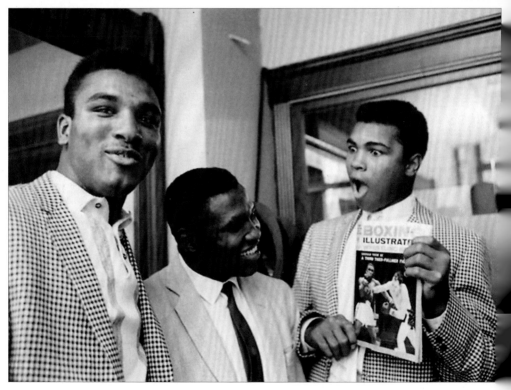

Above left: KO! Laying out The Beatles in Miami Beach's 5th Street Gym, years before my brother would try to reunite the Fab Four.

© Keystone / Gett

Above right: Pay-day! Depositing some money in Los Angeles' Bank of America.

© Richard Meek / Ge

Below: My brother and I clowning around with boxing champion Dick Tiger in Harlem New York, 1963.

Above: Malcolm X congratulating my brother after his victory over Sonny Liston. Two of America's most famous – and most infamous – black men, with yours truly sat on the right.
© *Bob Gomel / Getty*

Below: Muhammad and I deep in conversation with Nation of Islam leader Elijah Muhammad, sometime in the mid-sixties.
© *Bettmann / Getty*

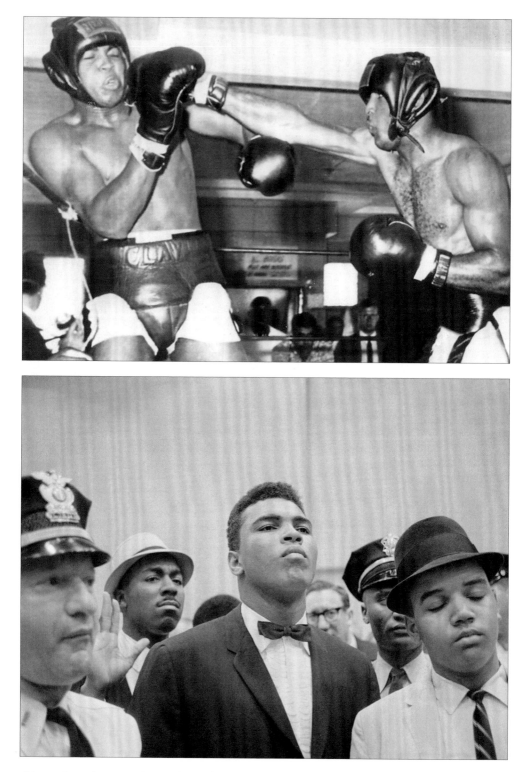

Above: Sparring practise at the training camp. Like I say, mostly he'd come out on top, but sometimes I'd get the better of him. . . I knew his style like no-one else!

Below: On the evening of his Sonny Liston fight, my brother had turned up at ringside in full evening dress to watch me fight on the undercard.

© Bettmann / Getty

Left: My brother and I paying a visit to our great friend, NFL icon Jim Brown, on the set of classic film *The Dirty Dozen*.

© Mirrorpix / Getty

Right: Always willing to make time for everyone, Muhammad signs autographs for teenagers in London in 1979.

© Charlie Hale

Left: Family portrait of Muhammad, Mom, Dad and I at Deer Lake in the 1970s.

© Neil Leifer / Getty

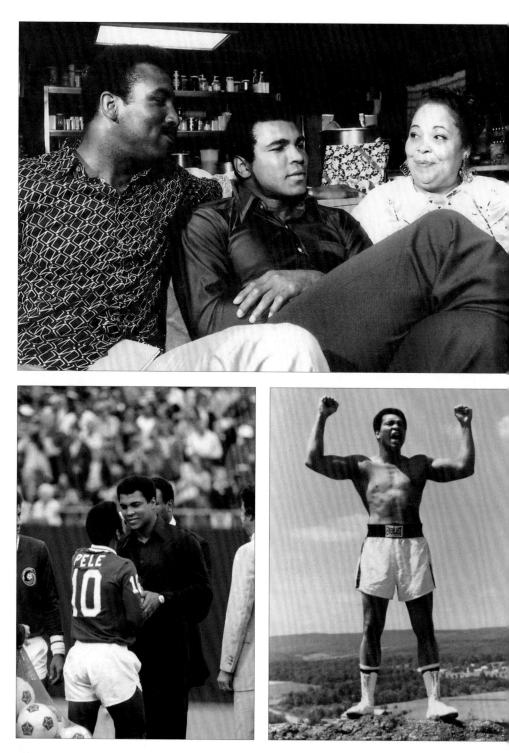

Above: With our mother at the new home my brother bought her in the early 1970s.

Below left: An embrace with Pelé, the soccer master. He was to his sport what my brother was to ours.

© Eric Schweikardt / Getty

Below right: Muhammad screaming 'I am the Greatest!' in the 1970s. Nobody could ever accuse him of too much modesty.

© Gene Kilroy

of everyone who orbited my brother. I'd be at his elbows saying, 'Don't give him more money; he isn't going to pay you back!' He would say, 'Let it go, Rahaman, I don't care. They need it more than I do, apparently.' And he'd keep giving. He was simply of the belief it was his duty to help others who were in dire financial straits. Although some of them had the aptitude for deceit, it was truly a sight to see.

Muhammad had a special affinity with strangers, an empathy and an appreciation for people's dreams and hopes, and it's part of why he was so loved. But it's also one of the reasons he was never financially comfortable, despite being the greatest boxer of all time. Honestly, it made my blood boil. Even to this day I have that character trait where I'm not too trusting because I saw first hand how many people took advantage of my brother.

Still, those moments of frustration were more than outweighed by the lives that he changed. Although Mrs Snowell, despite his great efforts, declined to accept his offer of a larger house, she eventually conceded to accept at least a little of his generosity. One of her relatives in another town had passed away without any insurance, and this relative's immediate family was in desperate need of cash, with no means of paying for a proper burial. Muhammad, without hesitation, decided to take care of this problem. He sent the deceased's son, and some of Mrs Snowell's other kids to the relative's town. He paid their airline flights and for the burial.

This incident, among others, helped my brother to establish a good rapport with Aaron Snowell, one of the teens of the family, whose thirst for knowledge was evident. 'Anything is plausible if you have the core belief in God,' my brother would say to this young man. 'And there's nothing impossible.' He instilled this belief in the youngster that he could pursue whatever he wished. If you show sincere and intense conviction and put trust in God, the impossible will manifest into the possible, Muhammad told him.

My brother, of course, epitomised this mindset himself. He battled insurmountable odds during his life, especially during the shaky period of being stripped of his title and being hated by a good chunk of America. He had shown a willingness to take surprising risks, and it was his belief that helped him triumph over adversity. With this in mind, he was talking from experience, not merely spouting platitudes about the virtues of Islam. In the end, Muhammad's good deed for the Snowells prompted them to take the shahadah, which is an Arabic word for accepting Islam. They became regular faces at Deer Lake. They would join him at the mosque, which sat up in the hill at the camp facing the proper way, and pray with him. Soon enough our mother and father met this family. They had the great pleasure of visiting the same household. Aaron became the chauffeur to our father, whom he held in high regard. The visit resulted in a close-knit friendship and a special bond between the two families. When Aaron grew up, he pursued the sport of boxing as a trainer and commentator and found himself working with some of the biggest names in the sport, including Tim Witherspoon and Mike Tyson. Muhammad, as he did with so many others, had strengthened this young man's resolve. It all boiled down to that connection with the Almighty. And it all started with a big briefcase full of money, and a prank from my brother.

DOUBLE TROUBLE AT CAMP DEER LAKE

Muhammad's daily routine was more or less the same for the entire time he spent at Deer Lake from 1972 until his last fight in 1981. He endeavoured to wake up at the crack of dawn, usually at 5 a.m. He'd kick the day off with roadwork. He was always accompanied by several members of his team, but often he'd find more than a dozen strangers in jogging attire ready to tag along with him. Even kids would make an effort to rise so early just so that they could jog with Muhammad. 'Fights are won or lost out there on the road,' Muhammad would tell them, as they laced up their shoes in the early morning air. 'Long before I dance under those lights.'

I would be the first one up with my boots on and ready to go. On the rare days – there weren't many – when Muhammad didn't feel like running, I would knock on his door and find him lying in bed. I'd wake him up and say, 'Oh no, you're going to get up. You're going to run today. We can't lose any fights. We've got to get ready.' Some days I would literally shake him awake. I was just ambitious: I knew what he could achieve, and I wasn't going to let him miss a workout.

For these morning runs, Muhammad would usually wear his favourite outfit: a light sweater, black pants and heavy black army combat boots. The boots, he explained, made his boxing shoes feel lighter in the ring, and seemed to pose little impediment even on tough runs. Those of us on foot would run alongside the busy highway while his business manager Gene Kilroy and several other camp members trailed behind him in a car. A trick he would often use was to sprint to a stop sign ahead of the rest of the group, smack the post with his palm and turn and run back. That way, he'd get a good workout in while letting the kids tag along, and nobody would be left behind.

After his run, he'd come back to the gym, do his sit-ups and wipe himself down. Muhammad's masseuse would rub and massage him while he lay on a long table, as he admired himself in the large mirror mounted on the wall. Slowly, he would drift off into a short nap on the table. Then he'd wake up and watch some TV before going back to sleep at 8 a.m. After waking at noon, the afternoon would be spent playing with his kids, relaxing, making phone calls and attending to any other business-related commitments requiring his attention. And at about two or three in the afternoon, Muhammad would head back into the gymnasium for his afternoon workout.

He'd always start by jumping rope lightly, for at least three rounds. This would be followed up with hitting the timing bag – a ball-shaped bag, attached to the floor and ceiling – for three rounds. Then he'd spend three rounds unloading on the heavy bag. As it got closer to fight night, heavy bag work would be eliminated from the schedule. Instead, Muhammad's focus would lean towards cultivating razor-sharp speed and precise timing. For this, he simply continued to employ the use of the double-end bag.

Finally, in would come the sparring partners, looking every inch as menacing as you'd expect. My brother liked to spar with a variety of partners, sometimes sparring with much lighter fighters to work on his speed. But when it was time for serious training, he enlisted the help of the best sparring partners in the sport. Larry Holmes and Tim Witherspoon – both went on to capture the coveted heavyweight title – were amongst the elite fighters who, at one time or another, sparred with Muhammad. Holmes, who was there from the beginning, spent four years at the camp and became a regular sparring buddy.

Starting off with one round with each, as fight night neared, he'd increase that to two rounds, three rounds, building up until he was enduring a total of nine hard rounds a night. These weren't usually easy sparring sessions, either. At times, my brother sparred using what he called 'pulled punches', focusing on developing his trademark blistering speed rather than using excessive force. But even during these light sessions, no one would emerge completely unscathed because of the sheer nature of the game. And at other times, my brother actually encouraged his partners to pepper him with hard blows. In fact, there was a general feeling among the sparring partners that they feared that Muhammad would fire them if they didn't deliver in the ring. If there was a downside to this approach, it was that it could seem rather ambiguous. One day you're thinking you need to back off, the next day you'd be required to unload on Muhammad if you wanted to keep your job.

He worked with me regularly. I spent an inordinate amount of time sparring with him. In fact, those who were around would attest to the fact that I was his best sparring partner. 'Rahaman, I need you to give me a good workout because I am going to be fighting a tough opponent,' he would say to me before our gruelling sessions. He encouraged me to dish out the best I had because, as he said, in the gym is where he had to get in the best shape for the real fight. 'Hit me as many times as you can,' he would say. 'I am going to try to block the punches but if you catch me, you catch me.' It was never easy, but I did have one edge – I knew his style and his tendencies better than anyone else. We had shared the ring ever since we stepped into a boxing gym when we were young boys, and so I could see things that others couldn't.

This meant that when my brother faced me, I was often able to evade his onslaught of punches and score on him with solid hits of my own. For my part, I would hit him with all my might. I knew when to land, how to catch him when he was least anticipating it, but even as the punches rained in on him, Muhammad would shake them off. His reflexes would kick in to let him evade my flurries, even as I pressed forward. 'Back off, you fool!' he would bark. But if he'd told me at the beginning of the session to push him, then it was my duty to deliver.

I will never forget when I once caught him with a big right hand so solid that it actually rocked him. Instead of bragging about it, I walked up to my brother after our brutal session to apologise. 'Hey man, I know we're trying to get you ready for the fight, but I didn't want the punch to be that solid,' I said to him. 'I hope I didn't hurt you.' I felt kind of bad. 'Don't worry about it, Rahaman,' Muhammad said. 'I have to be prepared for big punches like this. This is the business we're in. I don't want you to feel like you've done something wrong – it's the opposite. I could get hit by somebody else like that.'

Not everyone appreciated my brother's sparring style, of course. At one training camp – before Deer Lake – when we were both sparring, Cus D'Amato, who went on to mentor Mike Tyson, happened to be there, engaged in conversation with Angelo Dundee ringside. 'He lets himself be pinned to the ropes too frequently,' he told my brother's trainer. 'It's exactly the thing that he condemns in other fighters. He's too stationary, too happy to let the other fellow catch up with him. It's surprising – if it wasn't so repeated I would think that he's putting it on. I mean, to some extent he is, but he's being hit by too many solid punches for it to be a complete put-on.'

To some extent, this was true. I was constantly on the attack, pressing my brother and, yes, getting some shots in. But at the same time, my brother wasn't retaliating with the speed, power and accuracy that he was capable of, because this new style of fighting was all part of his game plan. When he wanted them to, his punches would fire out with the same speed and power when he desired to throw them. But unlike most boxers, he'd let you hit him. He was accustomed to being walloped. I knew it. The camp members knew it.

Angelo endeavoured to explain that Muhammad was trying to wear me out without throwing a punch. But D'Amato had a very critical eye, and something of an ego it seemed. 'You don't have to take that many punches,' he continued. 'He's been taking punches consistently round after round, twenty punches.' D'Amato just wouldn't let go. Apparently he didn't really understand Muhammad's style. He expected way too much from Muhammad while he was watching us. Muhammad's cornerman, Bundini, tried to explain, but D'Amato was seeing this from his own perspective. He did say perhaps Muhammad was being a little too lenient because he was sparring with me – his brother.

Still, even if he'd let you unload on him as he worked his defences, handling Muhammad completely in the ring was not nearly as easy. If you were of the thought that you could easily drop him, you were gravely mistaken. My brother, even in an era where sparring was harder than it usually is today, typically refrained from knocking his training dummies out flat. Certainly after he turned professional, he became known for his leniency on those who engaged in sparring with him as he moved towards mostly working on his defence. He couldn't see the sense in administering brutal punishment on what he saw as hired help. The same couldn't be said of some of his fiercest opponents he fought in how they treated their sparring buddies – if you sat in during their training sessions, you'd usually be watching a real fight.

Truthfully, my brother was always concerned about me. So was Angelo Dundee. After my first pro fight back in 1964 when Muhammad told me that I didn't need to fight ever again, he meant it – I could have never fought again for the rest of my life and he'd have taken care of me. Still, I wound up fighting professionally again, and so my brother had to resort to more extreme tactics. After my loss to Jack O'Halloran in San Diego in 1972, my brother divulged to me that he had actually contacted my opponent prior to our fight. He told me that he had advised O'Halloran to get me out of there. He told him to knock me out, but also asked him to refrain from hurting me too badly. In a strange way, this was him being protective of me. He didn't want me to take any more beatings in the ring or seriously get hurt, so he wanted me to retire. 'Rahaman, you need to get out of the game,' he said to me again after my loss to O'Halloran. 'You don't have to fight any more. I have enough money to take care of both of us.' This time I took his advice and stuck to it and never fought another professional fight. In an interview on TV not long before this incident, when the host had asked him about me and the family, he told her, 'He'll soon be one of the top ten heavyweights in the world.' The interviewer, of course, asked if he would fight me. 'No, I wouldn't fight my brother,' Muhammad said, deadly serious. 'I'd retire. If he's good enough to be the champ I'll retire and let him take over. I've been here long enough.' Of course, I was the one who ended up hanging up the gloves.

★ ★ ★

Although it was idyllic in many ways, staying at Deer Lake did present obstacles periodically. As part of the overall training regime, Muhammad religiously chopped wood, often going through an entire tree in a day. He cleaned out the front of the camp. Furthermore, Muhammad encouraged all of us boxers to follow suit. The rest of the pros and amateurs alike – all of us – were soon knocking big chunky trees down. This exercise, what some residing up in the mountains would refer to as 'hard labour', built Muhammad's shoulders and arms, but he also really felt one could cultivate full body torque with the axe.

Unfortunately, his tree cutting landed him into trouble one day. During his daily training routine he cut down a big tree, which fell on our closest neighbour's land. My brother owned five acres and the neighbour owned a couple of acres of his own. Though our camp should have been his first port of call, this individual made no effort whatsoever to converse with Muhammad, or any of us for that matter. Instead, he called the police and they wanted to arrest Muhammad. Of course, a visit from the police was the last thing my brother was expecting. He was stunned. Muhammad's intention was to just leave the tree there and then chop it up in a day or two: he didn't think anything of it. The neighbour, meanwhile, was busy claiming that my brother was trespassing on his property, which, of course, was absurd.

First, there was an argument over whose tree it was. After close scrutiny, the authorities established that it had been on the camp's property. This left the problem that the trunk crossed the property line. Let's be clear, here: it didn't fall anywhere near the guy's house or cause any trouble, it fell between other trees in the woods. It didn't damage anything, and yet this perfidious man stirred up such a fuss that the case went to the local courts.

My brother, of course, owned up to the charges without a fight. On the day of the hearing, he strolled into the courtroom declaring, 'I cannot lie. I can't lie! I cut down this man's tree and I'll pay for it!' In light of this, the judge ruled that Muhammad had to pay the accuser $1,000. This may not sound like a lot of money today, but back then it was all the money in the world.

All in all, for this man, who smirked all the way through the judgement, the case was a resounding success. As you've probably guessed by now, he was a staunch racist who had always shunned us. He had a disdainful attitude towards my brother ever since we set up camp, and I'm sure he abhorred the fact that so many black people were going up that hill. After this unfortunate incident, tension remained between the two parties. The property is still there, a nice barn and a house. Whether the same person is still the occupant or not I have no idea. If anything, I hope he has moved on with the times as far as his sentiments go.

This incident wasn't too surprising, since Deer Lake was predominantly a white area, full of what we at the time would have called 'mountain people' – or straight-up hillbillies. No one would give my brother racial grief to his face, and there were a few folks up on the hill who I always thought of as good people; but, at the same time, the ugly spectre of racism was never far from our camp.

Another problem back in those days was that a lot of the smaller towns in the vicinity of the camp were, I hate to say, basically run by the Mafia. And many particularly weren't fond of a brash black boxing champion. Sure, they'd have ingratiated themselves with the heavyweight champion if they thought they could squeeze his money out of him, but Muhammad wasn't going to be controlled by such people, nor let disruptive forces influence him. He had been controlled by certain individuals and organisations during the course of his career, and he'd learned enough to know that he didn't like it.

Another source of tension in our dealings with the locals was resentment at Muhammad's refusal to enlist in the army, which led to a refusal to call him by the name he'd chosen for himself. Even though my brother had proclaimed himself Muhammad Ali, people would deliberately call him by his original name, Cassius Clay – the name he had denounced. They knew full well that he hated being addressed by what he'd come to think of as his 'slave name', and yet he'd typically ignore them, or respond with a not-too-polite 'Yeah?' – a far cry from the politeness with which he'd greet most people who spoke to him. Some of these people, certainly, didn't understand why he had chosen to change his name, but others seemed to harbour a grudge against the black man in their midst, and would do any small thing they could to keep him in what they saw as his place. More than a few, I'm sure, would have jumped at the chance to make things escalate further, just as our neighbour did. Muhammad always had a way in with the more business-minded people in the local area, and even though many of them perceived him as a commodity, that gave him enough of an inroad with them to endear him to them with his trademark charm. Because of who he was he could do more than any other black man could have expected the white men around him to tolerate in the 1970s. And, for the most part, he was too thick-skinned to let it bother him. But even if we did our best to integrate with the entire community, some of them would never accept us.

Another indicator of the sensibilities of the time was the way Muhammad was treated on one of his infrequent trips to Reading, one of the towns closest to Deer Lake. This town was one of the first localities where outlet shopping became a tourist industry, but a more recent census showed that this town has the highest share of citizens living in poverty in the country. On a typical trip, Muhammad, who often had to fight off crowds of well-wishers in any city, might only be approached by one or two people, often out-of-towners. 'Reading is one of the few cities in the whole world where I can walk down the street and no one asks me for an autograph,' my brother once told George Dillman, who came from the city and knew it well. 'No one asks me for anything.' Everybody would stare, but nobody made any further effort to approach the most famous face on the globe. The vibe reflected what you would see in a western movie – a ghost town when an out-of-town gunfighter or total stranger strolled in. For my brother, who had a habit of approaching people and initiating a conversation, it was an unsettling experience to be left so deliberately alone. Everyone was aware who Muhammad was and that he had moved into the locality. So, the experience in Reading left a lasting impression on him.

Did my brother reciprocate the animosity that he was shown by the residents of Reading and some of our other neighbours? I like to think he rose above it. Certainly, in the eyes of some of the white populace, he was perceived as a racist hatemonger. Many of his views reflected that of the Nation of Islam, which couldn't help but stir up controversy. And yes, he had sometimes referred to the white race as 'white devils' since joining the group, which made people question his own sentiments towards racism.

When he originally invited Dillman to the camp for the first time, Muhammad actually warned him about how to speak with the black community there. 'When you're at the camp, you're going to hear the N word a lot,' said Muhammad. 'They're going to use it with each other, but don't you use it! It won't be the same.' Dillman took the opportunity to ask my brother about his own opinions. 'Do you hate white people?' he asked Muhammad. 'No. Why would I hate white people?' my brother responded. 'The man who got me out of the ghetto and made me a boxer was a white man – a policeman. Angelo Dundee who trains me and took me to fame is white. Everyone around me who's helping me is white. Bernie Pollack, who helped me build this gym, is white. You're my friend, you're white. And I know a lot of people here at the camp are prejudiced about white people, but I'm not.'

For my part, I witnessed a lot of the vile things that my brother had been subjected to that I thought were plain wrong. However, I was the protector and in my protection some people, if they didn't know better, actually perceived me as racist. They were of the thinking that if you were not black I didn't like you. It wasn't that I didn't like white people – not exactly – but the way they treated my brother for years because of his skin colour left an indelible stain on me. My small form of 'retaliation', if you can call it that, was that I simply didn't trust anyone that wasn't black back in those days. Of course, there were the few exceptions – white people I knew that didn't have a bad thought in their hearts or bone in their body – but still, I was wary of literally everyone around my brother. I wasn't prepared to take a risk by playing the nice guy. Muhammad wanted to eradicate racism, but I was a little behind when it came to turning the other cheek. 'They still hate us even though we've come a long way,' I would say. 'In their eyes we're still niggers.'

★ ★ ★

There was certainly one group of white people who loved my brother, and would seek him out at Deer Lake, though. Movie stars and celebrities would flock to the camp, either to train or to hang out and enjoy the fresh air and atmosphere. One of the members of my brother's entourage went as far as keeping a list of the famous individuals who visited, and from that I can tell you that more than a hundred of the music and movie industries' best and brightest walked through the gates of Deer Lake on a regular basis. Sammy Davis Jr. and Sr., the Delfonics, Nancy Wilson, Elvis Presley (someone my brother was a fan of when we were growing up), Frank Sinatra, the Jackson Five, Tom Jones and Richard Harris and countless boxing champions came to watch my brother spar or hang out as we chopped wood. Some would travel with entourages of their own and keep themselves to themselves, but it wasn't out of the ordinary to see an A-list star having a nap on the sofa in Muhammad's office while camp members walked in and out of the log cabin. It was surreal. There were no barriers separating the visiting stars and everyone else there.

As much as anything else, Deer Lake was a Mecca for visiting fighters. Upcoming pros and hall-of-fame fighters alike would flock to the champ, and Muhammad, of course, absolutely loved it. There was a huge fireplace outside that sat on the platform overlooking the valley. My brother would have a fire running as he mingled with the other fighters, and while everyone else lounged around talking boxing, he would spring up and start prancing around, demonstrating his lightning speed. 'What would you do against him?' he would ask one boxer, pointing at another. 'What would you do against that guy?' he would ask another. He'd do the same with fans milling around, most of whom never even laced up a glove, asking them what they'd do if they faced him in the ring. These social gatherings had a challenging, but playful, type of vibe. And at the end of the night, Muhammad would ring the bell that hung by the fireplace, signalling the end to the evening's activities. 'Why do you do that, ring the bell?' George Dillman's young son Allen once asked him. 'I ring the bell when I train,' my brother told him. 'Why do you ring it at night?' the inquisitive kid asked. 'I ring the bell to let everyone in the camp know that I'm going to sleep,' Muhammad replied. 'And if anyone makes a noise, they're my first sparring partner in the morning.'

★ ★ ★

Even if everyone respected the bell, there were still moments of tension at the camp. For the most part, everyone understood that it was crucial to gel: that, for the longevity of the camp, we all had to get along. But, as they say, you really find out what a person's like when you live with them, and as the weeks grew into months and years at the camp, there were the occasional arguments.

I remember Bundini Brown, in particular, would sometimes sneak out of the training camp and get drunk and come back in a very bad state. He was one of my brother's most trusted cornermen, a pillar of support throughout a large part of his career. Bundini was, no joke, the reason Muhammad won a lot of bouts that he otherwise might have lost: he pushed him to the limit, both in training and in the championship ring. His ultimate trick was to tell him he was losing a bout that he was comfortably winning; that unless he won the next two rounds, he was going to be handed a loss by the judges. 'How are we doing?' Muhammad would ask his cornerman. 'You lost the first three rounds so you'd better start fighting!' Bundini would scream at him, dripping with deceit. Other cornermen have tried similar tactics, but nobody could pull this ruse off as often, or as successfully, as Bundini. Fired up and furious at the prospect of a loss, he would go nuts, go out there and unleash hell on his hapless opponent. I feel if it wasn't for Bundini, Muhammad would have several more losses on his record.

Anyway, when Bundini lived in New York there were lots of little clubs on the West Side and he would go out just about every night. Now the thing is Bundini could stay up all night partying and hell-raising but still make training the next morning. An associate of Muhammad's, Leon Gast – who had become friends with Bundini and lived in the next street and would often drop by Deer Lake – went into the clubs a couple of times and asked the manager or the guy behind the bar, 'Excuse me, has Bundini been here?' And the guy would say, 'No, he hasn't been here. And if you see him, tell that motherfucker he's not welcome here.' Bundini could easily get himself in trouble because he's the kind of person who'd lose control after his first drink, and he wasn't averse to the harder stuff, either. It was a time when a lot of people were doing cocaine, though back then they called it 'milk'. And whatever it was called, Bundini wasn't immune to its charms.

Muhammad would get very upset at Bundini's drinking. My brother would try to explain to him about the bad influence of alcohol, which he'd seen take its toll on plenty of other men. He'd lecture him in the vain hope of getting him to see sense, but the words would make their way into Bundini's ear only to leave from the other. It just wouldn't register on his radar. Despite the arguments, the next morning Muhammad and Bundini would make up again. Then the same scenario would repeat itself.

There were the occasional extra-curricular fights, as always happens in the heat of a fight camp. The most brutal altercation in the camp started on a Wednesday night with Muhammad going to do a press conference in Philadelphia. At the media-packed gathering, three of his sparring partners – including Alonzo Johnson, the light heavyweight contender at the time – accompanied him. When my brother turned pro, he had locked horns with Johnson in a nationally televised fight in front of 6,000 fans in his home town of Louisville. That fight took place on 22 July 1961, and my brother beat the veteran in a unanimous tenth-round decision. Now Johnson was one of Muhammad's sparring partners. My brother would often help out pros in need of some extra cash or support by employing them as sparring partners and putting them on his payroll. The other two sparring partners were also famous boxers, maybe not on Johnson's level but certainly enough to give any fighter in the world a rough night.

At the press conference, Muhammad was set to spar three rounds against each fighter, for a total of nine. Realistically, at this kind of event it was mostly his brash and extrovert personality that sold the fights: he would launch into extended riffs to keep the assembled media's attention. But, sporadically he'd do open training sessions for the press, to remind them just how fast and agile he could be.

In that period, Muhammad would sometimes train with George Dillman in the morning or during the day. The day after that sparring session, which was a Thursday, Dillman was scheduled to join Muhammad for roadwork followed by a workout. Instead, he got a phone call from Muhammad, who told him that he wouldn't be up at the usual time of 5 a.m. because he'd be boxing the night before. It would be a light workout, my brother explained, but he still needed to conserve his energy.

Dillman arrived up at the camp the next day accompanied by his wife. On the walk to the gym, they happened to bump into Bundini Brown. Normally, they would have just said hi, but on this particular day Bundini cut the couple off going through the gym door. 'You'd better not go in there,' he warned. Confused and finding his gaze disconcerting, Dillman asked why. 'Muhammad Ali is pissed!' he replied, emotion obviously welling up inside him. Those are the exact words he used. 'What!?' Dillman asked. 'I've never seen him like this,' Bundini exclaimed. 'My whole life, as long as I've known him, I've never seen him like this. He's furious! He's lost it.'

Dillman was surprised. 'What's the matter?' he asked. 'Well, he's going to be fighting,' said Bundini. Dillman asked if Muhammad was going to be working out. 'Oh, yeah!' came the reply. 'He's going to be working out. But he doesn't really want people in there. I just thought I'd tell you that you'd better head home because I've never seen him like this.' Further pressed, Bundini explained that at the press conference the previous evening, the three boxers had tried to take Muhammad out.

It's still not clear what caused the ruckus in the first place. Sure, a lot of the media were present, and I'm sure Muhammad's partners didn't want to look bad. One possibility is that Alonzo Johnson was the ringleader and the impetus behind the assault, since he was certainly trying to knock my brother out in front of the gaping crowd. In the end, I later heard, my brother was forced into a desperate scramble to come out of the corner before he could get out and hit back. All three men were hitting Muhammad too hard, battering him, turning what was supposed to be a spectacle into something that almost mirrored a real fight. My brother thought the whole affair was supposed to be an opportunity for publicity, a chance to give the media a few quotes and pose for a few pictures. I mean, he'd taken part in countless events organised for press members, but never had he been subjected to this kind of treatment by his own team members, men that he paid for, housed and treated with respect. Bundini summed it up best. 'You know, George, sparring partners ain't supposed to show off.'

'So what's going to happen?' Dillman asked. 'Muhammad Ali's going to take on all three of them and beat them up today,' Bundini said, unable to resist a touch of theatricality even under the circumstances. 'They were told to be here at 12 o'clock. They're going to get in the ring, and we'll see what happens.'

At first, Bundini tried his best to dissuade the couple from entering the gym. He knew that the three boxers were going to be facing a brutal beating. However, after a moment of thought, he had a change of a heart and beckoned them to quietly slip in. As long as they refrained from uttering anything to anybody in there, he was fine with it. 'Just go and sit at the back and watch,' he said to them. A day which began sedately now began to unravel rapidly.

They made their way into the gym, saw several individuals milling around, and parked themselves right at the back for fear of attracting attention. In moments like these, I know from experience, one can sense trouble brewing, and the people who'd never seen my brother's darker side were in for a rude awakening. Moments later, Muhammad emerged out of the dressing room making his way to the ring. You could clearly see he was steaming, His face was flushed, and that ferocious look in his eyes, a look he seldom exhibited even in the prize ring, had surfaced. This look, as I know from seeing it myself, could've frightened off even the mightiest of men and made them tremble in fear. Muhammad had refrained from getting angry at the press conference. He had somehow managed to compose himself. But now he was mad.

When the three boxers came in, everybody was so quiet you could hear a pin drop. As a couple of other pros put on the wraps and gloves on the boxers, Bundini went over, gave Muhammad his gloves and wrapped his hands. Muhammad stepped into the ring and started bouncing and bobbing like he always did. The three culprits stood silently outside the ring. When he finally spoke, Muhammad's words stunned the crowd into silence. As he turned to the three boxers, he shouted, 'I want you first! I want you second! And you, Mr Big Mouth, you're last!' He continued as he vented his anger, 'Now I want the three of you fighting. You thought you were smart asses last night. Today you better be fighting. Now I want you to try to take me! I want you to hit me hard! I want to see what you got. Let's see what you really got. And you, Mr Big Mouth, you better be fighting for your life!' These boxers, my brother had decided, were going to go through hell and back. Only providence could save them now.

Muhammad wasn't putting an act on, which he was known to do in front of his usual crowds of fans. He was as serious as hell.

Muhammad went back to his corner, put his mouthpiece in, the wraps were on, and in came the first boxer into the ring. Muhammad hesitated for a split second. 'By the way,' he said, 'you guys better use headgear.' Bundini asked, 'You want your headgear, Champ?' Muhammad replied, 'No. I want to see what they got!'

When the going gets tough, while your natural instincts may tell you to resist in a fight, sometimes it may be safer to walk away and avoid a good old beating if the option is there. But these men had brought it on themselves. There was no turning back now. They knew now that there was no means of escape. All they could do was to wait patiently in line to get a taste of their own medicine.

The first boxer stepped forward and proceeded to fight. My brother unloaded on him, beating the living daylights out of him. And that guy was trying to hit him, tried to defend and pound him with devastating blows. This was no spar; this was brutality at its best. My brother cut him, beat him badly, knocked him down and dominated him for three rounds. The next guy came in. Muhammad beat him badly too, peppering him with blows knocking him down to one knee. The guy got up only for Muhammad to administer the same punishment. He was put in an untenable position as Muhammad totally obliterated him. The crowd's faces showed it all: this was war.

The third guy, Alonzo Johnson, the king of the culprits, got in the ring ready to rumble. 'Give it all you got!' Muhammad barked as the audience waited for the situation to culminate in a TKO. Johnson was a good fighter. He was trying to hit back in the vain hope of keeping Muhammad at bay. But his efforts were hopeless, as my brother sliced through his defence and beat him to a pulp. He got him on the ropes and beat his head like a timing bag as Johnson's defence faded. Muhammad knocked him down on both knees, went to pummel him again as he was down, but those who were outside the ring started shouting, 'Stop, Champ! Stop, Champ!' Bundini went in between them and shouted, 'You're going to kill him! You'll kill him! You don't want to kill him!' Johnson had endured such a beating that he couldn't even get up. He'd taken the most punishment as he disintegrated before the audience's eyes. The atmosphere was tense. There was a moment of silence.

Muhammad went back to his corner. They took off his wraps. He threw his gloves on the floor and marched straight back into his dressing room. The three badly beaten boxers got up, and were helped as they hobbled back to their dressing room. Dillman wasn't even aware if Muhammad knew of his presence. Well, not at that moment, anyway.

Something that not a lot of people know is that my brother had a two-way mirror fitted in his dressing room. He could look out, but if you were in the gym you couldn't look in: it was like the ones you have at police stations for identity line-ups. Even Dillman didn't know about this mirror. Muhammad saw the karate black belt and his wife sitting there like two well-behaved schoolkids who'd just had the shock of their lives, and he opened the door and marched over to them. 'Hey, what did you think of that?' he asked in a condescending manner. 'Was that an ass whipping or what?' Neither Dillman nor his wife had the words to reply.

On that specific day, I wasn't at the gym. If I had been there and found out that those three sparring partners had taken advantage of Muhammad, I would have taken a different approach. I would have said to my brother, 'We don't need them anyway. Let's kick them out of the camp.' That's the kind of person I am. I wouldn't have suggested that Muhammad fight them, but if I even got a hint that they were really trying to bring physical harm to him, you would have had to restrain me because I would have fought them, in or outside the ring. I was a straight fighter. I would kick your butt. So, I would've confronted them for sure. I would've said, 'You did that to my brother, I'm going to jump in and beat your butt my damn self!' In the end, Muhammad's way was more merciful, and in keeping with the way he conducted his affairs every day. He gave them a taste of their own medicine, and then kept them at the camp, letting them feed their families with the wages they made for training. And he gave Dillman, his wife and the small crowd that found themselves in the gym that day, one of the most intense displays of the sweet science they would ever see.

HOUSE PARTY

One thing that I'm certain my brother would have done in his life, if given another chance, would have been to spend more time with his family and kids. I don't think he'd argue that he neglected to spend quality time with his children during his boxing career; he spent more time away on the road than at home. Although they did visit Deer Lake, as I mentioned, they would leave early – I stayed right up until fight night and beyond. He was living a jet-set lifestyle, sure, but at the time he also felt it was the mother's job to bring the children up. Back then in the 1960s and 1970s, personalities travelled extensively to promote what they were doing, and Muhammad behaved much as anyone else did. The difference, perhaps, was that my brother loved children, and always had time for them.

Because of the amount of time he spent away, but also, perhaps, because of our own upbringing, Muhammad wasn't the best disciplinarian when it came to his children. When he was married to Belinda, she was the one left to enforce the rules, while Muhammad would play with the kids and let them run amok. One time in particular Muhammad and Belinda went to an event where Muhammad was promoting something, and they left their twin daughters, Rasheda and Jamillah, who were kids, in a hotel room in the care of the babysitter. While they were out, the twins threw all of their clothes out of the window from the balcony. Belinda scolded the little girls, but Muhammad refrained from any talk of discipline. He would just let any of his kids, more often than not, get away with little mischievous things. He just didn't have the heart to assert his authority.

He also wasn't up to scratch when it came to domestic duties. He didn't have a clue about the basics of looking after a baby. Often when he was at a TV studio appearing on talk shows, he had his wife and kids accompany him, and he'd hand off the baby the instant a diaper change became necessary. I think I saw him change a diaper once, at home, and on that occasion Belinda still had to take over halfway through.

On the other hand, what Muhammad was good at was showing affection for his children. When he was at home with them, he would kiss them or hold them, play with them and entertain them for hours.

Muhammad had three girls before his son came along, so he didn't know how to handle boys at all. One incident, in particular, illustrates the point. Nikki Giovanni used to work on a TV show called *Soul*, which was filmed in New York City. *Soul* was like *The Ed Sullivan Show*: they had singers, dancers, actors, interviews with famous black personalities. It was an hour-long variety show so people could see what was going on in the black community. Muhammad was one of the special guests who regularly appeared on the show at the time he was living on the East Coast. Muhammad periodically took his wife and kids along with him when he did TV studio interviews, but they didn't always travel with him. Anyway, Nikki had a little son about six years old whom she had brought with her to the studio. She had only one son so she could take him with her anywhere she went, especially if she was going someplace interesting, like Alaska or California.

The presenter who was interviewing Muhammad was peppering him with questions along the lines of, 'What do you think of the war?' This was in the era when Richard Nixon was going to get impeached, though he resigned before he did: apparently that was going to be broached among the hot topics. Muhammad was lounging around and Nikki's son was running around causing havoc, getting on everyone's nerves. Next thing you know, he picked the little boy up and whacked him on his backside. He didn't hit him hard; just to let him know he shouldn't be running around. And little Thomas went running to his mother, and he said, 'Mommy, Hammad Ali hit me!' He used to call my brother 'Hammad Ali' – he could never get the first name right. His mother said, 'That's between you men. I'm not going to get into that.' Then the child walked over to Muhammad, pulled his jacket and said, 'Hammad Ali!' Muhammad, still rather annoyed, looked at the little boy and sternly asked, 'What, Thomas?' He was really tired hence not in his usual jovial mood. Thomas pulled back his arm, made a fist and hit Muhammad in the knee as hard as he could. That was as far as he could reach because Muhammad, a towering 6 foot 3 inch individual, was standing. It was so funny. Muhammad was just trying to make Thomas shut up. He was just like any other child running around who shouldn't have been, and it was starting to get on Muhammad's nerves. It showed Muhammad's lack of experience in terms of dealing with a little boy misbehaving. He was used to his three daughters but had no real insight into handling little boys. The way he responded to Thomas was a spur of the moment thing. Muhammad said to me, 'One day I'm going to have a son.' And not long after his only son was born, whom he named Muhammad Ali Junior.

★ ★ ★

While Muhammad was spending little time with his family, he seemed to have plenty of time to entertain guests. Whether we went to special events or hosting parties – at his home or anyone else's – my brother would always have me accompany him. On one notable occasion, Muhammad, along with several friends, attended a Nation of Islam rally. The unusual thing about this rally was that four white friends had accompanied him to what was otherwise an all-black event – the first time, to my knowledge, that white souls had been granted access to one of the Nation's private gatherings.

Farrakhan was going to be the chief speaker. Muhammad, singer Nancy Wilson, the Delfonics and several other friends were all going along with Muhammad, but my brother also happened to mention to one of his white friends that he was going to this rally. Intrigued, his friend asked if he could tag along too. This was a dilemma for my brother. Muhammad knew that no white man could attend a Nation rally, or certainly that no man ever had – whites, for obvious reasons, were perceived as perfidious by the entire organisation. Muhammad, hesitant, told his friend that it was a blacks only event and, furthermore, that the attendees were likely to be talking in derogatory terms about the white race. My brother thought, wrongly, that this would deter him, but his friend was adamant and still insisted on attending. Muhammad, left with little choice, told him that he'd have to get the all-clear from party officials first. After conferring with a high-ranking member of the Nation of Islam, it was agreed that this friend could join him. So his friend brought his wife and another white couple along also.

Muhammad told his friends to meet at his place in the afternoon on the day so they could set off together. He also mentioned that he'd be hosting a party back at the house straight after the event, so they could just get together and have a good time to conclude the day, whatever else happened. Friends started arriving early about lunchtime all dressed up. Muhammad introduced his white friends to Nancy Wilson and the other distinguished guests who were present such as the Delfonics and they set off.

Like I said, at the convention the two white couples became the first ever non-blacks to attend this Nation of Islam event. And, sure enough, it wasn't all pleasant. There was a lot of what some today would call 'hate speech' broadcast that day. The speakers spouted some abhorrent views, which reflected on the injustices the black race in America had been subjected to ever since the slaves were shipped over to the place known as the 'Land of Opportunity'.

Truth be told, the white couple stood out like the proverbial sore thumbs. Every time Louis Farrakhan yelled, 'White people are devils!' four thousand black people in attendance would look at the table where the four white people were sitting. It was a cringeworthy moment to say the least. Nevertheless, the white couples sat there trying their best to be humble, keeping their placid demeanour intact. The rally was intended to recruit black people to join the Nation, strengthen the group, and stand up for the cause, and so emotions were running high. For my brother and I, this type of gathering was a fairly typical rally – the kind where, more often than not he was given a platform to expand on the principles relating to the organisation's ideology. My brother was obviously the organisation's money bag, but also he provided a powerful voice and star power. The platform he had gave the cause a bigger voice to make their views heard. Ever since we both joined this organisation, we had been members in good standing other than the time when Muhammad had a problem when he decided to pursue fighting again after he lost his licence. My brother would continue to spread the ideology of Elijah Muhammad.

★ ★ ★

After the event everyone made their way back to Muhammad's residence for a house party, including several of the ministers from the Nation of Islam and notably Louis Farrakhan. Muhammad always enjoyed parties. We were invited to dozens, all the time – from movie openings and famous musicians putting on private shows to gatherings held by friends, family and people from the neighbourhood or camp. When he was throwing a party at his home, though, my brother was always more relaxed. At other venues you might expect to see liquor flowing, or drugs being passed around, but Muhammad's house parties differed. Recreational drugs and alcohol were two things my brother never got involved with, two bad habits that Elijah Muhammad ensured my brother avoided. My brother was a human and had certain weaknesses, but he always believed that having a good time didn't mean you had to get drunk. Muhammad's 'drug', if you want to talk about what gave him a high, was entertaining others. His drug was boasting at press conferences and in front of the TV media. His drug was fighting in the ring. He got high on all those things. He might even have been addicted to them.

Not that he didn't have a good time at regular parties. He was the type of person who was always inclined to be the centre of attraction. And whether it was an innate ability or one he cultivated during our days growing up together, you'd have to say that he was phenomenal in that role. But at the same time, Muhammad's personality in front of the cameras or the crowds couldn't have been further removed from how he acted around family and close friends behind closed doors. The boisterous side of him was for the press and the public. If you said to him, 'Here come twenty people from the newspapers,' he'd go electric.

He would act like a wholly different person while the cameras flashed and the questions flew. The minute they departed, though, he'd say, 'OK, now we can relax.' Even at the wilder parties we attended, assuming the press wasn't around, Muhammad wasn't a party animal. Away from the crowd and limelight, he was most happy sitting around talking casually.

Most of all, Muhammad relished the peace and serenity of entertaining friends in his own home. This is something that most people have no clue about: my brother was never the type of person who, behind closed doors, gave you the impression how great he was. He certainly knew who he was, but he refrained from blowing his own trumpet, or inflating his own ego. He was very humble. 'The really great people never did boast that they wanted to be great,' he would tell us as we sat around, exchanging ideas. 'They wanted to be humble and close to God – Allah. They never consider themselves to be great.' My brother looked up to people like the Kennedys, Gandhi and Nelson Mandela. But as far as trying to impress other people went, he was happy to be himself.

The one-floor residence in Cherry Hill was beautifully furnished for entertaining. It was a French-style, octagon-shaped house with beautiful chandeliers gracing the ceiling of its large dining room, and a grand piano in the centre of the living room with a portrait of the honourable Elijah Muhammad above the fireplace. Muhammad had two guest bedroom suites in addition to his master suite, so that from time to time guests could stay over. There were half a dozen different rooms coming off from the hallway, and in the middle of the octagon lay a swimming pool concealed from the prying eyes of the media photographers, so that our family or guests could take a dip without finding themselves on the front pages of the newspapers. Small wonder, you might say, that so many celebrities enjoyed dropping by.

Something that had been on Muhammad's mind on this particular occasion, a pressing problem, was a speeding ticket that his wife Belinda had picked up. 'Hey, she's got a speeding ticket,' Muhammad said to his white friend. 'We're not worried about the fine, but she's going to get points. She was driving really fast. We don't want her to lose her licence.' His white friend, who had links with the police department, said, 'I think I can help with that.' So he later went down to the police station and he asked for the police officer who had issued the ticket. This resulted in the ticket being cancelled. Now all records are fed into the computers, but back then it was all paperwork. The ticket was pulled out by the officer, ripped up and he said to Muhammad's friend to forget about it. At the time Muhammad's friend was teaching unarmed combative tactics to the police. Thus he had a fairly good relationship with law and enforcement authorities in the area.

Speaking of parking tickets, I can tell you that Muhammad soon developed a habit of receiving about a dozen parking tickets on a monthly basis. He had this habit of parking his fancy car anywhere carelessly. It got to the stage where he managed to get an arrangement at the town hall with a high-ranking official where Muhammad would get a 50 per cent discount. All this just because of who he was.

Anyway, the evening of the house party Muhammad was on chef duties. Seldom one to immerse himself in domestic duties – something which, following the attitudes of the time, he felt was better suited to women – he was, nonetheless, a rather good cook. He could cook a few casserole dishes, but he also ate healthy food – steak, chicken, salad – and knew how to make it. He was second best to his wife, sure, but nevertheless, he tried his best, and you could tell when you ate one of his dishes. I certainly tried them and never really complained.

On this particular evening, though, there was some unusual food on the menu. As guests congregated in the dining room ready to dig into the feast, Muhammad unveiled a main course that was familiar to many members of the Nation, but completely unknown to his four white guests. To their astonishment he put on a big display of bugs – ants, caterpillars, cockroaches and grasshoppers.

This actually wasn't an especially unusual meal for my brother. Somebody had told Muhammad that, not only were insects healthy, but that they're loaded with protein – a vital resource for any serious athlete. In fact, cockroaches and grasshoppers have more protein than steak. The protein content in grasshoppers comes pretty close to that of a similar-sized serving of chicken breast, but with a bit of added fat.

Despite being less enthusiastic about the prospect of trying insects, however, the white folk eventually ended up devouring them at my brother's recommendation. At least one of them proceeded to taste every single bug on the menu, savouring the experience and the opportunity to try something new. As well as raw insects, there were deep-fried ones, cooked up well enough that if you were blindfolded you wouldn't have known what had just slipped down your throat. There were chocolate-covered caterpillars and chocolate-covered ants, and I'll be honest with you, you mostly tasted the chocolate. Then from the kitchen Muhammad brought in huge cockroaches, which had been deep fried, that had actually been imported from Africa. Muhammad, apparently, had done his research, as he proceeded to explain to his white guest which bug was associated with which tribe. It was a party, I'm sure, which those people never forgot.

★ ★ ★

Of course, Muhammad's biggest trait was that he was inclined to help you if you needed help. He would literally do almost anything for you. He demonstrated great empathy when it came down to communication with those who required a helping hand. Regardless of your colour or creed, if you were a friend of Muhammad's, he felt it was his duty to help those in need. What many are oblivious to is that he was always a good listener as well as a good talker. He'd listen to other people talking about their problems. Muhammad and Wilbert, one member of the Delfonics, were having a deep thought-provoking conversation. The latter knew that he could talk to my brother about any problem because of their friendship. Anything he said to Muhammad, my brother would take on board. Muhammad confided in Wilbert, too, and to this end he would tell him about his own problems. Muhammad always had Wilbert's back.

Of particular relevance was my brother's generosity and amidst their conversation attention turned to money. Wilbert asked my brother for some financial assistance. He knew Muhammad was the perfect person to ask, a man who never turned down any friend – a scenario that was all too familiar to me. If I was to count the number of times those who knew Muhammad would look towards him when they were in need of financial help, it would take me days. My brother was all ears as his friend explained his situation and asked if he could help him out. However, to his friend's great surprise, on this occasion Muhammad was unwilling to carry him on his shoulder.

To justify his reason, he said, 'Always people ask me for money, this, that and the other, can I get this, can I get that?' he said to Wilbert. 'I mean, everybody needs money. And they say Muhammad Ali's rich. You can't give money to everybody because then you'll be broke.' There were always scroungers surrounding Muhammad, but I don't know if this was Wilbert's intention. 'Sometimes you've got to let people know that,' Muhammad continued. 'I have more money going out than coming in. I can't help everybody.' This was not Muhammad's character. It was very unusual of him to say no. Disappointed but equally understanding of Muhammad's stance, Wilbert said, 'It's OK.' A lot of times you have to make a decision when you're thrust into a dilemma. Muhammad almost always didn't think twice. People thought that Muhammad had a lot of money, but if you've got a lot of money you've got a lot of responsibilities, too.

MURDER, MAFIA & MAYHEM

One very interesting character who played a part in Muhammad's life was Major Benjamin Coxson, – the 'Major' was his real name, not a military rank – an entrepreneur and power broker with ties to the Nation of Islam. In fact, Muhammad had purchased his Cherry Hill home from Major Coxson. My brother would later say that the 'Maj' was the driving force behind his family's move to the East Coast. Whether this was a joke is debatable. The two first met in 1968, when my brother was still in exile, at an event in Philadelphia, and later proceeded to join forces in an effort to get Muhammad back into the ring. Major Coxson's job, apparently, was to get the Muhammad Ali PR show back on the road, getting him back into the limelight after his exile came to an end. To be quite honest, I'm not sure just how much he could do to propel my brother further into the public eye because Muhammad didn't need anyone to accelerate his PR. He was his own PR machine and everyone knew it. I often saw people boasting that they were one of my brother's managers, representatives or close associates, just to jump on the bandwagon.

However, what was interesting about his flamboyant friend was that he was a long-time fixture in the East Coast underworld. Coxson had an impressive criminal CV. He was an automobile thief, fraudster and reputed drug dealer, but also a very confident and knowledgeable black man who attracted attention from all sorts of quarters. In collaboration with the Muslims at Temple 12 – the Nation of Islam mosque in Philadelphia my brother and I attended – he had a hand in setting up fake businesses as a front for money laundering. Moreover, this man was an aspiring politician who pursued politics and was running for mayor of Camden, New Jersey. Muhammad, meanwhile, had cultivated a great relationship with this criminal and they both became business partners when he moved to the East Coast.

Despite being aware of Coxson's background, Muhammad didn't shy away from endorsing his friend in public. There were plenty of local newspaper stories about the pair of them, which predictably confused people because those in the Philadelphia and New Jersey area knew that Muhammad's new friend was a career criminal who had served time in federal prison. The local populace knew this man was consorting with murderers and drug runners, yet, here you had Muhammad embracing him and supporting him openly. Honestly, it was very frustrating for many of Muhammad's supporters, and plenty of people in the New Jersey area were disconcerted with my brother because he was giving credibility and legitimacy to a known hustler.

Why did he do it? Let's put it this way: sure, Muhammad knew of his friend's under-the-table dealings, just like he knew who most of the Black Mafia members were. Like I said, my brother and I were frequent visitors to Temple 12. He knew that entire scene well. It didn't take the police department or law enforcement authorities to warn Muhammad whom he was dealing with. Although Muhammad's friend was affiliated with the Black Mafia, and dabbled in drugs and other illegal and dubious activities, my brother was in no way involved in those activities. Both men had forged a friendship in spite of their differences in outlook. I'd say Muhammad viewed Major Coxson mostly as a friend but also, at one point, called him as a financial manager. In the end, their relationship was a little of both – personal and professional.

Another man Muhammad was really close to was Jeremiah Shabazz, the man who headed up Temple 12. He was one of the most influential individuals in the Nation of Islam, a man who owned bakeries and food stores throughout the area around the temple. Several other members of Temple 12 Black Mafia were also heavily invested in narcotics, and it would later emerge that the FBI and police were keeping a close eye on their activities. Did my brother know about any of this? He certainly was aware of the drinking and drug use that some of these men, Coxson included, indulged in, and that it went against the tenets of Elijah Muhammad. But he certainly didn't take part himself. We both mingled with this fraternity, but would never be influenced by them.

It's also true to say that if you look at a lot of stars in showbiz back then, many of them – from the white community especially – were hanging out with hustlers. They loved the buzz of being in that world. Italian mobsters were constantly hanging out with high-profile celebrities, whether from Hollywood or TV or the world of sports. For his part, Muhammad found these people intriguing individuals. He loved the air of mystery they projected. Coxson had multiple bars and nightclubs. Those nightclubs were unique because this was one of the most racially divided cities in the United States. And yet, Major Coxson was so popular you'd see blacks mingling with whites, you'd see local sports stars, celebrities, it was an amazing thing he was able to pull off. Someone like Muhammad could have gone into any nightclub and it wouldn't have raised eyebrows; that was something Major Coxson was able to do with his power and influence. Everybody, I remember, would cause a commotion when the Black Mafia members or Major Coxson would walk into a bar. Muhammad, whatever else he thought of Coxson, could respect that kind of eye towards publicity, that ability to work a crowd and people's perceptions.

I don't think Major Coxson, for instance, ever completely divulged to anyone what he was getting up to. At one point, it was rumoured that Muhammad's friend owned a fleet of Rolls-Royce cars, and it was only after he died they realised these were just regular American cars, but he had replaced the Chrysler emblems on the cars with Rolls-Royce symbols.

To further complicate matters, Muhammad also decided to back Coxson in his quest to conquer politics when he ran for mayor of New Jersey. Of course, Muhammad understood that, with Coxson being black, it wasn't going to be plain sailing, but nevertheless, Muhammad and other prominent black faces from the area lent their support, perhaps figuring that any black face would be an improvement over the staid white men traditionally filling the role. Coxson, meanwhile, bought himself a residence in Camden district as a campaign office, painted the front white and called it the White House. Then he proclaimed that he was going to be the first black man in the real White House. Ironically, he purposely chose a spot next to the FBI building in New Jersey, the headquarters of the very people who were monitoring him. The guy, Muhammad felt, was crazy,

Eventually, Muhammad learned Coxson's campaign got in a mess because he owed so many thousands of dollars in back taxes, and even then my brother came to the rescue. The Internal Revenue Service, for instance, confiscated Coxson's fleet of cars because he couldn't document any legal income, and as soon as Muhammad heard about it, he wasted no time in giving him his own Rolls-Royce to use for the campaign. Muhammad was at the forefront of the campaign and soon the local papers jumped on the issue. My brother would take every opportunity to promote his friend. After he beat Jerry Quarry again in their second outing in June 1972, instead of saying anything about the fight he'd just won, his first words were, 'I want to dedicate this victory to the next mayor of New Jersey, Major Coxson.'

Since there was an inordinate amount of press surrounding Major Coxson pertinent to his criminal background, this became a key area which left Muhammad wide open to criticism. But my brother's PR and management at the time weren't like publicists today who control their client's image and might advise them against being associated with certain people. He was being advised by members of the Nation, Elijah Muhammad's children and the Black Mafia. It was difficult even for me to get through to him.

* * *

In the end, what brought Coxson down wasn't the FBI or the police – it was the criminal fraternity he was so enmeshed with. In 1973, he attempted to broker a drug deal between the famous Gambino crime family in New York and Philadelphia's Black Mafia. It was a $1 million heroin deal, a huge amount of money even now but immense back in those days. And the shipment vanished, apparently stolen. That caused a rift because, of course, the Gambinos expected payment regardless. Coxson assured his Italian associates that he'd find the shipment, and then contacted his friends in Philadelphia's Black Mafia, only to get another piece of bad news.

The two men who stole the shipment were found dead on the streets of Camden, New Jersey. The Gambinos weren't going to get their money and they weren't going to get the drugs. And, worse, the FBI was all over the murders. So, the Black Mafia stiffed Coxson on the money they'd promised him for locating the shipment, and now he had another problem. Sam Christian, the head of the Black Mafia, and Ron Harvey, one of his henchmen, didn't care about Muhammad's friend's dilemma. They didn't doubt that he got stiffed on the money, but they still expected to get paid for the services rendered.

These notorious men were not going to be merciful. Surveillance records showed law and enforcement was tracking Major Coxson every day, and if you look at the days leading to his demise it is very clear that he had no idea he was in any trouble and had zero fear of being taken down. He was still active, still out in public with Muhammad. He never resorted to employing bodyguards and acted no different than before. I think he wrongly assumed that because he was close friends with all these guys who he would let drink in his establishments they would for some reason treat him differently than any other drug dealer who got stiffed.

On 8 June 1973, a month after losing the Camden mayoral race, Major Coxson was found murdered in his own home. A group of masked men tied him up along with three family members and shot them all in the head. Worse, upon further investigation, the authorities concluded that there was no sign of forced entry. Major Coxson knew his murderers. He actually let them into his house.

The brutal murders made headlines across Philadelphia, and my brother was drawn into the speculation that followed. Muhammad's relationship with Coxson was well known, his house was a stone's throw away from his residence. Following the murders, rumours spread like wildfire that Muhammad was in fear for his own life. Meanwhile, Muhammad had his fighting career to worry about – two months earlier he had suffered a loss to Ken Norton and was preparing for a rematch to take place in September. Quite a predicament.

After a couple of days of press rumour and speculation, my brother moved out of his home in Cherry Hill. I don't think the move came from any sense of fear because he had no concerns about anybody coming to get him. He said to me, 'Rudy, let's move back.' He wanted to move back to Chicago.

'It's been reported that since the death of an associate of mine, Major Coxson, my life has been threatened,' he told reporters at a press conference. 'They've even gone so far as to say I'm fearful and frightened and I've been hiding. Even my wife and family in Chicago have been hiding. I'm here to say, I've called this press conference because it's not true. It's impossible for Muhammad Ali to hide.'

'Won't you be looking over your shoulder a little bit, though?' one reporter asked. Muhammad didn't seem amused.

'Howard Cosell gets paid for being an idiot, but what's your excuse?' he fired back at this reporter. 'Do you want me to be scared? I'm so great in boxing and such a positive image for my people and now you want to promote that I'm scared. You can't scare me.'

Ultimately, Muhammad wasn't concerned because he didn't deal with people on that level, although some of his friends and associates were of that fraternity. There was nothing for him to be frightened of, he felt; nobody would come after him. In the end, he told us, Major Coxson brought his troubles on himself because of his illegal activities.

'No, I wasn't a friend of his,' he told reporters after the murder. 'He wasn't a Muslim. I can only be a friend with a true Muslim.' Those who knew him, and the masses that had seen their relationship publicised for a couple of years, might have found this strange. Here's Muhammad who spent years hanging out with this guy, was seen all over in public, in bars, campaigning with him, but when he died he was saying, 'No, he wasn't a friend of mine.' Now, why he did this is speculative at best.

I would argue the main reason Muhammad was in Philadelphia and then New Jersey in the first place was because of Major Coxson. Even without the security concerns, I think after the murders Muhammad and his family said, 'We don't need to be here right now.' There was no longer a reason for him to be in New Jersey; it wasn't the only area where he could make a home for himself, despite the proximity of Deer Lake. I think it's probably a mixture of both. But his Deer Lake camp was within the vicinity of his residence. Moreover, the Nation of Islam at Temple 12 would've told him he had nothing to worry about. They were the murderers. Muhammad knew they did it – although I never heard them admit to him.

If you're law enforcement and you want the public to help you to prosecute people, but you've got someone like Muhammad involved with the people you're going after, either it confuses the public and they don't come forward, or it intimidates the public because they perceive this man as a legend in the black community. They would think, *Oh, gosh, if I go to the police and I tell them Sam Christian X is the murderer, who are they going to believe – me, a little person, or Muhammad Ali?* Part of the problem was that just by consorting with these people so publicly, Muhammad actually inadvertently 'helped' the Black Mafia in a sense.

Following the murders, Muhammad was offered police protection because they assumed he was a target. Muhammad turned it down flat. He always had not only the support and the physical presence of Nation of Islam bodyguards, but in that era he was considered untouchable because nobody messed with the Nation. Even without police protection or the FBI's help, he was one of the most well-guarded people in the United States at the time. I don't think the law enforcement authorities understood the essence of the relationship between my brother and his criminal friend, or the latter's to Philadelphia's Mafia. Had they known the nature and extent of the relationship, they wouldn't have thought for a minute that Muhammad would be in any danger. I never heard of my brother carrying a gun or owning one. He wouldn't have any need. Like I said, he was always so well protected. Don't forget he was not only part of the Nation, he was a resource. He was treated as untouchable by them. So I would be shocked if he did have a gun and I was unaware of it.

Belinda's reaction, meanwhile, was a little less calm. At the time of his relationship with Coxson, Muhammad's wife didn't realise that this diminutive-looking charming man was a notorious gangster. She was of the thinking that Muhammad's friend was merely a businessman. Major

Coxson and all his little friends just loved Muhammad, after all, and they had been very respectful around my brother's wife and kids. But after the death Belinda was watching a TV show called *American Gangsters,* and to her great shock they showed all these people – Major Coxson, Sam Christian, etc. – that she had cooked for, sat down with and fed in her home. She realised they were all murderers. They had murdered people. She was in total shock. Honestly, it was probably another of the things that eventually drove a wedge between her and my brother.

A STEP TOO FAR

Muhammad didn't want to fight Joe Frazier again. After his first loss to Frazier, my brother had fought and beaten both Jerry Quarry and Floyd Patterson for the second time, then lost a tough fight to Ken Norton which he avenged in his very next fight. In the meantime, Frazier had lost his title to George Foreman: a big, heavy puncher who seemed to have the shorter man's number. This led to the rematch everyone wanted to see: my brother was scheduled to face Joe Frazier for their return bout on 28 January 1974 at Madison Square Garden.

In some of the photographs of Muhammad that were shot at the training camp before the rematch, you see Muhammad looking down, looking a little despondent. George Dillman, who had been a regular visitor for the better half of two years, has his hands on his hips yelling at him because my brother wasn't going to fight Frazier for the second time. The first fight was so tough, so bad, so demanding that he confessed to Dillman that he wasn't going to go through with it again. He was going to quit rather than objectively assess the situation and decide firmly on an optimistic course of action. It's true.

'You don't see the press here,' Muhammad said to Dillman, 'What?' Dillman asked. 'The press is all at Joe Frazier's camp,' he said. 'They don't cover losers.' Muhammad felt dismayed by the attention given to his nemesis by the media. 'Muhammad, you're not a loser,' Dillman said to him. 'But if you think like that, then you will be.' He encouraged him to think like a winner, which would help him to have a more optimistic attitude. He said that with the assistance from the team, he could beat his adversary in their next outing. To console him, he made every effort to get into Muhammad's head by telling him that Frazier was slow and threw punches in round circles. The strategy they were going to implement was to shorten that distance. So, Dillman coaxed my brother into believing he could savage his opponent. Muhammad was going to outbox one of his fiercest foes and prevail. He was feeding him so much of Frazier so he would rethink his position.

In a time where pre-fight scuffles are a commonplace part of pre-match hype, it might be hard to understand just how unusual behind-the-scenes brawls were during my brother's era of competition. Nowadays, it seems almost expected that two fighters will get in at least one shoving match on the press tour to promote their bout, even if they're usually separated and the animosity seems manufactured. In my brother's era, such antics were much rarer, but when they happened, they most certainly weren't fake.

Muhammad would always get pumped up during the publicity before such a big fight. One of the key players involved in my brother's PR was a man named Bobby Goodman. He lived in New Jersey – in a place called Toms River, which was about forty-five minutes from where my brother was residing at the time – and Muhammad would have Goodman stop by and see him from time to time. They were very cordial together and Goodman became something of a family friend. Muhammad's kids would often join their father, and so when Goodman's kids would come to visit their father they would play with Muhammad's kids – it was all a very family-like atmosphere. Muhammad would notoriously go to camp early. He might go to camp two or three months before a fight – I was literally stuck to him like a magnet – and his PR man would too. So Muhammad was virtually living with his publicist for months before each fight – he was right in his face.

One reason for this was that, when arranging his PR schedule, Goodman and his team would try their utmost to keep the two fighters separated. Normally, they succeeded. Sometimes, though, it wasn't possible, especially in the case of Muhammad and Joe. The two of them just mixed like oil and water. Any time you had them together it was a potentially perilous situation, because Muhammad would needle Joe, trying to get under his skin, and, more often than not, he succeeded.

The most shocking incident before the second Ali-Frazier fight – maybe one of the most dramatic pre-fight interviews boxing has ever seen – happened in a Howard Cosell interview in a studio in New York. Cosell, in all his wisdom, wanted to interview both fighters together – something Frazier's trainer, Eddie Futch, initially refused to be part of because he didn't want to be around Muhammad with only several days left before the big fight. When Cosell found out that the Frazier camp was reluctant, however, he forced Goodman to play the middleman, telling the Frazier camp with great conviction that he would control the situation, categorically assuring Frazier and his manager that everything would be fine. Cosell, he assured everyone who would listen, would sit between both men, a buffer between them to prevent any undue aggression. Apparently this was enough to convince Futch and Frazier. And five days before they locked horns, both parties made their way up to New York to the ABC Studios, Goodman accompanying Frazier, me alongside Muhammad and his crew. Then the troubles started. And I, of course, had a front-row seat.

Firstly, apparently Cosell suffered some kind of short-term memory loss, because he didn't put his chair in between the two fighters for even a second; he had them sit next to each other while he sat well out of the way on Frazier's left. Next came the big idea: the two men, Cosell explained, would be reviewing the first Ali-Frazier fight, giving their round-by-round analysis as the bout was shown on a screen for the pundits, the audience and the folks at home. Then there was Cosell's final gambit. At the opening of the interview, he played a clip of my brother playing to the crowd in a public sparring session before his first fight against Frazier, declaiming loudly: 'If Joe Frazier whups Muhammad Ali, I'm gonna get on my hands and knees…and crawl to his corner, proclaiming you are the greatest.'

'That was almost three years ago, Muhammad,' said Frazier in the studio. 'You lost, but you never did crawl across that ring.'

'White people say I lost,' replied my brother, already looking agitated. 'Some white people. All black people know I won.'

From there, things got steadily worse. Cosell's aim was to get each fighter's critical input on what their opponent had done well or poorly, but of course my brother would never be content with a calm, collected analysis. You couldn't hear every word on TV, but Muhammad was constantly talking to Joe, undermining him with every blow that landed. 'See that, Joe, you're stupid. You're ignorant,' he said, watching himself skip blows off the shorter man as he came in. 'I can get you any time. Look at that.'

This, of course, didn't sit well with Joe at all. He was a man of few words, a laid-back character who was always happy to do his talking with his fists. Meanwhile, Muhammad, who'd never accepted the outcome of the first bout, took every opportunity to get under his skin. Even between rounds, when they cut for commercials, Muhammad refused to just sit there quietly. Instead, he would tap on Joe's knee and say, 'See what just happened? You're just ignorant. You don't understand what's happening.'

After ten rounds of this onslaught, Joe got sick of absorbing my brother's verbal blows. The continued onslaught was just too much. Joe felt he was being bullied in front of millions, and I don't entirely blame him.

'Why you picking on me?' he asked, standing up from his stool and moving into Muhammad's space. 'Why you picking on me?'

Muhammad was, I think, somewhat surprised that Joe got so serious, so quickly. Keeping his cool, and his seat, he politely told him to sit down. Meanwhile, I got to my feet because I was afraid that anything could happen, with Joe standing over my brother and menace apparently on his mind. I casually walked up to Joe as he stood there continuing to try to provoke my brother into a reaction, and he felt my presence immediately.

'You want some of me, too?' he said, glancing at me. 'I'll take you right now.'

'If you hit my brother now I am going to kill you, you son of a bitch,' I told him.

This was enough. Immediately Muhammad stood up, grabbed Joe around the neck with his left hand, and they grappled their way to the ground with a little help from me. Both of us had the same idea in mind

– to restrain him and diffuse the situation before it could escalate into an all-out battle. Several others, including security, intervened as the scuffle continued, and the next thing anyone knew Joe had Muhammad's foot up in the air and he was really trying to twist it like he was going for an ankle lock or something. Goodman had to jump in and pull Joe's hands off Muhammad's foot. 'Joe! Joe! If you break his foot there will be no fight!' Goodman was shouting. Meanwhile, I was gearing up to beat Joe's butt because I was angry that he was trying to physically attack my brother in what was supposed to be a publicity appearance. That would've derailed the big fight, but I was a prize fighter myself. Sometimes, your emotions just take over.

Security and myself aside, almost everyone else in attendance was in shock. A few might have thought it was an arranged pantomime at first, but it didn't take them long to realise the severity and seriousness of the whole debacle. Cosell was up on his feet, and the rest of the crowd followed, blocking the cameras as Muhammad and Joe were separated. Frazier and his camp immediately exited the studio with no intention of staying behind to resume the interview. Muhammad, of course, calmly sat down and finished his commentary on the fight, talking Cosell through the final rounds with a cool that you couldn't help but admire.

Later, I spoke to Muhammad about the event, and even if I was still spoiling for a fight, he couldn't help but find the comical side to the whole thing. He was just thrilled. He wasn't hurt, and he knew that when the interview aired, everyone would go crazy about the real altercation. The rematch hardly needed more hype, but it got some anyway. Muhammad, who was known to bait and fool around with every single one of his opponents during the pre-fight hype, finally had to back up his words outside the ring, and he'd done it handily. He wasn't certain what Frazier was going to do, but he realised the man was serious and potentially an all-out fight was possible. He'd handled it correctly, and I was right there to watch his back.

★ ★ ★

As everyone knows, my brother was the master of generating publicity. When you think of charisma, you think of Marilyn Monroe, Elvis Presley and Bruce Lee, those very few people that are blessed with that kind of persona. And Muhammad had that special aura, probably more than any other athlete of all time. And yes, a lot of it was simply him – the little boy who used to run his mouth back in Louisville, grown into a man who'd do it to adoring crowds – but it was also something he consciously worked on, he told me. For instance, everyone's aware of his lyricism at press conferences and publicity outings, where he'd tear into his opponents poetically before he ever ran rings around them under the lights – when he was talking, sure, he was nothing short of superb. But what people are oblivious to is that he also paid a great deal of attention to how he wanted to look in terms of what he wore, how he carried himself, how he acted. He was profoundly influenced by Gorgeous George and Little Richard, the wrestler and the singer, whom we grew up watching in the fifties, and watched every aspect of how they conducted themselves in front of a crowd. Muhammad's claim against Frazier – that he'd crawl across the ring and call him champ – actually came from one of George's promotion pieces against 'Classy' Freddie Blassie, where he promised to crawl across the ring and cut his hair off if he lost. And when it came to his in-ring appearance, my brother looked at Gorgeous George again. He liked the fact that George had white sneakers, at a time when everyone else was wearing black. Muhammad consciously copied that style, pairing his white sneakers with white trunks, all designed to catch your attention while he was throwing up his arms and saying, 'I am the greatest!'

My brother was a great salesman, too. To sell tickets, he said to his inner circle, he had to look the part of a salesman, a person that spoke well and could convince the public to buy what he was selling. He knew he was good, had no doubts that he was slick and talented and fast, but he wanted to embed the idea into fans' consciousness that he really was the greatest of all time. And it worked. His persona was just so strong that people bought into it, and followed him everywhere. People didn't just want to see him fight in the ring, but to hear him talk. They'd clamour to be near him at every opportunity, whether he was jawing off after a sparring session or holding court on the street. They were glued to the TV screens whether he was spouting his philosophy or verbally tearing into an adversary. Most of all, they wanted to see him fight, spending hundreds of dollars on tickets or staying up in the early hours of the morning as his bouts were broadcast around the world. He wasn't just a phenomenal boxer. He was an athlete who knew that his job was to entertain.

Another aspect of his skyrocketing popularity was that Muhammad became ever-more important to the careers of the sportswriters that followed him, giving them opportunities to get a scoop on their rivals any time they could get close to him. Many of them were grateful for that, and my brother began to see the press as part of his entourage, an important group of people who could catapult him to further fame. To this end, he made friends within the press giving them unprecedented access to his sparring sessions, his home and his life. He trusted some and had reservations about others, but he could also be manipulative, aiming to make some feel special and play them off against each other. He used to constantly think about things that would make for good stories, scenarios that would keep him in the public eye even when he didn't have a fight coming up. As happened with so many things, it was something he'd decided to become the greatest at.

The prelude to Muhammad's match against Buster Mathis in Houston, Texas, is a fine example of just how far my brother would go to get people invested in his fights. People didn't believe there was any real animosity between the two because Buster used to burst out laughing around Muhammad instead of responding to his provocations. Muhammad would be trying his utmost to get his adversary to say something back, and Buster would just giggle. The distinction from the Frazier fight couldn't have been more apparent, and Muhammad's press team were going out of their minds, trying to come up with something to get the promotion rolling.

'Champ! Champ! We've got to come up with something to get this promotion moving!' one of the entourage was telling him, I remember. Suddenly Muhammad's eyes opened up wide. 'I've got it! I've got it!' he said. For a second we all thought Muhammad had concocted some great idea, which he often did. 'It will get on the front pages of newspapers all around the world.' We leaned in, ready for this stroke of genius.

'You can have me kidnapped,' said my brother. 'Take me up the woods and mountains and set up a ring outside and set a couple of sparring partners up there; we can stay up there and a couple of days before the fight you can "find" me.'

There was a moment of silence.

'If you aren't there, we can't sell tickets to the fight,' said Goodman.

Muhammad had to think about that for a second. 'OK. We'll come up with something else.'

Occasional glitches aside, Muhammad was formidable at playing the promoter and the PR guy all packaged into one. He would look at the schedule with Goodman and discuss what he had to do the next day. As I mentioned earlier, Goodman would go to his house or Muhammad would go to Goodman's bungalow, whichever the case was. When they were on the road Angelo Dundee and Goodman used to stay in the adjoining rooms and would come by at night and ask, 'What have we got to do tomorrow, boss?' And they'd sit with Muhammad who would look at the agenda. Muhammad sometimes actually felt they were not doing enough. There were little things he wanted to add in and the PR team had to make adjustments. He had a great instinct for real publicity. But for Frazier, he wouldn't need it.

FACING BIG GEORGE

In his second fight against Frazier, Muhammad didn't come to play. He was a little slower than his butterfly best, maybe, but still plenty fast enough to keep away from Frazier while stinging him with his jab, and the sheer volume of punches he threw in the first two rounds nearly took Joe out early. He danced and moved, staying away from the ropes and clinched when Joe got close, minimising the damage he could do inside. Joe did more damage as the fight went on, but my brother kept busy, looked good and took home a decision that had many men clamouring for the pair to fight again. That would have to wait, though, as my brother immediately wanted to reclaim what he felt he'd been robbed of – to fight for his title again.

Muhammad's fight with George Foreman in Zaire in 1974, of course, will go down in history as one of the greatest fights of the century. Of all the fights Muhammad had, facing Big George was arguably one of his biggest tests, not just physically but mentally, in the preparation it took and the toll it took on both fighters.

Don King, then known as a shrewd and tenacious figure in boxing as well as a flamboyant character, was the man who made Foreman-Ali happen. He pleaded with Foreman to give him the opportunity to promote the George Foreman-Muhammad Ali fight. Apparently, the persistent King was on the shortlist with a handful of other promoters, but he wanted to get ahead of course. King wanted to jump the queue. He literally went crying to the then heavyweight champion, who eventually told him, 'Yes, if you can get Muhammad Ali.' King immediately got Muhammad on the phone and asked him if he wanted to fight Foreman. Muhammad, who was more than game, said, 'Yeah, I'll promote it.' So they signed the fight with that telephone conversation between the three of them.

Nobody should have been surprised. King was a very entertaining personality and he had the ability to suck you in. He would always play the race card: that we blacks needed to stick together and that we're all brothers was something I heard a dozen times. He would make you feel sorry for him, too – Foreman would say yes to a lot of things that he might not have otherwise, purely because of how persuasive King could be.

At the same time, King had a tendency to pay you more than any other promoter. That was one thing he certainly had going for him – big paydays for the fighters. If you asked him and all the other promoters for a fight, a promoter might offer you $1 million, but King would offer you $2 million. This man could outbid anyone. That was his main strength. And with that, inevitably, he lured fighters in. He'd sometimes even sign a deal putting himself at risk because he didn't always have the cash ready, so he would need to go out to find the money. He always did. Muhammad was his ultimate goldmine back then and he pursued him trying so hard to get a business working relationship going. I can reveal that my brother wasn't making the big money until Don King started promoting his fights, that's for sure.

★ ★ ★

Almost as soon as the fight was announced, doubts started to cloud Muhammad's mind. Foreman had obliterated every opponent put in front of him. He had developed a reputation for being one of the hardest hitters in the heavyweight division, and he didn't seem to have a weakness. One day Muhammad called the official Madison Square Garden photographer, George Kalinsky. It was 6.30 p.m. on a Monday evening. 'Can you wait for me, I'm coming up?' he asked Kalinsky, who he knew fairly well as a prominent member of the press who had photographed Muhammad on numerous occasions. They arranged to meet one evening at Kalinsky's office at the Garden. The arena was empty: when the crowds weren't around, it was a little oasis of undisturbed tranquillity. 'Muhammad, what's up?' Kalinsky asked him. And, for whatever reason, Muhammad had a startling confession to make that evening. 'In another month I'm going to be fighting George Foreman,' answered Muhammad. 'He's too big. He's too fast. He's too young. He's too powerful and there is no way I can win this fight.'

If this doesn't sound like the Muhammad the world knew as irrepressibly confident, nigh-on invincible, you have to remember exactly how feared an opponent George Foreman was. He'd knocked out nearly forty men before this fight and was looking formidable. In fact, whilst we didn't know this at the time, we were told after the fight that Archie Moore, who was the fight advisor in Foreman's corner, had actually been praying that his fighter wouldn't end up killing Muhammad. He felt Foreman was so dangerous, and so powerful, that the possibility of him ending Muhammad's life right there and then in the ring was actually a possibility.

And Muhammad wasn't the same man as he was before he lost to Frazier, to himself or to anyone else. Before that fight, he had developed an aura that when he walked down the street everyone thought of him as the most quintessentially powerful, strongest champion on the planet – the baddest man on earth. Everyone's perception of Muhammad was of this incredibly confident individual who never had a chink in his armour. But here he was confiding with this photographer, conceding he wasn't about to win a fight because all the attributes of his opponent at that particular moment outweighed his own. Here he was admitting his innermost thoughts behind closed doors to a member of the press. Kalinsky felt concerned for Muhammad now. Like virtually everyone else, he knew of the confidence that Muhammad always exuded, especially in front of the public and media members.

'You know, Muhammad, all your life you've been training for this fight,' Kalinsky proceeded to explain. When my brother trained with me or his sparring partners, one of the things we noticed was how Muhammad would let us consistently whack him in the midriff. We'd hit him and try to pummel him to oblivion. He seemed relatively unscathed, though. The photographer said that he had always wondered why Muhammad was letting sparring partners dish out this sort of punishment. Muhammad would keep his face covered so nobody could pepper his face with shots, but he would absorb plenty of solid shots in the midriff. And now, Kalinsky – he revealed that he had figured it out at last.

'When you get into the fight, you act like you're a dope on the rope,' he said to Muhammad. 'And with your back on the ropes, let him pound away like you let your sparring partners pound you in a workout.' When Foreman keeps hitting him he's going to tire himself out. 'And you have to act like a dope on the rope,' he continued. Muhammad interjected by asking, 'You mean, rope-a-dope?' When Kalinsky used the terms 'dope a rope; he himself didn't even understand it. It was spontaneous. 'Act like a dope on a rope,' Kalinsky repeated. 'I like the words 'rope-a-dope,' Muhammad said. 'OK, call it rope a dope,' Kalinsky continued explaining, 'The idea is you have to act like something's wrong with you. Make him think he's got you. Let him pound away and he will tire himself out.' It would work, Kalinsky knew. It was as if Muhammad was impervious to pain when he used to pull the same trick in sparring.

The press room they were having this conversation in had soda and water in a machine and Muhammad had a drink. Then both men walked back to his office. 'Muhammad, tell Angelo about this if you like the idea,' Kalinsky said. 'What do you think?' Muhammad was in favour of embracing the idea. 'It sounds like a great idea,' my brother replied. At the time no one had ever thought of that, not even Muhammad, even though it was something that my brother would more often than not do anyway in sparring sessions. So, Muhammad went back to Angelo Dundee and told him about this new-found strategy. However, at first Angelo wasn't keen on the idea. He wasn't impressed. However, about a week later he called the photographer directly. 'You know that idea of yours,' Angelo said, 'we're going to go with it.'

As the preparations for the big fight got under way, plenty of shady characters wanted to get involved in my brother's preparations. One guy, who looked about seventy years old, came to the gym a week before Muhammad left for Zaire, and bluntly asked my brother, 'Do you want to win this fight?' Muhammad replied, 'Yeah.'

'I've got something that'll make sure of it,' muttered this little guy, hat turned down like an old-school gangster from a 1930s film. He flashed some liquid in a little bottle that he took out of his pocket, so that only Muhammad and I could see it. 'Do you see this? You take this, if you get in trouble rub this on your gloves. You can't see it. You can't smell it. It's hot. And when you jab him, as soon as you touch him, first bit of perspiration, just the heat, it won't blind him or hurt him for good, but for a few minutes this man will actually not be able to see. You use it if you have to.' Muhammad palmed the bottle and said, 'OK.' My brother was never going to resort to cheating because he genuinely thought God would punish him even if he considered it.

Unbeknown to Muhammad, the same guy had been in Sonny Liston's corner the night it happened to Muhammad ten years earlier. And the same guy had been part of the Liston crew. He must have had a memory fade because he gave the secret to Muhammad now and Muhammad could've popped him on the nose or had him arrested. In the Liston fight for one round Muhammad was blinded. It didn't happen until the fifth round when Muhammad got Liston really in trouble. There was a widespread belief that my brother's chances of prevailing were slim, but Muhammad wasn't going to resort to cheating to win. I was going to ensure he was in shape for Big George. And, believe me, we worked very hard in the gym.

★ ★ ★

By the time we arrived in Zaire, the stage was set for the greatest fight of all time. Muhammad's and Foreman's relationship up until this point was somewhat neutral. They'd never had any real face-to-face arguments before, none of the psych-outs he usually used with his adversaries. That was somewhat unusual, I thought. Muhammad certainly dug in during the pre-fight hype, but when they finally met for the fight in the company of the President of Zaire in Africa, neither man was keen to engage in any meaningful conversation with the other. Even before the fight, my brother treated Foreman with some respect, as if he knew how seriously he would have to take Foreman in the ring.

Our team had already been in Zaire for a couple of months before the scheduled fight date. They had to set up the different training equipment we had shipped in on a special plane from the United States. Bobby Goodman met some people when the plane arrived so he could get them to set up the training facility. They didn't have anything like that in Zaire. There wasn't a gym there which we could work out from. So they set up the ring, the speed bag, the heavy bag and a mirror. Then when Muhammad arrived he made his adjustments.

Muhammad and I stayed at his four villas on the Zaire River. Foreman was staying in the hotel in Kinshasa and we were all staying at a government complex, like Camp David, on the river.

During our stay in Zaire, although Muhammad was seriously preparing for the fight, he continued to play the entertainer. We'd be in the gym and he'd be training in the ring and the next thing you know he'd start messing around with the locals. He'd be entertaining the little groups and the bigger crowds. I mean, any other fighter or athlete would have disappeared into solitary confinement to focus not only on the physical training, but mentally focus without anyone or anything becoming a constant distraction. On the other hand, Big George had somewhat retreated into obscurity. He was all too aware of keeping away from all the façade and mind games that would only lead to derailing him.

The atmosphere in Kinshasa was just amazing. The whole country had embraced Muhammad who mingled with the people. He became a towering inspiration. He often spoke to me about the importance of reconnecting with our African heritage. And one of the real reasons Muhammad brought this fight to Zaire was to get Africa in the spotlight. Muhammad said, 'Africa is my home. I live in America but Africa is the home of the black man.' From my recollections, I remember the people seemed to be very welcoming to us wherever we went. Women and men dressed in traditional African clothing, and young children performed traditional dances. Drums would be beating and Muhammad would join in. Naturally, he craved the attention and could mix with anyone, but the vibe I got was that he seemed proud and genuinely feeling at home.

Muhammad endeared himself to the kids. We would go for a run or a walk and we'd have all these kids and young men following us, running with us. This wasn't unusual because back in America this was a regular occurrence at the training camp.

It was such a vibrant atmosphere because part of the deal was that a three-day music festival would take place to promote the fight. Don King not only promoted the fight, but he was the force behind this festival. Just over thirty groups performed – some from Zaire and some from overseas – and James Brown and B.B. King were among the featured R&B and soul music stars headlining. I think it's fair to say that my brother fighting there put that nation on the map in a major way.

★ ★ ★

As the fight neared and the training camps started heating up, things started to get messy. During one training session Foreman got cut badly. In rising panic his team phoned Goodman telling him to come there with great urgency. He went running over to see what all the fuss was about. They let him in the dressing room to let him examine the deep cut. Dick Sadler, Foreman's manager, asked Goodman, 'What do you think?' Goodman said, 'Geez, I think we're looking at five, six weeks to let it heal.' Suddenly, there were sirens, marking the arrival of Mandunga Bula, the Zaire official who had been made responsible for supervising the fight that was going to put his country on the world map. Goodman, reluctantly, had to deal with him every single day and, believe me, he wasn't easy to deal with.

When he appeared at the door, Goodman just opened the door to let him in. And he said, 'Ah, hello, Mr Bula.' Bula, who was in a full panic, barked, 'What is this!? What is this about Foreman being cut!?' Goodman said, 'We're going to have to postpone.' This did nothing but fuel his disappointment. Bola said, 'Impossible! The fight will go on as scheduled. That's impossible!' Goodman had to explain that this was the heavyweight championship and it would be suicide if he fought with a cut on his eye. But Mr Bola was having none of it. To prove the cut existed Goodman proceeded to show him the cut was real. Mr Bola stood there shaking his head with sheer disappointment. So eventually they came up with a new date. And we were going to be there another six weeks now.

Everybody was down in the dumps, especially since most of the team members had already had been there for a while. The only person who wasn't upset was Muhammad, who handled it like a champion. Muhammad had been having problems with his hands, and the postponement gave him time to let his hands heal, as well as affording an opportunity for him to mingle with the people and go around sightseeing. It also helped him in his punching power. Believe me Muhammad lived on that heavy bag. I would watch him unload on that bag like a man possessed. And this might have, in addition to the rope-a-dope strategy, had a lot to do with the outcome of the fight.

In the meantime, Don King, who had a tendency to be a step ahead, had come up with an idea. A seventeen-year-old girl, Veronica Porsche, was introduced to my brother. She was one of the girls there to promote the fight. It was a strategy designed to keep him there because when Foreman got injured, King feared that the fight could all go up in smoke. Veronica was enlisted to keep Muhammad interested: that's how they met. Some people actually presumed that Veronica was a spy for Foreman's camp. Well, in spite of King's tendencies to resort to underhand tactics to achieve his objectives, I can tell you that she was not a spy – that myth can be eradicated. She was an intelligent student studying medicine at the time: making a little money, sure, but any interest she had in my brother was certainly genuine on her side.

★ ★ ★

On 30 October 1974, as the whole world watched, my brother knocked out Big George, the man many people thought was his fiercest foe.

I remember when the night finally arrived and my brother and I left our hotel room for the stadium. It was astonishing that the stadium was literally infested with policemen – both outside and inside. I remember it being very hot that evening. But I wasn't complaining. The atmosphere was euphoric. Prior to making the ring entrance, in the dressing room, Muhammad was pumped up, and he said, 'I can't wait to get Foreman.' And then it was time to go. Out of all the nights we walked together to the ring, we never had an entourage around us as big as the one we had to escort us that night. They all wanted to protect my brother. Our team was a close-knit group and, as he made his way to the ring, escorted by policemen, my brother was given a rapturous welcome. Everyone in Zaire that night was for my brother. They didn't like Foreman, and his intimidating persona only whipped them up more. We had never experienced anything like it.

Of course, my brother had a game plan all worked out. Personally I knew Muhammad would prevail. I knew he'd regain the crown. I always had confidence in him and I wasn't going to let doubt filter into my mind this time.

Throughout the fight, without the slightest sign of sympathy, Muhammad and the formidable Foreman just went for each other. Round after round, Foreman was punching himself out. Sooner or later Big George was going to gas out. I was feeling the extreme heat just being ringside, so imagine how dehydrated my brother must have felt in the ring as Foreman tried to smash him into submission. The thing with Foreman was that he punched from odd angles. His robotic style was predictable. But what he lacked in finesse, he certainly made up for with his ferocious power.

After intense rounds of exchanging blows and keeping everyone on their toes, Muhammad spent a lot of time on the ropes. He used the rope-a-dope strategy as he lay against the ropes and Foreman tried landing heavy blows. I could see that some of the punches were landing, particularly the vicious body hooks, but Muhammad had acclimatised himself to absorbing the punishment and making his adversary miss too, particularly those aimed at the head. Little did Foreman know that he was falling for my brother's bait. However, my brother's trainer Angelo became so nervous he literally felt sick seeing Muhammad on the ropes.

Then it came to round eight and with just under a minute left, Foreman tried to connect with a sneaky right hand and continued to pummel Muhammad as he lay on the ropes in the tight corner. I could see my brother was trying to protect his own face. Then with fifteen seconds to go Muhammad managed to break out of the corner and, out of nowhere, suddenly turned the tide with a right, left, right, left, right combination and Foreman went down. The knockout brought the crowd to fever pitch. Foreman failed to get up before the referee's count.

He'd defied the odds once again. I jumped in the ring joy with alongside everyone else, clinched and embraced Muhammad around the waist as he was swamped with people. Jim Brown, who was a guest commentator for the TV station, had actually predicted that Foreman would beat his friend. Muhammad liked to play these little games in the ring. He'd do certain things but was confident enough to not let side distractions affect his performance. He had been waving at Jim Brown winking all night because he knew Brown was of the belief Foreman was going to knock him out. Muhammad couldn't resist but say to Brown at the end of every round, 'Look at me, Foreman isn't going to beat me. I'm doing it.' Even King tried to ingratiate himself with my brother, abandoning his own fighter as he made his way towards the champ. But when Muhammad, out of the corner of his eye, saw King approach him with a big grin etched across his face, he said something to the effect of, 'Don't you dare.' King's demeanour immediately changed. His face fell. And Foreman, in front of the 60,000-strong crowd, walked away, dejected.

We made our way to the dressing room, which was cramped with our people. Gene Kilroy, Angelo and I stood on my brother's right side as he sat down, exhausted, as a TV reporter peppered questions at him. 'I kept telling him he had no power. I kept telling him he had no heart,' Muhammad was telling us. 'Guess what he did in the end, he started fighting really dirty. His thumb got me in the eye once. But I'm smart. I'm a pro. I reached in and took that thumb and made him quit.' Muhammad claimed he was too powerful and too strong for his dethroned adversary, that he had proved Allah is great and Elijah Muhammad was his Messenger. He would always throw in the Messenger's name. 'It wasn't close, was it?' Muhammad asked. The reporter responded, 'It wasn't a close fight.' Then Muhammad asked him if this was being beamed live. He told him that it was, and Muhammad said, 'Everybody stop talking now, attention! I told you, all of my critics. I told you all that I was the greatest of all time when I beat Sonny Liston. And I told you today I'm still the greatest. Never again say that I'm going to be defeated. Never again make me the underdog until I'm about fifty years old. Then you might get me.'

Muhammad went on to tell us all why he didn't dance. He had implemented the rope-a-dope strategy, he explained. He wanted Foreman to deplete his power. My brother, far from the nimble fighter that evaded almost every shot of Liston's, had won by telling Foreman that he had no punch and that he couldn't hit, all the while taking every shot that Foreman had. 'I want all boxers to remember this,' he said. 'Staying on the ropes is a beautiful thing with a heavyweight. You make him shoot his best shots and you know he's not hitting you, he can't hurt you. I would've given George Foreman two rounds if I was scoring, because after that he was mine. He was falling. He was missing.'

'What did you say to George Foreman before the fight?' asked the reporter.

'I told him he had no power. End of story. In the clinch I said, "Give me your best shot. I'm going back to the ropes." They told me he was strong.' Muhammad paused, then shouted to his team, 'Wasn't I stronger!?'

The reporter was curious and somewhat bemused about Muhammad's new strategy. 'Tell me, Muhammad,' he said, 'this is the thing that puzzles me. Why is it that when you were on the ropes that he could not hurt you, even when you were right there?' 'I was blocking and pulling back,' my brother grinned. 'I have a radar built inside me! I know how to judge punches.' Curious, the reporter asked, 'But tell me now, are you really going to retire?' Muhammad responded, 'I'm seriously thinking about retiring. There's nothing else for me to fight for.' Then, almost as abruptly, he said that he was going to hold the title for a few months. 'They took my title away unjustifiably!' he explained to the bemused reporter. 'If you want to know any damn thing about boxing, don't go to any expo in Las Vegas. Don't go to no gym, but come to me because I'm the man!' The atmosphere was just electric in that dressing room. We were all elated.

Eventually my brother and Foreman became good friends and saw each other many times. Foreman came to love him. Muhammad always had something up his sleeve whenever he crossed paths with his foe. The first time both met was in a boxing gym, six years before they fought each other. A young Foreman was in the ring training for a fight, and at the time Muhammad was in exile. Muhammad visited the gym, walked up the stairs and as he entered he shouted to Foreman, 'Hey, George, I want to show you something!' He said, 'Sit down and don't move.' Foreman stopped what he was doing and sat in the ring and Muhammad pulled out a big suitcase. Foreman thought, *Man, he's going to show me all the money in the world.* But when my brother opened it up there was one of those big portable telephones in the case. 'If you're going to be champion of the world, you're going to have one of these,' Muhammad said. Foreman thought, *Erm, I was looking to find money in there.* Seeing the funny side to it all, Foreman burst out laughing. He suspected Muhammad was going to show him something special or bundles of cash he was that excited and in suspense.

Foreman's childhood, my brother and I later learned, made our own look almost pampered by comparison. Big George grew up with six siblings in Houston's Fifth Ward, a notoriously rough district where Foreman headed towards the wrong side of the fence. His parents had broken up early, and there wasn't a whole lot of supervision for the young boy. For a young man who lacked confidence or positive role models, it took an innumerable amount of years and a lot of trouble to detach himself from the lifestyle that Foreman had run headlong into.

In his old neighbourhood, Foreman told us, everybody was looking to make a name for themselves. George, being big and accustomed to violence, would frequently get into scrapes, and it wasn't long before he became a bully. Believe it or not, he didn't win a lot of his encounters on the street, but eventually robbing and mugging people on the street became part of his lifestyle. It took a close call to turn him towards the light: he had to clamber out of the window of a house he was robbing to narrowly escape the police, and it was there and then, he told us, that he made a pledge to himself that he would never steal again.

Foreman's life would take a turn when he heard a commercial on the radio in which athlete – and friend of Muhammad – Jim Brown talked about the Job Programme. The teenager joined the programme when he was sixteen, taking him away out of his own state. There he heard about another California Programme and transferred there, where he met his first trainer, a man named Doug, who taught him how to box. Slowly, Foreman changed from a thug to someone trying to do something with his life. He eventually won an Olympic gold medal in the 1968 Olympics, turned pro the next year and fought thirteen times in 1969 alone, winning all his bouts – eleven via knockout. His bout with Frazier and run with the title didn't make him happy, but eventually he found his calling as a minister, and I could not have been happier for him.

That was all for the future, though. That hot night in Zaire, all I knew was that my brother was back on top of the world, where he belonged.

TRILOGY

Almost a year after triumphing against Big George, my brother was getting set to face Joe Frazier for the third time in their trilogy of fights. After the Foreman fight, offers came flooding in. The Iranian government offered $10 million to tempt my brother to fight in Iran. The Egyptian government was offering $6 million. Ever since my brother became the heavyweight champion for the first time, he became a symbol that Muslims could resonate with from all over the world. Marshal Mobutu, the President of Zaire, was also keen on putting on a rematch and was willing to put up $5 million. Muhammad knew these leaders were salivating at the prospect of luring the most recognised athlete in the world. Having my brother fight in their country would mean prestige and promotion; they weren't necessarily looking to benefit financially. And my brother understood this.

The fight was booked to take place in the Philippine Coliseum, Quezon City, and Muhammad and I both knew going in that Joe would come ready for the toughest fight of his life. Not that it started out that way. 'Thrilla in Manila' was originally Belinda's slogan, coined when my brother was a little too open about his then-girlfriend Veronica in front of his wife. 'I'm going to be a Thrilla in Manila if I see another girl around,' my brother's wife warned him, all too aware that her husband was having his female friend keep him company in the Far East. It was out in the open – Belinda even gave Muhammad a black eye at one point, sick of his shenanigans. I guess she learned something about punching in her years with him.

Still, if there's one thing my brother always knew, it was how to roll with punches. The next thing any of us knew, he was on TV using Belinda's own slogan for the fight. Even Belinda had to respect her husband's audacity – she bought him a little gorilla and he took it with him to his TV appearances, using it as a prop as he slung endless abuse in Frazier's direction.

As the behind-the-scenes tensions caught the press's attention making headlines, and Muhammad had to contend with his own domestic issues, my brother had a fight in the ring to worry about against a dangerous heavy slugger who had come out on top in their first outing. He trained hard, and I was right there with him leading to the fight.

The day of the fight was scorching hot. I was sitting ringside with great anticipation. My brother had trained hard and, of course, had the experience of fighting in Zaire, but it was still tough for any of us to know how either man would hold up under the conditions that prevailed. Frazier looked lean and mean for sure, bobbing and rolling as my brother fired off dozens of hard punches in the early rounds, aiming to teach him a lesson. In the third round, my brother started to employ the rope-a-dope, but if Frazier was worried about exhausting himself in the same way Foreman had, he didn't show it – he barrelled in close, tucking his chin under my brother's head as he fired off a series of hooks to the body that would have crippled any lesser man.

In the eighth, Muhammad tried to end it, firing off big shots, but Joe was too tough. After that, it seemed like both men accepted that they would just have to outlast each other – Joe sucking up punches on the way in, Muhammad leaning against the ropes to take his own punishment when Joe finally burrowed his way inside. Before the thirteenth round, Angelo said to him, 'You've got him, kid. This is it. He's going to quit. You can finish this off now.'

In the thirteenth round things turned around and Angelo knew his fighter could feel it. Joe just ran out of gas and you could see the tide turning. To his credit, Joe's shots were thundering. You could almost feel the shots at ringside, and Muhammad later told me it was some of the worst pain he'd ever experienced in his life. 'It's the closest I've ever been to dying,' were his exact words to Angelo. Both fighters were literally in a state of near-unconsciousness.

By the fourteenth, Frazier was stumbling and barely able to see. And then, well…

There's always been a rumour that before the final round, Muhammad said to his corner, Angelo specifically, that he wanted to quit. That he was ready to go out on his stool, in a state of despair. Let me refute that and set the record straight right now: that just never happened. Sure, the two men talked about quitting, maybe even said the word, but all their thoughts were on how to make sure Joe quit, not Muhammad. And it paid off. Frazier's trainer, Eddie Futch, threw in the towel just before the final round was ready to begin. I can't begin to describe that feeling.

Although Muhammad triumphed in the final fight of their trilogy, I think he had, again, taken this fight lightly. He didn't look great and didn't train so hard in contrast to some of his other major bouts. If I'm honest, he had this idea swirling around in his head that he was going to fight a guy who was washed up now. Muhammad was always in decent shape, and so he didn't come in looking terrible, but evidently Joe had taken the fight far more seriously. He was hungry to avenge his defeat. The interesting thing is, comparatively, Joe had looked terrible in his fights prior to stepping into the ring with my brother for the third and final time. This, I think, contributed to Muhammad's lacklustre approach. He really thought his adversary was done.

They sometimes say that everyone has the will to win and not everyone has the will to prepare to win, but I'm not so sure that's true. In their second fight Muhammad had looked terrible. He looked like he wasn't even trying. Then all of a sudden he pulls out this monumental effort. For the third Frazier fight, Muhammad didn't have the will to prepare, not like he should have, but when he walked in the ring he found the will to get it done. No other man could have taken as much punishment as he did and fire back enough to stop the freight train that was Joe Frazier.

Now, as much as my brother and Joe had their differences, they both respected each other. Muhammad said things that were not right in the prelude to the fight, but he always maintained afterwards that it was to build the purse. Whatever the truth, Joe took it personally. He clung on to this hatred for my brother well into his old age.

* * *

My brother's victory over Frazier, of course, didn't end all of his woes. Muhammad's motivation might have improved, but his money management was as poor as ever. Whether we went to another city in the United States or abroad, my brother, more often than not, took the financial hit. When we went to Germany for his fight with Richard Dunn on 24 May 1976, for example, Muhammad had sixty people in his entourage accompanying him. Butch Lewis, who had pinballed between being a street hustler and a used-car salesman before breaking into the promotion business representing Bob Arum's interest in the fight, was absolutely fuming at the situation, calling a meeting with my brother and bemoaning the situation at some length. First of all, the hotel we were staying at in Munich was a grand old place and damn expensive. Then there were those hangers-on. Some of our team members were eating two steaks a night and then ordering all sorts from room service on top, putting a dent in the promoter's own pocket. Lewis read the riot act, and Muhammad listened carefully to what he had to say. 'OK, we're going to have a meeting, call a meeting,' Muhammad told the concerned promoter.

Not long after, I was called into the room with the rest of the entourage. 'Listen, I don't want you guys to go hungry,' Muhammad said to his team, 'but if you're still hungry and you have one steak, don't just order another and take two bites and leave it. You've got to finish it. And cool it with the phone calls, you're running up huge bills. One call a day from now on.' What Muhammad didn't take into account, of course, was there were sixty people calling the USA every day from Germany, and they'd stay on the phone for an hour. Even if they followed his rules to the letter, it would still cost a fortune.

Now, the difference between Muhammad's entourage and the other boxers was that most of them would have a camp of six or seven guys, plus sparring partners. With Muhammad it was forty guys plus in his regular crew. That's a hell of an entourage, and that's not all. Invariably, he would pick up extra sparring partners because he felt so much compassion for the boxers who needed the work to put food on the table for their families. He would never complain, so it was left to the other senior members of the team to try and keep things under control.

To some extent, it's human nature to take advantage when you're being given special treatment, and in many cases these men had never had these opportunities before in their lives, and thought it was all on the company tab. So it was new to a lot of the entourage members who hadn't ventured abroad with Muhammad before and they soaked it up. Muhammad certainly felt good that he could give them this new experience, but this also meant that there were times he couldn't, or wouldn't, put his foot down and follow through with the rules he so cordially requested us to adhere to. He just wasn't programmed to turn people down. Lewis was certainly not on the same page, especially as he was picking up the bill.

In one memorable instance, the extended entourage caused an incident that went well beyond financial trouble. The weigh-ins, it turned out, were set to be conducted on a makeshift stage, which was about eight feet off the ground. Dunn weighed in without incident, but when my brother stepped on the scale, suddenly there was a rush of people trying to get on the stage, all members of the entourage trying to get a moment in the spotlight. I was trying to hold people back, but it was no use as everyone wanted their moment next to Muhammad, and, well, the stage went down like there was an earthquake. It was almost funny. One moment Goodman was weighing him in and the next, suddenly the stage was gone. He could have been hurt and the fight cancelled, but I'm damned if any of the entourage even learned their lesson. Muhammad went on to beat Dunn in the fifth round via TKO, and the next night they were right back to ordering their steaks.

★ ★ ★

Was my brother a gullible man? That, I think, depends on your point of view. He had a tendency to believe people, that's for sure. He treated people like he wanted to be treated. He wasn't sceptical of anything people told him. He was childlike in a way, if not childish. Muhammad was curious about everything and he believed people in his team or anyone associated with him when they insinuated themselves into his life by telling him fabricated stories. This goodness in him, inevitably, attracted the attention of devious people – pretty regularly, you'd see these so-called friends at the training camp trying their luck because they knew Muhammad was easily swayed into providing money or favours. Even so, he never changed. He didn't know how to change.

It makes me sad to admit, but sometimes my love for my brother and my hatred for what these hangers-on were doing to him caused a friction in our relationship. Many times, my attempts to protect him rubbed Muhammad up the wrong way. More than once I went off on one of the folks in Muhammad's entourage to the point that we got into an argument and he didn't call for me to come to the camp. It never lasted, but it happened.

Regardless, I remained a pillar of support for my brother, because those blood ties never truly break. Muhammad became softer as he got older and understood that his boxing was his platform to get what he really wanted, but I never really changed. I would be mean to people even after his career was over, trying to protect what was left of his money. When outsiders couldn't get to him directly, they would try to go through me and members of the entourage. It worked, too – certain members of our camp would actually charge people to see my brother train. It became pretty widely known that there were people in the entourage hustling to make a little extra money giving access to fans. Sportswriters who wanted an interview sometimes went to certain individuals in the entourage who would charge the reporter $50 for an interview, even though Muhammad would have gladly given it for free.

I remember when we were in Las Vegas training for the second Jerry Quarry fight. Las Vegas is and was back then a good boxing city for us because the organisers gave you what you needed for a fight. In some cities, just paying for the rooms and food for the huge entourage would take a huge chunk of cash, whereas if you went to Vegas they would give you rooms and the food as part of the contract. And yet, somehow, Muhammad would still lose money in Vegas.

One day, Muhammad was working out in a big ballroom in a ring erected just for the occasion. We would set up an area for about a thousand people to watch him train, and charge them something like $5 – this was supposed to go to charity, though whether that money ever made it outside the entourage or not, I couldn't say. Anyway, as Muhammad focused on his workout we saw a guy in a wheelchair rolling into the room. Something about him felt off from the outset. After spending a long time around hustlers and conmen, you get pretty good at spotting them when they come into a room. Muhammad, though, was his usual trusting self. While he was still in the ring he reached out to tug Angelo's shirt and nod.

'See the guy coming in? I want to talk to him.'

'Muhammad, that guy's a phoney,' said Angelo, who was as experienced as any of us at picking out a guy on the make. 'He can walk as well as you and me.'

'OK, fine,' said Muhammad, apparently losing interest.

After the workout, though, the story changed. Muhammad put on a blistering display of boxing, and when he stepped out of the ring, Goodman and Angelo sat down to field some questions from the press people in attendance. Moments later Muhammad broke off and started walking in the hallway on his own to his dressing room…and lo and behold there he was, the wheelchair guy in hot pursuit. This man had been watching Muhammad to make his move at the right moment.

Angelo cut the press people short, and raced with Goodman down the hall to Muhammad's rescue. Too late: my brother had his chequebook open and he was writing him a cheque out for what turned out to be $5,000, and by the time they got to Muhammad the guy was already on his way.

'Muhammad, we told you this guy's a phoney!' said Angelo, exasperated.

'Yeah, but he's trying so hard,' said Muhammad. He honestly didn't have a care in the world. He would give money away to the fraudsters as if they were his friends.

Now, I didn't have a problem when Muhammad endeavoured to help those in genuine need. For instance, he had an apartment in New York City, and he'd visit the Big Apple quite a bit. One day, he was hanging out with Bundini, Young Blood and a couple of other people while the radio was on in the background. There was a show playing where listeners called in with their problems, and it turned out that one woman's mother was losing her home because she was so far behind with mortgage payments. Bundini, at the request of my brother, called up the station to get the address of the station and find out where the home was. It turned out it was in Jamaica, Queens. 'Get a car, let's go out there,' Muhammad said to Bundini. And they drove out there. It turned out to be a home for the aged. Specifically, it was an all-Hebrew home.

Obviously, it caused a stir when Muhammad and his friends walked inside. The residents were trying to ascertain who these big black men were and what they were doing there. My brother just cut to the chase and told them he'd heard about their difficulties, then bluntly asked, 'How much do you need?'

'We're behind $7,500,' came the reply. Well, Muhammad took out his chequebook and wrote a cheque on the spot, saying, 'You can put this cheque in the bank today.' Then he flicked back to the chequebook and he wrote another cheque out for the exact same amount, and said, 'Hold this back for two days, then you can put it in the bank.'

Bob Arum, one of the most prominent boxing promoters, once made a remark that encapsulates my brother's charitable nature. He said, 'If I were to give Muhammad Ali $50,000 cash at my office on 50th Street, by the time he got to 49th Street he would've given it all away.' I saw him give cars away at the drop of a hat. He'd say, 'You like the car? Keep the car.' My constant conflict with him wasn't that he was helping others; I constantly argued with Muhammad because people – both around him and strangers – were ripping him off. Me being his brother, I felt I had a duty to protect him. But his compulsion to help others was also what made him so beloved.

'I'LL FIGHT ANYONE':
THE MMA MISTAKE

At the age of thirty-four, after sixteen years of being a professional and boasting a record of fifty-two wins with only two losses, Muhammad was still the hottest name in sport. Before he fought Norton in their trilogy match in September 1976, my brother was presented with one of the most unusual offers of his career. Two years earlier, immediately after he dispatched George Foreman, there had been talk of throwing the heavyweight champ in the ring with a wrestler or martial arts champion. The kung fu boom was at its peak, and suddenly everyone was curious about what these men who knew how to kick and grapple could do. At one point, Muhammad's management were in serious talks about him fighting a prominent karate fighter: the man, it was suggested, would wear gloves on his hands and the karate pads on his feet, while Muhammad would wear boxing gloves only, with no blows thrown below the belt to be allowed. This had caught Muhammad's interest and he had agreed in principle. He even asked if he would be allowed to grab his opponent's legs and take him down and punch him on the ground, which in today's MMA arena is referred to as 'ground and pound'. Anyway, on that occasion, nothing materialised.

Six months after that suggestion, my brother met the president of the Japanese Amateur Wrestling Association, Ichiro Hatta. Consequently the Japanese media ran headlines about Muhammad's challenge in which he boasted he'd offer $1 million to any fighter from the Oriental arts to fight him. He bragged that he could beat anyone – be it a wrestler or any type of a fighter. In the end, it was Japan's revered wrestler Antonio Inoki who accepted the challenge.

Unbeknown to anyone, I think it was partly Belinda that prompted Muhammad to agree to the Inoki fight. Whenever Belinda came to Deer Lake camp, she would frequent a local dojo twice a week, taking karate lessons. In fact, she ended up taking lessons from Jimmy Kelly, a world karate champion who became an actor and had appeared in *Enter the Dragon*. Although my brother knew she had been taking karate lessons for years, he had no idea that she had developed to a high standard. There she was treated like anybody else, blending in with the other students. She was tough and would spar with everyone. Anyway, on one occasion Muhammad was visiting her in Chicago and had the key to the house, so let himself in. His wife wasn't expecting him, so she thought there was an intruder in her home. She wasn't going to let anyone burgle her and she ended up flipping him up using a martial arts move. Muhammad landed on the floor and Belinda got ready to smash him before realising it was her husband. My brother was shocked, to say the least. Recovering from the fall, he sarcastically said to her, 'Oh, you're a karate person now? I'll fix you up and your karate.'

When Belinda found out later that he was going to be locking horns with a wrestler, she felt it was going to be a very dangerous fight and was actually in fear for Muhammad's life. She thought he could potentially die. She thought that Muhammad was trying to prove a point to her, trying to prove that boxing rules over karate. Belinda said, 'No. Don't try to get yourself killed just to prove a thing to me because that guy is too big. He's not really a karate guy, he's a wrestler. It's two different things.'

At the time, it was a fight he took seriously. So Muhammad enlisted the help of Freddie Blassie, legendary pro wrestling champion, and Jhoon Rhee, the tae kwon do master and a friend and training partner of Bruce Lee's. Even Vince McMahon, who would go on to own the modern-day WWE, got involved. He would have a hand in setting up the Chuck Wepner versus Andre the Giant bout on the same card.

Muhammad loved Japan. He took pleasure in mixing with the

common folk and revelled in the media attention. He would be in a limousine on his way to some promotional opportunity, and suddenly he'd begin to shout, 'Hey, I see some people in the street! Let me out.' Then he'd be gone, attracting people like flies. He got a big kick out of standing there for five minutes or so, until there were hundreds of people around him, chanting, 'Ali! Ali! Ali!' He couldn't speak Japanese, of course, but his kindness and smile and the gentleness of his nature did all the talking he needed wherever he went. He travelled with an interpreter, but he would insist on connecting through gesture, and always managed to get his point across.

Still, as popular as my brother was with the Japanese people, other events surrounding the fight would be challenging to say the least. There was a lot at stake. Inoki and his people had stipulated certain rules, which Muhammad's team wasn't in favour of. Muhammad and his camp had some sessions with the wrestling team, familiarising themselves with their training. But after watching Inoki stretch his partners, throw them all over the place and administer excruciating pain with classic locks and holds, it planted seeds of doubt. Discussing the safety of the fighters was of the utmost priority to our team, and toning things down was viewed as a priority by Muhammad's camp. Shockingly Inoki's people wanted to know if their man could literally pull bones out of Muhammad – and put on excruciating bone-crushing locks. My brother's team thought, *This guy is crazy, we're trying to put on a show, and he's talking about pulling Muhammad's bones out, ripping his muscle.* They didn't like the way they were talking about hurting my brother. In the bigger scheme of things, he was the heavyweight champion of the world – nobody wanted to mess up his life. The fight itself was promoted as more of a regular wrestling type of an event, but they were making it into a serious thing now, which gravely concerned my brother's handlers. It was alarming. Angelo had been dubious about the whole idea and very much pissed off because he knew it was going to be detrimental to Muhammad's health and career.

Angelo knew they were going to go straight for grappling manoeuvres, and he endeavoured to get the rules changed but to no avail. He tried to keep the rules to Muhammad's advantage but couldn't. He was convinced that Muhammad was going to get badly hurt. My brother was a boxer, not a wrestler. He didn't have any practical knowledge of even the most rudimental moves in the grappling arts. Angelo, meanwhile, was opposed to people crossing over in sports. When it came to the negotiating table, though, sometimes Angelo didn't get as much say as he would have liked – he was often left sidelined while the managers and promoters clung on to the power of decision-making. I know he always had the best interests of Muhammad at heart, not only because he was his fighter, but he took it quite personally if anything happened to his kid.

Herbert and the likes of Don King and Bob Arum and others, wrongly, thought it wasn't a big deal. Their understanding was that this fight would be an easy ride for Muhammad and fatten their bank accounts as it would my brother's. Arum felt the whole idea was going to be a light-hearted bout for entertainment, but a massive money generator. That notion was buried, however, when Muhammad's team realised it was far from a joke after they struggled to get the rules changed; no one was laughing any more. I think they thought it was going to be a WWE thing. But it was a total fiasco.

Much conjecture has surrounded this event as far as behind the scenes chaos is concerned, and there was certainly a good deal of confusion in the build-up. The pre-fight organisation, for instance, was awful. In an attempt to come to a compromise on the rules, Muhammad's team sat down with Inoki's representatives again after initial meetings, during which they utterly failed to come to an agreement. All this should have been straightened out before Muhammad ever got on the plane, but the rules at this late stage were still kind of loose and ambiguous. We knew Inoki was going to be barehanded or was just going to have his hands taped up, and they were looking for us to have Muhammad use boxing gloves. So we got Everlast to make a pair of special gloves, specifically for this fight, which were six ounces, as light as today's MMA gloves. Muhammad had to wear some sort of gloves to protect his hands and it was out of the question that Angelo would ever let him fight bare-knuckle. In the end it was agreed that eye gouging, punching to the throat, open-hand chops, knife hand and butting were not allowed. Then, at the insistence of my brother's team, throws and kicks from the standing position were also disallowed, as were joint locks on the floor. We all knew, though, that

Inoki would do anything he could to win. Tensions continued to simmer.

On 26 June 1976 the fight took place at the Nippon Budokan arena, broadcast, reportedly, to over 1.4 billion people in thirty-four countries around the world. It was reported that a staggering 54 million viewers in Japan watched it. Two million pay-per-view buys for closed-circuit TV were sold in the USA grossing $20 million.

Despite the fact we had tried to learn about wrestling techniques, nothing really came into play on the day. In the ring it wasn't like both fighters were mixing it up. They were both very fearful of each other and kept their distance – Inoki tried not to get hit by anything and my brother tried to avoid the leg sweeps that Inoki constantly tried to perform. To be honest, it wasn't pretty to watch as Muhammad's concerned team sat there wondering how it would all play out. The fight was a real debacle, truth be told. And everyone soon arrived at the same conclusion after they found it very boring with Inoki staying in a crab-like fashion on the ground trying to leg sweep Muhammad while my brother just tried to dance around and stay out of harm's way. But Muhammad sustained serious injuries. His legs were so severely bruised he could hardly put on a pair of pants after the bout when he was in the dressing room.

It was ridiculous that he had put himself in that position in the first place. His handlers should've done more before pursuing the fight, and certainly should have had the rules locked down far before they did. As it was, he was hurting for a while. When he got back to Los Angeles, Gene Kilroy took him to hospital.

Obviously, Muhammad would've liked to have done more and put on a show. This was his first time in a wrestling ring. He later told the family that he wouldn't have fought if he had known that Inoki was going to sit on his behind and just throw kicks at his legs. He said to me, 'Rudy, the guy was tough and rough. I had confidence in myself.' Although he had experimented with wrestling, Muhammad took the fight very lightly as far as hard physical training went. So, I don't think he was in great shape. He wasn't expecting the problems that eventually presented themselves in the ring.

At post-fight Angelo even said that Muhammad would fight again in a similar event, but this time it would have to be under different rules.

This statement was ambiguous as Angelo was one of the individuals who didn't want this fight to happen in the first place. He was completely pissed off. Without a shadow of doubt this event was one of the most embarrassing moments in Muhammad's career. Further claims have surfaced which basically say the Black Muslims had warned Inoki that if he hurt Muhammad, if he laid a finger as much, they would kill him.

★ ★ ★

Six months after the Inoki fight, Muhammad and Belinda's divorce was being finalised. During the period they had been together, Belinda often emphasised to Muhammad the importance of family life – what it meant to her and how strongly she felt it should be important to him. She didn't embark on the project of edifying him just because of her point of view, but because, according to her, he was, let's say, not fully taking responsibility as a man. The thing was for years some of my brother's entourage members gave him 'ideas', which meant that he did not fulfil certain responsibilities to his family. They planted the seed in his head that he could do whatever he wanted because he was Muhammad Ali – a powerful and famous man. Unfortunately, some individuals used this trick to ingratiate themselves with him, to use him because they knew too well of his weakness. That was his downside, that his weakness allowed him to be swayed. He was manipulated by certain men because they saw this chink in his armour. Whom you hang around with, the company you keep – it changes your life.

One of these men was Herbert, unfortunately. Muhammad had treated Herbert like a brother almost from the moment they met, and we both had mutual respect for Herbert. Belinda had known him since she was three years old. Spending a lot of time around Elijah Muhammad and his family led her and others to even call him 'Uncle Herbert'. Herbert had been good with her family from the start, but the more Belinda got to know my brother's manager the more she was able to ascertain how bad an influence he had become to Muhammad. Soon enough, she discovered that Herbert had been promiscuous. He had girlfriends and since Belinda knew his real wife she began to dislike him.

The thing is, Muhammad and Herbert were both open with each

other. Herbert said to Muhammad, 'You can do what you want in front of whoever. You're paying the bills. So you are the one bringing the money home for your family.' That was Muhammad's downfall later – being influenced by his friend. However, when it came down to the business side of things, in terms of third parties taking advantage, Herbert had been somewhat of a saviour. I didn't witness any crooked deals. Herbert used to keep his eyes on Don King. King could've taken a lot of advantage of Muhammad if Herbert had allowed it. But he didn't allow it. King couldn't fully take advantage of Muhammad because Herbert was in his way. To be honest, Herbert didn't warm to King. Then again, not many people did. There's something else that I can say about Herbert's management of Muhammad and that is that he was influential in ensuring gangsters couldn't take over my brother. This shielded Muhammad without a shadow of doubt from the claws of the underworld. And this is something Belinda, ultimately, and Muhammad and I, were thankful for.

Despite Muhammad's domestic issues, the public expect well-known public figures to behave in a certain manner. They feel sports stars are role models and aren't humans. But his wife felt he had the attitude, *I've done a lot of good stuff. I can do what I want.* And Muhammad did do a great deal of good. The sad part is a lot of these cracks in their marriage came about when Muhammad and Belinda were in their happiest moments. I must admit, there was a lot more effort Muhammad could've put in as far as family life was concerned. Those were the troubling times in their life.

I witnessed there were women who were just out to get Muhammad for money or position, and they were good at it. This further exacerbated Belinda's break-up with her own family. This was the hardest and most sensitive time that she had to go through.

When you realise that your partner doesn't want to correct themselves, and they continue to repeat the same mistakes, there's nothing you can really do other than accept it and move on. Belinda finally had to accept it and move on and let him go. So, although the cracks in their marriage had been present for years, it had now got to a stage where divorce was imminent. Muhammad and Belinda were a team in the beginning and went through plenty of battles together – they suffered, but came through despite insurmountable odds. Muhammad, according to Belinda, was a good family man in the beginning when they were struggling, a good husband and a good father. When Muhammad started making money and they got comfortable, then Belinda felt like he didn't want to fight for justice any more and he gave it up.

Now, his wife perceived him somewhat differently than how I saw my own brother. To me Muhammad could do no wrong. He continued fighting for justice. He loved his family, children and never went out to hurt a soul. They were married and had their own battles to fight, which is something I refrained from getting involved in. She believed if Muhammad ever fought for his family like he had fought against the war and the injustices in America, the marriage would've lasted forever. That was a turning point and Muhammad did not win that battle with his wife – he lost.

★ ★ ★

Muhammad knew Belinda wasn't going to allow some woman like Veronica to break up her family by getting in there. By now my brother and Veronica were living together. Belinda later said she never knew there were women like Veronica around. Belinda had grown up with and been around respectful women, devoted and loyal women. So to her it was almost beyond her comprehension that someone would come between her and Muhammad. She was naive because she was always around good women all her life. So, to see Veronica come into Muhammad's life didn't go well with her, of course. Belinda felt women like that didn't care about people's feelings. They're just out there for the money and notoriety, she personally felt. However, I know that Muhammad loved Veronica and didn't see it that way. And Veronica loved my brother and cared about him. Also, it wasn't Veronica doing the chasing of my brother in the first place – more the other way around. Over the years, I feel Veronica has received some unfair criticism.

Belinda felt that once Muhammad got what he wanted, he didn't care about the team. He just became manipulated by other women. My brother was easy to get manipulated. Although Belinda was manipulating him too, the difference was she was helping him in a positive way to make him better, to put him out there at the front. But the other women didn't care about that; they just cared about themselves and financial gain apparently. If Muhammad was scared of any one person, it was Belinda.

In January 1977 they divorced. Even after the divorce and eventually after departing from him, Belinda had made it clear to Muhammad that she wouldn't restrict him from seeing his kids. The children were in Belinda's custody. When they wanted to see their father, it was never an issue. Despite Belinda's personal views of Muhammad she felt he was still their father. She made it clear that there was no need for him to pursue the courts to see their children. 'If you want to see the children, that's fine,' she told him. 'You come here at any time.' And it was a good arrangement I felt. Despite their problems, I never witnessed Belinda use this against Muhammad when it came to their children. The problem with women today is they accuse the father of their children then the children get hurt in the end. But Belinda just never divulged anything derogatory about their father to the children. Furthermore, she thought they'll be able to see it themselves. But she refrained from highlighting negativity.

She said to Muhammad, 'Look, I'm going to divorce you, but I'm going to tell you something. We're soulmates. I might not be your wife any more but I'll be your sister. I don't want anybody to hurt you. We're going to be friends.' Years of marriage and producing four children had developed a sustained bond, even though both had more than their fair share of ramblings during the tumultuous period they were married. There was one warning, however. 'When I come to see you, get your women straight,' Belinda told her former husband. 'I demand respect, so you tell whatever ladies you've got hanging around that we're friends, like sister and brother, and nobody can stop that.' It was a direct approach, but sometimes that's what you needed with my brother, and in this case it certainly worked. Muhammad and his ex-wife mostly maintained an amicable post-divorce relationship, even if she seemed to rub him up the wrong way at times.

I think Muhammad could still confide in her. He would sometimes mention some women who had one thing on their mind – of attaching themselves to him and taking advantage. He would ask her, 'Is she stupid coming around here?' Belinda's response would be, 'But you're helping her.' Muhammad wasn't perfect – he liked women, and this is no secret –

but he felt what's done is done and you have to move forward, and he still loved his family, I know that for sure.

REUNITING
THE BEATLES

My brother first met The Beatles when the world still knew him as Cassius Clay. In February 1964 they were in Miami to make their second appearance on *The Ed Sullivan Show*, after a debut performance that saw them sing a few songs in front of a screaming studio audience that almost drowned out their lyrics. At the time, my brother was training in the 5th Street Gym, and so publicist Harold Conrad came up with the idea of having the boys drop by. When they arrived, though, my brother wasn't there – at that time, he was typically training once early in the morning and then again in the late afternoon, taking a nap in between. In the end, Muhammad arrived just as the boys from Britain were set to leave.

'Hello there, Beatles,' he said. 'We oughta do some shows together. We'll get rich.'

They all posed together for photographs, four smart talkers from the UK and one from Louisville, my brother pretending to knock them down with one punch. 'You're not as dumb as you look,' he told Lennon, only to be met with the response, 'No, but you are.'

As far as I know, my brother liked the boys. They treated him with respect, even if they were taking over America at the time. And so, when an opportunity to reunite them came around twelve years later, it's no surprise that he was willing to get on board.

By late 1976, my brother was still living in Chicago and The Beatles hadn't played together for more than half a decade. After the Inoki fight, Muhammad had been awarded a unanimous decision over Ken Norton in New York's famed Yankee Stadium, and he was still thinking about retirement and his other options for the future. One morning early in January 1977, he was having breakfast in a diner in Miami Beach with a couple of friends when he was approached by a young Jewish man by the name of Alan Amron. As I've hopefully illustrated already, my brother was never difficult to approach. He'd greet you cordially if you introduced yourself, of course, but he also carried himself in an easy manner that invited conversation. Not that Amron needed much encouragement – as it turned out, he had an idea in mind, and like many men driven by a purpose, he wasn't exactly shy about getting after it.

After introducing himself, he got right to the point, by asking my brother if he could help him get in contact with The Beatles. As it turned out, the young man – who was an aspiring inventor from New York – had just started a committee with the sole aim of reuniting the greatest music group. He had started by fundraising with an advert in *Village Voice*, a newspaper in New York City, spending $74 on a half-page ad asking every fan of The Beatles around the world to send him a dollar to help him pay the group to get back together to play one more time. *Rolling Stone* magazine had picked up on that advert and churned out an article pertaining to Amron's campaign and, consequently, dollars from all over the world started to pour in. Muhammad, with his diverse group of friends, had already heard this part of the story. So he knew what this guy was talking about.

Now, my brother rarely said no to anyone, but he also revered the Fab Four and felt that Amron's was a great idea. So he gave Amron his business card with the phone number for his manager Herbert Muhammad. 'Set it up with Herbert and come over to Chicago next week and meet with me,' he told this enthusiastic young man.

The following week Amron, along with his business partner Joel Sacher, flew to the windy city of Chicago. Herbert sent a limousine to the airport to pick up the guests to bring them to his house for a lunch meeting. Herbert's home, incidentally, was a little out of the ordinary. The tables and sofas, I can recall, were built into the walls, and the whole place was always very dark, making it an odd, subdued place to conduct any manner of business dealings. It could throw people off, and it certainly did with Amron. During lunch, as the three discussed the project, Amron blurted out a curse word mid-conversation. One of Herbert's burly bodyguards lightly grabbed the guest by the shoulder, and he said, 'We don't talk like that in front of Mr Muhammad.' Seeing the funny side, Herbert interjected, 'Oh, don't worry. Don't worry. Next time we have a meeting with Alan we'll just have it in the garage.'

During their discussion, Herbert was more interested in the monetary side of things: how much it was going to cost, projected profits, in addition to how they were actually going to pull off the feat of reuniting The Beatles. He moved straight towards the side of talking money, and seemed happy to leave the details to Muhammad and the two entrepreneurs. Everyone mutually agreed that this venture had the potential to make a huge profit, and The Beatles would make an awful lot of money. That, anyway, was the initial idea.

★ ★ ★

After lunch two burly bodyguards drove the two guests to Muhammad's house, which wasn't far from Herbert's place. Muhammad, holding his baby girl Hana who was only six months old at the time, greeted his guests and gave the baby to the housekeeper, then went into the kitchen and Amron and his friend followed. He was in a playful mood. As his visitors headed for the house's elevator, Muhammad darted for the stairs, taking them two at a time until the visitors got the idea and raced him to the top. Surprisingly, by the time Muhammad got to the top, he was huffing and puffing, breathing as heavily as he did after a few rounds of sparring. Amron, who was in a jovial mood, said to Muhammad, 'OK, now let me see if I can beat you. I think I can beat you now.' Muhammad was comparatively out of shape then. He wasn't in the top physical condition he had been in his peak years, and certainly wasn't in training. Regardless, the three convened in Muhammad's bedroom where he showed them a magic trick. Then everyone made their way downstairs to the lounge to discuss the grand plan to reunite the world's biggest band.

Whenever my brother was inside the four walls of his own home, he was always very relaxed and often walked around barefoot. You would never see him parading around like the Ali from TV. He was attentive and quiet as the visitors presented their proposal. Muhammad told them about his history with The Beatles, and said they seemed like really affable guys.

After that, it was Amron's turn to talk. Muhammad wanted his input. The reunion, he explained, would bring the British group together for one show, which would then be broadcast all around the country in movie theatres. Someone suggested that the video rights might bring in even more money, which really piqued my brother's interest. He was very proud of the fact that he was the originator of that particular money-spinner, the first boxer to have his fights shown in movie theatres. He told Amron that he had the contacts to do the same for a concert, as well as the capacity to contact the group members and get the financial backing necessary to put the whole thing together. Well, as you can probably imagine, Amron and his friend couldn't have been more excited.

Then came the problem. From the outset, Amron had conceived the whole thing as a commercial venture. What the partners proposed was that they raise a dollar from 50 million Beatles fans around the world: 90 per cent of a projected $50 million payday would go to The Beatles and the other 10 would be shared out between Muhammad, Herbert, Amor and Sacher, and any other party who was going to be involved. Still, Muhammad had a rather different perspective: straight away, he explained that he wanted to pursue the project for nothing but charity.

They argued that they were raising the money to get the group back together again – this was the sole reason. After contemplation Muhammad conceded, 'OK, we can give the money to The Beatles.' But what Muhammad really wanted to do was feed the children of different countries. Nonetheless both parties came to a compromise in the end. It was agreed that 10 per cent would go to charity, while the rest would be offered to the band.

Muhammad, as I've already explained, only cared about money to pay his bills; he really didn't care about the bigger picture. How much money he made from a fight was the least of his worries – that was always left to Herbert. Anyway, Muhammad explained where the 10 per cent of the revenue would go, and he asked, 'Alan and Joe, is that OK with you guys?' He, of course, later asked Herbert too. And in the end they all concurred because all those involved mutually felt this project would be momentous and, perhaps, some of the funds from the 90 per cent would find their way to a charitable cause. Muhammad and the rest of his team were of the thinking that maybe The Beatles would likely be generous enough to give a percentage from their cut to charity also. Anyhow, it was stipulated that the group was not obliged to. After the ball got rolling and with Muhammad's help, The Beatles' representatives initially agreed that they would do it for charity, in that some of the money would be donated.

As my brother continued the discussions a briefcase lay on the floor next to where he was sitting. Amor and Sacher were distracted by this and they couldn't help but gaze at his briefcase. On the other hand Muhammad's eyes were zooming directly at Amron's briefcase. Muhammad was curious to see what his guest had in his briefcase. Amron was equally curious because Muhammad was always seen walking around with that briefcase when he was living in Philadelphia, New Jersey, Chicago or Los Angeles, and wherever he travelled. By now he had created this image of himself in a suit carrying a briefcase. He strove to create that businessman image and looked the part. Muhammad and I would often wear suits. Literally everybody wanted to know what was in that briefcase. What was the secret? So Muhammad's guest felt he had an opportunity to unravel the mystery. Amron asked Muhammad, 'What's in the briefcase?' Next, my brother grabbed his briefcase and flicked it open, and he said, 'I keep cash and my lunch in there. If I'm hungry I eat my lunch and if I need any money I have it here.' Carrying cash was the norm for my brother. He was a cash man – old-fashioned.

As the day unfolded, Muhammad and Amron engaged in a deep conversation sitting on the stairs. My brother proceeded to enlighten his guest on the subject of religion, something he always liked to talk about. Muhammad had the tendency and capacity to be very philosophical on occasion, and on this one Amron was really taken aback by his vast knowledge. He was a young guy – what we called 'full of piss and vinegar', just full of aggression and a need to prove himself. Muhammad sort of took that tone out of him that day as the business meeting turned out to be a philosophical lesson. My brother left an indelible mark on Amron, for sure.

Before the guests left, they divulged something that made Muhammad laugh out loud. They'd been excited and jittery when they arrived, Muhammad knew, but he couldn't tell why. Well, they told Muhammad that when they were picked up by a squadron of burly black bodyguards with dark sunglasses, in a limousine with blacked-out windows they genuinely felt they were going to die. They didn't know whether to leap out of the car and make a run for it at some point when it stopped in traffic. The men, who were relatively new to business dealings at the time, had heard about Herbert being this Black Muslim leader whom the media had painted as a gangster and a thug. On the way to Herbert's house in the limousine both looked at each other and said, 'We are going to die.'

Muhammad just couldn't contain himself at this. He burst out laughing. He insisted on showing his guests around the house, chuckling all the while at their 'close call'. Then he had his driver take them back to the airport – with no need for protection.

Muhammad always made a huge impact on people. His guests left his house with a totally new perception of his character. He was not the Muhammad Ali everybody knows, all boisterous yelling and screaming. In person he was the polar opposite – so quiet and so subdued that it shocked these two men. In fact, before Amron met my brother, he told us later, he didn't like him. Muhammad came across as this boisterous, loud and somewhat mean man. But after spending merely three hours in his presence, Muhammad's guest discovered he had two personalities and the difference was astronomical. In public the created image worked for my brother, but when someone met him behind closed doors they'd go away with a total different perception and image of him.

★ ★ ★

Not long after this meeting, Muhammad was invited to an inauguration dinner gala for President Jimmy Carter. Carter had just been elected, and there were five of these events in Washington DC at the same time, all in hotels along the same street – President Carter, of course, made an appearance at all the venues. After receiving the official invitation, he wasted no time phoning his two associates and said to them, 'I'm going to Jimmy Carter's inauguration and you're coming with me.' Well, he picked them up in a car with no more said about it, and somehow all three men got into the event. The two men hadn't received any form of invitation whatsoever, but when you were with Muhammad nobody stopped you from entering a place – he had that power about him, that aura. I witnessed this many times. The event that Muhammad was invited to was the one with all the other celebrities from the worlds of sports and TV attending, and it turned out, unbeknown to my brother, that John Lennon and his wife Yoko Ono were among the celebrities in attendance. He didn't plan it, but it worked out – that was how a lot of things turned out with my brother.

At the event Muhammad, dressed up in his black tuxedo, spent some time mingling with President Carter, Lennon and his wife. He thought it was a great opportunity to discuss the proposal for the reunion with Lennon, and he approached the Beatle with a smile on his face and his hand extended. Lennon and his wife, I'm told, really liked the idea of doing the reunion for charity, especially after Muhammad explained about his own success with closed circuit TV (now called pay-per-view). Surprisingly, they didn't even discuss money – there was very little mention of dollars or cents in the whole conversation. Primarily what invoked Lennon's interest was the fact Muhammad was a part of the project – his questions were on how much he'd be involved, and what they could do together. Lennon told my brother that he would love to collaborate with him on the project. Then again, which star wasn't in awe of Muhammad's presence? I was around my brother more than anyone and the reverence celebrities had for him was far greater than any other figure in the public eye.

Muhammad, incidentally, thought Lennon was a terrific performer – exciting and inventive, and willing to speak his mind. Both had a mutual admiration for each other. You have to understand that Muhammad never really gushed – he wasn't a guy who was going to come at you all fawning, trying to win you over. He, by and large, treated everybody the same, as humans first and celebrities or whatever afterwards. But he recognised the fact The Beatles were huge, while never really conceding that they were bigger than him. He was always respectful of the fact how popular they were and how well known around the world. Muhammad was of the belief that the world needed more of The Beatles' music. The Beatles were making a contribution to world peace and love, he felt. Another thing that enticed Muhammad to this group was that they had embraced religion. Even though their beliefs weren't quite in sync with his own, Muhammad could empathise with their belief in something greater than themselves. Religion was important in your success in life, he believed – however it manifested itself.

When Muhammad fought Alfredo Evangelista four months later, he invited Amron and Sacher to the fight. After the fight Don King had to go home to attend to some business, so they went with him to his New York apartment. They pulled up in front of this really beautiful brownstone. The men went inside and then into his kitchen. Don and Amron were talking about how this Beatles thing could be really good for Muhammad. And how it would be great for The Beatles, not least how it would be great for Don King. Don saw that Muhammad's two new Jewish friends were on the favourable side of Herbert and Muhammad.

In the end, things dragged on Muhammad's side – he was always on the go, doing things outside the ring and preparing for fights. The Beatles' reps continued back and forth with communication. However, everyone was too busy doing their own thing and the idea faded into obscurity. Next thing you know, Lennon is assassinated and that shut down the project, for sure.

HOLLYWOOD

By now my brother's fight career was coming to an end, and he was contemplating his future. His business manager, Gene Kilroy, wanted him to get involved in the motion picture industry after his retirement. Muhammad and Gene discussed this. It seemed like a natural fit for someone so charismatic and recognisable, but Gene also felt that it was something Muhammad would enjoy. For someone used to being the most famous face on the earth, he thought, continuing to entertain millions via another medium would be a natural way to stay in the limelight.

Muhammad, of course, was keen. He'd dabbled with acting a little in his earlier life, and now was starting to give serious thought to carving out a career at it. Almost before anyone else knew it, the pair were collaborating on a Muhammad's first major effort, starring in his own film aptly titled *The Greatest*, a biopic focusing on his trials and triumphs from winning gold at the Olympics in Rome to his legendary bout with big George Foreman.

Although Muhammad would essentially play himself in the movie, the producers wanted to have a young man play him during his Cassius Clay years. And, of course, the process of finding someone to fill my brother's size thirteen shoes was a long and arduous one. Suddenly, there was a worldwide search for the right actor, including a TV campaign which resulted in 900 applications being accepted by the casting department at Columbia Pictures. Eventually, the producers set up a meeting for Muhammad in New York to meet two prime candidates for playing his younger self. One was an eighteen-year-old from South Central Los Angeles, from the hood, named Chip McAllister, who bore a remarkable resemblance to my brother. Up close, you'd notice that even some of his mannerisms were similar. The other candidate was relatively diffident, but also closely resembled Muhammad. He was the Golden Gloves champion, so came with the benefit of real boxing experience. Neither of them, I think, were expecting the audition experience they got.

Late one afternoon, the two candidates, along with a few assorted studio executives and hangers-on were lounging around waiting in an apartment, which belonged to one of Muhammad's friends, when all of a sudden there was a banging noise on the wall. I'm talking hard – these weren't little pit-a-pat taps; someone was hammering that wall.

'Who's that in the other room who's going to try to play me?' came the call through the wall. 'Boom! Nobody can play the greatest of all time. Boom! I'm Muhammad Aliiii! No one can play me!' Suddenly, my brother made his entrance, larger than life as usual.

Now, it looked like the other youngster's heart sank at this sight, but McAllister wasn't playing around. This confident young man stood up and started to mimic Muhammad. 'I'll whup you, sucker,' he said, 'You ain't nothing! You ain't nothing! I will beat you, sucker.' Next thing anyone knew, both of them were engaged in a war of words as they struck poses and beat their chests, feeding off each other's energy as they promised to whup each other. Moments later, a whole herd of paparazzi rushed through the door – there were about twenty cameramen and reporters. The whole thing had been set up with the press, and it couldn't have worked better. My brother's instinct for publicity had won the day once again. Right there, the young man from the ghettos stole the show in front of his hero. Muhammad took an instant liking to him.

Something very few people know is that a young seventeen-year-old Sharon Stone had caught Muhammad's eye at the Miss Pennsylvania Pageant, a contest she was competing in in Philadelphia. They both met and Muhammad was compelled to work with her. He was so adamant about getting her in the film that he called her father to offer her a part personally. Evidently, though, her father wasn't impressed at all. 'She is not going to be in a film,' her father told my brother in no uncertain terms. 'You may think she's not, but she is,' Muhammad replied, not taking no for an answer. 'You cannot hide that girl in a bushel basket. Her light is too bright.' Despite Muhammad's repeated efforts, the protective father refused to capitulate, as did Muhammad.

Finally, my brother had to do without this blonde young teen. Stone, who would cross paths with Muhammad decades later after she conquered Hollywood on her own merits, said to Muhammad, 'You know, I met you when I was a teenage girl?' Muhammad's recollection was second to none. He turned around to the beautiful blonde, and he said, 'Yes. And you were wearing a blue dress.' He vividly remembered their first meeting all those years ago. The Hollywood star was amazed at his razor-sharp memory. She obviously was embedded in his mind for all those years.

★ ★ ★

With the casting done, Muhammad was eager to start work on the film. We ended up travelling across seven different states to shoot the movie. On-set, my brother was every bit the entertainer he had been in every open workout and press conference he'd attended as a boxer. Everything he did was larger than life. At the same time, he wasn't exactly an actor in the real sense of the word, and so the director, Tom Grimes, often had to handle him with kid gloves. He urged Muhammad to make his performance natural, and spoon-fed him his lines to make the whole thing easier on everyone. I think most actors dislike like the term 'line reading', but Muhammad embraced it.

As everyone knows, you end up doing lots of takes for each scene when shooting a movie, but there was one scene in particular from *The Greatest* that none of us from the set will ever forget. I'm speaking, in case you haven't seen the movie, of the memorable scene in Kentucky where Muhammad rips a dress off his first wife, Sonji, played by actress Mira Waters, although under the name Ruby Sanderson. From the word go, Muhammad got right into the spirit of that scene. After one or two takes, he was still bouncing up and down, shouting, 'Let me do that again! Let me do that again!' He absolutely loved it – not for indecent reasons, you understand, but because the emotional content of the scene played so well with his natural exuberance. Wherever there was a fake argument on-screen, my brother came alive, and while shooting this scene in particular, we could barely hold him back. He didn't mean anything bad by it; he just found it all hilarious. Some of us stood there with big grins on our faces.

You see, acting came naturally to Muhammad because it had been a part of his natural showmanship ever since he became a professional boxer. He had been, to some extent, playing a part for years, running his mouth and putting on a show when part of him undoubtedly wanted to sit quietly and talk. That was acting. And so, Muhammad had been literally acting all his adult life. Considering he wasn't a trained professional actor, he did well, at least according to his contemporaries. On one occasion, I remember that George C. Scott was milling around the set just as another member of my brother's entourage was suggesting that he take acting lessons. 'No,' I remember George saying, fixing my brother with that stare of his. 'No, you're a natural.'

During the breaks from shooting Muhammad would sporadically take power naps. He slept a *lot*. He could take a nap right in the middle of the day. It didn't matter how stressful the shoot had been that morning, he'd head right into his personal trailer and be snoring two minutes later. But then, he would also relax by getting out and about with a couple of us accompanying him. Some people say that film-making is all about 'hurry up and wait', but my brother didn't like to wait for anything. Whenever he could, he would hang out with me, Gene Kilroy, Bundini Brown and Pat Patterson. And the funny thing was, each one of the guys was dying to be his favourite. If Muhammad asked for something, Gene would say, 'Oh, I'll get it for you!' and Patterson would be, 'No, nope, I'll do it!' It was hilarious how they literally fought to get his attention.

We had been filming for some time when I met Stack Pierce, the actor who had been hired to play me, Muhammad's brother, in the movie. He was a great actor and a really nice guy, but halfway through the movie, I put two and two together and said, 'Man, Muhammad's playing himself, why can't I play myself?' I was always in my brother's shadow, an introvert compared to him – while countless others around tried to exploit him, I was usually happy to hang in the background, but on this one occasion I felt like I had to speak up. The next thing anyone knew, I started standing closer to Muhammad more during the shooting of the scenes, jostling to get more screen time myself. Why not? I figured. I was an integral part of my brother's team and had always been close to him, certainly closer than anyone else on-set. Eventually, it worked – kind of. They took out whatever lines they had for Pierce in the script after I complained, but both of us, somehow, remained in the movie. Half of the scenes in the film had already been shot with Pierce, and nobody wanted to reshoot them, but with me complaining from the sidelines, he wouldn't get a speaking part. If you watch the movie carefully, there's never any specific and explicit reference made about me, Muhammad's brother. So, it's kind of ambiguous, but there were two people in the film who were both always with Muhammad. Sorry, Piers!

★ ★ ★

Now, the interesting thing is that the movie *Rocky* hit the big screen while we were shooting *The Greatest*. We were on location in Houston when Sylvester Stallone's film came out, and Muhammad was all too aware of this new boxing movie that was suddenly making waves. One day, out of the blue, he said, 'I want to go and see *Rocky*,' and so off we all trooped, his thirty-man entourage, to an evening showing at a local cinema. When we arrived there was a long line of people around the corner, and at first there was some nervous shuffling from the crowd. Just imagine a gang of thirty men, predominantly black, suddenly appearing when you're on a date – especially back in the 1970s. But then a few people noticed my brother at the front of the entourage and people's faces started to light up. Here was the real greatest of all times, here to see the same film as them! The 8 o'clock show was about to start and my brother was able to get the whole crowd to agree to let him and his large entourage see the movie. There was even some applause as we all walked into the cinema.

As I've mentioned already, I had accompanied Muhammad to the cinema an inordinate number of times over the course of our parallel lives. He was the same from childhood to almost the end of his life – whenever he was engrossed in watching a movie, he would be glued to the screen, totally focused with no time for distractions. *Rocky*, of course, was no different. 'You're not going to be talking,' he said, as the lights went down in the cinema, the smile gone from his face. 'You're not going to be making any noise.' Nobody was going to argue.

Anyway, to cut a long story short, my brother absolutely loved *Rocky*. We were of the impression that he was going to be critiquing the fight scenes – on the contrary, he was shucking and jiving in his seat right alongside Rocky and Apollo, doing everything except throwing punches as he got into the on-screen action. If he felt the movie had borrowed heavily from his own persona – it emerged later that Stallone had taken my brother's battle with Chuck Wepner as the inspiration for his story of an all-time underdog getting the chance of a lifetime against a brash-talking champ – he found it flattering rather than insulting. In later films, Stallone would borrow other elements of my brother's training regime for his own version of the greatest – the mountainside training camp and wood chopping from *Rocky IV*, the scene of Rocky running alongside a group of excited children from *Rocky II*, and of course Stallone's ubiquitous boots and grey sweatsuit all owed a debt to my brother. Even Bundini and Angelo Dundee had their similarities to Rocky's team.

Anyway, by and large, my brother felt *Rocky* was a great movie. Furthermore, Muhammad was very impressed with the star of the film, Sylvester Stallone himself. Of course the movie was good, and the writing was great, but what made the biggest impression and mark on Muhammad was that Stallone had insisted on playing the role himself, even if it meant taking a pay cut. Muhammad admired that stance. Very few people, he felt, would ever do what Stallone did. They'd compromise, take the money and let creative control slip away. So Stallone was a champion in my brother's eyes. *Rocky* didn't have a massive budget, but that didn't stop the film from exploding at the box office. 'I hope our movie is as good as this one,' he said to me as we walked through the lobby after the show was over.

After the film ended, we made our way outside only to be mobbed by the crowd – the power that Muhammad had with people emanating once again. I don't think I ever saw my brother turn down any autograph – unless he was going to miss an aeroplane, and even then I don't think many would have dared take off without him being aboard.

As the night wore on, next stop was to fill our hungry bellies. We ended up at a restaurant called Angelo's, a famous restaurant that Jim Brown was a huge fan of. Jim used to get seafood shipped from Angelo's to his house all the way in Los Angeles. Whenever Muhammad was out with his crowd and wanted to eat, Gene Kilroy would call in advance. Again it wasn't five or six days' advance notice, but Muhammad would just go, 'I want to do this,' and bam, Gene Kilroy would get on the phone right away: 'All right, I'm calling for the champ. Set this and that up.' Everywhere we went. It was crazy, like a circus. The table would be full of lobster, shrimp and prawns because Muhammad loved seafood. He would never even have to order anything again because the place would make sure the table was full of what food he craved.

In the end, my brother thought *The Greatest* was pretty good. The *Los Angeles Times* called it, 'Potent pop biography, lively and entertaining.' However, Muhammad's biggest criticism was that it depicted his life too fast. The editing was too fast from scene to scene, he believed, making it hard for casual fans to follow. Then again, when *Ali,* starring Will Smith, was released decades later, he thought that went too slow. Both of those movies were pretty good, but had their faults, in his opinion. *The Greatest,* well, it was just OK.

★ ★ ★

Muhammad didn't waste any time moving on to other projects. In 1978 he inked a deal to co-star in a movie called *Freedom Road* with Kris Kristofferson. Kris was a fight aficionado himself – he boxed during his tenure at Oxford University – and in 1960 he bummed a ride to Rome to see the Olympics where Muhammad won the gold medal. Back in America Kristofferson went on to fight in the Golden Gloves tournaments, and kept up his interest in the sport through its golden age. It was Gene Kilroy who met Kris and brought him and my brother together. The producer and director of this film had made contact with Gene, proposing the idea of casting Muhammad in this historical TV drama. He played an ex-slave and former Union soldier who returns to his home in South Carolina following the American Civil War and ultimately becomes a US senator. He enjoyed the role, and a few critics at the time seemed to think he'd done well, though he ultimately couldn't act with all the exuberance he brought to his sparring performances. Perhaps the most interest point about the TV movie is that at the time Kris was getting $5 million for a movie, but he did *Freedom Road* for a mere $100,000 and gave the rest of the money he received to the United Negro College Fund. He did this only because Muhammad's business manager asked him to, and to help Muhammad because he truly loved him. By then they had forged a close friendship. In fact, initially Kris didn't want to do this movie at all. He was one of the celebrity friends of my brother that wanted him to retire from the ring. When Gene apparently told him that Muhammad would go back to fighting if the movie failed, Kris agreed to do it.

For twelve weeks of work, Muhammad received $1 million. At the time, this amount was more or less a quarter of what he would usually earn in forty-five minutes in the ring. The total budget for the film was $7 million. While my brother was filming, the usual entourage was absent other than his new wife Veronica, whom he had married in the summer of 1977 in a fairly low-key event in Beverly Hills, and his two kids with her who would often visit the set. Furthermore, Muhammad made no real demands on-set unlike some celebrities who are inclined to make diva demands.

He was also offered parts in the endless black exploitation movies that were being made in the 1970s. However, he had strong reservations about accepting these parts. He strongly felt that titles like *Nigger Charlie*, *Cleopatra Jones* and *Black Killer* were detrimental to the black cause – that their scenes of nudity, sex and drug abuse exploited and degraded black women and men alike. All these were portraying the worst in our society. He exercised prudence as he didn't want to fall into the trap where he would make black people look bad.

Even outside of those films, Muhammad was choosy about the

projects he would take on. Promoting cigarettes, whiskey, partying or women of any kind being degraded – anything that might adversely affect the children, including taking pictures of blondes smiling as they were exploited for their looks, were not things he was willing to get involved in, which he made clear very early in his movie career. This was really just an extension of the way my brother always conducted himself. After a fight you never saw Muhammad or me sit in a bar revelling among a bunch of partygoers. We would have an orange juice and say a prayer to Allah. In that era, many black women and men had to do things they didn't want to do to make ends meet, and even the ones making successful careers in music, TV or the movies had to make choices they'd have rather avoided. Muhammad, though, wasn't going to be a sell-out, which was the key reason he was so hesitant in accepting movie roles, and the reason he didn't make more of a career of it. In those days, the opportunities for a black man to be on screen were few and far between, even if he was the greatest of all time.

And so, while initially he caught the movie bug hard and planned to become a star, his interest in making movies suddenly waned not long after *Freedom Road*. By the time he made *Freedom Road* he was really not interested in sitting around on a movie set doing nothing. 'I don't need these movies, Rudy, my life is a movie,' he would tell me. 'I star in my own movie. I don't need to be making somebody else's. I don't need it.' He'd appear on TV shows for the rest of his life, but he never really tried his hand at acting again.

★ ★ ★

Although Muhammad had moved out of our home town when he turned professional as a boxer, he would make frequent trips to Louisville to see family and friends for the rest of his life. The love for his town and those he left behind, people he had grown up with, was always there. Still, his thinking had changed – he didn't have too much time to stay there whenever he visited, he often said. He had been exposed to a bigger, more complex world, he told me, and it had changed his perceptions. 'The town looks so small and the people move so slowly,' he once remarked to me. He felt the friends raised there were still going through the same motions, still standing on the same corners. After all the travelling he'd done, the people he'd had opportunities to talk to and learn from, he found it hard to stay in any one place for too long, and after even a day in Louisville he'd be ready to leave. Or, as he once said to me: 'Even in jail I'm going to have a moving plan.'

Still, he would visit his home town whenever he could – and for the short time he was there, he would always make sure he was the life of the party. 'When you get big and make it and all of the people around the world know your name, and you have a big bank account, go back to your neighbourhood where you used to be nothing but a little boy playing in the street,' he used to say to anyone who had aspirations towards fame. 'Go back and find those people that you grew up with, and show them that you still care about them, and it will make you even greater. Go back to the same corner you were hanging out in the neighbourhood as a little boy with big dreams and plans to make them happen. Find those people that are still there, say hello, shake their hands and walk around with them to show that you're no different from them. And they'll love you for it.' That's the advice he gave countless people coming up in the fame game. And truth be told, the majority didn't seem to listen.

In particular, he'd make an effort to attend the Kentucky Derby, the most famous race in the world, which always takes place on the first weekend of May in Louisville. Muhammad could ride horses and would often ride with his kids and wife at Deer Lake. I remember that one afternoon at the height of his career Muhammad and I were in town and along with members of his entourage we all went to the races. On the top floor, some of the most famous people in the world were lounging around – presidents, Hollywood stars and anybody that was anybody in the corridors of power was at that race. You'd bet your bottom dollar that you'd bump into some A-listers.

My brother walked into that room with his circus and the room was swamped with hundreds of people from around the world. Muhammad stopped the room cold – everybody there came to a standstill when he emerged. He was undeniably the most famous man in the world. It was at the pinnacle of his fame. You couldn't get a more famous crowd and he literally took over. Just by walking into the room, his presence, his words, that unmatchable star quality, had brought the room to a halt. The celebrities eagerly walked up to him, shook his hand exchanging pleasantries and he mingled with anyone and everyone. Now, that was the period when I stuck to my brother like a magnet. Wherever he went, whomever he met, I was right there over his shoulder. But I have always been a bit of an introvert. I'm the brother that stayed in his shadow observing. While Muhammad would be the centre of attention, I rarely interacted. I was content to watch my brother soak it all in. That day he was in full performance mode. It was always a sight to see.

THE SOVIET UNION

In 1976 Muhammad had been on a TV show when he admitted that he wouldn't be voting in the upcoming US election, pitting incumbent Gerald Ford against the democrat Jimmy Carter. 'I don't know anything about politics,' he shrugged, 'nor do I want people watching this show to be influenced by my feelings because I don't know anything about it. This was, in some ways, an unusual stance for my brother to take. For one, of course, he'd been very politically engaged in his earlier days, and certainly had plenty of time for certain politicians. He loved the Kennedys, for instance, after a small kindness they'd shown him – when we were getting ready for the Zaire fight against George Foreman, Teddy Kennedy sent one of his secretaries to fill out applications and have it authorised. Until then, our parents never travelled overseas when Muhammad fought. The simple reason was they didn't have a passport – like many black people in America, they didn't have copies of their birth certificates. So our parents and Muhammad got a passport, under the name 'Muhammad Ali', because his original passport was under his previous name 'Cassius Clay', and he became a big fan of the Kennedys from that moment on.

He also admitted, later, that he was generally in favour of Gerald Ford's administration. Immediately after beating George Foreman he was invited to the White House where he met Ford and his daughter. I went with him. King Hussein was in the country at the time, and knowing that my brother was a Muslim he arranged to meet him and entertain him at the White House. This was enough for Muhammad – he said that if he had to do any voting, while he didn't know enough about politics, he liked President Ford. But soon, he'd have occasion to do a favour for another president…

In February 1978 Muhammad fought and lost to a young Leon Spinks, a boxer not terribly well known compared to the more high-profile fighters at the time. He was a favourite going into the fight, and had been training hard, hitting the road at 5 a.m. in the mornings, taking the fight seriously even if others didn't. Spinks applauded my brother as he entered the ring, but when the fight started the younger man was all business, my brother going to the ropes as Spinks pummelled him almost unchallenged. Spinks couldn't dance like Muhammad, and he wasn't even that big, but he knew how to pile on the pressure, and he landed hundreds of punches while my brother talked to him in the ring. Muhammad won rounds here and there, and the final round was an all-out brawl, my brother knowing he needed a knockout to win. When the judges' decision went against him, several commentators were ready to pronounce his retirement right there and then. Muhammad, of course, had other ideas.

'I'll fight him again, Rudy,' he told me in the dressing room. 'I'm going to be world heavyweight champ for the third time.'

The rematch was set for September. In the meantime, Muhammad was invited to what was then called the Soviet Union. In one sense the purpose of the visit was to increase his visibility – he was in the twilight of his career, and not quite able to command the attention he once had – but also my brother had a certain interest in a country that promoted and endeavoured to spread communism, a nation that America was compared to in power, but one that conducted its affairs very differently from the United States. He took Veronica, but also his lawyer, manager Herbert Muhammad and several members of his entourage. My brother made a point of going not only to Moscow, but also down to Uzbekistan where there is a large Caucasian Muslim population. That was another element of it: Muhammad was always enamoured with the idea of meeting Muslims around the world. He wanted to connect with his brothers in religion wherever he could.

Another wrinkle in the arrangement was that ABC Sports had entered into an agreement with Muhammad's management to shoot a short documentary revolving around his time in the Soviet Union. At the time ABC News and ABC Sport were headed by Roone Arledge, who was the President of ABC News and Sport division, while a man named Charles Bierbauer was the ABC news correspondent and bureau chief in Moscow. The deal was made to cover Muhammad's visit in a country that limited exposure to the West, and so Bierbauer, his cameraman and a translator followed wherever my brother went and reported the nature of his visit.

It soon became apparent that Muhammad was a big deal to the Soviets – the political fraternity as well as the general populace. They saw this as an opportunity to treat a world sports figure well, and they did it in style. To them, my brother was an African-American athlete who had transcended sport, and could help them promote their own message if he chose to. Did he believe in communism and socialism? I don't know. I think there are elements of what the Soviet Union stood for that appealed to him – things that he saw as more equal in the Soviet Union. And, at the same time, the Soviet officials were on their best behaviour, aiming to portray this visit as an experience which Muhammad would eventually take back with him to show the Americans back in the West what a great country the Soviet Union was.

Muhammad certainly threw himself into understanding the country while he was there. He walked through Red Square and visited the Lenin mausoleum – the resting place of the late Soviet leader. Lenin had died in the 1920s, but his body still rests in Red Square and in those days people went to see him, encased inside a tomb almost like something from Madame Tussauds. When Muhammad came out, he turned to his American companion, Bierbauer, and asked, 'Is that really him?' It was the same kind of incredulous question any tourist might ask.

The second thing that stood out about the trip came when Muhammad went to Uzbekistan. He was taken to a mosque in Tashkent, the capital. The guides were able to take him inside the holy place. You have to remember that in some places you could do that, but most places you couldn't – depending on the local relationships between the government and the religious leaders. In this case, they were able to – Muhammad was able to pray with the local Muslims, almost certainly because he was such a famed international figure.

He had ample opportunity to discuss things with the Americans who accompanied him almost everywhere he went. One of the most thought-provoking conversations he had, it turned out, surrounded the difficulties the Muslims might have been having in the Soviet Union. The reality was, there were very few practising mosques in the country, despite the fact that a significant minority of the population was Muslim. It was a similar situation with Christian churches – many were closed down under the Soviet regime, but the Muslims had it far worse. The Soviet authorities had restricted religious activities in the Muslim community, and mosque numbers had decreased dramatically – from 25,000 in 1917 to less than 500 in the 1970s. As a journalist, Bierbauer was keen to convince Muhammad that what he was being shown was more of a show than a reality. The government, he made clear, was trying to conceal the truth.

Muhammad, meanwhile, was just as happy and confident talking to the people of the Soviet Union as he was in Chicago or Miami. His ability to transcend cultures just knew no bounds. One night when they were in a Tashkent hotel there were a group of American college musicians, maybe twenty, who were on a tour, and Muhammad just sat there for hours mingling with them engaged in thought-provoking conversations. Another day, he might be talking to Russian schoolkids or people on the street. He could talk to anyone.

★ ★ ★

He also mingled with Russia's best and brightest, of course. Early in the trip, he met with Leonid Brezhnev, who was the first secretary of the Communist Party, at the Kremlin. The Kremlin is a fortress with walls surrounding it. Although Moscow is globally known for its unique buildings, equally some of the other cities and former Soviet states also have a Kremlin, a fortress, and use that same name. The Kremlin in Moscow is the symbol of government power and its historic architecture. It's hard not to be impressed in that regard, just as you would in Paris, London or Washington and the other leading world capitals. Muhammad found the Kremlin a very eye-catching place. It still is a highly decorative symbol of Soviet power, even though the Kremlin as an architectural piece predates by centuries the Soviets coming to power.

Muhammad, of course, wasn't the first non-political high-profile personality to be entertained by a world leader: boxers have been visiting the White House for decades now. The difference was that this was Moscow. The Cold War was going on and Muhammad was an American boxer. But his familiarity and fame transcended sport. Boxing is the vehicle that made Muhammad prominent, but he differed from any other athlete in that he had taken some very prominent visible and vocal positions on issues such as the Vietnam War, on Islam, on black athletes – all things that were part of his essence, part of the reason people were attracted to him and wanted to hear his ideas.

When my brother met Brezhnev, Veronica and Herbert accompanied him. The only other non-Soviets in the room were the American cameraman and correspondent – no other Western journalists were permitted. Leonid had his official translator. Actually, he was more than a translator; he was an advisor and subsequent party chief and his English was flawless. This man could shift from a British accent to an American accent smoothly.

Muhammad was very complimentary as he engaged in conversation with the leader who seemed very pleased to have a sports hero in his company. 'This is the greatest honour of my life,' Muhammad remarked to Brezhnev as he shook the president's hand and posed for pictures. It was a statement that, to the premier, probably sounded more impressive than it was intended to. Prior to that Muhammad had spent a lot of time in the company of Bierbauer talking about his international experiences. The American remembered, in particular, Muhammad telling him about, as a Muslim, walking hand in hand in Mecca when he had met the King of Saudi Arabia. Bierbauer was very struck by that story and in its juxtaposition to the words Muhammad chose when he met with the Soviet president.

Later that day at the news conference, Bierbauer started to needle Muhammad. Maybe he was genuinely curious, but maybe he wanted to make mischief. I believe it was the latter. 'Muhammad, you're a Muslim who has walked hand in hand in Mecca with the King of Saudi Arabia,' he said, 'yet you told the President that meeting him at the Kremlin is the greatest honour of your life. Did you mean that or were you just being diplomatic?'

Muhammad looked at him for a second, then got that old twinkle in his eye.

'If I told my mother I love her more than any other woman in the world and then tell my wife I love *her* more than any other woman in the world,' he said, smiling, '...then would you say I'm being diplomatic?' All this was being translated in Russian to a large audience of Soviet journalists that were present, and in front of all of them my brother grinned and said to the crowd 'Good answer, huh?' Even the normally serious Soviets couldn't help but crack a few smiles.

After the conference, though, Muhammad was less jovial. 'Why are you trying to make me look bad in front of the Soviet people?' he asked Bierbauer.

By and large, though, my brother's experience of Russia was very positive. He wasn't well educated – he barely got out of high school. He didn't speak any other language. But still, he could hold his own with everyone from journalists to political leaders to little kids. Undoubtedly, the fact he was a globally well-known figure, probably as beloved as any political or religious leader or celebrity, helped. But he also was able to transcend politics and geographical barriers and all those things because of his gentle, outgoing nature. He treated everyone just the same, whether they could do anything for him or not. That's something that everyone can relate to.

Everyone has their own perspective after reading about a place, and I know my brother went to the Soviet Union expecting certain things, but I think he was pleasantly surprised when he arrived. The hospitality of the Russian people was surprising and Muhammad immediately latched on to that. The people were always affable. He told me later that he was treated warmly everywhere he went. He was never met with any hostility, nor was he confronted by police the way he still occasionally was in America. He'd jog in the early hours of the morning, he said, and no one even gave him a second glance, let alone stopped him to question what a black man was doing running.

Of course, some of this was probably manufactured by his reception committee. Boxing and sport in general was an opportunity for Soviets to show their might in another way, and it was a tool for the government, which they exploited. To this end they invested heavily. All the communist countries in developing sport and their national athletes are a means of showing off the successes of their nation, people and athletes.

With that in mind, the visit wasn't going to be complete without a visit to a boxing gym or stadium. An exhibition match with a couple of Russian boxers at the end of his visit was set up. This had been prearranged and my brother was happy to get in the ring. It received positive attention. It was a good show. Muhammad understood that value he carried as a celebrity and an ambassador for the American people, if not for the government.

Of course it was a propaganda move on the Soviets' part to entice Muhammad to the Soviet Union. It was of great value for them to have him meet Brezhnev and have him say favourable things about their leader and this nation that was so isolated from the West. But Muhammad was not the only one to have walked that road. We've had presidents and prime ministers who have seen the value of having extremely popular and adulated personalities associate with them. I think what he did was good for Muhammad. It was beneficial for him to see a different culture and society.

This wasn't the last time my brother would go to Russia, however. By now he had American presidents trying to ingratiate themselves with him, and President Jimmy Carter sent Muhammad on a government-endorsed mission to the Soviet Union the next year. That year, the US boycott of the 1980 Olympic Games became a major international issue, stemming from the Soviet invasion of Afghanistan in 1979 – in return, the Soviets would boycott the 1984 Olympic Games in Los Angeles. This was an era when politics truly invaded the athletic sphere. It wasn't the first time countries had used athletics to fight their battles by proxy and it wouldn't be the last, but now my brother was in the thick of it. Suddenly, you had prominent world leaders inviting Muhammad to be part of their team, or at least to give them the illusion of respectability by endorsing their regimes. 'Brezhnev gave me a spot in the Russian Kremlin,' my brother boasted on one American TV show. 'Mobutu gave me a spot in his government building. Sadat gave me a spot in Egypt. Marcos in the Philippines gave me a spot in the Muhammad Ali Mall. I have a mall in my name.' The contrast, in his mind, from how he'd been treated less than a decade beforehand in his own home country, couldn't be clearer. Even if these strongmen had their own reasons for how they acted, they were undeniably showing him respect that no other athlete, or celebrity for that matter, had been shown before.

TURNING OVER
A NEW LEAF

By the late 1970s my brother might have been stepping into the political arena and rubbing shoulders with world leaders, influencing international policy and home-town voters alike, but his own business acumen was still sadly lacking. Time and again, I warned him that his status meant that he would attract leeches – that he couldn't trust just anyone who came to him with a business proposition, but his naivety never really changed.

As his financial situation spiralled out of control, Muhammad's new lawyers in Chicago started to play a pivotal role in his life. My brother always had a stubborn streak where he had a tendency to not listen to anybody, and an inclination to do certain things his own way – and that hadn't changed over the decades. Often he'd agree to do what you told him, but then do the opposite, reverse course and do whatever he felt like. Part of the reason he contemplated having a representative was that for the third Norton fight, in September 1976, he was guaranteed $2.2 million for the bout. One thing in Muhammad's favour was that he always made sure his taxes were paid, unlike some famous people who employ clever accountants to help them avoid paying their share. In all his previous fights he had, more or less, paid all his taxes up front so he didn't have to worry about paying them later. He was adamant on getting that out of the way.

And so, for the Norton fight, Spiros Anthony, who was Muhammad's lawyer at the time but turned out to be a real chancer, was handling the finances for my brother. Well, to cut a long story short, when he was eventually caught out, he told Muhammad, 'I invested your money because I knew that you weren't going to invest it, and I lost it.' The thing with my brother was he always forgave people who took advantage. He never held a grudge. And when his own lawyer cheated him, Muhammad didn't want to press charges against him. But then he was compelled to sue. No doubt it was one of my brother's advisors who told him to take legal action. As a result, Anthony settled out of court paying Muhammad just under $400,000. The lawyer was out of Muhammad's life after that.

After this debacle, Muhammad asked a friend, Tim Shanahan, 'Do you know a good Jewish lawyer?' His friend, who had Irish roots, said, 'No, but I know a good Irish lawyer.' Muhammad agreed to go with Tim to the First National Bank law firm, and Muhammad ended up with two lawyers, William Struthers and Mike Phenner, who formed a team to take care of the world's most famous athlete's finances. This well-established firm in Chicago had fifty-two lawyers in their organisation. It was a legitimate firm. Prior to this another lawyer named Charles Lomax, an African-American, had also represented Muhammad – and was Herbert's lawyer – with some legal matters. But when Mike Phenner took over, Lomax was really out of the equation. In fact, they were of the understanding that Lomax had been detrimental in Muhammad's business affairs, allowing my brother to get into these bad deals and putting him in an untenable position.

Robert Abboud, the CEO of the bank, loved Muhammad. Not long after my brother hired the firm's lawyers, this executive asked one of his assistants to invite Muhammad in for a consultation, where he assured my brother that he would have his trust department look through all of Muhammad's finances and get them squared away promptly. After weeks of sifting through papers, the firm decided that what they needed to do was set up a trust fund to take care of my brother and his family financially. By 1978 Muhammad had earned an estimated $60 million – which would work out today at about $304 million – most of it generated between

1970 and 1978, after his comeback. Somehow, however, Muhammad had blown enough of his earnings that his estimated net worth in 1978 was merely $3.5 million.

Whenever Muhammad would visit his new financial advisor, there would be interest from the ladies – even after all his wars in the ring, he was, of course, a very handsome man. My brother would come in and hug Robert's secretary, wrap his arms around her in a friendly manner, then he would sit in the office and Robert would discuss business with him. 'All these people are taking advantage of you,' a concerned Robert eventually told him, 'and what we need to do is any time anybody comes to you with a deal or proposition, both of us are going to have to sign.' Muhammad said, 'OK.' He had just lost the fight to Spinks and he had a rematch set up. 'You'd better go and win that,' Robert said to him. 'If you lose you're going to have to take me on.' Next thing Muhammad stood up from his chair, put his hands on Robert's head – they were big enough to cover his entire scalp – and with that old glint in his eyes, said, 'I won't even have to train.'

Generally, though, Muhammad was very respectful to this man who kind of felt like an uncle to him. He told Robert that in the first outing against Spinks he had let victory slip by, and said with great conviction that there wasn't any question he wasn't going to win the rematch. I don't think Robert was completely convinced, but I knew my brother. I'd seen his condition, and I knew he could prevail again. Robert was less sure, but his job, after all, was financial, and he was determined to do it right. 'If you come with us I'll make sure we protect your money,' he told Muhammad. 'Our goal will be that you have $3 million of government tax-free bonds. So you'll be protected for the rest of your life.'

Boxing and finance weren't the only things my brother and his financial adviser talked about, however. Muhammad was still used to holding forth on politics and world affairs, and Robert seemed to enjoy talking to him. He once told me that, although a boxer, my brother was a man with a wonderful mind, a very intelligent and articulate human being. He also realised that he let people walk all over him because of his generosity.

Meanwhile, another man by the name of Barry Frank of IMG talent agency, based in Los Angeles, was drafted in as part of a three-man team tasked with generating money for my brother. Robert had initially phoned Barry to get him on board as they had been classmates at Harvard Business School. 'I'm calling you because I have a problem,' Robert told him. 'And I need your help. Muhammad Ali has come to us and he wants to take out a mortgage on a home he wants to buy. But financially we couldn't support that. As I looked into his finances, I found out he's broke. So I have undertaken to put him on the right path and I'm forming a three-man team to work with him. I'm going to handle his money. We have a lawyer here in a Chicago law firm who is going to be handling his legal stuff. And I want you to handle his promotion and fundraising.'

Barry, of course, was delighted to be aboard. Together with Robert, he would be part of the team trying to get Muhammad out of the financial straits he was in.

My brother's paperwork was far from in order when the team first went through it. The problem, in part, was those who were supposed to have been managing Muhammad's finances before and making the deals on his behalf hadn't really done their job at all. As I've said Muhammad basically travelled with an entourage of hangers-on and grifters who kept on coming up to him with ideas and with 'financial opportunities' for him, with zero fear of failure because it wouldn't be their money they were investing. Every last one was financially unviable, and many were straight-up insane, while others were simply squeezing money out of him without him knowing. Robert and Barry certainly had their work cut out.

The initial plan was simple. The bank, we agreed, would have to sign off on any money my brother wanted to give away – whether it was to relatives or friends or complete strangers, it didn't matter. Moreover, Muhammad had to have the approval of the committee, which was three members strong, for any major deal or business venture. Muhammad agreed reluctantly, and an administrator for the law firm and the bank named Marsh Thomas was assigned to his day-to-day affairs. Thomas would later move out to Los Angeles from Chicago, living very close to Muhammad when he later moved and looking every day at his finances – what came in and what went out.

It was a start, but it wasn't easy. Prior to seeking the services of his new advisors, Muhammad had got tangled up in innumerable deals that firms were reluctant to make good on. And now, with his career in decline, Barry didn't exactly see the major offers pouring in. After some time, Robert agreed to allow my brother to take out a mortgage he wanted, under strict supervision, which felt like a turning point. Marsh was doing a commendable job – really, they all were. It was about time Muhammad had someone like these guys handling his financial affairs.

One problem was that every time Robert's team found out about any deal Muhammad was involved in with a member of his entourage, it resulted in arguments. Muhammad was loyal to the hangers-on he regarded as friends and didn't want to give up on them. So even though he knew intellectually that these were bad deals he was reluctant to say no to them.

'I can't just say no!' he would tell Robert, only to meet the latter's implacable face.

'Well, now you have somebody who *can* say no,' the money man would tell him. 'And that's me.'

The biggest problem, of course, was his long-time manager Herbert Muhammad. My brother had been Herbert's meal ticket from the day he became his manager, and now Herbert desperately wanted to stay with Muhammad and continue to do deals for him, despite the fact he was now being handled by very experienced men. It was a constant struggle for Robert and his team because Muhammad kept leaning towards and listening to Herbert, whose coaxing continued, as he saw him as his religious leader. Robert, to his credit, somehow kept him under wraps, while endlessly shooting down the deals that Herbert kept bringing to the table. Robert and Barry believed that Herbert was in it for Herbert, but Muhammad still felt a duty towards the man who'd accompanied him for so many years and still took a third of all of his earnings. Slowly, though, the team turned things around.

If there were any problems with this arrangement, they came from Muhammad. He'd still find ways to give money away, not only paying for the family's car and life insurance and sundry expenses, but handing out cash to cousins and friends whenever he had it. He would be under control for months and then get derailed. It was an uphill struggle, but my brother's advisors eventually got him to a point where he had $2 million in tax-free bonds in the bank. I can tell you that Veronica was relieved that someone genuine was taking care of their financial affairs at last. Not only Muhammad had been in need of help, as some of their staff had been caught stealing. Drivers would stroll into the bedroom and steal her jewellery and other valuables. The thing is, my brother refused to sack them. This, inevitably, had led to a huge amount of tension between the two, taking a toll on their relationship, and I could tell she was relieved to think that someone might finally be handling the problem.

★ ★ ★

Not long after first signing these papers, Muhammad, Veronica, Muhammad's friend Tim and his wife Helga, and Muhammad's two kids Hana and Laila moved from Chicago to Los Angeles in 1979. I would continue to live in Chicago with my second wife. It was what I would call a quiet life, far from the crazy days of following my brother to social engagements and media obligations.

When Muhammad first saw Veronica Porche, at an airport in Salt Lake City in 1974, he told me, 'I just saw the most beautiful woman in the world.' One thing that Muhammad always wanted was a wife that 'looked' like his wife – like part of the perfect couple that he always envisioned being. Veronica more than fit the bill – so much, in fact, that at first he was petrified to go up to her and engage in a conversation. That wasn't unusual because Muhammad might have been outgoing and outspoken with almost everyone, but beautiful women intimidated him more than anyone else, including the bruisers he'd regularly step into the ring against. Still, this time, he knew, he'd have to get over his nerves.

Veronica, it turned out, was shy too. She was certainly beautiful, but part of the reason my brother, I found out myself, was mesmerised by her was that she was reserved, not at all worldly. When Muhammad first asked Veronica to come and live with him, she was only eighteen…and she said that she had to ask her mother first! She was in that phase of transitioning from being a teenager to an adult, and it still wasn't out of the ordinary for her to ask her parents if she had to go some places – just like any schoolkid. So, Muhammad and Veronica phoned her parents and they got permission for her to move in.

Veronica was smart, too. This was something else my brother wanted, and valued, though only up to a point. She was going to go to UCLA – she was a straight-A student – and she wanted to go back to medical school when she met Muhammad, which was where the problems began. Independence, unlike beauty and brains, was something that my brother didn't value too much. In fact, it really worried him.

Because of this, he was adamant that the medical school idea wouldn't work. Ali and Veronica had been living together as husband and wife for about four years by now, and he would tell her with great concern, 'The wife of the heavyweight champion of the world can't be going to college and all these young white boys hitting on her. You don't want that, Veronica.' He added, 'You're my wife, school is finished. You're Muhammad Ali's wife, you're not a student.' Muhammad was very protective of her: almost too much.

After Muhammad divorced his second wife Belinda, and before he married Veronica, he expected some of his friends to take sides. This felt unfair to many. How do you take sides when you're friends with the husband and the wife too? As it happens, one of Muhammad's friends and his wife were travelling and had a stop at Chicago airport for five hours before their next flight. So they called Belinda and all three of them met at the airport, had dinner and talked. It had been, in fact, Belinda's idea. She said to the couple, 'Why don't I come and have dinner with you?' They told her that it would be a good idea. Muhammad found out and phoned his friend and in no uncertain terms said, 'Why would you go and have dinner with Belinda?' His friend said, 'What do you mean, Champ?' He said, 'Well, you had dinner with Belinda! My cousin told me. He took Belinda to the airport to meet you for dinner.' The stunned friend, in a defensive mode, replied, 'She called me. We talked about old times and we had dinner.' But Muhammad was all huffy puffy about the whole scenario. He got over it soon, though. So, my brother had that side to him when it came to his wives.

Eventually, Veronica had to accept that even though the one thing she wanted in life was to be a doctor, she would have to put that aside if she wanted to stay with Muhammad. She would eventually become a doctor, but only after she left him.

They had two lovely children, Laila and Hana, of course, and the children were the most important thing to my brother. He was at a stage where he could offer more time to his family and really cherish his children. By now his sports career was nearing an end, and he started to put the same work ethic he once put into training into raising his children. Whenever he was home he would make a point to be with the children, something he had failed to do with the children with his ex-wife. He'd drive them to school and pick them up. He would always have dinner with the family. Occasionally, when he wanted to make something special on a Sunday morning, he would make pancakes with butter and syrup. He started to settle down, and you could tell that he loved it. Being the most recognised face in the world, he wanted to make sure that he was a good father and a good husband to set an example.

Sometimes in the morning he got up early because he was an insomniac. Before he went to sleep his mind would be active, thinking about all the children that were going to bed hungry, one of the things in the world that he worried about the most. He would try to figure out how he could use his fame to help those children and eradicate hunger around the world. Because it was hard for him to sleep straight through he would get up in the morning before everyone else and he would make breakfast for his children.

For Muhammad, it was cornflakes for breakfast. He just loved them, maybe even more so than the kids. That wasn't the end of his sweet tooth, either – one drink that he always consumed every day was orange juice. It was almost mandatory for him to have his OJ. And he liked coffee too, really developing a taste for it after his training days were over.

Veronica was a late sleeper. Muhammad was always up before her and sometimes he would leave early in the morning and go for a ride. He loved to take the Rolls-Royce out on a cruise. When he was travelling and staying in a hotel, he would rise at 5.30 or 6.00 a.m. and he'd take a nice brisk walk to enjoy the peace and serenity. It was his escape mechanism. Nobody was on the street at that time so nobody could bother him. He would go sightseeing. Anywhere Muhammad went, he didn't care whether it was crowded or not, he wanted to see how normal people lived because he in a sense felt isolated because of the enormous fame attached to him. Muhammad had been idolised and he was curious to see what things were like without being seen. Above all he had a penchant for surprising people. He made their day. Just having Muhammad look at you, paying attention to you, was a big deal to any mere mortal. And I witnessed on many occasions the look etched on a boy's face. My brother said to me, 'People forget what you say, people forget what you do, but people will always remember how you made them feel.' He added, 'I never want anybody to feel like I did when Sugar Ray Robinson refused me an autograph.'

During his walks if he didn't look at people they wouldn't approach him, but once you made eye contact with him or he waved you over, one person would come, then two, three and then everyone would come over and gather around him. It was same when he had dinner in a restaurant. When he was out for dinner in Los Angeles with Veronica she would warn him, 'Don't start signing autographs before dinner because dinner will get cold!' He would always promise her, saying, 'OK, OK, I won't sign anything.' Because if he started to sign, we all knew, he'd never get to his dinner and it would be cold on the plate by the time the last fan left. Despite his vow to his wife, though, I never once saw him keep it. The fans would line up at his table and he'd sign every single autograph. He said, 'If you see Muhammad Ali come to a restaurant and they say, 'Oh, my God, that's Muhammad Ali,' and they've never seen a celebrity in their life and when you sign an autograph they'll remember it for the rest of their life and you've made their day. I never look down on people who look up to me.'

★ ★ ★

Not long after my brother moved to California, the Jacksons were on a tour that included a stop in Los Angeles, playing at the Forum three nights in a row. The day before their first concert, Muhammad was at home lounging around with Tim, who was a frequent visitor, when the gate rang Muhammad's phone to inform him that he had visitors. Muhammad asked, 'Who is it?' The man replied, 'They said, "We're the

Jacksons."' My brother told the man to let them in. Muhammad told his friend to follow him and they both got to the door and a white Rolls-Royce glided in. In the passenger side was Michael. Randy was driving and Tito was sitting at the back. Michael got out of the car, and Muhammad was on top of the steps barking to the neighbourhood, 'Look, everybody! Michael Jackson's here! My friend Michael Jackson's here to see Muhammad Ali! Everybody look, my friend Michael Jackson's coming up my stairs!' The only person who could hear him in this quite prosperous neighbourhood was a gardener across the street with a lawnmower, who waved and laughed.

Michael walked up to the door and entered the house and they gave each other a big hug. The two brothers followed, both embracing Muhammad. 'I can't believe I'm at Muhammad Ali's house,' was the first thing Michael blurted out. 'I can't believe I'm here. Remember when I came to visit you at Deer Lake and you came to meet us at the airport?' I had met Michael and all his brothers at the camp. They seemed like very polite and affable young men. Everyone settled in the room. A big white piano lay in a corner. Michael had just embarked on a solo career a year or two before, but now they had decided to regroup. 'Michael, you know, play my favourite song,' Muhammad told the youngest Jackson. 'I'll Be There' was one of my brother's favourite songs. So Michael sat down and he played the first verse and it was beautiful.

Next, Muhammad said, 'Dance for me, Michael. Do the James Brown.' Tim happened to have a tape recorder and he had a James Brown cassette in it. Tim had actually bought my brother the cassette, and whenever they were in his Rolls-Royce cruising they'd listen to Michael Jackson and the Jackson Five, Smokey Robinson, Aretha Franklin and James Brown. Michael said he didn't want to dance. But then Tim turned on 'I Feel Good' and Michael did a James Brown on the wooden floor – they pulled the rug out to set the stage. 'I feel good, I knew that I would, now. I feel good...' – Michael was singing and doing the James Brown – '...I feel nice, like sugar and spice... .... ' Muhammad was clapping his hands, laughing and having a ball while the others looked on with wide smiles. My brother loved anybody that danced. Jackie Wilson, James Brown and Chubby Checker were some of the musicians he adored. However, he had an affinity for Michael because he thought he was the best dancer he'd ever seen, even better than Brown.

There were two chairs and a couch in the office and Muhammad sat down behind his desk, the Jacksons sat on the two chairs and one of them on the couch with Tim. As the conversation moved towards the tour, my brother spontaneously and in jest asked them, 'You don't do drugs, do you?' Michael, in his baby-like soft voice, replied, 'No, man, we don't do drugs.' Muhammad said, 'Yeah, you don't need drugs; all these entertainers that do drugs, don't they know they're on a natural high when they're entertaining?' He continued, 'You don't need drugs to do that, you have the experience… you don't need to be sleeping and half dead when you're performing and making people happy.' I must add this was one of the things my brother promoted – no drugs. He didn't drink, smoke, he had no vices. The only thing he had a weakness for was women. Michael was the same way in that he was a health food nut and was conscious about what he fed his body. He asked Muhammad, 'You eat healthy?' Muhammad replied, 'Yeah, I eat healthy when I train. I have to eat healthy.' Then he asked, 'What do you do?' Michael said, 'I'm on a health food diet. When I'm in LA I always go to this health food store on St Vincent Boulevard.' He gave Muhammad the address of this place. 'We should go there sometime. I'll take you and show you the food.' This was a restaurant that served health foods. Since Veronica was into health foods too, she actually ended up going there with Michael instead. One day Muhammad wasn't home and Michael wanted to go to the restaurant, so he picked up Veronica instead.

Randy and Tito were shy and reserved. They didn't engage much. Instead, they were listening to Muhammad and their brother. They didn't interject at all. When Muhammad asked them a question they'd answer in a short sentence then let Michael take over. Michael was a born leader. No wonder he was the one who became more famous out of all the brothers.

Michael had to go to the bathroom, which was on the first floor right outside Muhammad's office. After he went in Muhammad got up from the desk and sneaked up outside the door. He thought it would be a good idea to play a prank on his unsuspecting guest. He put all of his weight behind the door, leaning against it, waiting for the toilet flush.

Michael tried to come out but couldn't open the door. He was jiggling the door knob, tried to push the door open but couldn't. 'Muhammad, the door's stuck!' he shouted in his baby-like voice. 'Muhammad, the door's stuck!' You could sense that he was trying to use his shoulder to push it open. After several failed attempts, it seemed like Michael had had enough. Muhammad ran back to his desk and sat on his chair, and he shouted, 'Try again!' Michael used his shoulder to push hard again and suddenly flew out like a rocket. Everyone burst out laughing. 'Oh, you got me, man, you got me,' Michael said. My brother loved to play this trick on guests visiting him. I remember he once tried the same thing with a sportswriter at his Michigan house years later. Muhammad's endearing sense of humour always cracked his victims up.

The Jacksons knew my brother was a prankster because they had spent time with him on numerous occasions before. They had not only visited him at his home in Hancock Park, but also when he was living on the East Coast in New Jersey. And, of course, they had frequented the training camp. Muhammad would go to their concerts and they would go to his hotel room and hang out. The Jacksons were only kids. He would always tell them that he was the prettiest in the group.

Michael loved my brother, just like all his other brothers did. Michael could be timid, but he was a strong person for his size. Michael could protect himself, so he would always say to Muhammad, 'Come on, Champ, show me some moves!' And they enjoyed messing around. They would hit him in the stomach. They would spar all the time and the champ would hit Michael lightly on the side of the head and Michael would try to get a lucky punch in. The brothers had taken martial arts lessons but their hectic travel schedule prevented them maintaining it. Jermaine actually became a fellow acting classmate of Veronica's when they both were taking acting classes.

There was an interesting development after my brother and Belinda divorced, however. Muhammad and Belinda had known Michael and the Jacksons for years. Michael loved them both and would come around to the Ali household when they were living on the East Coast. After Muhammad divorced Belinda, Michael went over to California with the intention of moving out there. She was shocked, though, when

Michael revealed that he had a crush on her. He was such a nice guy, and this was, quite honestly, pretty out of character for him. He wanted Belinda to go with him, wanted her to move in with him. She said, 'Wait a minute, baby. No, no, no. I don't like you like that.' He said, 'We'd be wonderful together.' Whatever else, Michael certainly had a thing for older women then.

So, they never got together, but Michael and Belinda became really friendly. She became very good friends with his whole family. They would sneak out to roller skating and did a lot of social things together. She found him a wonderful person and always cared about him as a friend.

Even decades later, with all the accusations and bad press the King of Pop garnered, this still didn't put a dent in their friendship. At the time, we believed Michael was innocent. Now, I don't know what he did or didn't do, but I do know he was a very troubled young man. He never loved himself, and never loved his own colour. That in itself is a very sad thing. Muhammad would always tell me, 'Black is beautiful.'

BUSINESS BLUNDERS

One thing about dropping by Muhammad's house was that you never quite knew whom you might bump into. My brother typically had one or two visitors lounging around, from Bundini Brown to members of the entourage to hangers-on who just dropped by and then inexplicably never left. It could be frustrating enough if all you wanted was some quiet time alone with him, but if you wanted to do business with him – well, it wasn't always easy. The man I most felt for in this regard was Barry Frank, the IMG agent who represented Muhammad across a couple of stints in the late seventies and mid-eighties. Whenever my brother wanted to discuss business, Frank would suggest sending the entourage elsewhere, only to get the same answer from him every time – 'These are my friends. They get to hear my business.' – and then be presented by whatever scheme Muhammad had been concocting.

On one particular day, Frank dropped by the house to discuss a business proposition Muhammad had been thinking about. The same old pantomime started again. 'No, no,' I remember Frank saying. 'We're not going to discuss business in front of all of these people. This is your personal business. I won't do that.' Muhammad was adamant. 'No, no. it's OK. They're my friends. They won't talk to anybody. They get to stay here and hear my business.' But Barry was unwilling and insisted, 'Well, I'm not going to discuss my business with you in front of all these people.

But if you have any business you want to talk to me about that's OK. They can stay and listen.'

As it turned out, Muhammad had a rather unusual idea that one of his friends had planted in his head. This friend, my brother explained, convinced Muhammad that he should sell his own car – an Ali-branded automobile that, my brother was quickly persuaded, would sell like crazy. I remember the incredulous look on Frank's face as my brother outlined his plan, alongside his exasperation when he tried to explain to my brother just how much it would cost to enter the automobile business. Barry really did try his best to explain the magnitude of such a project, only for Muhammad, who didn't really understand the intricacies of economics, to ask him, 'Well, can't we raise that kind of money?'

'No,' replied Barry. 'No one would put up the money. There are plenty of cars to choose from and you're not known – you're not a race car driver.'

'Yes, but my friend says it's a great idea,' said Muhammad.

'Well, I'm telling you it's the worst idea I ever heard,' said Barry in an assertive tone. 'I won't let you do it.' Muhammad said, 'Well, what do I do? What do I tell this man? What are we going to say to him?' It seemed like he was more concerned about letting his friend down. Barry bluntly said, 'You tell him that I said it was a crazy fucking idea, forget it.'

Next up, there was a guy who had convinced my brother that there wasn't just a market for a Muhammad Ali soft drink, but that it would be more popular than Coca-Cola. He pitched it to my brother as Barry listened in, and Barry, who was used to this stuff by now, couldn't help but butt in: 'Do you know how much money it would cost to get into that? How much would be required to spend on advertising?'

'No, how much?' my brother replied.

'Millions and millions of dollars.'

'We can make that. We can raise that,' said Muhammad, once again. Barry did his best to make it clear that this was a preposterous notion, but again it was difficult to escape the idea that my brother's main interest was looking like a big shot in front of his friends. In fact, Barry had come to see him with the intention of discussing important things, so he kept waiting in the vain hope that the people lingering about would vanish, but they didn't. Barry's impression was that Muhammad was mostly concerned with conveying how important he was, how dominant he was and how he could make this white Jewish guy listen to him and pay attention to his ideas. Muhammad wanted to show off in front of his entourage – that's what that was all about, Barry felt.

On that day, the entourage was comprised of Muhammad's usual group headed by Bundini Brown, who was still a close friend and advisor and kind of head of the entourage. After discerning that Muhammad wasn't going to budge, and his friends were not going to leave to give the two men privacy for a confidential business chat, Barry had had enough. His voice full of despair, he said, 'OK. That's it. I'm done, Muhammad, goodbye.' He left after being there for an hour and a half.

For years my brother had taken some heavy financial blows when he started investing in business ventures, and especially in businesses that had no chance to prosper. At one point, someone had lured him into investing in a business they named Ali's Trolley: a trolley car which was converted into a chicken restaurant, like a fried chicken restaurant to go. At the time Muhammad was preparing for the third Ken Norton fight, and the guy who came up with the concept was a friend of his. He said that he had the secret recipe from Kentucky Fried Chicken, which would have been a big deal at the time. Was it true? I doubt it, but my brother believed it. Well, I must admit the chicken was good, for sure, but there was no future. It was a small place which had six tables inside and it was a takeaway where you sit down. On top of that, the individual that they hired to manage the place was absolutely terrible.

It was good food and people liked it, albeit it was located in a place where there was no hope of getting a huge crowd. The site was a well-off area and not what you call an average neighbourhood where you would expect the public to go in to eat. It was a very poor decision that Muhammad had made. Muhammad's friend Tim Shanahan tried to dissuade him beforehand about this venture. 'This isn't going to be very successful,' he warned him. 'How many chickens do you have to sell each day to make a profit?' Yet, my brother went ahead and pursued this venture anyway because he liked the guy who came in with the idea. Moreover, he considered him a friend and it was hard for him to let down a friend. Anyway, this ran for under a year I think. They closed it down because they found themselves pumping in a colossal amount of money every month and not making anything. I think he lost $90,000.

This failure didn't stop him as other business proposals came flooding in. After the food business a guy came up with Champ Soda. This was just a soda company that would manufacture a soft drink using Muhammad's name and image. This factory was in Detroit as the guy who came up with the idea was from there. The scheming individual was definitely a crook, and the reason he got to see Muhammad was that he had befriended Jimmy Ellis. The crook promised Ellis a part of the business if he sealed the deal for him. So Ellis, with sincere intentions, brought him to Muhammad to present the proposal. That's how this venture all started. Muhammad trusted the guy because he came as a recommendation from Ellis. Muhammad, not surprisingly, gave the green light thinking millions would be having a drink with his name on. That lasted about the same amount of time. I think Muhammad invested about $100,000 in this one. They got it up and running, but it didn't go anywhere. They got the cans and soda manufacturing process started, but, again, poor management was part of the problem. Another dead end.

By now certain individuals were piling in with offers of business opportunities for the heavyweight champion of the world. The business pitches came rolling in when Muhammad's friends and associates realised their famous friend was the man to get to invest in their ambitious ideas. Other things such as exercise-related products and gimmicks followed – even Muhammad Ali spas in hotels. One of the most unusual ones was when he was plunged into a deal with some shady character where he was going to invest in Saudi Arabia in water, believe it or not. A group of people persuaded Muhammad that in Saudi Arabia water was more important than oil. So they were going to get him to invest in Mack trucks to transport water all over the country. 'There's definitely a need for water,' they told him, 'because of the desert.' Again, a lot of money went down the drain. Anything that was brought to Muhammad, whether it was with sincere or ill intentions, he seemed to blindly embrace it.

UNUSUAL ENCOUNTERS

One of the things Muhammad's new team of advisors had diligently focused on was to plan his retirement. They did a retirement special on TV, in which Muhammad officially announced his withdrawal from the sport of boxing in June 1979. A month before announcing his retirement, he did a tour of Europe, which was basically a nine-day trip with my brother fighting three-round exhibition matches in each city. This was Muhammad's farewell tour, and he was expected to make a lot of money from it.

Veronica, I know, was totally opposed to him ever fighting again. So were our parents, who were always conscious of the toll earlier fights had taken on him. His inner circle was more mixed: Bundini and Dundee, I'm fairly sure, would have been happy to see him quit the ring for good, but he knew they'd always be there to support him if he was determined to come back. Herbert, Don King and the rest said the same – that they'd have no choice but to support a comeback – but I suspect the prospect of one more payday had to appeal. Barry Frank and the new financial team, however, certainly wanted my brother to stay retired this time.

As plans for the tour of Europe kicked off, Bundini wanted to tag along. However, Barry had strong reservations and succinctly said to Muhammad, 'No. Bundini is not coming.' Muhammad, who always welcomed his close entourage members, was insistent. 'Bundini wants to come,' he insisted. 'We're bringing him.' Barry said, 'I'm not paying for his airfare. I'm not paying for his hotel room. I'm not going to take Bundini to Europe.' Muhammad was adamant and told Barry, 'Well, Bundini wants to come and I'm paying for it.' And so Muhammad facilitated it. Bundini was looking to make the most out of the trip and he brought a chest of drawers with him, and in there he had lots of Muhammad Ali memorabilia – T-shirts, boxing gloves, jockstraps, you name it. Having been the cornerman, anything Muhammad had used while training and boxing, Bundini had carefully preserved. He'd follow my brother around and would pick up stuff he'd worn and thrown away. At these exhibition fights in Europe, he exploited the opportunity of getting up close and personal with the champ's biggest fans. He made bundles of cash, just another crazy friend that Muhammad let hang around and exploit him. To some extent, my brother knew it was happening, but he didn't have a problem with that as he considered his friend an integral part of his circle. Apparently, Muhammad's agents did have a problem, and by now had had enough of these men.

The thing that surfaces above anything else about that tour of Europe is Muhammad discussing history with Barry. One of the places they went was Denmark. Barry was a Shakespeare fan and when he was with my brother he wanted to go and see Hamlet's spiritual home. He decided to leave the rest of the entourage to do their own thing for a day and he went and checked out the country. When he came back, Muhammad questioned his agent, 'Where were you?' He told him. And my brother, curious, asked, 'Why did you go there?' And he replied, 'Well, because I wanted to see where Hamlet was from.' Muhammad, who had no clue who Hamlet was, asked, 'Who is Hamlet?' Barry proceeded to tell him the story of Hamlet and Muhammad was clearly fascinated. The thing with my brother was when he was having a conversation with someone and the person didn't grab his attention early then he often had a tendency to not pay much attention. He especially did this with journalists who were somewhat drifting towards mundane questions – but something about the story of this Danish prince gripped him. Muhammad kept on asking Barry questions: 'Why did Hamlet do this and that?' In the end, Barry spent two hours talking about Hamlet with him.

At the end Muhammad said, 'Thank you. That was really interesting.' You see, my brother had a curious mind and he liked things like that. It was a fairy tale to him, but he knew Shakespeare was somebody to be respected and if that was his most famous work then he was interested in it.

★ ★ ★

In England Muhammad and his handlers stayed at the Hilton Hotel in Park Lane, which was where he'd eventually meet another fan who'd introduce him to a whole new world. Charlie Hale, a mixed-race youngster from the north of England, was sixteen when he got a sniff of Muhammad's visit and couldn't resist making a trip to the big city to meet his hero. It was a big thing back then going to London, when travel was tougher, but Charlie and his friends made it – and then started to strategise about how to meet their idol. Taking charge, Charlie said to his friends, 'Leave it to me.' He further warned, 'If you look nervous, they're going to pull you out.' He had a trick up his sleeve and told his friends that if they could convince the hotel staff and the security that they were part of the hotel, then they could just saunter in with relative ease.

When they made their approach, Muhammad, Bundini, Howard Bingham, Jimmy Ellis and a couple of others were sitting around this large table on the ground floor of the hotel savouring lunch. It's a scene my brother and I had often experienced with his jet-set lifestyle, one he was well acquainted with by this stage of his career. Despite the elegance of the hotel, Muhammad was in a red tracksuit with black stripes. He liked to be comfortable.

Charlie's plan worked, somehow. He managed to slip in confidently and told his crew to wait outside for his signal. He peeked into the room in the hope of spotting Muhammad. It didn't take long for him to figure out where the crew were and he wasted no time sauntering back to the door and winked to his gang who were eagerly waiting, holding their breaths. 'Follow me,' the young man told his crew. The visitors walked up to the table and Charlie greeted Muhammad, who was more than welcoming and shook the young man's hand. 'I came to see you spar with John L Gardner,' Charlie said. 'Remember I was shouting?' Without much hesitation Muhammad replied, 'Yeah, yeah.' My brother's disarming smile would always make anyone feel at home.

Understandably the young man thought Muhammad would have forgotten him. But my brother's memory was sharp and he remembered his first encounter with this effervescent young man the year before. You see, Muhammad crossed paths with so many people and mostly he'd forget them, but sometimes he did remember them. With reporters, whom he bumped into fairly regularly considering they'd show up at press conferences and his fights, he remembered faces but often had a hard time remembering their names – and these were men who were in constant contact with him. Nevertheless, whenever a person met him for the second or third time and tried to get Muhammad to recall their initial meeting, he had a tendency to say, 'Oh, yeah, I remember you,' while in actual fact often he didn't have a clue. So he would tell a little white lie. Primarily he did this because he wanted to make that person feel worthy.

Anyway, this guy's face hadn't eluded my brother due to a memorable incident that had taken place. His memory was as sharp as a razor. Muhammad had fought an exhibition fight for charity at the Shaftesbury Theatre. It was more of a sparring match with John L Gardner. At the time Charlie was a young teenage professional footballer who had signed on for a professional club. After the bout, which by the way was attended by several thousand fans, all packed out, Muhammad and his conditioning trainer Luis Serra were hanging out in this rather small side room on the first floor. Several people were coming in and out sporadically. Then Charlie walked in. His first impression of Muhammad was he thought he had darker skin than he had believed. He had always thought that Muhammad had the same colour skin as him, which was fairly light brown. But when he laid his eyes on my brother for the first time he was stunned. Muhammad was a few shades darker than he had realised.

Anyway, Muhammad had been receptive and engaged with him, listening to the young man talk about how he'd spouted a poem imitating him on a TV show. Then he proceeded to do the dazzling Ali shuffle, which impressed Muhammad. To make him feel good, Muhammad said to him, 'Your feet are faster than mine.' My brother was on the verge of being an over-the-hill fighter by then; he wasn't the fighter he once was. He said, 'I'm tired, I'm tired. I can't dance any more. My legs can't dance.' But my brother wasn't going to let this teenager do all the gloating. He didn't just stand there talking while others garnered the limelight. No. Muhammad was compelled to throw punches, shadow-boxing and was in a jovial mood. That was my brother. Whether he was in front of millions on TV or conversing with a couple of people, he yearned for the spotlight. You weren't going to be showing him something and not let him interject to show you who was really the brashest, boldest man you'd ever seen. 'You're the greatest in the ring,' Charlie said, mesmerised by his charm, 'but you're even greater outside.'

As Muhammad mingled with this enthusiastic fan and his masseuse looked on, suddenly three young men approached them. And they singled out Muhammad to try to pull a fast one on him, given the fact he was known to say yes. The so-called leader said to him, 'We run the Gerald Sinstadt Boxing Club, Muhammad, and we're looking for some donations.' Gerald Sinstadt was a famous football commentator on TV. However, the problem was he didn't have a boxing club. Charlie, curious, jumped in straight away interjecting, 'Muhammad, I know Gerald Sinstadt. He doesn't have a boxing club. Don't give them anything.' He was trying ever so hard to dissuade Muhammad, and he continued, 'These boys are having you on. I know Gerald Sinstadt. He's a friend of mine.'

Anyway, next thing you know these three guys' faces went whiter than white because they realised they had been rumbled. My brother apparently didn't take much notice of the warning, but Charlie was adamant and said, 'Muhammad, they're conning you, believe me.' The culprits, trying to conceal the truth, attempted to put up a verbal fight arguing, 'There is!' Charlie said, 'No there's not.' One of them was speaking while the other two were hiding their heads in shame. Regardless, Muhammad took some money out of his pocket and actually gave it to them. A bemused Charlie said, 'Muhammad, look, there's no boxing club.' My brother just shrugged his shoulders as if to say it didn't really matter. So Muhammad hadn't forgotten his first encounter with the young man who tried to warn him of deceiving individuals on his last visit across the pond.

Anyway, now their paths had crossed again and my brother held his hand out beckoning Charlie to sit down. The rest of his flock followed. 'I'm a little tired at the moment,' Muhammad said to Charlie. The hectic travel schedule and flying had resulted in jet lag. He wasn't the usual bright, brash man that day; he was weary but wasn't going to turn these men back.

★ ★ ★

As Muhammad shared pleasantries with Charlie, the rest of his group listened on. He was just finishing off a bottle of Coke, and suddenly a guy emerged out of nowhere, and with no real warning proceeded to poke Muhammad in the chest, which caught my brother off guard. With it came a tirade of verbal abuse. The lunatic was barking at my brother, 'Joe Louis is better than you!' The guy was only about 5 feet 7 inches tall and in his mid-forties. Muhammad just glanced at him before looking away in an attempt to ignore him. Those sitting at the table were stunned into silence – nobody reacted verbally or physically. It was if everyone froze. Charlie, being the young man at the time full of vigour, sprung up and pushed this guy so hard he flew to the other side of the room landing on his ass.

He stood back up, dazed and startled, having been caught off guard himself, and walked out in a rage barking about his alleged hero Joe Louis. Charlie was shouting back, 'Get out, you arse-witted moron!' before sitting back down. Next thing you know, Muhammad was laughing at him and giggling because he found Charlie's impulsive reaction amusing. My brother liked the idea of a young man having a great affinity towards him and standing up for him in his defence. And the way that guy went flying could've given any man a good laugh. Muhammad's crew were more or less soaking it all in. The guy was trying to provoke a reaction from my brother. But Muhammad had refrained from falling for his bait, but the fact he didn't react in any way was surprising. Knowing my brother, if anything, he would have reacted verbally. He turned around to Charlie and said something very poignant. 'Look, the man is wrong,' he said. 'Sugar Ray Robinson is the greatest of all time. I'm the greatest heavyweight. I would've beaten any heavyweight.' Muhammad, who had completely ignored the guy, continued, 'You don't give anybody like that

Left: Training with Clarence Griffin at Windy City Boxing Club.   © *Montell Griffin*

Right: Muhammad loved engaging his fans in conversation at the Deer Lake camp. As here, they'd often just knock on the door.

© *Kareemah Andrews*

Left: With his corner man, Bundini Brown, preparing for the Larry Holmes fight in 1981.

© *Kareemah Andrews*

Left: My brother loved listening to his reel-to-reel tape player when relaxing at Deer Lake.

© *Kareemah Andre*

Right: Everyone was welcome! Here you see Muhammad clowning with one of the kids, who'd decided to stare him down.

© *Kareemah Andrews*

Left: Bundini Brown, myself and the team surround Muhammad after a hard training session at Deer Lake.

© *Kareemah Andre*

Right: Muhammad play-sparring with current WBC president Mauricio Sulaiman. Early 1980s.

Photo courtesy of WBC / Mauricio Sulaiman

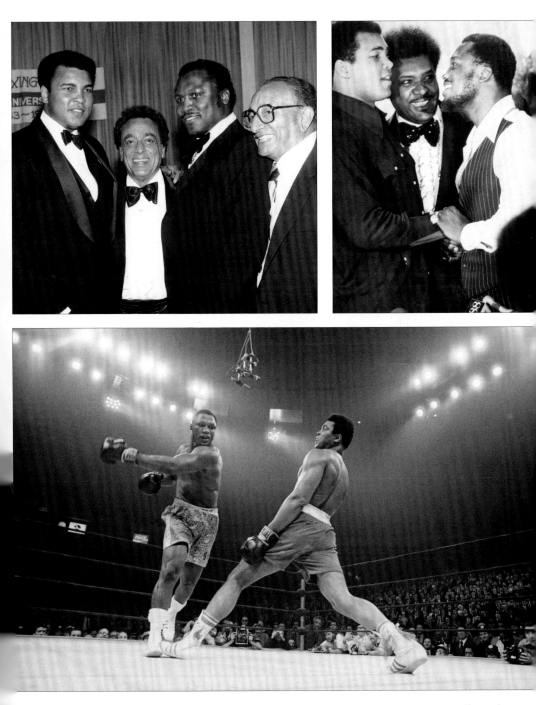

Above left: The relationship between my brother and his greatest rival was complicated, but ultimately ended in mutual respect. Here they pose together at a WBC gala dinner.

Photo courtesy of WBC

Above right: Don King orchestrates a press conference between Muhammad and Joe Frazier before the Thrilla in Manilla.

© New York Daily News Archive / Getty

Below: Frazier: Part I. In my opinion, one of the greatest sporting photographs of all time. Just look at the grace – the pure geometry – of my brother's movement here. The 'sweet science' at its very best.

© Bettmann / Getty

Above left: Sweaty training for the Rumble in the Jungle in Zaire. I work a heavy bag in the background whilst Muhammad puts on a skipping exhibition for the press.

© Agence France Presse / Gett

Above right: A photo that captures the heat and brutality of the legendary fight with Foreman. Just look at that sweat fly.

© Bettmann / Gett

Below: Foreman hits the canvas as my brother prowls the ring.

© Tony Triolo / Gett

Left: I accompanied my brother everywhere he went. Here, we were in New York on one of our many business trips.

Right: The giant Antonio Inoki aims a flying kick at my brother's knee. You can see what he was up against in this strange but dangerous fight.

© *Takeo Tanuma / Getty*

Left: Muhammad being interviewed by American ABC News journalist Charles Bierbauer in the Soviet Union in 1978.

Photo courtesy of Charles Bierbauer

Right: Muhammad, his second wife Belinda, and their four children – Rasheda, Jamilah, Maryum and Muhammad Ali Jr – in front of their Cherry Hill home, in 1973.

© Neil Leifer / Getty

Left: My brother and his third wife Veronica with journalist Harold Bell.

Photo courtesy of Harold Bell.

Right: My brother with flamboyant boxing promoter Don King and the then heavyweight champ, Mike Tyson, at a WBC event in 1988.

Photo courtesy of the WBC.

Right: My brother comforting his daughter Laila at the 2005 Butterfly Ball event in Atlanta. © *Tom Grason*

Left: Muhammad clowns around with my friend and manager, Ron Brashear. © *Tom Grason*

Right: My family and I visiting at my brother's home. I am truly grateful for how close we remained until the very end.

Left: With Muhammad's former business manager, Gene Kilroy. Nicknamed 'the Facilitator', he was a huge figure in my brother's inner-circle.

© *Gene Kilroy*

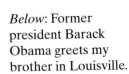

Left: Caroline and I with a frail Muhammad at the 2013 Muhammad Ali Humanitarian Awards.

Below: Former president Barack Obama greets my brother in Louisville.

© *PA Images / Sam Upshaw Jr / USA TODAY*

Above left: Muhammad and his wife Lonnie at the grand opening of the Muhammad Ali Center, in 2005.

© *Tom Grason*

Right: My brother officially crowned 'King of Boxing' at a WBC event in 2012. A champion – my champion – right until the very end.

Photo courtesy of the WBC

All photos courtesy of Rahaman Ali's personal archive unless otherwise indicated.

attention. That's what they're looking for.' Muhammad explained how he would have beaten Louis, but how he loved and revered him.

Surely, if it was one of the other boxers instead of my brother then this guy wouldn't have dared poke them in the chest. The boxer would've punched him in the face. But he knew Muhammad was a gentleman and wouldn't resort to physically attacking him, hence this guy tried it on. He took advantage. Nevertheless, he was expecting a reaction from him, but instead he got it off the young teenager. Everything was serene till this guy barged in. Of course, if I had been there with my brother I would've taken care of the situation myself. I wouldn't let any odious character get close enough to Muhammad to physically push him around.

Although Muhammad was flying country to country on what was a retirement tour of Europe, rumours had already started to fly about his potential duel with his long-time sparring partner Larry Holmes. As he resumed the conversation with Charlie, the discussion centred on potentially hanging up the gloves for good. Charlie was itching to pepper him with the ultimate question. 'You're not going to make a comeback, are you?' he asked. Muhammad burst out laughing. 'You're definitely retired?' Muhammad affirmed, 'Yeah, I'm not coming back.' Charlie said, 'There are a lot of rumours circling that you're going to fight Larry Holmes. You don't want to fight him because he's not fit to lace your boots. He's too young for you. You don't want to be fighting anyone your own age now never mind someone younger.' Muhammad said, 'No. Don't worry I'm not going to come back.' Still not entirely convinced, the young man further pressed, 'Is that definite?' Muhammad's reaction was priceless as he rolled his eyes and replied, 'No, I ain't coming back.'

Before the George Foreman fight, my brother had a verbal slanging match with Archie Moore. He said to him, 'Archie, I'm not too old to win the title against Foreman.' In all honesty Muhammad knew that and even admitted that one day he'd see that day, but he was the champion of the world and soaking it all in. Basically, my brother felt he should maybe carry on fighting till he started to get derailed, losing fight after fight.

If Muhammad had beaten Holmes and Berbick he would've come back and fought somebody else. It was always, 'One more, one more.' Maybe till he hit the fifty-year-old mark. He may have even ended up fighting Mike Tyson. But Muhammad kept reiterating he was retired. At the time he was of the belief that fighting Holmes was tenable. During the conversation he never said anything good about Holmes – that he was a good champion or highlighting his attributes. He merely replied to this enthusiastic man's questions, a man who was convinced that Muhammad had no chance of triumphing against his old sparring partner. Truth be told, if you watch my brother in the ring during that particular era, it was like the end of an era as his skills diminished. I was still training with him and he was no longer even close to his peak.

As he entertained his young guests, there were some eager fans milling around now waiting outside to meet a hero. But the security and staff members wouldn't let them in. Jimmy Ellis, who occasionally travelled with Muhammad, sometimes unofficially acted as Muhammad's security man if I wasn't with him. A thing that my brother was often curious about was where someone was from. He had a knack of finding out about an individual's heritage, their lineage. Having travelled the world he was exposed to diverse cultures and people. So he asked Charlie his origin. Although he was born in England, he traced his heritage back to Africa. 'My dad was born in Ghana, Africa,' he told him. As it happens Muhammad and I had been to Ghana. Africa was always in my brother's heart and mind, and he loved the people there as they looked up to him. As a matter of fact, my brother and I had even met President Nkrumah after Muhammad was crowned the heavyweight champion. Furthermore Charlie's uncle, Johnny Hansen, was actually the Minister for Politics for Ghana. Muhammad learned that Charlie's family was well connected. 'There is a lot of royal blood there,' he proudly told my brother. This really impressed Muhammad and roused his interest as his eyes lit up.

My brother absolutely adored his fans in the UK. And every time he flew over across the pond, they embraced him with open arms. Making small talk, Charlie asked, 'How do you like England?' He replied, 'I like coming to seeing my fans here in London. I've always had support here.' After the two Henry Cooper fights that we went there for, Muhammad always garnered support. He obviously had a fondness for England because the country supported him through his draft. 'I love English people,' he proudly said.

Muhammad would often joke about wanting to go to Buckingham Palace. He'd boast to us, 'The king needs to be in the Palace and I'm the king.' Whenever Muhammad visited England, paying a visit to the Queen was always on his mind. Muhammad revered the British monarch, whom he had met several times. In fact, he was intrigued with the British royal family in general. He always thought very highly of the royal fraternity and thought it was great to have a royal family. He, particularly, seemed to be impressed with how they conducted themselves. He considered Buckingham Palace the equivalent of the White House in Washington. In fact Muhammad once revealed privately that he'd love to box at Buckingham Palace. He said, 'Can you imagine Muhammad Ali boxing live not at Madison Square Garden but at Buckingham Palace,' and then bursting out laughing. Having the Queen ringside was a dream of his, but my brother obviously realised that would be pretty much impossible. He said, 'I would like to have invited her ringside to watch one of my fights – the whole royal family. I know it doesn't really work that way – you don't even get American presidents ringside normally.'

Another prominent member of the royal family that Muhammad seemed to be quite fascinated with was Prince Charles. He thought he was a man of dignity and really liked him. His accent, in particular, was something that seemed to invoke my brother's interest. 'I like the way he speaks,' he said. 'I like his accent.' And the Duke of Edinburgh was a gentleman, Muhammad thought.

Our great-grandparents were of Irish origin and Muhammad and I were really proud of our Irish roots. My brother had fought a fighter named Al 'Blue' Lewis in Dublin in 1972. During the conversation with Charlie, Muhammad said, 'I'd love to be President of Ireland. I'd stop all the trouble and get them all to love each other.' I don't know if I'd go that far, but Muhammad had certainly endeared himself to the people of Ireland.

The funniest thing happened earlier. Veronica, who was accompanying her husband on the tour, wasn't present – she had gone horse riding, something she'd do passionately. She had encountered the group of teenagers earlier on in the hotel and engaged in a short conversation. Apparently she had been joking about Charlie's eyelashes because they are very prominent. As it happens she had mentioned this to Muhammad before she left the hotel to horse ride. So Muhammad jokingly said to Charlie, 'I believe you've been sweet with my wife.' And he started laughing.

THE FINAL BELL

My brother was never supposed to fight Larry Holmes. After some contemplation, Muhammad came back and signed on the dotted line for the Holmes fight behind his agent's and financial advisors' backs. Understandably, Barry was frustrated. 'Muhammad, you can't do that because we retired you,' he said, exasperated. 'And you made a lot of money and told a lot of people all over the world that you were retiring.' Muhammad, to be quite honest, didn't really have a good answer to this. He said, 'No, but I signed for this fight.' 'Why did you do that?' asked Barry. 'Too much money,' came the reply. The offer, a staggering $8 million, had been too enticing to turn down. In fact, I remember him telling me, 'A sixty-year-old who was dying in his bed would get up and fight Larry Holmes for $8 million.' Concerned for his well-being, I tried to talk him out of it.

The tour had been a huge success and they had collected a lot of money. As a matter of fact, they made $13 million for Muhammad – $5 million more than what he signed up to get for the Holmes bout. Muhammad's financial agents had bailed him out financially, but he had gone against what his team had agreed. Seeing this as the final straw, Barry said, 'I can't do that, Muhammad. I can't be part of it. Goodbye, good luck.' Barry ripped up the contract to declare it null and that was that.

'You can't,' Muhammad protested, but Barry stood firm. 'I'm not going to have this any more because you made a liar out of me. It's not just that you said you're retiring, but I put my own reputation on the line and arranged all these outings for your retirement.'

Frank wasn't the only person upset by my brother's change of heart – it caused a serious rift between the two and the rest of the team. Muhammad's lawyer Mike Phenner was despairing by this point, but was also determined that my brother should hold on to the money he had. 'Muhammad, you can't keep doing this,' he would tell him. 'We've got to keep on this programme. You can't keep giving your money away.' My brother, though, would listen with one ear and out it would go from the other. The bottom line was: he wasn't going to cooperate.

In the end, Mike and Bill's plan lasted less than three years. Aside from that Robert had left the bank in 1980 and then there wasn't anybody there to protect Muhammad, so other people took control and what his team had put together really came apart. Muhammad, meanwhile, was right on the verge of hanging up his gloves for good, but he was still a hot property. To give you an idea of Muhammad's popularity, by 1980 he had surpassed Lincoln, Christ and Napoleon as the most written about individual in history. This was recorded in the *Guinness Book of World Records*. There were still, in the eyes of his less scrupulous handlers, plenty of chances for cashing in on his name. He was still a golden goose for many.

When the notion of fighting Holmes surfaced, most of us who were prepared to be realistic looked at the situation with a premonition of doom. Muhammad was in no real shape to be in the ring – I knew it, and so did anyone who'd seen him spar, which he'd barely done since his win over Spinks. Sig Rogich was the chairman of the Nevada Athletic Commission. Pre-fight, Muhammad had engaged in numerous discussions with him. Taking into consideration Muhammad's safety, the commissioner made it clear to my brother and Angelo Dundee that he would have to go to a first-rate medical clinic to make sure he was physically fit to fight. So the commission sent him to the Mayo Clinic for his physical. This place had an esteemed name and a great reputation for integrity.

To his detriment Don King was one of the individuals who didn't warm to the idea of safety checks. I guess there were certain individuals around my brother who didn't want any major obstacle that could potentially prevent him from fighting. An astute businessman, King was in the boxing business to make money. He loved money and money loved him. But later on we were all glad that we did it to give credibility to Muhammad's health. He couldn't have gone to a more reputable institution and received a clean bill of health. So from that standpoint it was good to get that out of the way.

Finally, the Nevada Athletic Commission received Muhammad's medical records from the clinic. In these documents, apparently, it highlighted that when Muhammad tried to touch the tip of his nose he missed the target. The Commission sanctioned the fight on the basis of this report, but didn't make the report public.

As the training camp got under way, my brother had promoters pushing the fight. Rogich went to see him train in New Jersey Silver Lake. He went there a couple of times and it was packed with the press. Muhammad was coming back with this fight. It was a monumental fight which garnered international coverage. I think my brother was more concerned with looking like he used to look in his heyday, so he took a lot of diuretics. He looked unbelievably in pristine shape in his training sessions. It's a view Sig shared also. But what wasn't apparent to the commissioner at the time was that Muhammad was losing weight at a rapid pace because he wanted to look like he did when he was a young Muhammad Ali. That sapped him of his strength it would later emerge on fight night.

Angelo did have some reservations about it too and expressed those to Sig a couple of times. The Commission endeavoured to do everything in their powers to ensure Muhammad was safe to be in the ring again. Fearing for my brother's safety, Sig would call Angelo to ask, 'Hey, Angie, how's he doing?' Angelo would say, 'Believe it or not, he's doing great. He looks a lot like his old self. He's moving around good.' And he was. I could see it myself. Angelo gave the commissioner good reassurances. Muhammad stepped into that ring looking amazing. He looked handsome. He lost all that weight. When he weighed in he was 212 pounds or something.

On fight night, I remember, it was a hot day and it was an outdoor event. As soon as Holmes threw his first punch of the fight, Muhammad wasted no time in starting the psychological warfare. Taunting his former sparring partner, I could hear Muhammad shouting, 'I'm going to fuck you up!' He continued verbally terrorising Holmes, 'You ain't no fighter and you never were!' He was back to his best with his psychological warfare that had derailed many adversaries in his prime. The harder Holmes started whacking Muhammad, the more raucous and dirty the cursing got. Unfortunately no pressure was going to derail Holmes this time. Muhammad wasn't doing anything. Next, I could hear Angelo screaming at my brother to hit Holmes or he was going to throw in the towel. Muhammad shouted back at him, 'No! No! No!' They stopped the fight in the tenth round, with Angelo insisting the referee call it off as my brother sat on his stool. Bundini was adamant on letting it continue – he asked my brother if he wanted to carry on. But a feeling of intense irritation was visible as Angelo demanded the referee end it. Angelo was mad as hell. Even Holmes didn't want to keep fighting him as the fight went on. He was beating Muhammad so badly. Holmes loved him. Everybody in the business loved him and it was agonising to see him crumble. I didn't want to see him go down like that. Muhammad didn't win a round.

In front of a packed arena – and some of Muhammad's children who had never seen their father fight at an arena before – Holmes had beaten the hell out of my brother. It was a great disappointment for people who were pulling for Muhammad to kind of redeem himself after all that time. Prior to entering the ring, he had been all business in the dressing room. I could see he looked comfortable. He looked confident. He looked unbelievable. If you look at his pictures he looked like a young Muhammad Ali.

I think this fight did a lot of things. It defined Larry Holmes to a degree that I don't think he had been defined before. Everybody thought Holmes was very good, but they didn't know he was great. He was a great champion. He had a left jab just impossible to defend against. One thing about Holmes, which I must add, is that he has often proclaimed himself as the greatest boxer, and occasionally has made comments about my brother which don't sit well with some people. Despite showing great respect, he gives the impression he was definitely better than Muhammad. He can have his views, but not many would embrace them – even if in retrospect the thought of watching the fight makes me curl up like a pretzel. It would later emerge that Holmes didn't want to fight my brother; the promoter pushed him to.

Ferdie Pacheco had been one of the most prominent members of our team. He just wanted to look after Muhammad and he was committed to him but was totally against this fight. He was kind of an eccentric guy and was controversial in some ways. He had acted pragmatically in response to circumstances so he left our camp after the Ernie Shavers fight three years prior because he felt Muhammad should have retired for his own good. He expressed great concern. Before the Holmes fight, he had actually warned my brother not to fight otherwise he would never have a normal life. After the result he said everyone involved in the fight should've been arrested for letting Muhammad get back in the ring. He felt a crime had been committed.

★ ★ ★

Anyway, on at least one occasion Muhammad got into another fine mess that could've landed him in jail. While still in Chicago Muhammad had come into contact with a guy named Harold Smith – his real name, it turned out, was Ross Fields – but we wouldn't learn that until much later. Harold looked every bit the businessman. He was around forty, a black man dressed up in a nice suit and carrying a briefcase. And somehow he talked Muhammad into having a friend pick him up at Chicago airport so that he could pitch my brother his master plan.

Harold's idea, it emerged, was a Muhammad Ali Amateur Sports Program, an initiative designed to scout out the best young high school and college-age athletes, even if they weren't in school. Harold told Muhammad that he was looking to get Olympic athletes through this process. It would start as an amateur programme, but eventually evolve into an organisation dealing with the world's best athletes. He wanted to use Muhammad's name to add credibility, of course, but another crucial consideration was that this was intended as an entirely for profit organisation; it wasn't a charity. The prime purpose, even from the outset, was to make money.

Still, the biggest selling point Harold used to convince my brother and bring him under his spell was that this was going to help people – it would help young, aspiring athletes to realise their dreams. A Florida-based sprinter, Houston McTear, who held the national record for the hundred-metre dash, was held up as an example. Harold convinced Muhammad that this young man would be the first guy that they were going to sign up. Muhammad had a burning desire to help people, and was also convinced that his name would be immortalised by this organisation that could make a difference to people's lives. Harold was a straight-up bullshitter and there was nothing guaranteed. My brother was a dreamer himself so he believed it. It wouldn't be the last time it happened.

If I'm being completely honest, Harold probably didn't need to try so hard to lower Muhammad's guard – my brother was easily talked into projects, even after so many bad experiences – but he continued to bait the trap. Somehow, he had acquired $40,000 in cash, neatly stacked in this briefcase of his, and this was what he presented as he talked through his plan with my brother. 'I'll pay you now,' he said, over the stacks of bills. 'If you sign these papers now I'll give you $40,000.' With no manager or agent present, other than his good friend Tim Shanahan who sat there listening to the whole business deal, Muhammad signed the proffered paper – a one-page document – and Harold handed over the money.

Now, the reason Harold brought this money in a briefcase was that he knew a similar tactic had worked on my brother in the past. Don King, when he wanted something from Muhammad, would barge in wherever he was staying with a large amount of cash in a briefcase, flash it and have my brother sign on the dotted line there and then for a fight. Once he brought $100,000 and he had him sign papers, promising Muhammad some exorbitant sum that almost certainly ended up being less after the fight was done.

Muhammad had already asked Tim to head his non-profit organisation called World Organization for Rights and Dignity, and set up a headquarters in LA. Harold was already based in the city, and by the time Muhammad moved there both men were officially bound by the agreement and were now business partners.

Unfortunately, now that he had Muhammad in his grasp, Harold was ready to progress to the next level of his deceitful plan. Another of his aspirations, it emerged, was to become a fight promoter, using my brother's name and image to add legitimacy to his fledgling set-up. He also, unbeknown to any of us at the time, proceeded to make an arrangement with Wells Fargo Bank to set up an account in the name of the company he had been made the CEO of. Somehow, the manager would just give this man money with no collateral but Muhammad's name. And Harold ended up promoting a series of fights and in the beginning he made things happen. But eventually his efforts started to decline as he continued promoting but with very little comeback. Ultimately, Harold ended up scamming Wells Fargo for a staggering $21 million using Muhammad's name to build trust and a track record, and all under Muhammad's eyes.

By early 1981, when the bank realised they'd been scammed and the FBI was called in, the first thing they did was pay Muhammad a visit at home. My brother was shocked to see a pair of G-men on his steps because he had been oblivious as to what had gone on behind his back. His first call was to Tim, who arrived at his house a half-hour later to find two FBI agents were sitting at Muhammad's desk. They told them about the scam Harold had pulled, leaving no doubt about what a serious mess everyone was in.

No doubt to Tim, anyway. Muhammad, always happy to see the lighter side, said, 'No nigger can steal $21 million from Wells Fargo Bank with all those smart Harvard graduate businessmen protecting our money. Hell, ten niggers couldn't steal $21 million from the bank.' It was, honestly, beyond Muhammad's comprehension that someone could steal $21 million using his name. 'Because of your name, Muhammad. Your name's what did it,' the FBI men told him, but he just laughed. Sure enough, it seemed like a hairy situation, but it emerged that the FBI wasn't going to take further action as they were eventually able to ascertain my brother's innocence, so jail was never a serious possibility. What they did pursue was the culprit. The FBI raided his Santa Monica office. Eventually, Harold was caught and convicted. He got eight years, and ended up spending six behind bars. Muhammad, on more than one occasion, told me, 'It's always my black "brothers" that take advantage of me. It's never the white folk.'

★ ★ ★

After Holmes defeated Muhammad, my brother was itching to fight again in Las Vegas, only to be told by the commissioner that he wasn't going to grant him a licence. We had a hearing and the commission had to show at the hearing as to why they should or should not give him a licence to fight. Rogich knew he had the support of his commissioners – there were five of them on the commission – to revoke Muhammad's licence. During the hearing – and there were a lot of press there, probably fifty to eighty press people – Muhammad was relaxed and demonstrated his levitation tricks. He sat ten feet away from the Commissioner. He knew he could see him. And Muhammad would look at him and he'd do his little one-foot balance, apparently not caring one bit about the forces arrayed against him.

At one point, Rogich called a recess and went into the bathroom with Muhammad and Gene Kilroy. Scrutinising the situation with objective eyes, he tried to dissuade them, saying, 'You guys are not going to get a licence here. And I don't want to embarrass you. If you will withdraw your application I'll end the hearing and we won't take any action.' After conferring they asked, 'Will you do that?' Rogich replied, 'Yes, I think I can get the support to do that.' So the three made their way back to the room, and the Commissioner announced, 'Mr Ali has withdrawn his application and we've ended the hearing.' And he closed the hearing. They, rightly, took away his chances to fight in the United States. For a moment, I was almost relieved. Then Muhammad did something that seemed almost inexplicable.

He went to the Bahamas and fought there anyway. It was a repellent decision, just crazy. I think that fight – against Trevor Berbick, who was relatively unknown at the time – did as much to hurt him as any other fight he had. Trevor Berbick just beat the hell out of him – my brother's jab didn't work like it used to, and when he went to the ropes Berbick would batter him without a sign that he might get tired. My brother was rocked several times and only showed one flash of his old brilliance, trying to shuffle in the opening sessions of the final round. Berbick won a lopsided decision, and even my brother had to admit he'd been bested.

Why did my brother continue to fight? He didn't want to end his career with his loss to Holmes, but the money was honestly a part of it. He was fighting for money a lot, in those days. He'd never learned the value of it early in his life, and now that he finally had an inkling of how much a lifetime of bad business deals had sucked out of him, the big paydays were past. And still, all of us – and finally, Muhammad too – were adamant that he'd never again step inside a ring to box.

SUMMER HOLIDAYS

Despite my brother's celebrity status, instead of using chauffeurs he would often make an effort to drive his children Hana and Laila to school, and pick them up. Like any other parent there, he would eagerly engage with their teachers and ask them if his little girls were good girls and what type of students they were. Notably, he started taking more of an interest in his two girls now that he had consciously made an effort to be part of a normal family ever since moving to Los Angeles. Given the fact that his ring exploits were behind him now, he was in a position to make up for lost time.

For their part, his two daughters were proud of their daddy and sometimes went the extra mile to make it known to the other kids in their class that they had an important father, the Greatest of All Time. 'My dad is Muhammad Ali,' Hana would say to her fellow classmates, puffing herself up in the way she'd learned from her dad. Laila, meanwhile, had no low opinion of her own abilities. On one occasion, Muhammad found himself talking to another little girl called Cheyenne who was five or six years old because she had some problem with Laila, and both had got into a little fight. He asked her kindly, 'Are you friends with my daughters Hana and Laila?' She replied, 'Yeah.' He said, 'What did Laila do?' And the little girl bluntly replied, 'She hit me!' Laila, who was standing in the background, interjected, 'I didn't hit her. She hit me first then I hit her back.' Muhammad then looked at Cheyenne and said, 'Cheyenne, are you a bad girl?' Well, little Cheyenne didn't say anything. Instead she pouted. He said, 'It's OK. Don't be sad. I'm bad sometimes too. You just can't be bad all the time.' Well, that raised a smile on that little girl's face.

In the years after Muhammad moved to Southern California, he made sure all his kids from other women – his ex-wife and the two women he had kids with out of wedlock – came to visit him not only on special occasions such as birthdays, but to spend a prolonged period of time in the summer holidays. Whether it was at his Los Angeles residence or later up at the Michigan farmhouse, my brother would religiously fly his children over. Initially Belinda had some reservations about letting her children visit their father in Los Angeles, but eventually she conceded and allowed her four children to join their father and the other siblings.

Despite the fact that Muhammad's eight blood children had four different mothers, his ultimate vision was for all of them to get to know each other – love each other, and bond together, and ultimately maintain contact with one another without him. He was always resolute in this regard. And despite their differences, they do to this day. Khaliah and Miya were two daughters born out of wedlock to two different mothers. They both seemed alienated from the family at first, but my brother endeavoured to include them as much as possible. You'll hear stories that he literally abandoned his two children out of wedlock. The fact is he loved them too.

Muhammad always felt that summer holidays were ideally the time for everyone to get together, and so in summer the Fremont Place mansion was swamped with kids. He didn't particularly have specific 'dos' and 'don'ts' his children had to adhere to at home. The most important unwritten rule was: they all had to get along. Otherwise the only real rule had to do with his concerns for the children's safety: don't swim in the deep end of the pool. It was mandatory to always have the presence of a lifeguard onsite at the house when the pool was being used by the children. Equally Muhammad always had concerns, consciously or subconsciously, when the children were playing on the streets out of sight because he was afraid of potential kidnapping attempts. After all, a man of his position in the public eye was a potential target. By and large, Muhammad was a fun father and he let his children spread their wings. Raising them with moral and ethical principles was of the upmost importance, but they were allowed to have their fun.

★　★　★

Some of the fondest memories I have of my brother in the holidays were of everyone lounging around watching movies on the third floor in the media room of his house. Everyone would eat together hanging out in the home office, a significant place that became the playground for the kids, the grown-ups, everyone. It was like paradise for me.

Muhammad's library was in his office where he would spend time on a daily basis. Despite not being a big reader he accumulated plenty of knowledge of life in general, and when he found something that interested him he was more than happy to look it up in a book.

One of his oddest habits, though, was his way of lighting the fireplace in his office. Instead of using a match he'd grab a piece of paper from his desk, walk all the way to the kitchen, light the paper and then he'd walk through the house with this small piece of paper burning in his hand, paying close attention, and light the fireplace. The nine-bedroomed mansion was 11,000 square feet so the kitchen was quite a distance from the office. One had to walk through several rooms to get to the kitchen. And this was a daily occurrence. Many times, he almost wouldn't make it to the office. For him, I think, it was almost like a personal challenge to see if he could get to the office without burning the mansion down, with the paper burning his hand. This stunt might have made some people's wives or partners irritated, leading to a war of words, but Veronica was oblivious to her husband's habit till one day their daughter told her mother about her father's little game. Apparently Veronica didn't even get mad. She was always happy to see her husband's playful side.

Typically Prince and Michael Jackson songs blared as the daughters would show their father the intricate dance moves they'd learned or concocted on their own, shaking, shimmying and sliding to the beat. Salt-N-Pepa and Cyndi Lauper were among the popular artists for the older girls. While his daughters and son were growing up influenced by pop culture, Muhammad preferred to sit at his piano and play the more basic tunes he had a knack for.

Although the office was the spot in the house where he spent his time talking on the phone with business associates, it didn't deter him from letting the children run wild in there. It wasn't uncommon to see him engaged in an important conversation on the phone on worldly issues with President Jimmy Carter, or trying to free hostages in Beirut, or discussing business deals while Laila or one of the other kids danced or leapt around the room, engaged in some craziness. You would be hard-pressed to hear him say to his kids, 'You can't jump on the couch.' Or, 'You can't do this,' or 'You can't do that.' Most of the kids could hardly sit still for ten seconds. Regardless, the office door would always be open for the kids who would come in and make noise. Even if there was complete pandemonium, Muhammad would just never kick them out. He didn't clip their wings, but let them be kids.

Of course kids typically misbehave, but when they all came together they bonded well. If their father saw them have a little argument here and there, he'd sit them down and in his restrained fatherly voice would remind them, 'You're all sisters and brothers. You should love each other and get along. Be friendly to each other.' Having said that there were hardly mammoth squabbles between them; they were just typical kid arguments, which was never anything to worry about it. Nonetheless he still took everything seriously regarding their interpersonal relationships, and taught them very early in life to work things out between them.

One sticking point was that some of the kids sometimes didn't get along like they should have with Veronica. It was understandable because of the history between all the adults involved. Still, Veronica had a way of keeping her cool more so than most would in her position. Belinda's children on occasions made it clear to their stepmother that this was their father's home and she couldn't say anything to them. They did sometimes vocalise their opinions and their condemnation, so there were occasionally minor tensions. But, then again, it's not unusual under the circumstances because they had a strong reason to believe this woman was responsible for their father parting ways with their mother. So, the twins being rude to Veronica wasn't out of the ordinary. Veronica would try her best to stay composed. Often, I think, she felt it better to maintain a distance than blurting something out and later regretting it.

Muhammad had missed his four children with Belinda. So now was the time to get to know them a little better. A recurrent outing was to take all the kids around with him in Beverly Hills, riding in his Rolls-Royce with the top down. Muhammad particularly enjoyed cruising down Wilshire Boulevard, the symbolic spine of Los Angeles, and all over. It wasn't an uncommon scenario to see people, who were in their cars going about their daily business, get a shock when they turned around in traffic to see the face of The Greatest grinning back at them. They'd quickly lower their car windows and ecstatically chant, 'Ali! Ali! Ali'. My brother would proudly without fail respond with, 'Hey, these are my kids,' while pointing to the children.

In fact, my brother was so proud of his kids that when he was travelling with his children he was inclined to thrust them into the spotlight giving them attention. He particularly had a penchant for walking up and down the hotel lobby with them to attract everyone's eyes, not just to him, but to his kids. It was a regular drill. They'd be sitting in the hotel room and he'd suddenly say to them, 'Let's go walk around together.' Muhammad would take them all down to the restaurant and have dinner, making sure to get a seat in the middle of the room. I certainly feel like he relished being out and about with his children compared to today's celebrities who constantly strive to shield their children and shy away from interacting not only with the public but the paparazzi – and in some cases hurl abuse at the photographers who pursue them.

Frequenting restaurants with my brother was always an exhilarating experience, though finishing a meal could be difficult. Fans would often interrupt without any sense of personal space, coming over to Muhammad as he ate with his flock of children and asking, 'Hey, Muhammad, I'm sorry to interrupt but can I have a picture and can you sign an autograph?' As was always the case, he would oblige as the kids would be mumbling in the background. On top of his fame, he frequented eateries on the busiest street in Beverly Hills. It's not surprising that it was very difficult for him and the kids to get in the restaurant without fanfare and a task for them to exit because of the crowd wanting to stop and engage with Muhammad. But he soaked it all in. He had that affinity towards people.

★ ★ ★

Hana was really a difficult child as a little girl, in particular on shopping trips. She would scream and shout because she wanted virtually everything from the shops. Whenever she resorted to this behaviour, her father would just look at shoppers as she threw her tantrum, and would calmly say to the onlookers, 'She'll grow out of it.' If Veronica was with them she would be embarrassed to the extent she'd want to leave the store, but Muhammad would have so much patience with his daughter that instead of getting mad at her he would gape at her and cry back, 'Ahhhh.' The bewildered child would gaze back at her father and think, *Why is he crying?* Often just this was enough to calm her down. Muhammad would often come out with this kind of off-the-wall solution in how he handled his kids when they were naughty or demanding. Neither Muhammad nor Veronica were strict disciplinarians. There was none of the severe punishment that my brother and I were subjected to when we were growing up. Instead, Muhammad practised exercising patience by sitting his daughters and son down and talking to them, almost lecturing at times. He would explain the contrast between good and bad, acceptable and non-acceptable, and so forth. He would put them in the corner and make them sit and listen to him.

One morning Hana woke up and was eager to take her pretty dolls to school with her. Reluctantly Muhammad sat her down and told her, 'You know, Hana, don't take your nice dolls to school. These are for you to play with at home. There are a lot of kids at school that can't afford them and may feel bad when they see yours. Don't try to show off by showing people things that you have that they may not have. As you get older you feel something good because you have something or get a kick out of showing people something good they don't have; you should want for your friends and people the same things you have.' She was only seven years old, so very young, but these were the kinds of lessons Muhammad felt it was important to reinforce at an early age.

My brother was inclined to impart life lessons wherever he could, to keep the children conscious of the value of life. As Hana grew up she used to walk around with nice clothes and handbags, like young girls do. Her unassuming father would ask her, 'How much did that purse cost? How much did that shirt cost? How much did those pants cost!?' She would reply, 'Twenty dollars,' or, 'a hundred dollars.' He would point out to her the true value of the item by telling her, 'Well, it costs $2 to make it. How much did those pants cost?' She would answer, 'Thirty dollars.' 'Well, it cost fifty cents to make those.' Muhammad would explain to his daughter and her siblings how people were working hard in impoverished conditions in third-world countries for meagre money to make these classy, expensive items that might sell for twenty times the cost. Despite their opulent surroundings, my brother strove to shape his children's minds so they were conscious about valuing things. He aimed to plant seeds in his children's heads, something thought-provoking. Even when the kids were still relatively young, it didn't deter Muhammad from being adamant about teaching them about the most important things in life before they could fully comprehend the concept of what he really was conveying.

Of course, it wasn't unusual for the children to ask their father for money as kids do. What's interesting is that he had a little safe in his office desk and he would write the combination of the safe on the little brown chest of drawers because he'd forget things. He had a propensity for writing on wooden furniture. He'd scribble on the cabinet people's telephone numbers in every house he ever lived in. That's one thing he had a tendency for and never could grow out of it. Whenever one of his girls asked for money, Muhammad would open the chest, look at the combination and open it up and pull out a fifty-dollar bill – all he kept in there were fifty-dollar bills – and he'd give it to his daughter and she'd go on her bicycle with her friends and buy candy.

My brother loved the idea of gifts – giving and receiving them. Of course, he could literally buy whatever he desired, but he liked the idea of being on the receiving end of a gift. Whether it was his wife buying him something strikingly gorgeous for his birthday, or a friend or a head of state showering him with a surprise gift, Muhammad would make a show of drinking it all in, showing how much he enjoyed it.

Maybe not surprisingly, then, my brother actually let his children –

the two who lived with him – have Christmas, which is frowned upon by Muslims. They'd go as far as having a tree displayed in the lounge and nicely wrapped gifts. However, he made it clear to his daughters, 'I let you have Christmas because everywhere you go you can't get away from it. But we're not celebrating it in the same tradition that other people do. We don't believe that Jesus was the son of God; he was an important Prophet.' So he'd explain the reasoning behind his behaviour.

Now, Veronica was Catholic and my brother a Muslim. So, of course, he wanted the children to be raised as Muslims. Muhammad believed it was imperative for him to start the kids on the right path when they were really young and he demonstrated this. To this end, when Hana and Laila were only five and four, he would wake them up really early in the morning to begin their teaching – as you can imagine, this would be torture for such young souls, but when it came to teaching them the true principles of religion he would be far from frivolous. One morning as Muhammad rose up to submit to God, as was the norm at the Ali household, he woke his two kids to join him. But that day he said something which was flustering and would leave an indelible impact on Hana. This was the first time the little girl realised that her father loved someone else more than her. And she never forgot what he said to her which left a stain on her that was almost unbearable. He said to her, 'Stop messing around playing, you should love God more than you love anybody, more than you love me. I love God more than I love you.' Muhammad's little daughter's heart just broke because she just couldn't comprehend it. The disenchanted little girl asked, 'What!?' She never forgot what he said and, even now, that day is embedded in her head.

So this made her curious about what God was. She thought to herself, *What's God?* Always playing the role of preacher, Muhammad vowed to – for her personal edification and intellectual enrichment – teach her. He began to justify the need for such sacrifice, the kind some would find rather torturous. In his quest to make her understand the importance of God, he said, 'That sofa, that bed you sleep in, did that make itself? Just spring into existence?' She replied, 'No.' He said, 'A person made that. Who do you think made the stars, the moon, the oceans and the universe? That's God's creation.' So that's how his daughter understood a little better, although it was beyond her comprehension to fully absorb and appreciate what her father was telling her.

Muhammad continued making every effort to ensure his daughter soaked it all in. He continued, 'God made that sun that shines. God made stars. God made the beautiful mountains people climb on such as Mount Everest.' He proceeded to name the mountains. 'All those were made by God.' Then in contrast to this he said, 'You are going to get people in life tell you that there is no God. You don't judge them, some people are lost and you make sure you always keep the concept of God in your heart and mind.' As a concerned father he worked tirelessly towards teaching his children these life lessons as he felt it was crucial to mould them into good humans with an understanding of the reality of the world. As growing concerns mounted, Muhammad enrolled Hana and Laila in a Muslim academy. This would give him more of peace of mind to ensure his daughters would not get derailed with worldly influences as the school they were attending, understandably, did their bit which reflected Christianity.

While summer holidays were filled with fun and frolics, equally the father of eight perceived this as an opportunity to edify his children. Again, they'd have found it too intricate at that age, but he said to them, 'If you think about how short life is, you don't have much time. Think about all the time you spend sleeping – eight hours of your life has gone by not living. Think about the time you have to spend going to school, how many hours, six or seven hours a day? All that time you're learning about the trade you are going to do in life when you grow up. You're going to grow up and get a job. So, you have eight hours of sleeping, six hours of schooling. You don't have much time in the day left to live. We have very little time to make a difference in this world so utilise that time because you don't have much of it. It will be gone someday.'

Sitting on his chair in his office, Muhammad's constant highlighting of how the world might treat them better because the fact he, a famous celebrity, was their father, gave them something to contemplate. He strove, however, to make it clear that no one was better than anybody else, except perhaps in their hearts. Being good to people was the ultimate goal.

Muhammad also felt compelled to explain the importance of being humble. 'No matter who you are, Hana, people will treat you better because you're my daughter,' he told his daughter. 'Because of who your father is. Always remember that not fame, not wealth, not money, nothing makes you better than anyone else except your heart. Always have a good heart. Be good to people, be compassionate and be humble. God will always love you. In life you're going to have advantages, but that's how the world treats people because of the fame, because they love your father, because of who I am. They respect and admire me, but that shouldn't make a difference to you.'

Warming to his theme, he continued, 'If you want to feel better and be better than anyone, you work on your heart and being the best you can be.' This was one of the core lessons he emphasised to his children constantly. Muhammad didn't merely spout words; he believed you had to practise to be humble. He said you have to remind yourself you're not great, God is great. The more famous you are, the more you are thrust into the limelight, the more responsibility you have to help make the world better. You can't just go sit in your house and lock the door and not give anything back to the world. That's why my brother strolled down the streets without bodyguards; he wanted people to see him. He said to Hana, 'You can't help God. You can't serve God. The way you serve God is to help people, so bettering other people's lives.' This was something my brother would constantly express. Muhammad would delve into great philosophical lessons as a loving father, and the teaching he imparted stuck with the children for the rest of their lives.

After the summer holidays were over, Muhammad would drive them all to the airport and put them on a plane back to their mothers. Not only would they leave elated and cherish having been with their father and the rest of the siblings, but they'd take away life lessons. Before they left, he'd religiously tell them to make sure to tell their mothers that they want to go see their daddy again in the holidays because they had a marvellous time. 'Don't say that I said this to you,' he'd tell them, as the mothers might be reluctant. 'Tell your mothers that you really want to visit again.' For Muhammad, the summer was one of the happiest seasons of the year.

ENTERTAINING STALLONE

Not many people are aware that Sylvester Stallone shot some scenes for *Rocky III* at Muhammad's mansion in Los Angeles. There's a misconception that it was the sequel, but it was actually the third film. Being an amateur boxer and a huge fan of the sport of boxing, Stallone's intended purpose was to do something which would involve Muhammad. He knew that using Muhammad's house as Rocky's house, as heavyweight champion, would be momentous. It was a little story Stallone wanted to do between them to add an element of authenticity. Stallone had invited Ernie Shavers and Joe Frazier to his own house for auditions for the role of Clubber Lang. Both men literally almost put Stallone in hospital. He couldn't handle them. In the end it was Muhammad's bodyguard Mr T. who ended up getting the part. I wonder what it would have been like had Muhammad fought Stallone in the movie.

Stallone had Muhammad's phone number, so he got his producer to call him and tell him that they wanted to rent his house. The Hancock Park mansion was only required for a week. Muhammad got paid $3,500 for the week. Back in those days that was a lot of money.

My brother had met the Hollywood actor at the Academy Awards after the release of *Rocky*. Sometime later, I met Stallone – who became a friend of mine – with Muhammad in New York City when the actor was filming there. He shook my hand, gave me a hug and said, 'Nice to meet you,

Rahaman. You're Muhammad's brother and I love you both.' The actor was among the celebrities who adored boxing and attended my brother's fights, including the Ernie Shavers and Leon Spinks duels. Stallone's brother Frank, who was close to him like I was close to Muhammad, and their mother Jacqueline were both on-set. Frank Stallone was and still is a massive boxing fan like his brother. He had pursued a singing career, but it was short-lived. He wasn't very good. Stallone's mother told the story about her son Sylvester and how he was going to have monumental success. She would always read people by starting with a letter. 'I see an R and there's going to be a lot of Rs in your life success,' she claimed. Stallone, of course, eventually had enormous success with *Rocky* and *Rambo* – some of the biggest Hollywood franchises of all time.

As the film crew took over the house, Muhammad and the Stallones hung out in between scenes mingling with each other. That day the actor Burgess Meredith was there. It was a small crew because they were only shooting a few scenes. Muhammad's office, dining room and the driveway were used for the scenes. Those scenes involved Stallone in the office talking on the phone. In one of the scenes Stallone walks from the office to the driveway. They also filmed in Muhammad's and Veronica's bedroom. Muhammad had a little old-fashioned black car he called 'Put-Put'. In the film you see Stallone sitting in the car in the backyard in a scene. All the catering trucks parked up and tables were laid out with the food for the cast and crew while Muhammad's two daughters ran around.

Stallone told my brother about the brawler Muhammad had beaten, Chuck Wepner, whose boxing heroics were the inspiration for the *Rocky* film. He explained how he was a struggling actor who attempted to peddle his own story, but nobody believed in his ambitions. Muhammad listened to Stallone as he explained how determination and being persistent had finally got him to where he aspired to be. He said to Muhammad, 'It was a dream of mine, doing this movie and for me to star in it.' Muhammad, who could empathise with this, said to him, 'You have to have dreams. If you don't have dreams you can't achieve anything.' Further, he added, 'I wanted to be a boxer and I wanted to be the heavyweight champion of the world. I dreamed about it every day. That's why I made it. I dreamed about it happening. If you believe you can do it, you will do it.' Muhammad had always shared his dreams with me, ever since we were young kids. Stallone listened to his words of wisdom that seemed to resonate with his own. Then he questioned my brother, 'What if you don't believe it?' Muhammad responded, 'Then fake it.' The idea of Stallone making this movie after innumerable hurdles left Muhammad full of admiration.

He was also impressed with how Stallone garnered the attention of the opposite sex – how they flocked to the movie star. 'You're not married and you've got all these women after you!' Muhammad said to the action star, half in jest. 'How do you handle it?' Stallone, trying to maintain a humble attitude, replied, 'Well, there's not that many. People are interested in you because you're a celebrity and a star. It's very difficult to find a woman that can want you as a human being rather than just a star.' My brother, who was all too familiar with being in the star's position himself, remarked, 'Once you're doing as good as you are, it brings in the foxes.' He meant if you'd get so many women throwing themselves at you that you can't handle them any more. Muhammad once said that women were the destruction of men. Temptations and urges, after all, can derail any man.

There were all kinds of rumours circulating about Muhammad and women in his peak. I can remember the way they looked at him. It was like, *I want to eat you up, I want to be with you. I want whatever.* I can't say he took advantage of it to an extreme level. In our youth, our mother would tease Muhammad. She would always say that I was more handsome than him and that I was stronger athletically. Muhammad would be fuming, but he also didn't have the confidence with women to do anything about it. When he was a young man in his early twenties, he really got into women. He was no longer the bashful boy that grew up with me. His confidence shot up tenfold. All I can say is that the ladies desired my brother. Women just lost their minds for him, I can tell you that without a shadow of a doubt. I don't think there was one who didn't literally love him. Muhammad looked kind of identical to me in a sense and we both had good physiques, but our personalities were polar opposites. So women flocked to us and men wanted to be around us because they knew women would be there. When Muhammad would be at a public event, sometimes the bouncers would have their hands full trying to control all the females. We were social butterflies.

As my brother's fame grew, he realised that he couldn't go anywhere without women trying to get close to him. A lot of celebrities hung around us during Muhammad's career, and even the celebrities wanted a piece of my brother. Regardless of how big their name was, it was nothing compared to Muhammad – nobody was bigger than my brother; he was the biggest celebrity around. In my eyes he actually found pride in that.

Women aside, Muhammad and Stallone were interested in discussing training. The *Rocky* star, who was and still is an advocate of hard training, was into eating healthily and he worked out on a daily basis. Their conversation also leaned towards the type of food they consumed. Stallone asked Muhammad if he worked out every day. He, wrongly, assumed Muhammad hit the gym on a regular basis. But Muhammad revealed that if he had a fight then he'd train every day, but after the fight he didn't train at all. This, I assume, surprised Stallone. 'You have to do that,' Stallone said to him, 'because once you stop it's so hard to get back. You've got to do it every day. You have to force yourself. Do something every day and that way you'll be used to it so you'll want to do it. If you stop, then you're going to find it much more difficult to get back to it. So never stop.' Before pursuing boxing, Stallone had been heavily influenced by Steve Reeves, who was the bodybuilding legend and star of the Hercules movies back in the 1960s. So he had been a serious iron pumper ever since he was a teenager. Speaking of weight training, my brother never really took to lifting weights. In fact he felt that was the worst thing a boxer could train with because it tightened the muscles. On the contrary, as sports science advanced, training correctly with weights improves one's performance. But it was never my brother's thing.

Nonetheless, the most Muhammad would do in the form of training when home and not in training camp was to go for a nice run. He wouldn't do boxing and nor did he have a home gym in his Los Angeles mansion, although later when he moved to Michigan he had one set up which housed a heavy bag and speed ball. And he would intermittently go in there and do his thing. Stallone, who looked in top physical condition and was allegedly sparring eighteen rounds daily, advised Muhammad, 'You've got to do it every day.' However, my brother was just not motivated to work out if he didn't have a goal – there had to be a fight. 'Imagine being in the ring,' Muhammad said to Stallone. 'You have to imagine being under those lights to put in the work outside of them.'

Between takes, and their in thought-provoking conversations, Muhammad would get up and box a little with Stallone once in a while; they'd throw playful punches at each other. Muhammad would give him the mean look he always did when fooling around. Stallone is an interesting individual with an inflated ego, but I think he admired Muhammad more than anyone. He really idolised my brother. He was just so happy that the real-life heavyweight champion had let him use the house for the movie scenes.

When the movie came out the Ali family didn't watch it together. My brother was such a big celebrity that he wouldn't really get too excited seeing his home in a film. However, he was apparently more excited because Stallone based a lot of that film on him with the Creed character. Indeed, Muhammad's two children were excited when they watched the film. Hana would shout, 'Hey, that's Put-Put! Hey, that's my father's patio. Hey, that's my parents' bedspread.' They'd changed the bed sheet for filming. Muhammad had been sleeping in another room that day as his bedroom was being used for filming.

When my brother went to see a private screening of the sequel, though, he had been severely critical about Stallone and the way certain things were portrayed. Accompanied by film critic Roger Ebert, Veronica and their daughters and a friend, they watched the film at Paramount Studios. He argued that a real boxer can detect that Stallone wasn't a real boxer. What he meant was the movie star, although a well-conditioned athlete, lacked the real moves and the way he carried himself in the ring. But Muhammad had no hesitation in commending Stallone's acting. Among his critical views, he mentioned how the old trainer was being portrayed wrongly. Basically, the boxing in the film did not accurately mirror that of an authentic professional boxer. Indeed, he was much more critical of *Rocky II* than he had been of the first film. When I watched the first film with him, he did nothing but praise it. But then, my brother always did reserve the right to change his mind.

ANOTHER DAY, ANOTHER DOLLAR

After Muhammad announced his retirement after his defeat to Berbick, when he finally hung up his gloves, it was the start of a new chapter in his life. Ironically he returned to Barry Frank at IMG again, the man he had broken up with earlier. A young agent named Jean Sage was working with Barry at the time. She was working in the broadcasting division and they had forty broadcasting clients. A lot of the ex-coaches, ex-football players and personalities who wanted to be sportscasters were on her books. As part of Muhammad's renewed focus on commercial interest, he was assigned to this young lady at IMG. As athletes were starting to retire – and in Muhammad's case he now had the signs of Parkinson's, his voice subdued, though he still could talk – Jean's job was to secure endorsement deals.

Muhammad's agent had worked for a commercial agency before she made the transition to IMG. And she was working for actors and getting them commercials so she dealt with a lot of advertising agencies in New York and the casting directors. Not long after joining the agency, Muhammad inked a Polaroid commercial deal. Back in those days, Polaroid was a camera which had an instant picture slip out after you took it. His agent would usually deal with Muhammad through Howard Bingham, and then Howard needed time off. I can't remember whom she dealt with after that. Howard came back into his life some time later. But at the time Howard was kind of fading himself out a little.

In the fall of 1983 Muhammad flew to New York with Veronica. They were scheduled to meet the agent at the airport who had been given the responsibility to bring him into New York City and make sure he got to the shoot location. I guess they wanted somebody from the agency to meet him and welcome him as a client as soon as he stepped off the plane. That day there was a blizzard but Jean had made her way to JFK in a limousine. It took forever to get Muhammad. My brother, of course, was an outgoing person who could connect with anyone. But the young agent didn't know what to talk about with Muhammad. She sat there in the back of the limousine thinking, *Oh my God. I'm here with Muhammad Ali*. In fact, she was terrified. Her nerves had taken over.

Muhammad had his agent set up the shoot stipulating certain conditions, taking into consideration that my brother was a devout Muslim. It was an absolute necessity that he got his prayer in. 'We need to have a separate room because he is a devout Muslim and he will interrupt the shoot because he does the prayers and he needs to have that space,' the agent told the company representative. That was his only condition. It was way more important than the monetary side because by then he had embraced the Sunni sect of Islam and had voraciously studied the true teachings behind the religion he had first converted to. Muhammad's devoted attitude seemingly impressed Jean who had great admiration for him because back then, in the 1980s, there was a period when a lot of the black athletes were converting to Islam following in my brother's footsteps. It was an empowerment sort of thing. Yet, not everybody practised it, but Muhammad was devoted. That was a major source for his life. Whether he was at home or travelling he endeavoured to follow this fundamental pillar of prayer. And I would join him by praying with him. We took it very seriously.

The next day, the day of the shoot, the 33-year-old agent and her driver picked Muhammad up to take him to the shoot. Again, Muhammad was sitting in the back of the limousine with her and they were being driven to uptown Manhattan. He leaned over to his agent and asked her, 'You want to see how famous I am?' in that sort of low voice. And this woman was literally terrified as her nerves hadn't left her from the day before. She was thinking, *Oh, God, now what.* She didn't know what was going to happen – what Muhammad had up his sleeve – but she knew how famous and unpredictable he was. The driver slammed the brakes on at the lights and Muhammad got out of the limousine and just stood there. People were passing by, and as you can imagine this was the centre of one of the busiest cities in the world.

Not long after, passers-by realised it was Muhammad Ali. I swear to God women in mink coats, police officers, people from all backgrounds going about their business, created a traffic jam in the middle of Third Avenue. My brother absolutely craved that attention. What was of paramount importance was that people still recognised him and he still had that power over people. It was one of those moments you just go, *Wow.* Jean had never seen anything like it, even with all the famous people that she had worked with; nobody had that power emanating that Muhammad had. 'Muhammad,' she said very concerned, 'we've got to go to the shoot,' as she struggled to get him back in the limousine.

This was when his physical prowess had begun to wane, so part of him wanted to convey to her how famous he was even after he had hung up his gloves. I feel my brother needed that injector boost. All he now to do was stand on the street corner and he would create a traffic jam. Jean sensed Muhammad's devilish sense of humour, something that I had seen so often. She told him he had to get back in the car, but he was saying, 'We're fine, we'll get there.' Life was a great adventure for my brother. After about five minutes she finally literally dragged him back into the limousine.

One thing is for sure: Muhammad didn't want to embrace the bullshit that goes with fame – diva qualities and isolating oneself from the masses. Instead, he was comfortable with being himself. He was more comfortable with people who handled him, such as agents, who didn't push and pull him in situations. And his agent basically realised this and she was thinking, *Do what you want, I'll get you there in time.* She didn't push him to be other than what he is because she knew she wasn't going to get anywhere with it anyway.

Needless to say, they arrived late for the shoot. The Polaroid executives were there because everybody was eager to meet a sporting icon. The casting director, the director, make-up person, writer, and there were lots of others including the secretaries. The shoot went well and Muhammad broke for the prayers in between. He went into the empty room. Then they wrapped up. After the shoot they drove back to the IMG offices based in the General Motors building on 59th Street and 5th Avenue. When they both got out of the limousine my brother wasn't done. Compelled to continue his entertainment, he said to Jean, 'Come with me. We're going to go over.' He wanted to take her with him to 5th Avenue, but he didn't get further than the building next door as he got flocked by fans. 'I've got to get to work, good luck,' she said as she made her getaway back to the office. In the meantime, Muhammad was surrounded by people.

When she got back to the office, she told Barry that she had left their client on the corner of 59th and 5th Avenue. 'You've got to go back and get him,' Barry insisted. But she said, 'No. No. No. There are too many people around. Ali does not need me to be a babysitter and I am not Ali's bodyguard. He just doesn't need me.' Following Muhammad all day had been a relentless task. She just couldn't keep up with him because he was like the North Star that everybody gravitated towards. He was like the wind. He went where the wind blew him. He could go anywhere. This was in the days when he wasn't so programmed by having to do promotional things when we were constantly going from city to city. The fact that he wasn't boxing meant he wasn't required to do specific fight promotional stuff. So, Muhammad was let loose and went and did what he did. Apparently he wanted to take Jean to Harlem. He had told her, 'You need to expand your horizons. I'm taking you to Harlem.' She had to decline the offer because he wanted to go late at night at 11 o'clock and she had to get up for work in the morning and she had two kids to get to school. So she said, 'I can't go. I'd love to do it.' Some actor!

★ ★ ★

The next day in the *New York Post* on page 6, which is the celebrity gossip column, there was a derogatory piece on my brother. Basically, it read that Muhammad did this Polaroid shoot and was being inappropriate with the girls. When Jean saw the accusations levelled at Muhammad, she went utterly nuts. Muhammad's agent had been there with him, and she knew the story was patently false. No one had complained. Everyone was fine when they had left. This was back in the day when you didn't expect people to say untruths, not like today where rogue stories persist about unacceptable behaviour. As anger ran through her veins, she didn't waste time calling up the editor of page 6. She screamed, 'What are you doing! That was not true. I was there. He went in and did his prayer. How can you print this about Muhammad?' In spite of her complaint, it seemed they didn't care what she had to say. They had no intention of listening and didn't retract it. The agent was just appalled and thought, *Wow, how many other things have been printed about Ali that aren't even remotely true?* She was trying to defend Muhammad not merely because she represented him, but she knew there was no substance whatsoever in the piece. They just categorically told her, 'We don't care, whatever. We're not retracting.' She quipped, 'What do you mean, you don't care!?'

Muhammad was a larger-than-life character in the public eye, so he was prone to attract lots of controversy. I often encountered members of the press who had bad intentions. It was simple. I used to say to them, 'Leave my brother alone. If you want to say anything bad I don't want to hear it. Are you crazy? What's wrong with you? I remember once one reporter fired back at me, 'What are you going to do?' I said, 'A whole lot. Are you threatening my brother?' Needless to say, the guy backed off.

And that was just as shocking back then to his agent. Interestingly she didn't bring this to my brother's attention, nor talk to him about it. Besides, Muhammad and Veronica – who wasn't present at the shoot – had left for Los Angeles the next day. Even if she had brought it to his attention, I think – and this is what she thought too – Muhammad wouldn't have cared. But she cared and wanted to set the record straight. He had got used to people spouting untruths about him over the decades and he had been swamped with controversy, so I think he just had an attitude, *It is what it is.* I don't think things like that mattered to him and he was so used to the media-induced negative publicity in addition to good publicity. Nonetheless, Muhammad's agent was right behind Jean and her furious attack, because the newspaper wasn't even remotely accurate. All he was doing was praying in another room. He never missed his prayers, and being a devout Muslim after you've just prayed to the All-Mighty, the last thing on your mind is looking at scantily clad women.

Muhammad and Jean knew that people exaggerated or they just told outright lies in the column. So, back in the 1980s when she saw this and people would read it she thought, *How can you write that that wasn't even true, get your facts right.* That was an eye-opener to say the least. I think what it demonstrated is when you're that famous you're just going to take hits from wherever whether they're true or not true. My brother understood that better than any of us and just let it roll off his back.

★ ★ ★

Later, some people prodded Muhammad's agent to divulge the more derogatory revelations about him. They wanted the dirt. Except the agent said, 'There is no dirt on the man.' Whatever his flaws and limitations they are there for the world to see. And every time anyone was in his presence, they always felt elated. Muhammad had that magical thing about him. Even though it looked like my brother had this massive ego, those who really knew him never translated it into ego. Barry might have another take, though. Muhammad never ever suggested that he was better than anybody, I can assure you of that. It was this that really humanised him to the world. In some ways he could be the greatest narcissistic maniac in the world, but all the people would still love him. That ego was a healthy ego. Now, here's the thing: anybody that had power, he would always give them a pile of shit – that was his thing. Howard Cosell, Barry, etc. And because they had power he would let them know who was in control. 'You may have a certain degree of power, but not over me,' he would tell them. Moreover, he did it without nastiness. It was a remarkable thing to witness. Some were fortunate to see a personal side to him that not everybody saw.

Anyway, during Muhammad's second stint at IMG they tried to maximise his earning potential, but Muhammad didn't really care. When Jean was assigned to him she was told, 'You've got to get commercials. He needs the money.' She was trying to get commercials, but he'd be going here and there without a care in the world. So for the most part they wouldn't work out and he ended up not doing a lot of commercials. They did, nonetheless, have numerous charitable related things Muhammad would be inclined to do – that's something he enjoyed doing. For these, of course, he didn't get paid and he was absolutely fine with it. He would say, 'Oh, I will do that for charity.' He didn't care about commercial endorsements and money; he was concerned about his image, how people perceived him and how he wanted to be remembered. Moreover, at that stage of his life, he had a devoted faith and everything else was just gravy.

Muhammad's motivation for commercials diminished. Although he wanted to make money – and the idea of making money was really important – it was the idea that seduced him, not the end result. I think there lay the problem: following through with it. *How are we going to do this for you to do it?* was the question. I think that was the push. Of course, Muhammad could've earnestly pursued more commercials in his quest for bringing in loads of dollars and laughed his way to the bank. I just don't think he was motivated. He knew he was famous and he could do anything he wanted, but it was also the beginning of his physical decline. Perhaps that's why he didn't pursue them with as much vigour as he maybe would have done when he was in his prime.

FATE: FROM ILLNESS TO DIVORCE

By the time the 1984 Olympics came to Los Angeles, Muhammad was fully in the throes of a retired life, but little did he know that he was about to do verbal battle with an old adversary. It started when George Foreman, who had forged a deep friendship with Muhammad in the years since they locked horns a decade earlier, happened to have a deep conversation on the phone revolving around my brother's condition with *Sports Illustrated* writer Gary Smith. George expressed his concern for my brother's health in grave terms – as one of the men who'd seen him most over the years, he thought his faculties had deteriorated considerably. More to the point, George felt somewhat blameworthy. He was of the notion that his punches in the Rumble in the Jungle had contributed to Muhammad's decline, that the beating he had handed out during the war in Zaire were to blame for what he was seeing on his TV every time my brother was interviewed. George, by this time, had developed a disdain for boxing – before his comeback, he went through a period of feeling sickened by the violence of this sport he'd been part of. You have to understand, too, that George idolised my brother. His concern was genuine.

'I need to go talk to Ali,' he told Smith. 'I need to kind of come to some sort of resolution around all these feelings I'm having.'

Always receptive of guests, Muhammad was delighted to see both when they turned up on his doorstep a matter of hours later. He sat them down cordially, and the pair started chatting just like old friends, with Smith happy to fade into the background. Moments later, though, George threw out his first jab.

'You need to turn your life to Jesus Christ,' he told my brother, following up with a series of homilies from the Bible. Muhammad, who never appreciated being preached at in his own home, hit straight back with a quote or two from the Koran. And, well, things just erupted from there as the two started going at it full swing. It was Rumble in the Jungle II, except that this time both men were slinging Biblical and Koranic quotes instead of punches. George, who had become a staunch Christian, was trying to convert my brother to Christianity, while Muhammad, who'd never really lost his own staunch Muslim beliefs, would absorb his arguments and throw them right back. Smith, caught in the middle, had a ringside seat for these two heavyweights going at each other again.

The subject of religion, of course, was something Muhammad and George had broached before. Muhammad loved needling people by pointing out discrepancies in the Bible, while George, who always carried a Bible, was always happy to start preaching. At the house, however, Muhammad had had enough of this to the extent that he told him to leave him alone.

'Look, that's enough,' he said, finally. 'I don't want to hear any more! I followed Elijah Muhammad and Malcolm X converted me and nobody else is going to convert me. If God wants me to change, let him tell me.' Apparently George got the message because he refrained from ever pursuing that route again. Round two of their rivalry, you'd have to say, ended in a draw.

The strange thing about Muhammad's relationship with his former foe was that Muhammad refrained from ever engaging in a meaningful conversation with him pertaining to boxing – particularly their own fight. George might occasionally attempt to drift into a conversation about the sport, but Muhammad was never inclined to go down that route. My brother once told George that he knew God would give him victory over Sonny Liston and Joe Frazier. George, being the humble man he became and showing great reverence, said, 'I understand you had a victory over me too.' At this Muhammad closed up. His friend might not have minded talking about getting dethroned by Muhammad, but my brother had reservations on lighting that fuse again. Despite their religious belief differences, both men had mutual respect for each other.

★ ★ ★

Even once my brother retired, going to visit him was always an adventure. You might spend the afternoon quietly lounging around and talking in his house, or he might wave you into his car to take you on some madcap escapade. On a day not long after the Foreman visit, Smith visited Muhammad, and as soon as he parked up on the driveway my brother beckoned him to get into his own car – with a twelve-year-old Muhammad Ali Jr., who was visiting with his sisters, parked in the back seat – and take a drive. It turned out that he wanted to see the boxing workouts of the Olympians who were in town – in particular Mark Breland, the five-time Golden Gloves champ who was favourite to take the gold. The visit went pretty much as expected – Muhammad appeared at the gymnasium and everybody had a fine afternoon – but the aftermath left Smith with more cause for concern.

While driving back home on the Santa Monica Freeway, Muhammad's eyelids suddenly started to close. Smith, who was in the front passenger seat, was startled but before he could react, Muhammad's hands dropped off the steering wheel and the click, click, click sound of the tyres clipping the lane dividers signalled that they were drifting left and right. The car was going sixty miles an hour and drifting, other drivers honking their horns, and Smith straight-up froze. *Could this be a trick? Do you grab the steering wheel from the Greatest of All Time, the champ?* He glanced over again to see Muhammad's eyes still closed, his hands down on his laps… and then, just as Smith was about to reach over for the wheel, a little pair of hands came up from the back seat. Muhammad's skinny little son had reached over his dad's shoulders and tried to take the steering wheel to drive the car. All of a sudden, Muhammad's eyes popped open and he took the wheel as calmly as if he was getting in the car for the first time. He had that little devilish smile he often wore after a good prank, and that only made it tougher to divine what had actually just happened.

Had my brother really fallen asleep at the wheel? Smith was well aware that Muhammad was taking medication for his Parkinson's disease – still not officially announced – which could make him very drowsy. But, at the same time, it could have easily been a prank. *It must've been,* part of him thought. *He must've worked it out with his son. They worked that little routine out, how many times must they have rehearsed it?* To this day, neither Smith nor I know the answer to that question.

Whatever the truth, the one thing his medication hadn't robbed Muhammad of was his sense of hospitality. Moments after the drama in the car, people in cars who had dodged Muhammad's vehicle were peering in the windows of the car, trying to get a peek at who this lunatic was trying to cause a crash on the highway. It's not uncommon in Los Angeles for someone to pull a gun out in a road rage incident. They were about to get two surprises – the first when they realised it was Muhammad Ali, and the second when they realised that he was already urging them to form a line behind him. Before you know it, my brother had ten different cars lined up behind him. He started a convoy and signalled his new 'followers' to accompany him to his mansion.

In that period, my brother was still living in LA's Hancock Park, 55 Fremont Place, a nice little gated community full of prototypical Hollywood-style mansions. The house was set up to Veronica's taste, through and through – my brother's new wife had given it a traditional theme with old-style regal furniture, chairs that were nicer to look at than to sit on, decor designed to show opulence rather than create comfort. It was a place to marvel at, not to make use of – it just lacked that ambience and warmth. Despite the opulence, you could feel that Muhammad didn't rely on this house, and he didn't have very much input. My brother had said – and anybody who knew him well will attest to this – that he could live under a car. He didn't need nor really care for luxury. That had never really been his goal in life, and now he was past it almost entirely.

Anyway, Muhammad invited everybody in. All of these total strangers congregated into the room, amazed to see where they had found themselves. Muhammad moved straight into the role of entertainer, going behind people's ears to produce coins and making cards and keys disappear in his hands. For Smith, who earlier was in fear for his life, this was a welcome respite. As Muhammad mingled with the people, Smith saw this as an opportunity to introduce a hardcore fan to Muhammad. His good friend, Radomir Kovačević, who was a judo Olympian, was in Los Angeles for the Olympics. This guy was huge, over 6 feet, weighing in at 290 pounds. So Smith grasped this opportunity to make his friend's dream come true. He excused himself, jumped in his car, drove back to the Olympic village, picked the judoka up and brought him back to the house.

This athlete was a three-time Olympian hailing from Yugoslavia. He had ventured into the Far East living in Japan and became a champion there while training at the university. He had always had this great admiration for the Greatest of All Time. And as a young man growing up in Eastern Europe, Muhammad was this great warrior he'd read about. For him, it was a dream to meet him.

Once Muhammad set eyes on Radomir and saw this giant of a man, a big character with a robust personality, it was only a matter of time before he realised this guy was no ordinary man. Basically, it started to sink in for Muhammad that this guy was a warrior. Muhammad proceeded to perform magic tricks for him too. And he engaged in a conversation about life with him. This guy was a huge character himself, and he wasn't going to sit there with his mouth open star-struck. He was going to engage Muhammad and start talking to him about life. He cherished this rare opportunity. Ironically, my brother had a tendency to talk about you, the guest, not himself – he was always full of questions.

In this stage of his life, Muhammad was often quiet and contemplative – like I said, by this time his condition had become more visible. He would act like he was napping but he'd be listening to everything. And then, when it was least expected, he'd come alive and fool everyone. This act happened so often that his closest friends and family – me included – learned not to lower their guard around him or to say anything that they didn't want him to hear, about his condition or anything else. Still, though, it was difficult for us to disguise our concern, day to day.

Having people in his home always brought him alive, though. He'd light up as he mingled with fans, answering their rapid-fire questions or quoting uplifting verses from the Koran. His fists and fast talk might have faded, but he was still an entertainer, always looking to find another way to thrill his audience, even as his condition overtook him.

He enjoyed telling jokes to people that I'd heard a hundred times. Yet, each time if you laughed and said to him, 'I've heard that one before,' Muhammad would respond, 'You heard that one before? I heard it ten years before. I heard it six years before.' His act was always the same, but the people closest to him enjoyed it regardless. He had a way of putting a smile on people's faces; even if you weren't a fan of Muhammad's, after a couple of hours in his presence you couldn't dislike him.

Veronica, meanwhile, was more reticent about entertaining than her always outgoing husband. She would come and go very quickly when there were guests around. As glamorous as she was, she didn't seem to enjoy entertaining in the same way Muhammad did. Honestly, the marriage wasn't thriving and cracks had finally started to surface by then between him and his third wife. She wouldn't ignore guests entirely – if they were famous or old friends of Muhammad's, she'd do her best to present the respectable front a family needs. But you could tell her heart wasn't really in it. Even some close members of my brother's camp felt she wasn't very friendly. But, I suppose, everyone's entitled to their opinion. Veronica just happened to be a reserved individual.

★ ★ ★

When Muhammad was first diagnosed with Parkinson's, a couple of months after the Los Angeles Olympics, he wasn't entirely ready to accept it. We first noticed it as a tremble in his left hand – nothing more than that, but still something noticeable to anyone who'd known him for as long as his family. It got worse, then spread – until finally, it was bad enough for everyone to notice. My brother's mind was unaffected by the disease that was ravaging his body, at least at first, but there came a point where nobody could deny its existence.

When Muhammad first started getting the shaking signs, whenever he would phone his ex-wife Belinda he would mumble. She would ask, 'What did you say?' So for a long time she actually thought he was playing games, as he enjoyed messing about and this diversion wouldn't have been out of character for her. She had no idea he was ill. When she finally learned of his illness, it was traumatic for her because she felt she was his soulmate despite the fact they were divorced by then.

When I first heard he had Parkinson's, I was surprised. I had no idea. I said to myself, *If he's got it then it's God's will. He controls everything in the world. He made the world.* Muhammad actually said that he was maybe being punished with his illness because he wasn't faithful. He thought, 'OK, it's a blessing. God's punishing me here on earth so I can spend eternity in heaven.' This was his thinking and he believed in it.

For my part, I had seen Muhammad shaking more and more, and it weighed on me a great deal. One thing I certainly have in common with my brother is that when someone calls me for an interview, I don't always think before blurting out what's on my mind. One day, an interviewer asked how I felt about my brother taking punches, all those hits he absorbed over years in the ring. I told the guy that it made me sad to see my brother shaking and slurring his speech, and without intending to I confirmed that Muhammad had Parkinson's. At that time, my brother's condition wasn't official, and my family certainly didn't want to deal with the press, but next thing you know the tabloid press took what I said and were running with it. That caused rifts that, in some quarters, have never healed. I know the whole family, including every one of Muhammad's children, still acknowledge and accept the fact I'm their uncle, and they all know that I mean well despite what I sometimes say. I've had my own set of issues, but they also know that I have occasionally been misquoted or coerced into saying things they wish I had not to the media. That has caused some friction, but along the journey family matters. It wasn't malice on my part but unfortunately I was targeted somewhat, as interviewers knew I wasn't as savvy as some.

It was true, though. There was no disputing it by that stage. He had been diagnosed at a hospital by Doctor Stanley Fahn, a month after the Summer Olympics. My brother had been admitted to Columbia-Presbyterian Medical Center, where he underwent an examination for several days for Parkinson's and the doctor, a neurologist at New York University, suggested that he seek the opinion of a Doctor Abraham Lieberman, who worked at the same hospital.

On the day of meeting Doctor Lieberman, accompanied by Yolanda 'Lonnie' Williams, a friend who was taking care of my brother,

Muhammad had one more chance to see his fans before anyone would know that the worst was happening. After conferring with the doctor, Muhammad made his way downstairs to the hospital cafeteria and sat down to eat – only to be quickly surrounded by well-wishers. News spread quickly around the hospital, and suddenly hundreds of interns, doctors, nurses and patients were jumping at this rare opportunity to meet the champ himself. While Doctor Lieberman wasn't a boxing fan, he was entirely aware of Muhammad being a famous boxer, but this was to be his first taste of just how appealing my brother was to people from every walk of life. Muhammad, of course, was accommodating as always as he was approached by people, even when the requests got strange. At one stage, one of the technicians from the radiology department came up to Doctor Lieberman and begged him to get my brother to punch him in the arm. Somewhat taken aback, a bemused Doctor Lieberman went down into the cafeteria to relay this unusual request – and sure enough, my brother ended up giving the crazy fan a tap on the shoulder, just hard enough for him to feel the impact of the left jab that once ruled the heavyweight division. For the next couple of months, Doctor Lieberman later told us, this man went around boasting, 'I was hit by Muhammad Ali. He punched me right here and I didn't fall down.'

Almost everyone has heard of the story when my brother, whom I was accompanying at the time, was refused an autograph by the legendary Sugar Ray Robinson. However, what people don't know is that when he was a young boy he would go to St Louis where he went to a game and he requested an autograph from a baseball player only to be refused. Muhammad vowed that when he became famous he would never refuse an autograph. And, believe me, he kept his promise till his final breath on this earth. He was no different in that cafeteria, even waiting for what was likely to be the worst news of his life. It was how he lived. On this occasion, though, it would do more good than simply giving a few dozen people a story to tell for a few weeks.

★ ★ ★

Meanwhile, my brother's third divorce was clearly on the cards, even though he loved Veronica dearly. Some people felt that Veronica left

Muhammad because she knew he was getting ill, but to my mind that's a viewpoint not even worth entertaining. Veronica herself said she'd had enough of Muhammad's old ways, and I'm certain that's part of the reason it happened. But another part was Veronica's own independence. She had her own ways and a penchant for many things – music, horses and acting – and wanted to pursue a career and not merely be a stay-at-home wife. They both loved each other and the connection between them remained long after they were no longer married – that part of their love didn't fade away – but marriage by now just wasn't right for them.

When Veronica told my brother she wanted a divorce, he sobbed for an hour straight. He found the prospect of separating daunting, and had no inclination to take things as far as divorce whatever happened, but he knew he would have to respect her wishes.

Another consideration, though, was their young daughter, Hana, who was only eight at the time. Even though Muhammad could still walk, talk and otherwise get around pretty much normally, every now and again he would stumble and get off balance, and it was something that really worried his little daughter. She saw this look in his eyes whenever he stumbled – just like a blur. She could sense something wasn't right, but she couldn't put her finger on it. It must have been alarming for her, but to console his daughter, Muhammad would just smile, shower her with kisses, and tell her, 'God takes care of me.' Eventually, little Hana would go as far as asking other people around her, 'Why does my dad talk that way? Why does he sound like that?' Nobody, as far as I know, ever told her the truth. Instead, they would concoct little white lies, designed to spare her. 'Oh, he fell off a scooter when he was young. He'll be fine, he'll be OK.'

Veronica, worried about her daughter and the impending divorce, arranged for her daughter to see a psychologist: but in the end, this led to an even crueller turn of events. In one session at the psychologist's office, without knowing that his patient had been kept in the dark, the psychologist asked the little girl, 'Hana, how do you feel about your parents' divorce?' Hana, with no knowledge of any potential divorce on the cards, was left stunned. Back at home Hana came running to her mother gulping back tears.

'I'll be a good girl now,' she told her mother. 'Please, I'll be a good girl.' Veronica explained to their daughter that she loves her father but people grow apart. Hana, as naive as an eight-year-old girl can be, said to her mother, 'Oh, but you both like popsicles, you both like movies. So how are you different people?' It was, understandably, beyond the scope of their daughter's imagination.

In the summer of 1985 Muhammad and Veronica decided to pursue the divorce. Despite the fact I knew they had their set of issues, I was surprised that they actually went ahead with it. Six months before the divorce, Muhammad went to visit Veronica and their daughters at their house – by then Muhammad and Veronica were living separately. Muhammad was finding the whole situation torturous. He knew there was no other plausible solution. As the divorce finalised he left some belongings at the office for Veronica. Muhammad had with great effort scrawled out, in a diary-style format, everything he and his wife had done together during 1985, the last year they lived together. Underneath that, there were a bunch of letters, covering every month from 1983 to 1985, penned by my brother asking Veronica for another chance, expressing how much he loved her, and how repentant he was for the mistakes he'd made. He wrote of how he gravitated towards praying on a regular basis, and how he hoped to see his wife in the life hereafter.

Why didn't my brother directly bring the letters to Veronica's attention so that they may have salvaged their marriage before their divorce was all but unstoppable? I can only speculate. I assume Muhammad felt Veronica would never take him back – forgiveness certainly never seemed on her agenda at that critical period of time. Muhammad and I, meanwhile, had grown up seeing with our own eyes our father dallying with other women, my brother once telling me that he was only four years old when he first witnessed one such unfortunate incident. Our parents could've split when Muhammad and I were still little boys, but they stayed together for the sake of their two sons. As an adult when my brother asked our mother about whether she would take our father back, she replied like a dam suddenly bursting, 'Oh, never, never, never!' So, I think part of that may have been the reason why Muhammad might have been apprehensive about throwing the dice because he thought it was too late – what was done was done, and Veronica wasn't going to forgive him. Nevertheless, he left the letters behind for her to discover them and maybe she'd come to truly understand the deep love he still had for her. But as it happens she apparently never did get to read them. When she eventually did get her hands on them, it was too late.

★ ★ ★

The divorce finalised in 1986, even though Veronica and Muhammad had been living apart for over twelve months by then. The same year, the woman who would go on to be his fourth and final wife moved in with my brother permanently – they married on 19 November 1986. Lonnie Williams had been friends with Muhammad since his youth in Louisville – her mother and our mother were friends and they lived across the street from each other in Louisville. So she had met and been around Muhammad when she was eight years old. She was always around, even if not physically, and had gone on to become Muhammad's carer when his symptoms worsened in the early eighties.

Back in Chicago, before his career started to decline in the mid-1970s, Muhammad wanted a training camp near Chicago. As a result he had bought Berrien Springs farm in Michigan. He called it 'The Farm'. For this eighty-one-acre sprawling suburban estate, which at one time was owned by Al Capone's bodyguard, my brother paid around half a million dollars. He had a gym there right between the house and his office where I would join him for training camps, which doubled as a retreat.

Muhammad, along with his new wife, moved to Michigan. It wasn't long after that Muhammad invited Gary Smith to his Michigan home. Smith was writing a story on Muhammad's former entourage members and what they were doing with their lives, but also wanted to speak to my brother, even though by then Muhammad had withdrawn from much of public life.

By now, Muhammad was still on medication and shaking more noticeably. He still made a point of showing his guests that he still had juice left in him, and on this occasion, with a man who'd known him for several years, he was itching to demonstrate his skill. Just as he had years before in LA, he beckoned him to the car and had him drive to a boxing gym, though this time it was old and abandoned, practically falling apart.

Muhammad unlocked the place and pulled his watch off as he walked inside. He started to hit the black leather heavy bag, slowly at first and then with increasing speed, little pit-a-pats slowly shifting into the thunderous blows of my brother's glory days. He was moving fast, dancing, doing the Ali shuffle and flicking out jabs with some effort, Smith calling out the time at the end of each round. In the third, Muhammad's tempo increased until the whap-whap-whap of the bag sounded like thunder. In all this, Muhammad hadn't changed into workout gear; he was doing this in his black shoes, black pants and black shirt. He managed a smile as the final seconds ticked away, and one last lightning-fast combination on the bag.

The whole thing took maybe half an hour. After the show, Muhammad locked the place up and they headed back to his car, and then his body finally betrayed him. My brother, Smith saw, could barely get the key in the car door, shaking as he tried to do this simplest of things. This was a man who, at the height of his power, demolished his opponents with his iron fists. Now he couldn't even open a car door with the keys. We all saw it, at various times – glimpses of the man my brother once was – but his day-to-day struggle was a sight sad to behold.

Muhammad drove slowly on country roads on the way back, but he had one more surprise for Smith. In the barn that abutted the house, he had dozens of photographs framed from his career, but they weren't hung up gracing the walls in any manner whatsoever – just lined up on the floor against the wall. It was as if someone had just moved into the property and was still settling in. All these great moments in Muhammad's career were right there, but my brother had not taken care of them at all. No one had made any effort to really preserve their condition. As he walked around he realised the pigeons had been crapping on them and they were all streaked with bird crap. He had no reaction to that at all like, *Oh damn I knew that…* When Muhammad saw the crap, he slowly looked up at the rafters and didn't murmur a word. Instead, one by one, he slowly turned every picture against the wall. One thing Muhammad loved doing more than anything was looking back at his own career via the medium of film and photographs. Reminiscing, he would flick through photos with me – and his family members – which brought back great memories. He'd do the same whenever he had guests around.

On this day, Muhammad continued walking around with Smith following behind. Now you could see the back of the photos. It was like the lights going off one by one from the whole of my brother's career. Still with no remark at all like, *I gotta take care of them,* or *Damn, how did that happen?* Not even a word. It all happened real slowly like a slow-motion movie clip. Then Muhammad just walked out and his guest followed him quietly. The crapping on his whole career, never complaining or in any desperation, Muhammad's attitude was, *Oh, that's how it is. I'm just dealing with it and moving on.*

A NEW VOICE

As my brother settled in Michigan with his new wife, he was more or less out of the public eye. Still, he'd make occasional appearances. Muhammad was always a promoter's dream, with an extraordinary ability to fire up the fans and sell any show he was a part of. In the 1980s, he might have slipped from the public's consciousness somewhat, but his name continued to attract considerably large fees for public appearances, and promoters were always keen to recruit him. The real problem was that he would show up for next to nothing. It seemed insane a man of his calibre lending his name when he had the capacity to potentially generate a considerable amount of income for himself. By now he had left IMG.

In 1988, for example, a boxing-focused dinner event with the Canadian heavyweight champion George Chuvalo, who had the dubious pleasure of sharing the ring with Muhammad twice, was organised in Toronto. Chuvalo, after his bouts with my brother, had tallied up a total of ninety-three professional fights and was never knocked out in his entire professional career, even with big hitters like Joe Frazier and George Foreman on his résumé. When the organisers pursued Muhammad to ask if he would show his support by making an appearance for his old foe, he readily agreed. Muhammad was asked what monetary compensation he required. 'Get me a room, get me a ticket and I'll come,' he told the stunned promoters. 'I won't charge you anything.' The promoters got him a first-class return ticket on Air Canada and booked him a room at a 5-star hotel, but he'd have probably taken less. That was just how my brother operated. Maybe on this occasion you could chalk it up to sympathy for Chuvalo – but similar things happened again and again.

Anyway, Muhammad was adamant on helping his Canadian friend. The event sold out with 1,300 people. Businessmen, doctors, lawyers, financiers and sports fans filled the room out because they were yearning to meet a sports icon. Before the organisers announced Muhammad's name they had already sad 300-plus tickets. Then once they announced that Muhammad was going to be attending, numerous radio and TV shows proceeded to interview him. As a result, within twenty-four hours all the tickets were snapped up.

A former boxer turned radio show host, Spider Jones, who was one of the key people responsible for securing my brother's visit, along with a Polish guy named Eddie, picked Muhammad up from the airport in Toronto. Muhammad donned a suit, looking neat, and had Howard Bingham with him. At the airport Muhammad bumped into actress Shirley Temple. When she saw him she ran up and hugged him. She loved my brother. Here were all these baggage handlers, regular Joes, but he took pictures with them and laughed and joked around. Despite the fact he was jet-lagged, it didn't stop him from clowning around, putting on a show for spectators and onlookers who were mesmerised to be in the company of a famous man. He was more subdued when he was in the car. Parkinson's disease was progressing and his health was dwindling – he wasn't the same man Spider Jones had encountered twenty-two years earlier.

Along the way Jones sprung a request on my brother. 'Muhammad, I know there's a Polish woman who adores you whose husband passed away a couple of months ago,' he said. 'He was your biggest fan. Do you mind dropping by just to say hello?' This woman was actually Eddie's mother. Muhammad was more than game. He would never really reject such requests. People knew Muhammad was a people person and those who associated themselves with him to whatever degree were hardly hesitant to get what they could out of him. So they stopped by the house. They knocked on the door and a little woman, about 5 foot 3 inches, emerged. She was in her seventies and looked dejected. As she looked up she got the fright of her life, a pleasant surprise, when she realised Muhammad was standing there right in front of her face. 'Muhammad! Muhammad!' she screamed hysterically. He hugged her and kissed her on the top of her head four or five times. She invited them all in and made them a cup of tea. They sat around for about fifteen minutes and talked with the gleeful lady before heading to Toronto.

For the next two days, that was Muhammad's new home. During the course of his stay, Chuvalo and Jones – who had their own little entourage – took care of and paraded my brother around while he was their guest. What followed was two days spent in a whirl of feverish activity. One time when they were out they walked on the main street of the city and people flocked to him like bees to honey, resulting in a traffic jam on both sides – a scene I had witnessed with my own eyes countless times. Unlike other fighters and famous personalities, Muhammad started dancing like he used to in the ring and challenged a random guy by provoking him to get out of his car. He almost always took the initiative; no one would throw down the gauntlet. This guy was more than happy to comply so he got out of his car. Next thing you know, Muhammad started playing around with him. Both men were exchanging non-contact blows. Before you know it, the traffic built up as onlookers tried to figure out what was going on. Not long after the cops emerged out of nowhere. My brother started dancing around them in a playful spar manner. They were laughing.

People were screaming out of their car windows as they realised it was Muhammad Ali. You could hear shouts of, 'Ali, I love you! Ali, I love you!' My brother had the city in turmoil. The scene was vibrant, just like the first time he went over to Toronto to fight. Muhammad had a special affinity towards Toronto and he told the people that he loved their city. He said, 'I'm here and in my own country they treat me like I'm a criminal, but in Toronto they show me nothing but love.' Ever since his first experience there he had cultivated this warm relationship with Canada because the populace there had always treated him with dignity, while he had felt a deep resentment towards the US when the authorities revoked his licence.

Muhammad and his handlers would step into barber's shops,

restaurants, and everybody would follow like he was the Pied Piper. Everybody loved it! He'd always dig deep into his own pocket, take out a bunch of notes and hand them over to total strangers in the street. I must point out that to Muhammad it was of paramount importance to go down to the black community in whatever city he visited. He made every effort to mingle with the ghetto people. The hustlers on the street, the pimps, they captivated him – because although my brother grew up facing racial discrimination, he didn't grow up in that sort of street life . He had an insatiable curiosity for interesting people.

For him, the streets of Toronto became his playground, often challenging guys in the street to a fight. Of course, it was all in a playful manner. And when a guy would square up to fight him, he would run behind Jones's back and holler, 'Don't let him hit me, Spider Jones! Don't let him hit me.' He pulled that trick all the time to people's amusement. From the corner of his eye he spotted a white guy in the crowd, he must have been maybe twenty, twenty-one, and Muhammad barked at him, 'I remember you!' The somewhat bemused white guy said, 'I've never met you before, Champ.' Muhammad said, 'I remember you; you the one who called me a nigger!' Everybody burst out laughing. Muhammad had a strong tendency to use this line and he said to this guy, 'I'll whup you.' Amidst Muhammad taking his jacket off, the guy caught on right away and he took off his jacket slowly as if to take on the champ. Next thing you know, Muhammad ran like a scared baby behind Jones again. 'Don't let him hurt me!' and the crowd went into hysterics; it was just hilarious. It was something that teenagers would do. Muhammad spent some time with Jones in Detroit and Philadelphia and the latter witnessed a similar scene.

At that stage of his career, Muhammad went through several individuals who took on the role of 'manager' or 'agent' – including Richard Hirschfeld, an audacious lawyer who became a fugitive after federal tax and conspiracy charges…and who, it emerged had been imitating my brother's voice on the phone to smooth over his felonious transactions. Others wanted to ensure Muhammad got paid as well as lining their own pockets, but Muhammad was a giver and it wore him out.

The phone never stopped ringing, people asking for favours, to show up at events, people with business pitches. Virtually all of his money had disappeared by now. By the time he married Lonnie he was living comfortably, but he wasn't getting any better with money management, and the cracks were starting to show. Eventually, Lonnie undertook the responsibility of handling things, and did her best to stop him being exploited so easily. She got rid of the Black Muslims, but it was like fighting a hydra – you stopped one head, and two more popped up, demanding money. Not long after his visit to Canada, Muhammad visited Pakistan. And a year later, in 1989, he was invited back, this time as a special guest at the Fourth South Asian Games in Islamabad. Boxing may have been a fringe sport there, but literally everyone knew who my brother was.

★ ★ ★

Back in the 1980s Muhammad would attend boxing events whenever he could and I would sometimes accompany him. He missed fighting, sure, but also had a strong urge to be in the public eye. Being out of the limelight was killing him. Going to boxing shows was one place he knew he'd always make a stir.

At one time he was with Eddie Mustafa Muhammad at a fight. The Mirage hotel had opened up in Las Vegas and there was a big fight taking place at the venue, with a bunch of other celebrities invited. Muhammad, along with his friends, was walking in the hotel lobby and fans instantly recognised the world's most recognisable face. Sensing this was the chance of a lifetime they approached him to get autographs. Next thing you know, Muhammad stood there signing autographs for about an hour. When passers-by saw an assemblage of people they, naturally, were curious of what was going on. And they joined the line. Next thing you know, there was a long line of autograph hunters. It became apparent that Muhammad was going to be there for much longer. So Eddie told one of the staff, 'Can you bring a chair and a table because we're going to be here for at least another two hours signing autographs.' So a table and a chair was set up right there in the lobby. This was something unheard of. My brother sat down on the chair and commenced to sign. Now, had this been another famous star they'd have walked off, or their handlers no doubt would have taken control of the situation shielding the star.

But Muhammad signed every single autograph – about four hundred autographs. He told Eddie, 'If it wasn't for these people who pay the money to see us fight, we wouldn't be where we are.'

He told Eddie, 'You're a world champion, you belong to the world. You no longer just belong to your friends – no, you're bigger than that.' He continued, 'They see you on TV and they want to get next to you, they want to shake your hands and give you a hug.' Muhammad said to his young friend to always be courteous. You have to realise that he was a world-famous athlete. And in order to be a guy of Muhammad's magnitude you have to be able to go around the world where people admire you and mingle with them. Muhammad knew people just want to be in his presence and want an autograph. So, my brother was more than merely a world champion; he belonged to the world.

IRAQ

Our father passed away on 8 February 1990. I still miss my father today and I think about him often. It was difficult, and it left me really sad, for a long time. At the time he passed, my parents had been married for forty-nine years, so were very close to celebrating fifty years of marriage. Muhammad was forty-eight at the time and I was forty-six.

Whatever his failings, I had always looked up to my father with a great deal of admiration and respect. My dad always had my back and was there for me. I was one of the pall-bearers at the funeral, which took place on 12 February. It turned out to be one of the most difficult things Muhammad and I had ever dealt with in our lives. I had doubts whether I would get through or not at our father's funeral, but I held it together long enough to carry the casket, praying for strength to make it through the funeral even as I felt its weight on my shoulder. I felt as if there was a fresh hole in my heart. Eventually, life had to go on, Muhammad and I thought, though we continued to grieve long after his passing. Six months later, Muhammad finally had something to take his mind off the passing of the most important man in our lives. A mission that he believed in, albeit one which could put his life in danger.

I don't know if my brother knew who Saddam Hussein was before 2 August 1990. That was the date most of us heard about him, after all: the day the Iraqi dictator invaded Kuwait against the specific instructions of George Bush Sr., claiming to be providing resistance to 'Kuwaiti revolutionaries'. Almost simultaneously, his troops took fifteen American hostages from a local General Motors plant – regular engineers and petroleum workers whom Saddam promised to murder if Bush acted. For a few days in America, things were on a knife edge.

By that stage, Muhammad had been openly suffering from Parkinson's disease for six years and was living in relative obscurity, but he still retained some contacts who would reach out to him occasionally. One was Ramsey Clark, a former US Attorney General and by this point a real pacifist, who was trying to figure out an avenue to circumvent a bloody war. He was very apprehensive about the possibility of a major conflict in the Middle East. And so, after exhausting a few other avenues, he eventually contacted my brother to ask if he was interested in pursuing some behind-the-scenes diplomacy to prevent this war from escalating. Muhammad, a man of peace and a devoted Muslim who empathised with the entire Muslim world, didn't want to see war break out between the United States and the Muslim countries, and he readily agreed to do anything he could to utilise his fame and status to help. One thing led to another, and suddenly he was booked on a flight to Baghdad.

At the time, many of his friends and family counselled against the move. But he said, 'You can't live life in fear. You have to live life trusting God. If I lived in fear I wouldn't be able to do anything. If someone wants to shoot me and kill me, no one can save me, no man or bodyguard can protect me. So I have to live my life with trust and that I'll be taken care of as long as I am here. God gave me too much fame and love in this world, so with the fame I have I've got to help people. This effect I have on people, if I can help and save people and I didn't, it would be a sin.'

Muhammad and his team – including Herbert Muhammad and Brian Becker – arrived in Iraq on 23 November, more than a hundred days after the crisis began. Back at the White House, George Bush was apparently strongly disapproving of Muhammad's activities. His advisors regarded Hussein's activities as propaganda, and insisted that Muhammad was playing into the hands of a dictator by indulging this man's whims. Segments of the American press described what Muhammad was doing as 'loose cannon diplomacy', opining that a sports personality shouldn't be getting involved in such a potentially explosive conflict. Muhammad would compound the problem, was the general consensus.

While in Iraq, a man named Vernon Nored, the liaison for the camp my brother was staying in, accompanied Muhammad everywhere he went. This African-American government official had a strong understanding of the conflict and the parties involved due to his long tenure in the country, and Muhammad was strongly advised by him to venture out to meet the people of Iraq – to go to schools and talk to kids. My brother took this advice and was treated graciously from the outset. The populace swarmed around him everywhere he went. The Iraqis loved to have a sporting hero in their midst, he told me later, and were nothing but friendly towards him. And so, Muhammad walked the streets, met people and paid visits to mosques.

One thing that was paramount in his mind was to take back home an account of the real Iraq, so that on returning to the United States he could give a fair account of the country. The West had no real feel for the Iraqi people, he thought, and only knew the country through its troubled history. He wanted to change that and did his best, endearing himself to the Iraqi populace, who gravitated to him just as crowds did all around the world.

Still, not everything on the trip ran so smoothly. Saddam hadn't given Muhammad a specific date for their meeting, and as my brother's trip wore on, the meeting with the dictator was delayed again and again. My brother continued to mingle with the populace, but now there was a fresh concern. Muhammad had a very short supply of his medicine to control his Parkinson's, which was escalating by this point. The heat drained his strength, and at several points, I heard, his energy was so low that he could hardly talk. Again and again, there was no choice but to extend the trip, and concerns mounted. Seven days after he arrived, he could barely get out of bed. Luckily, Muhammad had encountered a group of Irish nurses and doctors in the dining area of a local hotel on the first day of his visit, and his team eventually managed to replenish his supplies. All the doctors asked for in exchange were photos with him.

Not long after that, Saddam's people told Muhammad's camp that he was ready to meet with my brother. Muhammad, accompanied by

Herbert and a couple of others in his team, arrived at Saddam's palace for a meeting. As talks got under way, Muhammad strongly expressed to the dictator that he wanted to avoid war. The time he had spent in Iraq prior to meeting him, he explained, had really opened his eyes, and he promised to take a good account of the country back to America. As discussions continued, he asked for something, a gesture of good faith from Saddam. He wanted, of course, to take the American hostages back with him to the United States to show that the dictator was capable of fairness. He played his final gambit quickly: 'Look, I'm going to go back and say the Iraqi people are good people,' he said. 'And tell America that we should not be sending planes and bombs into the country.'

Saddam, for his part, recognised that Muhammad was perceived as a leader of Muslim people globally, and that it was in his own best interests to have a positive interaction with him. Saddam, my brother believed, respected him, or he would not have taken the meeting. But at the same time, his hostages were extremely valuable. Despite Muhammad's frequent inability to talk clearly he tried his best, via the interpreter, to convey his message. The host talked for quite some time as his guest listened on.

Saddam, the translator finally explained, didn't feel that the captured Americans were hostages: that they were simply staying in the country as a matter of expedience. One of the things that the dictator wanted to impress my brother with was that he had been a good host. 'We, the Iraqis, have provided our American guests with movies to watch on VCR,' he explained via the interpreter. 'Do these look like hostages to you?' The reality, of course, was these civilians had no interest in anything but going home to their families. They had been kept from leaving and held against their will, however 'well' they were being treated. Muhammad knew that Saddam must understand this, and yet the negotiations were slow.

The meeting was relatively short – from start to finish, the whole audience took less than 60 minutes. As it came to an end, Saddam refused to make any formal declaration pertaining to releasing any hostages, but he did say to Muhammad, 'My, brother, I'll do something.' Muhammad, at this stage, had no idea whether his whole trip had been in vain.

One day later, word came through that Saddam had agreed to release all of the American hostages in his care. They were brought to Muhammad's hotel room, where my brother sat on his sofa, exhausted from the symptoms of his Parkinson's, but delighted to see them. One gentleman named Addie Henderson, a Vietnam veteran, told my brother that he vividly remembered Muhammad refusing to be inducted into the army back in the 1960s, and being angry with him at the time, because he felt that no one should be exempt from service. Now, he told my brother, he had re-evaluated his decision. He thought Muhammad did make the right decision for not joining back then. Other hostages thanked my brother and praised him, but his response to all of them was the same. 'You don't have to thank me, you don't owe me anything. I'm here as a Muslim and a man of peace. God works with people and God works for me to help you.'

Bush and the White House could hardly celebrate when they heard the news, but the press coverage of the event experienced an abrupt about-face. After being criticised for meddling in international affairs, suddenly Muhammad was being praised in some quarters, while in others, criticism persisted as some continued to tar him claiming he had done it for publicity. Critics claimed that Muhammad was really there just to benefit his own image. My brother had a book coming out, they said, or Muhammad just couldn't step away from the cameras, he was addicted to the cameras and fame. I can tell you one thing: when it came to serious matters, especially helping others and anything relating to Muslims, he took it seriously indeed. No book deal would have been worth the way my brother risked his health and well-being in Iraq. He did it for the hostages – and for the people of Iraq.

When war broke out on 16 January 1991, Muhammad was left desolate. He had kept his word to Saddam, speaking to reporters about what he saw in Iraq – the smiling children he saw in schools and the peaceful religious assembly in mosques. In the end, it didn't help. Whether the ultimate reason was oil, political interests or the safety of Kuwait, the US seemed determined to invade and bombard this country into a shadow of its former self. One member of Muhammad's delegation told him at the time of his visit that the American government was thrilled hostages had been taken. It would, he explained, lend public support to the forthcoming invasion. America had made its mind up.

I had no idea that Muhammad had actually gone to Iraq until I found out at the same time as everyone else. I was shocked, but not entirely surprised. I think there is absolutely no other celebrity who would have, or could have done what my brother did. Later, I talked to him about it and told him that I was very proud of what he'd done. He would try again, making his first and only visit to Iran in pursuit of negotiating the exchange of soldiers held prisoners of war after the Iran-Iraq war in 1993. In 1985 Muhammad, along with his friend and CIA agent Larry Kolb, went on a mission to Beirut to secure the release of hostages. Being around Muhammad, I wouldn't be surprised if people realised he had more friends, associates and connections in high places than any other celebrity.

And even if he couldn't stop the war, he could remind America – or, at least, some of America – that there were people in Iraq who didn't deserve the same fate as Saddam Hussein.

BECOMING A DAD AGAIN

L ess than ten months after returning from Iraq, there was a reception for Muhammad at Gracie Mansion, the official residence of the mayor of the city, in New York, where the mayor was among the guests. Chuck Wepner, who had fought a hard fifteen-round fight with Muhammad, was also in attendance, and for a moment it seemed as if his presence might cause an issue. Wepner had unquestionably been tough, but he was also not above resorting to dirty tactics in their fight. How could I forget this? He had been awarded a knockdown against Muhammad, but really it looked more like he had actually stepped on my brother's foot. At several points, he hit Muhammad on the back of his head with an open hand, which had further aggravated Muhammad. At the time, my brother was furious. But what would he do now?

Seeing my brother, Wepner started to walk away towards the exit in an attempt to leave the party. Unbeknown to him, though, Muhammad had been spying on his old foe from across the room. Suddenly, he ran all the way over to Wepner and in a very elaborate and humorous manner, he stepped on his foot. After that – smiles everywhere. All was forgiven. That was a wonderful example of my brother's decency and good humour. Wepner was thrilled.

To some people there was no difference in the public Muhammad Ali and the private Muhammad Ali. I can tell you that he was pretty much on when he was very much aware he was dealing with the media and his adversaries. However, there were times over the years he was cranky. There were times he didn't want to talk to anybody if he was moody. But he wasn't petulant. For the most part, he was very pleasant. You see, Muhammad was somebody who wanted to be loved and admired. Muhammad was somebody who craved attention. He emanated this aura about him. Unless he was particularly annoyed about something, he was jubilant and receptive.

This particular event was in aid of creating a Muhammad Ali Day. It was an outdoor garden party. The weather was good, the food was great and people were standing and chatting. Everyone dressed well. In attendance were a lot of people from the New York area, certainly a lot of journalists, some prominent boxers and politicians. Everybody got the chance to shake hands with my brother. Accompanying my brother was his wife Lonnie and a small kid named Asaad, whom they had just adopted when he was five months old. When Lonnie moved in with Muhammad, her sister was caring for a friend's baby, Asaad. Lonnie just fell in love with this adorable baby and she and Muhammad decided to adopt him. It would be Asaad who would go on to live and spend the most time with his adopted parents from all of Muhammad's children. Despite this, he has always stayed out of the limelight. On this day, though, there was some kind of strange vibe because even though they were bringing this kid out in public, they requested to the reporters present not to mention him. It was still some sort of a guarded thing. I don't think any honest reporter kept this a secret despite Muhammad's and Lonnie's wishes. How can you trust the press on something like this?

By now Muhammad had begun to slur his words. At the event he didn't make a major pronouncement. His deterioration physically and particularly verbally was more and more apparent. And towards the end, certainly after the Olympics in 1996, you'd see less and less of him in public as he fell by the wayside after his time in the spotlight. Undeniably, on that day Muhammad was the most famous person in the room. Certainly in the 1960s and 1970s he was at the fore of the sporting world and the most recognisable face on the planet. I think it wasn't until later, the 1990s and the 2000s, that you had to start explaining who he was to some people. In high schools now when you talk to kids, they remember Muhammad as a face from the past. Maybe they have an image of him as a fighter. Maybe they saw him light the Olympic torch. But they have no sense of the controversy he fuelled in the 1960s when people despised him. Certainly at the garden party Muhammad was the most famous face – people still had memories of him. Remember that anybody in the 1960s around college age about to be drafted or join the army abhorred Muhammad. He was perceived as an ungrateful celebrity, because they were going into war and he wasn't. I think as time goes on and people get further and further from the moment of his glory days, it's hard to remember quite how much passion he stimulated – one way or another. Because of that, it was great to proclaim a Muhammad Ali Day to cement his legacy as a positive force in America's history. And in June 2019, I was proud to be, together with Lonnie and my other relatives, at the ceremony unveiling the official logo for the Louisville Airport, now renamed the Louisville Muhammad Ali International Airport, in recognition of the way my brother put our town on the map, before he went on to change the face of the United States forever.

★ ★ ★

Though my brother almost always had time for everyone, I know that one thing he regretted in later life was that, in his early years, he didn't spend more time with his own children. His first children, with Belinda – Maryum, Muhammad Ali Jr. and the twins, Jamillah and Rasheda – were very young when the two divorced, with Belinda and the kids moving back to Chicago. When Muhammad and Veronica got divorced, their two kids – Hana and Laila – were very young also. And Miya and Khaliah hardly spent any time with my brother during their formative years.

It wasn't until the children were older, of course, that they realised that they would have to share their father with the world. Several of them remained oblivious to the true magnitude of the impact their father had on the world until they were in their teens – he was out of the news and the public eye, even if millions of people around the globe remembered his fights and the stand he took for his beliefs by refusing to go to war.

Although the press did their best to delve into his personal life in his heyday, by and large their intrusions were something he managed to shield his children from. On the subject of his children being exposed to the media, Muhammad once told an interviewer, 'I think it can present a serious problem… that if everywhere you're going people are saying this and that… but if you keep quiet and don't publicise it, then people won't know who you are. Joe Louis's daughter was handling some job in Chicago and nobody there knew who she was until she told somebody. So if you just keep quiet it shouldn't be much of a problem.'

Muhammad was always conscious of the pressure his children were prone to. He felt bad about it. It was something we often talked about. And so, although he couldn't always be around, my brother did his best to ensure they were raised in an environment that was what you'd hopefully call 'normal'. Part of this, of course, was the circumstances of their upbringing. Because of my brother's divorces and the fact that the kids were living away from him, they were naturally kept out of the limelight.

His four children with Belinda, for instance, were raised by their grandparents from their mother's side. They didn't grow up in Hollywood, or have that type of lifestyle where you are exposed to the glitz and glamour and come to think of it as the norm – the environment the Jackson kids grew up in, say. They attended the same schools as other kids, grew up practising whatever sports they wanted to, had to save for things they wanted just like normal kids. Nothing was just given to them on a plate because of their last name. Part of this, as I say, was circumstantial, but Muhammad couldn't have been happier about it. 'This life is just a test,' he would tell them. 'You can't take materialistic things with you. The important thing when you die is your soul – that's what counts.'

That's not to say that my brother was always above helping his kids out using his name. He was living in Michigan, for instance, when both twins applied for the same position in an office and – though they didn't know this till later – instead of hiring one candidate the company decided to hire both sisters for the same position. This made the salary almost insultingly low, and when Muhammad was visiting Jamillah, and happened to talk about it with her, he was shocked.

'That's slave labour!' he told her. 'You can do better than that.

Why don't you quit your job and travel around with me? I'll get you networking.' After that, the twins sporadically travelled with their father, not just domestically but abroad, and came to learn more about him.

One memorable day, Muhammad, accompanied by Lonnie and the twins, decided to show his daughters that he still had it in him to gather a large crowd, and maybe give the girls a taste of the fame their father had enjoyed in his heyday. They were going to an exhibition for the award-winning sports photographer Neil Leifer's photographs in New York on 5th Avenue at a very nice bookshop. Leifer was the young up-and-coming photographer in 1965 who ended up shooting the best sports photograph ever, the iconic picture of Muhammad standing over his fallen foe Sonny Liston in their rematch. Muhammad was the guest of honour, and when the exhibition was over they went out to dinner. Then they all got into a limousine that was waiting to take my brother back to his hotel, which was in midtown Manhattan.

When they got to 7th Avenue and the corner of Times Square, though, suddenly Muhammad asked the driver to stop. He stepped out, casually walked to the corner of the Square and stood casually in the street. I had seen him do this countless times. It never took long before someone recognised him, which prompted them to stop and shake hands, and after that the effect would just snowball. It happened in the smallest towns, but in Times Square the effect was immediate, and crazy. Moments later, people were shouting, 'Champ, champ, champ!' running over in the hope of getting an autograph or a few words with Muhammad. Before long there were dozens of bodies flocked around my brother. There were no mobile phones back then, of course, so only the few tourists who'd come equipped could take a picture. All the rest could hope for was an autograph, or a simple handshake. But for many, that was enough.

Before long, the crowd moved out into 7th Avenue, blocking traffic. Taxis were beeping their horns, but Muhammad was savouring every moment, posing with his fans and well-wishers as his daughters watched in awe. The only interruption to his reverie came when a police officer walked by, but this man in uniform wasn't planning to stop the impromptu gathering. 'Champ, can I ask a favour?' asked the policeman, politely enough. 'Could you move onto the sidewalk? You're holding up the traffic in Times Square.' Muhammad got a round of applause from the fans as he strolled to the sidewalk and the crowd followed. He spent at least another ten minutes mingling with that crowd, while Lonnie and the girls watched, knowing that this was the kind of thing Muhammad thrived on. Eventually everyone got back into the limousine to go back to the hotel. In the car, someone asked him, 'What made you do that, Muhammad? Why did you want to stop?' He turned to them, happy, and said, 'I just wanted to show my daughters that I could still stop the traffic in New York.'

★ ★ ★

As his daughters started seeking their own paths in life, Muhammad still found every opportunity to let them travel with him abroad. In 1992, when the twins had both graduated but before either of them had started to carve out a real career, the family flew to England. This time it was for Muhammad to promote a book and a restaurant. The first place they went to was Manchester, where they stayed for a few days to enjoy the tranquillity of the near-countryside – and got one hell of a surprise.

My brother, as I've mentioned, always loved horror movies – Dracula movies in particular. He'd mock-throw up his hands in fear at the scary parts, and shush us if we even tried to talk. His favourite Dracula, of course, was none other than Christopher Lee. And, it turned out Mr Lee was a good friend of the restaurant owner, who'd invited him over for a visit.

Well, when he laid eyes on Christopher Lee, my brother's eyes just lit up. He was so animated – asking him to do the Dracula pose, and then imploring him to act like he was Dracula. The whole setting – the house, the secluded area, the trees surrounding it – felt like a set for a Hammer Horror movie, and the twins loved it so much they almost didn't want to go to London. Later when they were back in America, they'd joke that they wanted to live there.

While Muhammad was fulfilling his contractual obligations, he was also having fun. They were in a small room in a hotel on Deansgate in the city centre. Unbeknown to Muhammad he would be bumping into someone he had encountered as a then teenager for the first time thirteen years earlier – Charlie Hale, the young man who first came to his rescue when a jostling, boisterous guy walked into a London hotel room with the intention of initiating an altercation with Muhammad. If you saw Muhammad travelling, the chances of his best friend Howard Bingham of being on his side were pretty high. Howard, with a camera hanging around his neck, was in sight. He was always quiet and would fade into the background. Lonnie and the twins were having a light-hearted conversation with this man, and Lonnie asked him, 'What do you do?' He explained that he'd been on TV and did impressions, that he was a comedian. Curious, she asked him, 'Who do you take off?' He replied, 'Muhammad,' and he took his hat off, which got Lonnie and Muhammad's daughters chuckling. Lonnie further pressed him, 'Who else?' Charlie, who was an ardent boxing fan, revealed Mike Tyson. He did a remarkable impression of the notorious heavyweight champion. It was amazing that Lonnie was so impressed that she was signalling for Muhammad, who was in a suit mingling with someone nearby, to join their little group. My brother, Lonnie and Howard, had this secret signal which they used to do between them with their tongue. They would make weird noises to get one another's attention in a public place.

Muhammad sauntered over and Lonnie enthusiastically said to her husband, 'Listen to this guy's impression of Mike Tyson.' So he repeated the Tyson impression and Muhammad was absolutely choking, and I mean choking with laughter to the extent he could not contain himself. It was as if it wasn't enough so he kept asking him to do it over and over again. In the end the comedian must have repeated the same act twenty times. Muhammad was really relishing it. Jamillah gazed at her father and saw this happiness etched across his face that had eluded him for a long time. She remarked to the comedian, which was in a sense good but equally a desolate feeling, 'I wish you could come around with us because I've not seen him laugh like that for years.' Muhammad continued rolling over laughing with a mirthful laughter. Muhammad's other daughter Rasheda turned to Charlie remarking, 'My dad said to me that he's still got restless leg syndrome.' Meaning he wishes he was still fighting. One of my brother's greatest fears had always been being away from the limelight and being plunged into obscurity. It absolutely terrified him. At the time Tyson was the king of the ring and Muhammad talked about him in an admirable manner. He said, 'He's a great fighter, he's ferocious.' Charlie, whether he believed it or not, or was merely saying it to ingratiate himself to my brother, said, 'You would've whuped him.' Nodding his head Muhammad burst out laughing as if to say he didn't agree with Charlie's view.

Mike had been convicted for the well-publicised rape by that time, but Muhammad and Lonnie said they felt sorry for him. Muhammad and Mike had mutual respect for each other. Muhammad said that he was a great fighter, and that he didn't belong in jail. It's a shame what went on for everyone's sake, the woman, the whole situation, Muhammad was saying to Charlie, as he was shaking his head. It wasn't good, the whole thing. In my brother's eyes, Mike was innocent.

My brother stood there chatting to this comedian and his attention quickly shifted to non-American sports. Muhammad wasn't too familiar with the world's most popular sport – soccer. He never really had any interest in American sports other than boxing. He asked Charlie, 'They play soccer here, don't they?' Charlie replied, 'Yeah, we call it football. In America you refer to it as soccer, I suppose.' Muhammad asked him if he could elucidate further. It was funny because the British sport Muhammad was intrigued by was rugby. Muhammad asked, 'It's not that crazy game where they run at you and they flatten each other's noses is it?' Charlie replied, 'No, that's rugby.' Charlie told him that he used to play for Manchester City as a professional soccer player. He told him that there are two clubs in Manchester – Manchester United and Manchester City.

If you named some of the top players Muhammad would have no idea whom you were talking about. However, my brother and I had actually met the greatest of them all, Pelé, in New York at the Yankee Stadium a day after the third Ken Norton fight. A fight that some had a notion Muhammad had really lost but was given an undeserved decision. There had been quite a bit of a stir in the aftermath. Muhammad mentioned to Charlie that he had met Pelé, and that their paths had crossed numerous times. He said, 'I've met him a few times. He's the best soccer player in the world. Best there's ever been. Pelé is a great man.' Meeting this great sportsman was an experience for me. I found him to be an affable man. My brother introduced me and Pelé said, 'Rahaman, it's nice to meet you. I love your brother very much.' Pelé turned around to Muhammad, and he said, 'You're the greatest.' My brother, being the humble man he was, said, 'You're the greatest.'

My brother and Pelé, although they didn't spend an inordinate amount of time together nor forged a really close friendship, developed mutual respect for each other. Their iconic status in the sporting world and skill endeared themselves to the legions of fans. In fact, when my brother was voted The Greatest Sportsman of the Century, Pelé took the second spot. Soccer, as I said, was an alien sport for Muhammad. Despite his extremely limited knowledge of the game, he wasn't oblivious to the fact that Brazil were the kings of soccer and Pelé was the god.

As strange as it may sound, and it's not something the wider public knows about, Muhammad's favourite English soccer team was Everton. How did my brother come to 'support' this team? Well, when we were in England in June 1963, when he fought Henry Cooper for the first time, we got talking to some random fans at Wembley Stadium who told him about this team. I remember how blown away I was when I laid eyes on Wembley Stadium. Muhammad and I had previously heard about this famous and large stadium, but being there just made me realise the true scope of this place. Curious, Charlie asked Muhammad, 'Your favourite soccer team is Everton?' And Muhammad just grinned and answered, 'Yeah. They're the only ones that I know.' Muhammad then asked, 'They're the ones that play in the blue, aren't they?' Charlie replied, 'Yeah. They're nicknamed The Toffees.'

Muhammad met almost every big sports star you can imagine during his heyday. At one time it was arranged for him to meet George Best, who to some is the most talented soccer player from Britain – maybe even the most talented player to ever don a soccer shirt. When he was supposed to meet him for a dinner date, though, Muhammad was left hanging around. It left my brother bemused because he had, to my knowledge, never been stood up by any other celebrity. Once, it looked like Elvis might fail to show up for a planned visit to the Deer Lake camp, but he eventually turned up, very late, in the early hours of the morning, drugged up and under the influence of alcohol. Even the King of Rock & Roll wouldn't bail on my brother.

So, anyway, after George's no-show, Muhammad had been adamant on sending an open letter to the *Manchester Evening News,* a prominent newspaper in the star's home town. *Dear George,* it read, *I know you are to Manchester what I am to the whole world.* Muhammad was taking a jab at George, although in jest he wanted him to know who the bigger man was. Whether George ever saw that letter, I can't tell you.

Anyway, the incident was brought to George's attention when Charlie spoke to him about the mishap eight years later. George, apparently, couldn't stop laughing at my brother's response. Muhammad's humour had endeared him to the soccer star.

'Yeah, I had a dinner date with him, but I couldn't make it,' George admitted, 'That's one thing I really regret. It would've been just me and Muhammad having dinner. I'm really, really gutted I couldn't make it.' Charlie rubbed salt into the wound when he showed George his photos with Muhammad. George peppered Hale with questions. Gazing at the photos with eyes wide open, he said, 'You're very lucky to have photos with the greatest sportsman ever. I love everything he does. I love his fights. I love the way he talks and his personality. And I love what he stands for.' Talking about Muhammad really got George excited. You couldn't talk about any soccer star and invoke an excitement in George. But when you brought up Muhammad's name he was suddenly all ears.

To George's mind, Muhammad changed the whole of sport – which, of course, he did. The soccer icon traced back his adulation to the Liston fights when he was on the brink of making a name for himself at a very, very young age. Watching Muhammad Ali fights, George said, 'It was a huge thing in our house.' His dad revered Muhammad and they never missed his fights on TV. Muhammad endeared himself to the whole Best family.

George never compared himself to Muhammad openly. He enjoyed boxing and Muhammad was his favourite sportsman ever. 'Do you know that Muhammad has Irish roots?' Charlie asked. George replied, 'Yeah, I do know that.' He then said jokingly, 'That's why we've claimed him.' Muhammad had asked Charlie if he knew George. Charlie replied, 'I know him, I work with him.' So Muhammad said give him my regards.

Like I said, Muhammad knew very little about soccer. At first he brought up rugby when Charlie brought up soccer. But he obviously knew of George because he knew about Brian Clough. 'Brian Clough, he talks too much,' Muhammad once told me. He was aware of George being a superstar, that's for sure – the first soccer celebrity, like Muhammad, went from the back sports pages to the front pages. I heard that George's now ex-wife, Angie Best, went to see him in hospital after he had an accident outside the world-famous department store Harrods. He'd been drinking. Angie walked in and George was on the bed being relieved by a nurse – she was pleasuring him. Horrified, she rushed straight out and straight on the plane to America.

Unlike my brother, George was insecure and intimidated apparently. So despite the brilliant soccer genius that he was, maybe he didn't want to meet the greatest sportsman. What was apparent is when someone discussed Muhammad with George or Pelé, their eyes would light up. I later learned that my brother and George did get to meet finally years later in London.

★ ★ ★

The Ali family had a grand old time in England. After a good tour it was time to fly out. Call it a pure coincidence or whatever, but George Michael happened to be passing through the airport in London. When the twins spotted the pop star, they ecstatically told their father how much they loved George Michael. Muhammad was embarrassed about that. They said to their father, 'George Michael's there, can you introduce us to him? We love him!' Of course, although he initially acted like he wasn't pleased with that, Muhammad could not resist so went up to the pop star. Next thing you know the twins literally ran away. Then again, I don't think my brother was embarrassed because they said how crazy they were for George Michael, but I think he was just being funny. When Muhammad went up to him and told him about his daughters, their excitement faded to a sheepish demeanour. Both sisters were literally jumping up and down. Being huge fans of the pop star, they were dying to meet him and now an opportunity presented itself. Sometimes Muhammad's daughters would divulge to their dad which celebrity they admired profoundly. To this end he would make an effort to introduce them to the person. It's more likely the celebrity knew Muhammad or is a fan of his – that just made it easier for his kids to meet other celebrities.

There was another case, as far as top celebrities are concerned. David Beckham was invited by Muhammad to his seventieth birthday party at a swanky dinner gala in Las Vegas. Two thousand revellers had congregated. From Samuel L Jackson, Puff Daddy, Snoop Dogg, LL Cool J, to boxing personalities Sugar Ray Leonard and Bob Arum. One man on the twins' mind is an icon in his own right – David Beckham. The sisters very much had great admiration for this soccer superstar who garnered a huge global following.

Again, they were dying to meet him. They saw him saunter up to their father and Muhammad engaged in a conversation. The twins were standing by Muhammad's side and could not resist but interject. They said to David, 'Oh, we love you. Thank you so much for coming.' He was so gracious and very honoured to be there, he told them. David's been a huge fan of Muhammad's and their paths had crossed numerous times. He was also one of the special guests to take the podium and speak at the event that evening. The twins were able to meet him formally with their father and he was just so down to earth. The impression he made on the twins meant they loved him even more after that. Considering he was a soccer superstar and a global celebrity, he was so down to earth, so nice and humble just like their dad. Some people disappoint you, but he was great. Plus he's gorgeous, the twins thought. He took the time to take pictures with the sisters, when some celebrities who meet Muhammad just say, 'Let me just take a picture with Muhammad.' They don't really pay attention to others standing around Muhammad. My brother is the central attraction and everyone wants a piece of him.

A GIFT OF GIVING

O ur mother's life continued for another three and half years after we lost
our beloved father. She passed away on 21 August 1994 at a Hurst-
bourne Health Center nursing home. Mom had been disabled by a stroke
six months prior. She was the anchor and glue of our family. It was hard
for me and Muhammad to accept that she wasn't going to be around any
more. To be in a situation where both our parents were now deceased
was a trial for us both. We required strength and love to get through it.
Personally, I try to reflect and hold on to the most wonderful, uplifting
memories of her life, knowing that she was proud of what we became
and glad that she got to see it. She was the one constant in our lives, the
one person that Muhammad and I knew we could go to regardless of
what we were going through in our lives.

At the funeral a local reporter by the name of Bob Hill made
Muhammad briefly come to life. When he first sat next to Muhammad,
my brother was very sober and silent. When the reporter asked him about
our mom, though, Muhammad kind of lightened up a little bit. Bob
interviewed him briefly. They talked about our mom and Muhammad
told him how much he loved her. My brother said people think he's the
greatest, but he thought our mother was. Muhammad was extremely
close to Mom throughout his life. She was the only person in the whole

world who could talk down to him and get away with it. She had the power to literally make Muhammad crumble.

Now, though, my brother had his own chance to do something for other families going through their own hardships. Doctor Lieberman, it transpired, was part of an organisation dedicated to fighting against Parkinson's. Some years later the organisation came to learn that he had a connection to Muhammad, and so they asked the doctor if he could convince Muhammad to be a spokesperson for Parkinson's – with an eye towards elevating fundraising. Lonnie thought it was a fine idea, but Muhammad had strong reservations. 'I don't want to be a poster boy for Parkinson's!' he told the family, explaining that he didn't want to be remembered as a man ravaged by disease but as a family man, friend to everyone and a champion. Not prepared to give up at that, Lonnie invited the doctor to their home in Berrien Springs in the vain hope of convincing Muhammad. My brother, of course, quickly divined the good doctor's intentions, and the conversation was soon getting strained, with my brother's stubbornness coming to the fore. He was a very independent person, and the last thing he wanted was for people to feel sorry for him. He didn't want to represent an illness. People constantly showed pity for him, but he did not want that. I can tell you with great conviction that if you wanted to get on the wrong side of Muhammad, all you had to do was show him pity. He detested it.

Still, Muhammad was never anything but cordial to Doctor Lieberman. They had lunch and then snacks, and continued to talk long into the afternoon and evening as my brother took the measure of this man. In the end, the doctor spent upwards of eight hours with Muhammad at the house, talking about boxing, his travels and his many experiences. He must have worn Muhammad out because in the end my brother reluctantly said, 'Look, write me a letter,' just to get rid of his guest. The strategy – if it was a strategy – had worked.

Doctor Lieberman went back home to Phoenix and he thought to himself, *What am I going to write to Muhammad?* He started scribbling on a piece of paper, trying hard to pen the opening sentence but with great difficulty: Muhammad Ali, Dear Mr Ali. Dear Muhammad. He contemplated how to put down on paper something compelling enough to invoke Muhammad's attention, focusing on why Muhammad initially refused to be the spokesperson. So, he wrestled with this and he woke up the next day on a Monday morning with an idea circling in his head. He said to himself, *You know, I will write him a poem.* Muhammad himself was a fan of poetry and was a strong believer that if you worded it correctly in line with what was in your heart, then it represented something coming from God. Doctor Lieberman didn't write poetry, but was determined and proceeded to pen his letter in poetry form. Basically, what he expressed in the poem was that Muhammad was not really afraid of getting old. You have the ability to help people with Parkinson's, the poem said, and you must meet this challenge. When you go to your grave, as we all must, it's not going to be enough that you were the greatest boxing champion in history if Parkinson's disease lives on. The doctor concluded the letter with a challenge to Muhammad, knowing that my brother would never be able to resist.

Doctor Lieberman wasted no time in sending his letter by fax to Lonnie, and didn't have long to wait. About an hour later Lonnie called him. To his delight, almost her first words were, 'Muhammad will do anything you want, just tell us.' On reflection, Muhammad had come to terms with that he had the capacity to help even more people in his life by being a spokesperson for a disease that was, at that time, little understood. This, he felt, was more important than some people feeling sorry for him, more important even than his own feelings. Anyway, it was the right thing to do, he decided, and from that day on he resolved to channel his thoughts and actions into helping others. Subsequently, he became a spokesperson and he was very receptive from there on.

★ ★ ★

In Phoenix there was a prominent charitable businessman, named Jimmy Walker, who headed a foundation called Fight Night. Later, it became Celebrity Fight Night. This was the organisation that raised money for sufferers of Parkinson's. Boxers who were down on their luck took part in the boxing event. It wasn't uncommon for the event to raise $50,000, most of which would go to boxers who weren't doing too well – towards their health insurance and medical problems, among other things. As it happened, this entrepreneur was a friend of Doctor Lieberman, and in late 1996 Walker used an introduction from his friend to ask if Muhammad had any inclination towards joining forces in a quest to raise money for charitable purposes. Walker asked if Muhammad would come to his Fight Night. Muhammad didn't know Jimmy and hadn't met him before, but that didn't matter because, as ever, Muhammad was always a gregarious person, and always happy to help. It wasn't long before Muhammad was introduced to Jimmy at an LA Lakers game. Muhammad had come under the spotlight in the spring when he had lit the Olympic torch at the Atlanta Olympics, which endeared him to millions who watched this touching moment on their screens. It was definitely the right timing for Jimmy to lure my brother in.

Eventually, Muhammad paired up with the two men, and the first Fight Night he attended the year after raised more than $100,000 – double the amount they were raising before my brother came on board. It was just terrific. The next year they raised a quarter of a million dollars, and after that well over a million dollars. Eventually, Walker, who was also part owner of Phoenix Suns, used my brother's celebrity to convince other famous athletes to attend, drawing football, baseball and basketball players – such as Kareem Abdul-Jabbar – and eventually celebrities ranging from Arnold Schwarzenegger to Jennifer Lopez. Whenever I attended, I would always see the 'who's who' of sport and entertainment. About 1,100 people attended each event, paying high prices for their tickets. Eventually, Fight Night also moved abroad, with an event in Italy that attracted a cheque for $500,000 from a man in Russia who is a Muslim, a very wealthy person, who wanted to give money to Muhammad. This individual didn't even attend the event, but wanted to honour my brother by making that donation to his charity. Muhammad's name alone had the power to attract big dollars.

I think it encapsulates Muhammad's giving nature that when he was fighting he did hospital visits to cheer people up, but also his infallible optimism that he continued to do it when he himself was struck down by disease. Whatever his own state of health, he always had something optimistic to say to people who were suffering. He just possessed this aura that made you feel good about yourself. Once, when he was still boxing, an entourage of about twenty of us went with Muhammad to a hospital. As the gang walked through the hospital Muhammad suddenly stopped and asked the hospital officials, 'Who's in that room!' And the hospital officials unenthusiastically replied, 'You don't want to go in there. It's just an old man who hasn't spoken to anybody for five years.' Muhammad insisted, 'No. I want to go in there.' Muhammad walked in the room and he saw an old African-American man was sitting in his chair. Going up to him he asked rather loudly, 'Old man!' The man looked up. 'Do you know who I am!? The man replied, 'Yeah.' Muhammad asked, 'Who am I?' He said, 'Joe Louis.'

Muhammad, somewhat surprised, turned around and proceeded to walk out of the room. 'You know, if that old man thinks I'm Joe Louis,' he said to us, 'and it gives him pleasure to think I'm Joe Louis, then I'm Joe Louis.' You've got to realise that even though Muhammad had an ego, he had a heart and refused to hurt anyone's feelings. The other thing that I remember was my brother was affable to everybody. Whether you were a billionaire or down on your luck he treated you equally. He visited the sick and elderly and gave a damn about them when most others in his elevated position wouldn't bat an eyelid.

After coming on board with the charity, Muhammad dived headlong into this new avenue of philanthropic work. He was always upbeat, and he would go to the clinic, Muhammad Ali Parkinson's Center, which is part of the Barrow Neurological Institute, whenever he could. This is a 3,000 square feet place, there's a rehab centre and they have an exercise area and a laboratory. People would especially visit this place for the sole purpose of getting a peek of Muhammad when they found out he was there. People wanted to proudly say, 'I saw Muhammad Ali.' He would saunter in with Lonnie, or whoever was accompanying him, and exude that smile. And people around him would smile. He was like a beacon. He really was. In the last fifteen years or so among friends he would speak, although he didn't say much in public gatherings. Muhammad, you have to understand, was a perfectionist. If he wasn't 100 per cent sure about an approach, he preferred not to pursue it. I mean, there are a lot of people with Parkinson's, but I don't think many people battled it with Muhammad's perseverance. His zest for life never diminished.

Lonnie still does a lot of travelling raising funds. She's very committed to raising money for research, but Muhammad and Lonnie were adamant on raising money for patient care specifically.

'I get very good care because I'm Muhammad Ali,' my brother once told the family. 'I want everyone else to get the same care.' Eventually, the family came up with Ali Care, an organisation with the sole purpose of paying for prescription drugs for those who couldn't afford them. Lonnie was very concerned that there were many people who had trouble getting to the clinic, so she started a service that catered to patients at home. Additionally, of course, they have a clinic at the Center where everything is done the same day. Muhammad and Lonnie were very clear that the money they raised would be spent on patient services. They said, 'Look, Michael J. Fox is going to raise money for research, we're not in the business of doing research. Let Michael do that. We're in the business of taking care of people and giving them the same level of treatment as Muhammad.' Lonnie's a very smart, very thoughtful person. She has a lot of insight into people. She can ascertain who's bullshitting her and who's not. Celebrity Fight Night has raised close to $30 million for the institute. It's a huge part of Muhammad's legacy.

* * *

Muhammad's daughter Hana had moved to Michigan to live with her father in the year 2001. She ended up staying for just over five years – even after his rapidly declining health resulted in him having great difficulty talking. Muhammad's routine on a regular day back then was pretty simple: he'd get early up in the morning, sometimes as early as 5 a.m. He'd go downstairs and have a snack, watch a little TV and around 7 he'd go back up to bed and then get up at 8 or 9. He'd go back down to have breakfast and then go outside, and walk up his driveway to his office. Sometimes he'd take his little go-cart, the kind you use at the golf course. Muhammad and his daughter would ride that together. He'd go inside and wish his staff a good morning and then sit at his desk, sift through and read his fan mail. Back then you received fan mail through the medium of post. And, believe me, Muhammad received a lot considering he had been out of the spotlight for a very long time by then.

His other main hobby was exploring and researching his religious interests. One of his hobbies was finding contradictions in the Bible. Hana would often help him with that. 'Daddy,' she would say, 'I'm going to learn the Bible better than I learn the Koran because of how much I'm reading it trying to find these contradictions.' My brother, meanwhile, would patiently make a list of them. On the occasions I saw him work, it was like watching a scholar or professor. Muhammad would, of course, respond to a lot of the fan mail, often with his own personalised touches. But often, when he provided an autograph he'd slip in an Islamic pamphlet titled something like: 'Who Is God?' or 'The True Meaning of Islam'. Sometimes this would backfire, as even ardent fans would write back and say, 'Don't you ever send this crap to me again!' While others would be kinder and write back saying, 'Thank you. You're doing a good job, God's work.'

Anyway, fan mail and religious study would take up a considerable amount of time for my brother. Afterwards, Muhammad and his daughter would take a stroll. Hana would help him walk although he could walk on his own. Muhammad's eighty-one-acre property was, you could say, staged for idyllic nature walks. He enjoyed the peace and serenity. Frequently he would sit and drive the go-cart around his land. He always enjoyed taking drives and his enthusiasm didn't diminish over the years. He would say to Hana, 'Take me to where the black people are.' They'd go to the black neighbourhoods and Muhammad would get out of the car and mingle with everyday people. He'd talk to them and they'd be delighted to be in his presence. Frequently, Hana would take him to get his hair cut. He particularly liked going to the barber's shop. So Muhammad was engaged in regular everyday living.

Ironically, the year that Muhammad finally settled into a life of obscurity was the same year that Will Smith portrayed my brother in the Hollywood movie titled *Ali*. Muhammad, along with Hana and other family members, attended the premiere. I think this was great to keep my brother's legacy alive, but a lot of people had to be shocked to see the condition he was in. A month after Muhammad attended the premiere, he received his star in Hollywood on the world-famous Hollywood Walk of Fame. When Muhammad was approached about this, he was hesitant to have his name on the street with people trampling over it. To this end he did the unthinkable – Muhammad told the official committee that if they wanted to honour him with the star then they'd have to put it up on the wall. Today, my brother's star on the Walk of Fame is the only star which is not on the street but on the wall of the entrance of the Dolby Theatre. No other personality has been granted this request and probably never will be.

★ ★ ★

In February 2005, an event for the Muhammad Ali Center took place. It was the first fundraising event for the upcoming centre, which was scheduled to open nine months later. This was another venture to preserve his legacy and continue to raise funds for charity. It was called the Butterfly Ball and it took place in Atlanta at the Hyatt Regency. The tickets were very expensive – a table set you back $10,000, while even the cheaper tickets set you back $500 a time. The event raised a ton of money, and major heavyweight sponsors such as Adidas and Coca-Cola came aboard. My brother's name, evidently, was still attracting the 'heavyweight' brands. Personalities in attendance included Jesse Jackson and Andrew Young – Mayor of Atlanta.

Several members of the Ali family were in attendance. Lonnie was there, of course, but so was Laila. So was Lennox Lewis, who was one of the first supporters of the Ali Center. The former heavyweight champion donated a million dollars. They brought Laila in for a press conference. The media outlets interviewed some of the prominent personalities. Muhammad saw my business manager Ron Brashear there and when the press conference was over and he was in a jovial mood, he put his fist on Ron's fist resting on his nose. He had a gift of making you feel like he was as impressed to meet you as you were him.

Next they escorted Ron and his photographer, Tom Grason, to a special ballroom. Nobody was there, other than Muhammad, Lonnie and security personnel. At that point Muhammad could not eat in public because they had to put a bib on him – without it, he had a tendency to spill food on his tuxedo – he was always dressed sharp at events. So they go into this room and Ron brought him gifts. He gave him a DVD autographed from his late uncle, Carl Brashear. It was the movie *Men of Honour*, based on his uncle. Additionally, he gave him some pictures and Muhammad signed his boxing book. Ron was in tears, literally. Muhammad meant so much to Ron and to other African Americans. Muhammad was one of the first public figures to really stand up to the establishment. They made us feel like we were cursed because of the colour we were, but my brother gave us a platform.

Lonnie's nephew Corey was helping Muhammad, alongside Lonnie, of course. Time was ticking and the officials needed to get Muhammad into the hall across the ballroom. Muhammad was supposed to go onstage at 7 p.m. because the whole event was being broadcast on live TV. In an attempt to get him there fast, they started marching my brother across the hall in the hallway. As he was making his way, there was this little kid with his dad who wanted Muhammad's autograph. This little white kid was ten or eleven and he was dressed sharp. He might have come a long way because his father had a foreign accent. As he approached my brother with his eyes shining, the entourage and security moved in and said, 'Sorry, we can't, we've got to get him into the ballroom.' But Muhammad stopped and said, 'Wait a minute, wait a minute,' even though he was late. Not only did he take this kid's paper and sign an autograph, but he drew an aeroplane, drew water, drew birds in the sky and then he signed it. He didn't give a damn about getting onstage in front of a roomful of executives who'd paid through the nose to get there. Instead he stopped to make a memory for this kid, and leave him something he'd remember forever. The kid was grateful, of course, but his father seemed almost as overwhelmed to meet the champ.

'How do you do it, man, you're all over the place,' the father questioned Muhammad. 'You've got Parkinson's; you never rest?' No one there will ever forget my brother's words. Muhammad leaned over to the kid and the father – in his later years he had a tendency to lean over and whisper to you – and he said, 'When this life of mine is over, there will be plenty of time to rest.' At the time Muhammad still had command over his facial features, so he could still write and talk even though he had signs of shaking – and he had a twinkle in his eye. And the look on this kid's face was just something unforgettable.

A DAUGHTER'S FIGHT
& THE FALL OF A FRIEND

My brother never pressured his children towards pursuing any particular career. None of his children, for instance, ever really gravitated towards a boxing career other than, eventually, Laila. People used to ask him, 'What would you do if your son wants to become a boxer?' His response was, 'Well, first I'd do everything I could to dissuade him. Then I'd do everything in my power to help him if I failed.' Muhammad grew to hold the belief that education was indispensable – it could ensure you'd never have to rely on your body for your upkeep, or to face the inevitable consequences when your health declined. Muhammad once jokingly said, 'It's impossible for him to be as good as I am.' My brother, I think, never contemplated any of his daughters would ever gravitate towards boxing – although one of his twin daughters was inclined to pursue professional wrestling.

Laila, of course, went on to enter the ring and made great strides. In June 2005 Muhammad and I went to watch her fight in Washington DC when she locked horns with an Irish-American girl called Erin. Mike Tyson was headlining in what would turn out to be his retirement bout against Kevin McBride. Mike had by then lost that touch and motivation for boxing, to be honest, and was ready to drift into obscurity as far as fighting in the ring was concerned.

People have their own sentiments on the subject of women fighting.

Muhammad, I can say for sure, felt women didn't belong in the boxing ring, and the fact that his own daughter was fighting was a grave concern for him. On the surface he acted like he was very supportive of her, but the truth is he was discomfited with what she was doing. It wasn't that he was merely concerned about her getting hurt badly – the prime factor was that Lonnie and my brother were practising Muslims and neither of them thought that women belonged in the boxing ring, particularly dressed the way a fighter has to be. Muslim women, in the eyes of strict adherents to the faith, just don't dress in trunk shorts and show off their flesh – their dignity is brought into question. So Muhammad felt it was the wrong thing to do.

Like I said, publicly he was supportive and refrained from making a fuss, but behind the scenes he was constantly trying to convince Laila not to box. In an attempt to get her to rethink her position, he would say, 'Look, women have breasts, they give birth. You're delicate, you're not meant to be in the ring. Women shouldn't get in the ring and box. It's a man's sport.' He may have come across a little chauvinistic, but he only wanted the best for his daughter.

And yet, as strongly as he felt, in the end his daughter came first, and he treated her just as he always said he would his son. After he did everything to reason with her, he didn't turn his back on his daughter. He offered support. This wasn't the only fight of Laila's that Muhammad attended. He'd go because he, naturally, cared about her and her well-being. His attitude was, *We only get one life, and so we have to make the best of situations that we don't always like and can't control.*

Interestingly, women were boxing at my brother's camp in Deer Lake alongside the men way back in the 1970s. We would be training with the ladies right alongside us, which isn't an unusual sight now, but was almost incomprehensible to outsiders back then. As the spectators lingered about in the gym, one woman was introduced as a boxing champion of Los Angeles. I'm sure the bemused fans were thinking, *Do they actually have matches where women box?*

Anyway, before the fights got under way, Muhammad was brought into Mike's dressing room to meet him and wish him the best of luck. Both men's paths had crossed innumerable times previously, and I had met Mike a couple of times too. But still the aura and the presence of greatness that Muhammad exuded clearly awed 'Iron' Mike. He's a big fight fan and an admirer of great pugilist champions before him – Jack Dempsey and Joe Louis to name a couple. And he adored my brother. In fact it's not an overstatement if I said Mike treated Muhammad like royalty, and he made no effort to conceal it in public.

Mike sat on the bench while his assistant wrapped his deadly fists ready for battle. Mike stood up and embraced Muhammad with a hug of affection. Mike looked into Muhammad's eyes and you could see it – the kind of adoration that you can't put into words. Their mutual respect shone through. They talked about Mike's career. Muhammad was astute enough to know that Mike's career was coming to a dead end and I think Mike knew that his time was up soon, that his career was on its last legs. There were confident words from my brother that basically conveyed: you've had an illustrious career, you've achieved greatness before getting out of the sport, which is the most important thing. The wonderful words of inspiration from Muhammad wishing him well were welcomed by Mike.

My brother could resonate with Mike because he reflected back on his own final bouts – against Larry Holmes and Trevor Berbick – which were some of the real low points of Muhammad's ring career. Muhammad told Mike how it was hard to exit this sport, a brutal combat sport that becomes a major part of one's life. All good things come to an end, and time always catches up with us, he added. We all knew that Muhammad was preparing him mentally for what was likely to be his last fight. As it turned out, it was the last time Mike would enter the ring, an arena he had ruled with a heavy hand in his heyday back in the late 1980s and early 1990s. Muhammad couldn't leave a gathering without making those present laugh and uplifting their spirits. 'Let's go, I can take you right now, Mike!' Muhammad challenged in jest as Mike let out a diffident smile. My brother then went to Laila's dressing room – where Veronica was keeping their daughter company – to spend some time with her as a concerned father. I think him being there for his daughter meant a lot to her. It gave her that boost.

★ ★ ★

Gene Kilroy had introduced Muhammad to Mike when the latter was still a teenager in 1979. Muhammad happened to be in New York City with his manager when out of the blue Gene received a call from a lady running a small school – 2,000 students or so – in the city. 'Nobody ever comes out here, no celebrities,' she told Gene, who was, of course, inundated with requests for appearances, 'It would be great if Muhammad could pay us a visit.'

Gene brought this to my brother's attention, and Muhammad, who was always up for school visits, was eager to make an appearance. So Gene informed the lady who sent a driver to pick them up. There they played Muhammad's film *The Greatest* on a big projector screen. All these twelve- and thirteen-year-old wild kids were jumping around with excitement. The place was filled with unbelievable scenes of jubilation. Mike was among those teenagers. And that's where the shy little teenager met Muhammad for the first time.

About a year later, Gene took a call from Mike's coach Cus D'Amato. Cus was friends with all the old-time fighters. He stood up for the rights of boxers and against the powers of those who sought to abuse them, and consequently, every fighter had a great deal of admiration for this coach among coaches. So, yeah, Cus and Muhammad often talked on the phone. On this occasion, though, he had something special in mind. 'Lightning's struck twice,' he told Gene. 'I have a young kid here who is going to be the heavyweight champion of the world. And he knows you.' Gene, trying to refresh his memory, said, 'Put him on, where do I know him from?' Mike got on the phone and in his little squeaky voice said, 'This is Mike Tyson. You came to my reform school. I wanted to be the big man, but when I saw Ali I said, no, man, I want to be a great champion like Ali.' Muhammad's visit had uplifted Mike. My brother had made him feel special, like he did so many other children. Many years later, he would say that Muhammad made him feel special during that first meeting, at a time of life when he badly needed it.

In return, Mike vowed to vanquish the men that had beaten Muhammad when my brother was nearing the end of his career. The night before Cus's call, Muhammad had just tasted defeat at the hands of Larry Holmes, and Muhammad was in no mood to talk tactics.

Muhammad said he wanted to speak to Cus, but Cus said, 'Hold it. I've got a fourteen-year-old black kid here and he's going to be the champion of the world. Tell him listen to me, OK. Tell him listen to me!' Then Cus handed the phone to Mike. Muhammad didn't tell the young aspiring boxer to listen to his trainer, but instead his conversation centred on his own defeat against Holmes and how he was going to come back and knock him out next time. Now Mike was gulping back tears as he listened to my brother unreservedly divulging details. A very emotional Mike pledged, 'I'm going to get him for you. When I'm big I'm going to get him for you!' Cus, along with Mike and several others, had driven an hour from the camp to watch the fight on a close-circuit TV.

Mike, an avid student of the sweet science, had been following my brother's career ever since he got into boxing. Up in his room at the Catskill training camp, the young up-and-comer spent an inordinate amount of time viewing footage, taking advantage of an enormous collection of boxing film footage. Bill Cayton and Jim Jacobs – his management team at the time – had accumulated the biggest collection in the world of every possible fight you could think of. For Mike it wasn't enough. He would make comments to his friends and sparring partners while they watched: 'If that left hook had connected it would've changed the history of that weight division.' Mike was a walking encyclopaedia of boxing, and he had nothing but admiration for my brother. 'Muhammad can box,' he would say. 'He can fight on the inside. He can punch. He can fight technical, or he can brawl.' Mike used to marvel at Muhammad's footwork and his hand speed, his boxing ability and his boxing brain. He would talk about Muhammad constantly. He always said with great conviction, 'Muhammad could've ruled any era of boxing.'

★ ★ ★

In the end, Mike kept his promise to avenge my brother against at least two fighters. He demolished Trevor Berbick, who beat my brother in a unanimous decision, in two rounds, and then eventually beat Holmes six years after the man beat Muhammad. He went on to amass thirty-seven wins before falling against a fighter who had some similarities to my brother – Buster Douglas, who moved well around the ring and had a long, rangy jab. By the time Laila was fighting, his career was in decline, and he lost his final fight to McBride as we watched. Muhammad was sitting quietly in the second row with Veronica and a bodyguard on each side of them. I could see he was very observant. I was at ringside watching in great anticipation. Muhammad, I know, felt somewhat despondent to see his friend suffer a defeat because I think it brought back painful memories of the day when his own career was over. It was sad to see Mike losing the way he lost to a fighter whom he would have demolished in his prime.

Meanwhile, it was the perfect timing for Erin to fight Laila because the latter was going through a divorce at the time. Her mind was obviously full of concern about her father's illness – and this girl Erin could fight. So there were three things in her favour. She had a very experienced fighting background, but Laila's class was too much. We were treated to three exciting rounds, but Laila got the better of her adversary, stopping the fight in the third round. She had her father's blood running through her veins, the Ali family blood – a great pedigree. We were there to support her and she appreciated it. Even at that time of her career with all the distractions, she still put on a superlative performance, beating a good fighter.

Following Laila's victory I stepped inside the ring with Muhammad. And sure, these people in the arena had been buzzing with anticipation to watch Tyson, or were there to watch Laila, but when The Greatest stepped in the ring you could feel the affection and the emotion they felt. It was uplifting. Muhammad, of course, showered her with tender kisses while she was still glowing from the fight. Laila did her dad proud that night, outclassing her opponent with speed and power. 'It's wonderful any time my dad is there,' Laila said at the time. I know every child wants to do their parents proud, and I know when she was boxing she wanted to do her father so proud. She wanted to emulate her dad and achieve titles like him. 'It lights a fire in me,' she told the ring announcer. Then he asked Muhammad, who was standing directly in front of me, what his thoughts were. 'She's bad,' he told the assembled crowd. 'It runs in the family. She talks like me.'

After the fight a post-fight press conference with the world's media took place. Suddenly Muhammad emerged and every member of the media present was clamouring to pepper him with questions. Mike and Kevin, who were already sitting onstage ready to take questions, realised that this man was going to steal the limelight, steal their time. Nevertheless, they were happy they had The Greatest at their press conference. 'We are in the presence of greatness,' Mike said, proudly. 'We are privileged and blessed to be in the presence of Muhammad Ali.' Muhammad was so dignified in his appraisal of Mike, of Kevin's victory, of Laila's skill and Erin's tenacity. He was complimentary and optimistic towards every fighter, even as he expressed his sadness for Mike's loss.

My brother had four burly bodyguards with him, but they were very professional. They knew Muhammad loved his fans and had always been very receptive, so these big protectors were courteous as they let fans shake Muhammad's hand. After the press conference concluded, Muhammad and Mike had some private time. My brother consoled the notorious heavyweight knockout artist. Every fighter knows when it's over. And Mike knew it was the end of the road.

Probably one of the biggest debates in the boxing world that has persisted for decades is: who would've prevailed if my brother and Mike had locked horns? 'I know I couldn't beat Muhammad, and Muhammad knows he couldn't beat me,' Mike once said in a private gathering. 'People argue over it, but it's a pointless argument. We're never going to fight each other. It's a pointless argument because it's never going to be proved.' What was Muhammad's sentiment? According to George Foreman, Muhammad really believed Mike hit extremely hard. When George revealed to Muhammad he was pursuing a comeback, the first thing Muhammad said was, 'Man, Mike Tyson can hit.' Mike's ferocity really impressed Muhammad and the power the 5 foot 10 inch dynamo could generate made him pause. According to George Muhammad once told him that he couldn't have beaten Mike. But I disagree. My brother would've beaten Mike. I can say this with great conviction. I think he was just being humble. Muhammad had a granite chin and would've unequivocally beaten any boxer. And whenever he fought, every time he got knocked down he would be up. During his pro career Muhammad was never knocked out cold. I tallied up many sparring rounds with Muhammad and know what he was all about.

Now, finally, we have another Ali family member who is destined to reach the top ranks of boxing. Muhammad's daughter Rasheda, who initially attempted to steer her son away from the sport of boxing and instead wanted him to pursue a career in American football, really wanted her father to be there for her son Nico's fight in Arizona well before he passed away. Although he was in Arizona for her son's first fight, he was ill so he couldn't attend. So he gave Nico some advice afterwards and made a promise by saying, 'OK, we'll make it to the next fight.' But, of course, he couldn't make it. She really would have loved for her father to have seen Nico's first victory. That was one of her dreams. He was able to see Nico play football briefly but never battle it out in the ring.

ROAD TO HEAVEN: A LIFE WORTH LIVING

In the year 2013, Lonnie helped to put together the Muhammad Ali Humanitarian Awards as an annual event in Louisville, with my brother's blessing. The event was a fundraising gala, created as a way to publicly recognise and celebrate the greatness of people from around the world – honouring those making significant contributions towards securing peace, social justice and human rights. Eventually, the awards would grow to recognise young adults, too – people under thirty acting as advocates and role models within their own communities, upholding the same values my brother held most dear.

The second show was at the Marriott downtown in Louisville, and Lonnie invited me and my wife Caroline. Even in his later years, Muhammad continued to visit Louisville regularly. Although he had moved to Scottsdale, Arizona, in 2005, where he spent most of his time at his mansion in Paradise Valley, a year later he purchased an additional home in Louisville. And so a strong connection has always existed. For everyone else, tickets sold for $1,000 a spot, but that didn't stop people purchasing them and it was jam-packed. I was wearing the white suit I keep for special occasions. People always say I must have inherited my flamboyant dress sense from my father. I remember Gene Kilroy cracking my business manager Ron up by making jokes about how I looked like Colonel Sanders, founder of Kentucky Fried Chicken, but that was my favourite suit, and I was sure as hell going to be donning it for my brother's big night. When we got to the venue the whole red carpet thing was in full swing, with cameras flashing everywhere and TV crews up in my face straight away. Well, I worked that carpet like there was no tomorrow. That was a good day for me: it was an event to honour my brother, and I was dressed my best. Watch the footage now, and you can see my self-esteem lifting right on camera.

Anyway, it was a great night. Of course, there was only one man everyone was really there to see, and the ovation Muhammad received when Lonnie brought him into the ballroom was amazing. Lonnie introduced us together: 'We're happy to have members of the family here today in attendance, Muhammad's brother Rahaman and his wife Caroline,' and I received a round of applause as my name was mentioned. It felt great, even to get that small bit of recognition for my part in his career.

By this time, though, Muhammad's health had rapidly declined. He sat there in his wheelchair with his dark shades on, and it wasn't clear at all how much of the proceedings he was taking in. I went up to him to tell him I loved him, but I got no reaction – that was how out of it he was. I just wanted my own small moment with him, to hug him and let him know that I was there, but it was very emotional to see fans who adored him seeing a man who looked nothing like the world champion they'd seen on their TV screens so often. Many looked genuinely concerned or sad to see the champ. As a well-wisher, you couldn't really get close enough to interact with Muhammad that day, and so a lot of the people in attendance came to me instead, to say hello or have their picture taken. I just soaked it all in. The day, the attendees, the whole event was incredible. To have an international event recognising so many people for their humanitarian achievements was amazing, certainly something my brother would have wanted. I was overwhelmed.

The day before, Friday, Jim Brown had come to the Ali Center because he and all the special guests had arrived in town. Jim came up to me and we hugged and we talked. I believe if it hadn't been for Jim, the Supreme Court possibly may not have overturned Muhammad's case, because in their eyes they thought they were right. Jim Brown was on top of his game back then when he created the Cleveland Summit. It was an honour to see him there and receive his award.

So, that day at the awards it was great to see people acknowledge those who merited it. And to continue to recognise the world of good Muhammad had done.

★ ★ ★

One otherwise fine day in May 2016, my phone rang. It was Lonnie, sounding as distressed as I've ever heard her. She was calling me to inform me that Muhammad had been hospitalised. He was in a critical state, she said, and nobody quite knew what was going to happen. I guess everyone gets at least one call like that during their life, but it's still never an easy thing to deal with. I was devastated, of course. I've always been emotional, and this was my brother, the man I'd grown up alongside and spent so much of my life with. Even if I'd known this day was going to come, it was difficult to comprehend that it was finally here.

While I was still processing the news, Lonnie was informing the rest of the family. Jamillah was at work in Chicago when she got the call, and walked out the moment she heard the news. Her twin sister Rasheda was in Las Vegas at the time, and started packing her bags as soon as news reached her. And so it went with all the other kids – one by one, they dropped what they were doing and rushed to airports, or hired cars, convening on Arizona to see their father for what was likely to be the last time.

Meanwhile, I was thinking, *I don't know how I can accept this. I'm not prepared. How do I prepare for this?* Eventually, I took solace in the teaching of Islam, which teaches that death is part of life. Everyone's going to take that road, and everyone has their time. We had to bring ourselves, I realised, to accept that the man we love was going to go. I could accept it logically, but it still felt like a hammer blow to the gut. I had known Muhammad all my life – you couldn't separate him from me. Though I reasoned logically that he'd be in a better place, I couldn't even start to comprehend what it would be like when he wasn't on the same physical plane as me.

These thoughts had been with us all for a while by the time the call

finally came. Nine months before this moment, he gave us a real scare –
on that occasion, he was in the hospital for three days non-responsive,
and many of the family had made the trip to Arizona as Lonnie thought
the end was near. In the end, it turned out that one of his doctors had
misdiagnosed him – he didn't have pneumonia, as we all originally
thought, but a severe urinary tract infection, and after the doctors
administered the proper medication he made a recovery that seemed
almost miraculous. He was animated enough, even in his hospital
bed, that as Muhammad's son-in-law, Mike Joyce, who is married to
Jamillah, went to shake his hand, my brother faked a little punch at
him, the way he sometimes did. The day he regained consciousness the
doctors were talking about moving him, and when Mike asked, 'Are
you moving him into another room?' they replied, 'No, we've got to get
him out of the hospital because he's driving the nurses really crazy. He's
flirting with them, he's joking with them. He's causing a commotion.'
There was never a situation so serious that my brother wouldn't try to
bring humour into it in one way or another. When Gene Kilroy used to
see my brother in bad shape as his illness escalated, he told me, it really
affected him emotionally, but all of a sudden Muhammad would say
something funny and the usually stern Gene would crease up as the two
laughed like it was old times. *God*, he would say to himself, *let this man
stay here as long as he wants.*

At the same time, Muhammad was never afraid to talk about death.
He started telling his daughter Hana that he would die, that everybody
one day is going to die, when she was only five. She was really too young,
but he always wanted to teach his kids about the realities about life –
that all we ever did in life didn't mean anything compared with what we
would do for God.

When we watch Muhammad in documentaries and on video
showcasing his dazzling skills, we told each other, that's how he wanted
to live on – not as the shell of a man he'd become. My brother didn't
want to be dependent on anybody, but over the last decade of his life,
he'd become almost unable to operate without assistance. Some days he
spoke perfectly well, but other times we couldn't understand anything he
was saying. Some days, he showed flashes of the coordination he'd had on

the world's biggest stages, but others he could barely get out of bed. And, overall, things were getting worse. *Would Muhammad want to remain on this earth and suffer?* we asked each other. The answer, each of us believed, was no. When you die and return to Allah, it's believed in Islam, your health and youth is returned: my brother would be able to speak again, move again, float and dance and smile again. Those were the thoughts that gave us solace.

As the closest members of the family waited for the rest to arrive, everyone's attention shifted to prayer. Muhammad was on respiratory machines that were keeping him alive, but everyone knew the end was near. A doctor explained that the machines were keeping Muhammad alive, and asked if they had any questions. 'Is he in any pain?' asked Muhammad's son-in-law, to which the doctor shook his head. He explained that, once the machines were shut off, Muhammad would be gone almost immediately. Bowing their heads, the family congregated around my brother.

In Muhammad's last hour on Earth, all of his children and grandchildren gathered around as he lay in the bed motionless – a few brief moments of reflection before the end. He was unable to speak, but his countenance would lighten up as his daughter Rasheda whispered in his ear. His eyelids fluttered open at one point, acknowledging the daughter he had perhaps the deepest bond with. His children shared and reflected and laughed and cried together at his bedside. They talked for hours and hours and they prayed together. Some of the last words that his children told him were that they would try their best, as Muslims, to carry on his legacy in the best way possible. 'On the other side,' Rasheda told her father, 'You're going to be young, handsome, fast and pretty.' Then at 8.30 p.m. on 3 June 2016, the doctors switched the machines off because it was time to let him go. Even then, Muhammad wasn't quite ready to give up fighting. In the end, he kept breathing for another hour and a half, no quit in him. And then, finally, he was gone. My brother had a favourite saying, 'Service to others is the rent we pay for our room here on earth.' Finally, his service was over.

I wasn't there the day my brother died. I should have been, but I couldn't afford the flight. When I was informed of the news that my brother had died, I cried. My emotions were set off like fireworks. Losing a loved one can very easily plunge you into a state of desolation. I wanted to be left alone and grieve alone. I had the support of my wife who had always been by my side.

Yet I do remember our last conversation with some comfort. While shaking heavily, my brother asked, 'Rahaman, how do I look?' I said, 'You look the same to me. You look the same, even with all that shaking.' He said to me, 'I'm in no pain. No pain.' Then he said, 'Don't cry for me, Rahaman. I'm going to be with God. I made peace with God. I'm OK.'

★ ★ ★

Even though Muhammad passed away in Scottsdale, the funeral took place in our home town of Louisville. It was a dilemma for Lonnie – on the one hand, Muslim tradition dictates that the deceased be buried as expeditiously as possible, but on the other, she knew that the whole world would want an opportunity to pay their respects to my brother. One thing that emerged in the days leading up to the funeral was that Muhammad had planned his funeral years before he passed away. He wanted, I guess, to be the man in charge even in death. It happened while he and Lonnie were watching TV. Out of the blue, Muhammad told his wife that he wanted to have his funeral in a big stadium, so that anyone who wanted to could attend. He insisted that there be representation from all faiths and peoples, including an address from Native Americans, a people he'd always had a great respect for. He had a hand in the final speakers, and the members of the family who would speak. In the end, the funeral didn't take place until two weeks after Muhammad's passing, and there was some genuine behind-the-scenes bitterness among people who felt that the Muslim tradition had been disrespected.

Eventually, our family aligned. We agreed that the Janazah, the Islamic funeral prayer, would be conducted the day before the actual funeral ceremony, allowing mourners two full days to pay their respects. And even then, I don't think any of us expected as many people as arrived – on the first day at the Janazah, they packed the Freedom Hall Arena out. Lonnie, at one point, said she expected around one thousand people to attend. In the end, more than 14,000 made the trip.

The next day, the funeral itself took place at the Yum! Center, probably the only building in town big enough to have a hope of accommodating the crowds. When you hear the word beloved, it comes with a certain set of connotations, but I don't think it does justice to the way people felt about my brother. People from all walks of life had their lives touched by him – from presidents, movie stars and sportsmen to children and families who'd only ever seen him in passing, but still caught one of those many moments he made special. Sugar Ray Leonard, Lennox Lewis, Mike Tyson and Don King were all in attendance, but so were world leaders including Jordan's King Abdullah II and former president Bill Clinton. Barack Obama, whom my brother met several times and who had followed Muhammad's sports career very closely, couldn't make it because of his daughter's graduation. Among the roster of speakers was President of Turkey Recep Tayyip Erdogan – but for some reason he was taken off the list. Billy Crystal spoke about my brother's ability to build bridges instead of walls, and Clinton talked about his bravery in the face of the disease that had dogged the last decade of his life.

Mike Tyson, Will Smith and Lennox Lewis, who were among my brother's ten pall-bearers, all hugged me when they brought the casket in. Behind my dark glasses, I couldn't stop crying.

From the family side, both of my brother's surviving ex-wives were in attendance – Belinda and Veronica. It was good to see family unity in that setting. My children were there, alongside my ex-wife and current wife, Caroline. Muhammad's children Rasheda and Maryum went onstage to speak about their father. Every one of the children was dignified in front of the world, however much they'd cried behind closed doors. Then there were the regular people who'd had their lives touched in some way by Muhammad, flooding the streets to pay their respects. We had recently opened the Muhammad Ali childhood home to the public, and people just poured into the West End of town: they lined up for blocks, camping out, vendors selling T-shirts and memorabilia. They just took over, converging on 3302 Grand Avenue.

Amidst all of this, I was doing my best to hold things together. I had lived in my brother's shadow for seven decades and now I became the centre of attention, and it was overwhelming for me. I was being approached constantly by members of the press, having a camera stuck in my face at every turn, seeing faces looking at me everywhere in the crowd. I'm very emotional at the best of times. What you see is what I am, and I don't make any apologies for the fact that I had to fight back tears that day. I did one interview with the BBC and couldn't continue as I broke down on camera. The whole family knew that I would fall apart, and so I stayed away from the centre of the action. There's no way I could've held it together.

Something almost no one knew at the time was that, by the time of the funeral, I'd been struggling with Parkinson's for several years myself. At the time, I wasn't sure if it was some sort of inherited defect in our family genes or just the fact that I'd spent so much time doing the same things as my brother growing up – playing around the lead-tainted paint fumes from my father's office, living and training at the Deer Lake camp when it was being sprayed with pesticides, and of course sparring with my brother on a sometimes daily basis during my own boxing career. All I knew was that it was something I had to deal with, and that it affected me slightly differently from my brother. If I don't take my medication on time, for instance, my temper is short. I have always been known to be stern and aloof, and although I've calmed down a lot as I have got older, I can still snap when I get upset. The day of the funeral, of course, was one of the hardest days of my life. If you gave me a podium to stand in front of, you'd be rolling the dice because you didn't know what I might say or do. Not everyone knew about it – even my agent Ron just knew I was being more snappy than usual – but everyone knew something was wrong.

So, yes, there was tension behind the scenes at the funeral, but the family put on a united front outwardly, determined to give my brother the send-off he deserved. As the day unfolded, after the funeral, the VIPs and the family went to the Ali Center. Food was being served, and I remember seeing Lonnie in all black, regal and elegant, even on this toughest of days. At one point, I overheard her as she leaned towards Ron and said, 'Please, look out for Rahaman.' He said, 'I'll do what I can, Lonnie.' He did his best, but when he came over to talk to me I blurted out, 'Don't touch me! Don't touch me!' That's when he realised that I was in a bad place emotionally. I was lost in my own little world, not thinking straight. I left not long afterwards.

At the end of the day, my grief on the day of the funeral was twofold. It wasn't just that I had lost my beloved brother, but the emotion of not being there by his bedside when he passed had added to my grief. It left me wretched. It's something I'll have to live with for the rest of my life.

★ ★ ★

Muhammad's finances had been shaky at the end of his career, but there was still money floating around his estate – even if he would never have been able to tell anyone where it was. Lonnie has been astute. When Robert Sillerman, a billionaire who was buying up the rights to American icons like Marilyn Monroe, Joe DiMaggio, Elvis Presley and Frank Sinatra, was contemplating approaching Muhammad, a friend of my brother's, Tim Shanahan, brought a possible deal to his attention. He was right to be excited – in 2006 Sillerman gave Lisa Marie Presley $100 million for 85 per cent of the rights to Elvis's image. 'You're bigger than that,' Shanahan told my brother after explaining the dynamics of the deal over the phone. 'You're popular on five continents; Elvis was only big across three. There are more people going to be recognising your name than his, especially in the Muslim world. So don't settle for anything less than $150 million.'

'OK,' said my brother.

'Seriously,' Tim reiterated. 'Nothing less than $150 million.'

Well, Sillerman did pursue Muhammad – and Tim later found out that my brother had settled for $50 million.

'Why didn't you just wait?' he asked, exasperated, when he finally got my brother on the phone. 'They would've given you $150 million.' Muhammad, who never did give a damn about money, replied, 'Wouldn't you settle for $50 million if you could see the looks on your children's and brother's faces when you wrote out a cheque for a million dollars to each one of them before you die?' Apparently Muhammad was content with, what he deduced, was a fair offer, which would help secure his children's and my future. He felt that was enough money to distribute among those he loved so dearly so they could live comfortably.

After my brother's death, Lonnie had the right to attorney, and did a commendable job. From the Sillerman funds, the pay-off was allegedly $10 million a year to Lonnie and Muhammad for the next five years. So in 2011, they apparently had $50 million paid from the company. When Muhammad died, there were rumours pertaining to a family feud of who was going to get how much from the will. There were reports that Muhammad's children were allegedly going to get several million each.

All I can say is, like any family, internal problematic issues were our private business. It was none of any outsider's concern. Next thing you know, cruelty suffered at the hands of the tabloids, the media-induced negativity, was something our family could've done without. Anyway Muhammad's children received some money. And Lonnie sometimes helps me out financially, for which I am grateful. I really appreciate her support.

IN PURSUIT OF A BETTER WORLD

Muhammad was reportedly worth $82 million when he died. That was a contrast to how I'd been living – I had been struggling financially for many years. Muhammad had taken care of me financially virtually all his life when he was in charge of his mind and body. When I first joined my brother's team in Miami I wasn't actually on a salary; I was simply there to get him in shape for fights and look to protect him. Eventually, Muhammad became the heavyweight champion of the world and money came rolling in and he would lavish me with anything – suits, jewellery, cars, clothes – everything. He kept me sharp just like he would keep himself immaculate. We both loved to dress well. Still, you can't spend millions on clothes, so where did the rest go? Well, bear in mind I have been married six times now. My first wife was a Muslim lady, all the way back in 1966. Muhammad, of course, was thrilled that I married a Muslim and bought me a brand new house in Chicago, throwing in a new car for good measure.

Well, that marriage didn't endure. The next thing you know, I was divorced and lost the house and ended up not having the car, but, not learning my lesson, I turned right around and got married again to another sweet Muslim lady. Muhammad turned around and gifted me another new house and another new car. Again, that marriage didn't endure, either. When I got to my third wedding, I didn't get a house or a car. Apparently, I couldn't handle my women *or* my money.

During Muhammad's retirement years, he continued to take care of me financially regardless of whether I was with him or not. I never had a long-term job to support myself so I really depended on him. And Muhammad always used to say to me that he wanted to make sure his brother would always be taken care of, even though he knew that I had my own set of issues. Things somewhat shifted after he lost his voice as a result of his illness persisting. I believe with a strong conviction that if Muhammad had his own mindset intact, had he not suffered from the illness, I would be in a better position financially because he would've put his foot down to make sure that I, his brother, was better financially taken care of. I admit that I had been negligent in handling money – I left most of that to my wives, and I still see that as one of my shortcomings today. I still don't handle money in that respect – Caroline does. I dearly love her, of course, and trust her.

Growing up, my brother and I both entertained the idea of one day being in the limelight, surrounded by everything we wanted. That's the mindset of a young black youth. Maybe any youth who grows up modestly, the dream that one day you are going to conquer all and want for nothing. Well, Muhammad did it, and we both reaped the rewards. But it had to end one day.

★ ★ ★

As I struggled financially, Muhammad's children were doing their own thing, living their happy lives. But his son had the worst of it. Muhammad Ali Jr. had lived an isolated and sheltered life since he was a young boy. The family kind of kept him out of the eyes of the public virtually all his life, and he remained out of the spotlight as he grew up. Later in life, he was unemployed for the most part, getting a job at a fairground and a few other places to pay the bills. Most of Muhammad's children seem to have bonded to at least some degree, but Jr. seems more isolated. I wish I could do more to help.

One of the saddest occasions I remember involved my nephew trying to purchase some of his dad's memorabilia from a boxing memorabilia seller. During a trip abroad he stayed at this guy's house for a night because he was making an appearance at the local boxing club. This guy showed him an impressive collection of his dad's memorabilia – from signed framed gloves to classic pictures all endorsed by the hands of Muhammad. As the conversation shifted to memorabilia, Muhammad Ali Jr. left the man stupefied when he said he wanted to buy some of the items. 'Yes, I know, but I don't get anything signed off my dad.' The man realised some things had gone on in the family, but it was none of his business so he refrained from delving into it. He was just taken aback that Muhammad Ali's son wanted to buy his dad's memorabilia, the man who was the most famous person in the world. Anyway, he didn't end up purchasing it in the end. Needless to say, he couldn't afford to. The man explained his dad's memorabilia had cost him a lot to acquire. He wasn't going to let him have it for free. Nonetheless, this man couldn't really fathom what he had just heard.

Muhammad never spent much time with his son as his career took precedence over family life. And the son never gravitated towards boxing at all in the hope of following in his dad's footsteps. He admitted it would've been hard to live up to his dad. He remembers all the attention as a little kid and everywhere he went with his dad there were cameras. As a little boy he was thrust into the limelight, something he never wanted. He just wanted to be a normal child, but there was no getting away from it; he was always Muhammad Ali's son. Later when he was growing up without his dad around him, it seemed very strange when there were no cameras when he went out. The pressure he has encountered with people expecting him to do what they thought he would has been burdensome. It was very difficult for him growing up, knowing who his dad was, wanting to live up to it but not being able to. I remember Muhammad telling me that he wanted a son. And not long after God blessed him with his only son. He did say that he wouldn't want him to box, though. Instead, he preferred his son to delve deep into studying in the hope of producing a wise son.

Unfortunately my brother didn't study at school like he should have. He wasn't motivated to read and write. 'I hated all that studying,' he said, 'all that book work and reading. All that test work. I don't know what I would have done.' He once said if he was back at twelve years old and he had a chance, and he was told he wasn't going to prevail in boxing and if he had a choice, he said, he would've been a doctor. Helping people, seeing a human being in pain and knowing that he can help them, relieving them of pain, was something he was inclined to do. Surprisingly he might have even become a lawyer or a policeman, he said.

When we were both growing up our own mother just wanted us both to get a good education, stay out of trouble, stay out of bad gangs and try to be somebody in life. When it came to his turn, Muhammad strongly encouraged his children to go to school and learn. His third wife Veronica was very intelligent, very educated, and, at least partly inspired by her, he wanted the children to focus on their studies.

When he fought in the ring his mind always gravitated towards how he could help the black man. This is why he ultimately fought – using the sports platform to make a stand. Be heard. Make a change. He would tell me that boxing was merely a platform for him to do bigger things.

What's interesting is that when his son was born, Muhammad said he would want his children to have enough money to be comfortable. He didn't want to think of his children working in a meagre job, prone to criticism: 'How did they end like *that*?' Muhammad was convinced that this was never going to happen. I mean, money had been flowing in, he had fought around the world, and he was the hottest property in sport. How can he not take care of his own family? It was unfathomable. Unfortunately, as much as I regret to say it, this is exactly what happened with his son. It's been a life of constant grind for him.

★ ★ ★

We are living in critical times right now. In February 2017, Muhammad's ex-wife Belinda and their son Muhammad Ali Jr. were stopped by TSA officers as they were returning home to Deerfield Beach, Florida, after attending a Black History Month event in Jamaica. The officers interrogated them separately for nearly two hours, asking questions like, 'Where did you get your name? Are you Muslim?' despite the fact that their passports were perfectly in order. Eventually, Belinda was released after producing an old photo of her with Muhammad – the authorities were still not convinced she was telling the truth – but Muhammad Jr. was still detained. At the time, there was speculation that the officers were trying to enforce the travel ban instituted by President Donald Trump against seven predominantly Muslim nations. Although my nephew was, of course, born in Philadelphia, he'd spoken out against the ban, and some people thought that his detention was some kind of retaliation. At the time, I wasn't sure about any of this, but when Muhammad Jr. was briefly detained again a month later, it got tougher to be dismissive of these theories.

Trump, at least back in the 1980s and 1990s, used to act as if he was friendly with my brother. He was a boxing fan, and had briefly dabbled in promoting the sport in the 1990s, when Muhammad attended some of the bouts he put on in Atlantic City. I think Trump was impressed by the fact Muhammad was a global figure as he always wanted to associate himself with people who were high profile, and so at ringside and after-parties he would seek out Muhammad. Of course, back in those days, he wasn't spewing the Islamophobic language he later became known for.

Let's be honest – Muslims have never been popular in America. They have come under heavy fire for decades, but I think it's just one of our trials. Muhammad often spoke on this subject to his close friends and family – whether it was due to a terrorist attack or something else, he said, people will have their misconceptions about Muslims, and all we can do is try to live as we should. True Muslims aren't terrorists. Our religion is a religion of peace – that's where the meaning of the word comes from.

Those who have any intelligence know this, but there's always a percentage of people who will seize on the worst aspects of any religion, just as they might with Christianity or Judaism. They characterise the image of Islam in the Western world as dominated by conflict, but every religion has bad apples, and Islam is no different.

So, while some people need to take the time to learn about Islam, it's also our job to do the best we can to be great representations of true Islam. Muhammad loved everyone regardless of their race, creed or religion and he taught his kids to do the same – to love everyone regardless of their affiliation or group. He wasn't perfect, but I think for the most part he was sincere and he did showcase the great values our Muslim religion teaches.

I believe if Muhammad were here today, as difficult as it was for him sometimes to articulate his views, he would go on national television to let people know that what's happening to us, the Muslims, is horrible. He was always quick to inform the public about misconceptions regarding our religion and he constantly spoke against bigotry and racism in this country.

Is Trump a racist? I don't think so. I met him with Muhammad and I think he's actually a nice man, despite the fact that his off-the-cuff remarks and speeches have compounded the problems we have been having in America. He has strong views, of course, but to label him a racist, someone who hates the minority because of their colour and where they're from, is not right. Muhammad met him numerous times and even went to his wedding – and my brother never had anything to say to me regarding Trump being an individual that had any disdain for other races.

Personally, I refuse to be drawn into this maelstrom of criticism. Unlike Muhammad I have never been a vociferous individual unless my family was in danger. I always left all the talking to Muhammad. And, as I understand it, he did make his voice heard so to speak, that he wasn't warming up to what Trump was doing in terms of the Muslim travel ban, and his condemnable views relating to Muslims. Personally, I've got nothing bad to say about Trump, at least not specifically. I do, of course, wish that we could all get along a little better.

★ ★ ★

There were some white people who labelled Muhammad a racist because he advocated segregation, and wasn't shy about hurling prejudiced remarks at the white race. In my opinion, any time a criminal calls the victim of his crimes a criminal, it's a way of deflecting discussion. The idea that Muhammad was a racist because he talked openly and unreservedly about racism in American society and the impact of white supremacy on the status of black people in this country – well, to me, that's outright fabrication. The white populace in America, unfortunately, bought into a racist ideology that goes all the way back to the arrival of the Europeans who came to this country and went back to report that they had discovered a new nation. Never mind that there were people standing onshore watching them get off the boats. At the end of the day, the original sin of American society is white supremacy, not slavery. Slavery was born of white supremacy. People who perpetrated it and turned around and called people such as Muhammad a racist are just ridiculous.

How do I feel about the way perceptions of my brother changed in almost forty years of his life after hanging up the gloves? It's interesting. These days, he's praised by almost everyone, pointed to as an example of the way a sportsman and a human being should conduct himself, and looked at as a hero. Is this because of changing perceptions, or a new generation coming to be opinion formers? I don't believe so. To my mind, it has to do with the traditional American way of handling those who challenge the racist status quo and survive.

There are two things America is very, very good at. One is rewriting history so that a person or people's existence, struggles, biography and so on, essentially become non-existent. They simply ignore it. The second, if a person becomes high profile, is to project a viewpoint which makes it look like America was always on the right side of history, that this individual when struggling had the support, if not of the whole nation, then of enough of the population to let America keep its self-image as the greatest country on earth, one where the good always prevail in the end. And so, while Muhammad and I saw racism and discrimination in all their forms during our upbringing, and suffered its effects during his career, it's often portrayed as a series of isolated incidents: of a few people in power who made bad decisions, in a situation that could never happen again.

Over time, this is what I heard from a lot of black activists and opinion formers – as the ones who survived grow older and are perceived to be less of a threat, the attacks on their character diminish and people start building statues of them. Bill Russell has a statue, now, alongside Jim Brown, Tommie Smith and John Carlos – the two athletes who raised their fists on the podium at the 1968 Olympics. The mainstream narrative about them has changed now, and plenty of people are keen to make it look like they've always been supportive of what they stood for, which, of course, is an outright fairy tale.

At the end of the day, everyone has to do their homework. Muhammad was not always revered, honoured and adored. He was victimised, he was vilified, and – like many other black athletes – he was criminalised. Yes, the movement against racial discrimination made great strides during my brother's lifetime, laws changed and the rights of blacks were fully established while many people's attitudes shifted. People recognise now that the Vietnam War was a mistake for our country and that we should've got out of it long before we did, and Muhammad was right about it and took the sensible course of action. But it's important to remember that, at the time he was speaking out, my brother provoked widespread outrage and many sectors of the public loathed him. And the same thing is happening, in different ways, today – racial discrimination is still prevalent, and black athletes are still being vilified for standing up against it. Plenty of people, I'm sure, will tell you in ten or twenty years that they were always against the police discrimination being protested about on America's sports fields, and that they supported the athletes who did something about it. What are those people doing right now? Only they know.

EPILOGUE

Muhammad may have gone, but his spirit lives on.

Once, Jamillah tells me, she went to her father's gravesite in Louisville, Kentucky, and was talking to him as if he was right there in front of her. The whole cemetery was closed for that day, but the staff had kindly agreed to open it, just for a little while, just for her. Standing there with mixed emotions running in her head and tears running down her cheeks, she remembers saying aloud, 'Daddy, some parts of my life are a struggle. I just want you to be there for me. I wish you could see me.' It was summertime, so there were butterflies everywhere – almost as if he was reaching out to her. She dreamed about him a couple of times after that – she said she knew it was him. He was healthy and he was speaking perfectly well. Now, when she's in her car, she tells me, she'll sometimes see a butterfly and think of him. And sometimes when she's got obstacles in life she sits down and asks herself, *How would Daddy handle a situation like this?* His spirit is always there for her, as it is for all of us. Whatever challenges we face, we always kind of look to him for inspiration. We're happy that he's safe.

The rest of the family, I know, miss him just as much. I would say rarely a week goes by that we don't hear his name, or see his image, be it in a commercial, in a sports story, on the radio or TV somewhere around the world. My family misses him every single day. By the same token, during the last year of his life his health deteriorated to the point where there was a lot of suffering, but he never complained once. I think our family thought that as much as it has been a loss for us, we felt it was his time. Although we might have wanted him to live forever, he had to leave us. He's beyond any suffering now. The reality is, we all miss him, miss talking to him, miss hugging him, kissing him, all that. You can't do that any more, you have to sacrifice that, but he's still alive – he's moved over to a new home. He's achieved his mission and goal in life. So, honestly we can't be selfish and want him to stay one day longer. God had decided it is time. And God makes no mistakes. If God said it's time to come home now we have to accept it. That's how you deal with it. We live to die, that's our end from the moment we're born.

For me, it's hard because I've never had to live without him. In my room I have pictures of him with me spanning way back – from the earliest days of our childhood to the beginning of his career and after. How do I remember him? I remember him as the mischievous boy, the ringleader, the committed student of the sweet science, the Olympic champion and the braggart whose mouth the world wanted to see closed. I remember him as the proud man who proclaimed that he wouldn't fight another man's war, and the champion who fought his way through some of the toughest boxing matches anyone will ever see. I remember him as the man who would give away his money even when it infuriated the people closest to him, sign endless autographs and do magic tricks to entertain one child when he had an entire stadium waiting for him. And I remember him as The Greatest, of course, the man I looked up to most in the world, the one I'd never have wanted to live my life without. Not because of what he did in the boxing ring, or in front of any TV camera. Because he was my brother.

ACKNOWLEDGEMENTS

First and foremost, I would like to thank my late loving parents, Cassius Marcellus Clay Sr. and Odessa Grady Clay, who provided so much love for Muhammad and me. Secondly, I would like to thank my wife, Caroline, my love and my best friend, who has always supported me and shown me unconditional love. I care about her dearly.

I would like to thank my good friend and business manager, Ron Brashear, who is like a brother to me and continues to guide me. I'm ever so grateful for all his help and guidance. I would like to thank my friend and my brother's former business manager, Gene Kilroy, who, like me, always cared for and endeavoured to protect Muhammad. I'm grateful for his help and enduring friendship.

Thank you to my ghostwriter, Fiaz Rafiq, who spent an inordinate amount of time working with me on this book, making this a reality. A special thanks to my agent, Charlie Brotherstone, who played a pivotal role in having this idea manifest into a reality. Fiaz and I would like to thank Joel Snape for editing the manuscript. A big thank you to Mike Tyson for his support. I would like to thank Jim Brown, the greatest NFL player of all time, and his wife, Monique, for their support. Lastly, a big thank you must go to John Blake Publishing and to my editor, James Hodgkinson, for all his hard work.

INDEX